hokum

hokum

an anthology of african-american humor
edited by paul beatty

BLOOMSBURY

All pieces reprinted by permission.
Permissions information is listed in full on pages 463–468.

Published by Bloomsbury Publishing, New York and London
Distributed to the trade by Holtzbrinck Publishers

All papers used by Bloomsbury Publishing are natural, recyclable
products made from wood grown in well-managed forests.
The manufacturing processes conform to the environmental
regulations of the country of origin.

Library of Congress Cataloging-in-Publication Data

Hokum : an anthology of African-American humor / edited by Paul Beatty.—
1st U.S. ed.
p. cm.
ISBN-13: 978-1-58234-434-8
ISBN-10: 1-58234-434-5
ISBN-13: 978-1-59691-148-2 (pbk.)
ISBN-10: 1-59691-148-4 (pbk.)
1. African American wit and humor. 2. American literature—
African American authors. 3. African Americans—Literary collections.
I. Beatty, Paul.

PN6231.N5H65 2006
817.008′0896073—dc22
2005048183

First U.S. Edition 2006

1 3 5 7 9 10 8 6 4 2

Typeset by Hewer Text UK Ltd, Edinburgh
Printed in the United States of America by Quebecor World Fairfield

contents

(nothing serious) just buggin'

black absurdity

People laugh when you fall on your ass.
What's humor?—Jean-Michel Basquiat

back in college a friend once asked if she could tell me a joke. A sure sign of a bad joke is one which requires permission to be granted in order for it to be told, but I agreed. After all, she'd put up with me stalking her for a semester and a half; the least I could do was listen to a quip that, judging from the "Okay, okay . . . wait a sec" preamble and her finally resorting to reading the joke from what looked to be a mimeographed first-day-of-class handout, was going to be a groaner. "Okay, I'm ready. You listening?"

"If listening means I haven't choked you to death yet, then yes."

"All right, two black guys, George Washington Robinson and Roosevelt Lincoln Kennedy . . ."

I smirked, and a noise that sounded like something between a chuckle and a snort rumbled from my throat.

"You're laughing. I knew it!"

"Knew what?"

"Professor Boskin said you'd laugh."

"Professor Boskin? Who's Professor Boskin?"

"Today in class he said there were forms and styles of humor that only people of certain demographic groups find funny."

"What group, and more importantly what joke?"

"You're in the African-American group and you laughed at a joke designed to appeal to African-Americans."

"You haven't even gotten to the punch line yet."

"That's the joke."

"'Two black guys, George Washington Robinson and Roosevelt Lincoln Kennedy,' that's the entire joke?"

"You laughed, so it must be."

"I was laughing to please you."

"I forgot. You don't have a sense of humor."

"If I had a sense of humor, I'd be laughing my ass off that you and Professor Boskin would think that anyone African-American or otherwise would think that two black guys named George Washington Robinson and Roosevelt Lincoln Kennedy is funny. That's the real joke."

"Okay, fine, but then *why* is it supposed to be funny?"

Why indeed? If it was so damn funny, why would Lincoln Theodore Monroe Andrew Perry have adopted Stepin Fetchit as a stage name? That disconnect between our humors has stayed with me for some time, and although I slightly exaggerate this twenty-some-odd-year-old conversation for effect, it's a fair example of how, over time, my sense of humor has developed through a confluence of resentment and unsated libido. I didn't find a joke about two black guys named after dead American presidents funny, partly for reasons of minstrel triteness, but mostly because I resent the idea of a people, in this case African-Americans, being thought of as having not a collective consciousness but a collective funny bone. I especially resented that the omnipotent whiteness of the joke's reference point had nothing to be resentful about. The joke is dependent upon a baseless fear, a fear of finding the other too similar to oneself, too American. No matter how heartfelt, white interpretation of Negro humor and Negro existence is often too black. It's Vanilla Ice slant-rhyme jive black. It's poor, beleaguered Bill Clinton pleading temporary blackness and bivouacking in Harlem among his people of non-Rwandan ancestry. It's the in toto blackness of *Uncle Tom's Cabin* and *Check and Double Check*, a blackface so pervasive, so complete that even Amos and Andy's and Topsy's palms and fingernails are shoe-polished to a grease-monkey pitch.

My resentment has become so overbearing that these days I'm unable to take anything seriously, much less humorously. Everything is satirical. Not *Mad* magazine satirical but Orwellian dystopic. The stand-up comedians are indistinguishable from the trade paperback satirists and the round-table news pundits shooting one-liners at each other like Jack Benny and Rochester. They're embittered middle-aged infants, as abrasive as Spanish-language punk rock, as perceptive as Neville Chamberlain, and about as funny as *The Patriot Act: The Movie*. Much of today's humor seems to be based on the "laugh or else" crime-boss-and-underlings model. A mean-spirited joke gets told and the heartiness of audience response is based not on its cleverness but on its offensiveness. Not to say offensiveness can't be funny, but everyone is so insecure we're afraid to laugh at ourselves and for anyone to laugh at us. Fuck 'em if they can't take a joke. Fuck 'em if they can't tell a joke. Fuck 'em if you can't fuck 'em.

Two guys, their names are Eleanor Madonna Nixon and Deng Xiaoping O'Malley. They may be guys, women, transsexuals, omnisexual, Hopi, black, Latin, white, transracial, Cablinasian, selfish, stupid, Republicans, or other, in any combination and permutation, but nothing would make me happier than if they were funny. Apart from the five minutes of weekly brilliance on *Chappelle's Show*, the *Onion* newspaper, Sarah Silverman, and George Lopez, there isn't much to laugh at these days. The best I can hope for is to chance upon some unintentional comedy. Nothing the chitlin circuit Kings of Comedy have said in the past five years was funnier than football Hall of Famer and angry black-man-in-residence Jim Brown's response to a radio host's suggestion that he calm down and enroll in an anger management class: "What are you talking about, man? I teach anger management!" No one brought more levity to 9/11 than Christine Whitman, ex-governor and then administrator of the Environmental Protection Agency, when she stood amid the still-smoldering ruins of the World Trade Center and calmly assuaged my downtown New Yorker paranoia with, "We are very encouraged that the results from our monitoring of [cough, cough] air quality and drinking water conditions in both [ahem, ahem, aaackk] New York and near the Pentagon show that the public [pant, gasp] in these areas is not [wheeze] being exposed to excessive levels of asbestos or other harmful substances. Given the scope of the tragedy from last week, I am glad to reassure the people of New York and Washington, D.C., that their [hack, cough, gasp, hack] air is safe to breathe and their water is safe to drink." And then there's Iron Mike Tyson, the Henny Youngman of unintentional humor, who after losing to Lennox Lewis answered a question about his boxing legacy by saying, "I guess I'm gonna fade into Bolivian."

I compiled this book because I'm afraid that American humor is fading into Bolivian and that Will Smith, the driest man alive, will be historicized as the Oscar Wilde of Negro wit and whimsy. Three years ago I was in a Berlin bar commiserating with an expatriate black author of some renown. We were doing what African-Americans who live abroad do, which is to castigate the entire black race (apart from ourselves and Thelonious Monk and Harriet Tubman, of course) and all of its overhyped contributions to society, from fire to record scratching to the touchdown celebration. Inevitably, after a few red wines and a sound thrashing of Stanley Crouch, I slurred, "Niggers ain't as funny as they used to be."

"Ain't no such thing as niggers."

"You're right. Well, unicorns ain't as funny as they used to be either, but we should start a humor magazine."

"Yeah, a *National Lampoon* for black folk."

"We could call it *Coon Lampoon*."

"*Mad as Fuck Magazine*."

"*Readers Digress*—Laughter is the World's Best Medicine Next to Morphine."

"*Hokum: A Seriously Funny Magazine*."

I returned stateside bandying about the idea of starting a humor magazine to people who, thankfully, knew better than to take me seriously. At the time I was reading *Oreo*, an incredibly hilarious novel written by Fran Ross. I'm usually very slow to come around to things. It took me two years to "feel" Wu Tang's first album, even longer to appreciate Basquiat, and I still don't get all the fuss over Duke Ellington and Frank Lloyd Wright, but I couldn't believe that *Oreo* hadn't been on my broad, albeit balky, cultural radar. The relative obscurity of *Oreo* and some prodding from my agent inspired me to think about compiling an anthology of African-American literature. All the other black tropes, such as eroticism, crime, hair, athleticism, blackness, real blackness, blue blackness, black gay eroticism, black gay thug eroticism, black eunuch and post-menopausal eroticism, have been anthologized to death, creating this nappy-haired, virile Frankenstein monster who growls in a bluesy a-a-b rhyme scheme but has no sense of humor.

Not being ticklish, I see laughter as a learned response and not a reflexive one. However, it's far easier for me to recall learning when not to laugh than learning when to laugh. Don't laugh at the hippies along the Venice Beach boardwalk. *Slap*. Don't snigger at your grandmother's proclivity to attach an "er" to the end of her words. "This yell-er Tropican-er banan-er is for your sister Ann-er." *Wallop*. Above all don't laugh at the other neighborhood kids getting smacked around as they learn their lessons as to what is and what isn't funny. *Blam*.

I suppose the first thing I was allowed to laugh at without fear of repercussion was myself. I was the butt of the first joke I'd ever heard.

"Why are you so dark? Because God left you in the oven too long." This also was an affront to my atheism, but I let that slide, since no one was directly teasing me for my lack of faith, and if they had I suppose I'd let that slide too. The worst part of the racial ridicule was that the time-tested rejoinder "I'm rubber you're glue, whatever you say bounces off of me and sticks to you!" is useless when you're surrounded by a bunch of cowlick white boys calling you "jungle bunny." I could never come up with a good punch line for "Why are you so white?" It was like asking, Why is the sky blue? There might be a scientific explanation, but it sure as hell wouldn't be funny. There was nothing negative about being white, but thank goodness there was some shame in being Polish.

When my friends exhausted their supply of nigger jokes, my debasement was quickly followed by the schoolyard ridicule of an invisible ethnic group known as Polacks. None of my white playmates were of openly Polish descent, so I finally had a shield to hide behind. In those days on the spinning rack in the rear of the corner liquor store you could find *Mad* magazine paperbacks, seventy-five-cent smutty novels, and the paperbacks with fluorescent covers and titles like *500 Ethnic Put-Downs, 1001 Polack Jokes, 1001 More Polack Jokes, 1001 Polack Jokes Not in the Other Two 1001 Polack Joke Joke Books*. The Put-Downs book was no good to me because I didn't know any "ethnics" other than maybe David Eisenstadt, my best friend and a gangly, Fudgsicle-brown kid, who due to a complete lack of ethnic identity (other than thinking he was a WWII fighter pilot) never took offense to anything, so I developed an encyclopedic repertoire of Polack jokes. I knew so many versions of the "How many Polacks does it take to screw in a light bulb?" riddle that my answer was liable to be anywhere from one to one thousand. The longer I told Polack jokes, the longer my friends stopped laughing at me, the longer I stopped laughing at myself. Are Polack jokes told by a resentful black kid African-American humor? Are Mad Super Specials #4 through #22 literature?

By the time the family moved to the significantly more urban Westside of Los Angeles, I was a fairly literate eight-year-old. I'd read all the books in my mom's library, Bellow, Heller, Doctorow, *Grey's Anatomy*, but had only two literary heroes with whom I could identify, Encyclopedia Brown and the black spy from *Mad*'s cloak and dagger cartoon, *Spy vs. Spy*. Whenever Encyclopedia Brown, the boy detective, solved the case of the missing roller skates, or the earthenware pig, or the natty nat, it was a victory for all Browns, both surnamed and those, like me, left in the oven too long. I shamelessly rooted for Antonio Prohias's black spy; relishing every spring-loaded boxing glove that smashed the white spy's pointy insect proboscis and blackened his beady eyes into X's. A triumph by the duplicitous, conniving, diabolical, plunger-pushing, Mickey Finn–slipping, dynamite-stick-lighting punk-ass white spy was enough to send me to my room to continue my quest to coin a biting ethnic slur for Whitey. Surely the progeny of the people who invented jazz, the hot comb, blood plasma, and the knock–knock joke could come up with something better than *honky. Blue-eyed hoogy, inside trader, lipless Larrys, snow niggers* . . .

My out-of-doors life in the new neighborhood was a reanimated version of the *Spy vs. Spy* espionage except that all the spies were black. Even the white, yellow, brown, Polish, and Pamela Kennedy, the lone Eskimo, were black spies. We didn't toss pipe bombs at one another but hurled firecrackers, dirt clods, and insults that would sting well past high school. Again I was laughing at myself, at my blackness, only now my color was less amorphous. It was defined by the height my pant leg dangled above the high tops of my sneakers, the shape of my skull, the whop-ness of my bicycle rims, the width of my nose, the emptiness of my wallet, and the circular outline of the unused condom permanently imprinted on its inner fold.

Nigger-themed jokes still filled the lull between school bells, yo mama this and yo mama that, but these gags had a different tone than the ones told in the old neighborhood. They were lyrical, united joker and listener rather than divided. They probed rather than goaded, and if told right I'd no idea I was listening to folklore.

Acculturation

A little black boy was in the kitchen watching his mother fry some chicken. Seeing the flour, he dabbed some onto his face. "Look at me, Ma," he said, "I'm white!"

"What did you say?" said his mother. He repeated what he had said, and his mother gave him a resounding slap. "Don't you ever say that!" she said, yelling, "Now you go to your father and tell him what you said to me."

Crying furiously, he made his way to his father. "What's wrong, son?" asked his father.

"Mom-Mom-Mommy sl-sl-slapped me," he said.

"Why'd she do that, son?" asked the father.

"Be-be-because I-I said I was w-w-white," said the boy.

"What?" said his father, slapping him even harder. "Go tell your grandmother what you said! She'll teach you!"

Shaken and confused, he approached his grandmother. "Why, baby, what's wrong?" she inquired. "They-they-they slapped me," said the boy.

"Why, baby—why'd they do that?" asked his grandmother.

Repeating his story, his grandmother slapped him so hard she almost knocked him down. "Don't you ever say that!" she said. "Now what did you learn?"

"I-I learned," said the boy, "that-that I-I've been white for only two minutes and I hate you niggers already!"

My introduction to black, excuse me, Black literature happened during the summer between eighth and ninth grades when the Los Angeles Unified School District, out of the graciousness of its repressive little heart, sent me Maya Angelou's *I Know Why the Caged Bird Sings*. It was the first book I'd ever opened that was written by an African-American author. Notice I said "opened" and not "read." I made it through the first couple of pages or so before a strong sense of doom overwhelmed me and I began to get very suspicious. Why would a school district that didn't bother to supply me with a working pair of left-handed scissors, a decipherable pre-algebra text, or a slice of pepperoni pizza with more than two pepperonis on it send me a brand-new book? Why care about my welfare now? I ventured another paragraph, growing ever more oppressed with each maudlin passage. My lips thickened. My burrheaded afro took on the appearance and texture of a dried-out firethorn bush. My love for the sciences, the Los Angeles Kings, and scuba diving disappeared. My dog Butch yelped and growled at me. I suppressed my constant craving for a Taco Bell Bellbeefer because I feared the fast food franchise wouldn't serve me. My eyes started to water and the words to "Roll, Jordan, Roll," a Negro spiritual I'd never heard before, poured out of my mouth in a surprisingly sonorous baritone. I didn't know I could sing. Quickly, I tossed the book into the kitchen trash. For a black child like myself who was impoverished every other week while waiting for his mother's bimonthly paydays, giving me a copy of *I Know Why the Caged Bird Sings* was the educational equivalent of giving the prairie Indians blankets laced with smallpox or putting saltpeter in a sailor's soup. I already knew why the caged bird sings, but after three pages of that book I now know why they put a mirror in the parakeet's cage, so he can wallow in his own misery. After this traumatic experience I retreated to my room to self-medicate with Clavell, Irving, Wambaugh, the Green Lantern, Archie and

Jughead; it would be ten years before I would touch another book written by an African-American. As my wiser sister Anna says, "Never trust folks like Maya Angelou and James Earl Jones who grow up in Walla Walla, Mississippi, and Boogaloo, Arkansas, and speak with British accents." Thank goodness they didn't send me her poems.

Still I Rise (and unfortunately write)
by Bayou Angel-You

> You may force feed me earth mother bullshit
> With your bitter, twisted dreadlocked lies
> You may stomp me into poverty personified
> But still, like my bloated bank account, I'll rise . . . (and
>   unfortunately write)

The Lido Theater on the corner of Pico and La Cienega was an old-time movie house complete with velvet curtains, squeaky seats, and marble men's-room urinals that were five feet high and two feet wide and ornate as Egyptian sarcophagi. The summer that I discarded Maya Angelou was the summer the Lido developed a reputation for being rowdy. Once the genteel venue for G-rated Disney fare like *The Love Bug* and *The Bad News Bears* and highbrow comedies—think *Harold and Maude*—in the seventies the Lido, feeling the pinch of the recession and the Westside's changing demographics, had changed direction. Now the double features were either splatterfests like *The Exorcist* and *Beyond the Door* or pornography like *Looking for Mr. Goodbar* and a scratchy print of *Last Tango in Paris* passing as art, but it was the havoc of the blaxploitation weekend marathons that filled their coffers and became part of Westside lore. I received my advanced learning in when and when not to laugh in that five-hundred-seat lecture hall.

For forty-nine cents it was Friday night at the opera, the county fair, the Improv Room, and Intro to African-American Studies all in one. The movies were just an excuse for public assembly. In a seat usually toward the back, but not all the way back, and next to the aisle just in case, I sat alone in the dark, a nervous but attentive member of an audience that was far more entertaining than the movie. In the Lido nothing was off limits; anything, no matter how cruel, could be funny. If the beating of someone's cousin wasn't funny at the time, by Monday, the first day school rolled around, it would be. The heckle, the firecracker, the gunshot, the "fuck you, pig"—it was all a matter of timing.

One weekend, not long after Nica, my friend Toi's sister, developed an adolescent *je ne sais quoi* known as "butter," a bunch of us went to the Lido. Since every Crip-in-training was courting Nica, and Toi was her brother and I his friend, for the first time I sat in the back. The back back. This was like living at the top of the hill. The Coke bottles got more roll, the spitball enfilade was glorious, the acoustics made Steve Miller's "Fly Like an Eagle" almost sound live and not Panasonic-transistorized. The main feature was *Coffy*, a pimp/ho tragedy for which Pam Grier's bosom serves as the Greek chorus. The scene where pimp/dope pusher King George gets his comeuppance wasn't played for laughs, but when his mutton-chopped, white-turtlenecked, suit-that-looks-like-it-was-knit-from-a-Mondrian-painting-wearing ass gets tied to the rear bumper of a Ford Fairlane and is lynched by being dragged through the winding streets of Holmby Hills at sixty miles an hour, hitting every eucalyptus tree, curb, and garbage can along the way, everyone but me cracked up so hard I couldn't hear the screech of the tires or the white henchman's own wicked cackle. But by the time King George's skinless corpse finally came to a stop at the bottom of the hill I found myself rolling in the aisle. Was it the peer pressure? The obvious crash-test dummy staging? Freudian displacement? I don't know. That was one of the blackest nights of my life. There was a feeling of vengeful liberation in laughing at all that senseless pain and blood, but underlying that sense of liberation was caution, a sniggering warning that I might be next.

Quality of Life

A little black boy was sitting at a curb playing with a rather large pile of shit. Noticing him, an Irish cop inquired as to what he was doing. "I'm making a policeman," replied the boy, nonchalantly.

"A policeman?" said the cop, incredulous. "And just what sort of policeman would ye be makin', huh?"

"I'm making an Italian policeman," said the boy. At that, the cop broke into peals of laughter. "Wait here," he said. "Don't you move."

Making his way back to the station, he ran to his colleague Tony, who was, in fact, Italian. "Hey, Tony," he said, "come with me, I want you to see something."

Finding the boy yet at his task, he said to Tony, "Ask him what he's doing."
"Hey, boy—what are you doing?" said Tony.
"I'm making a policeman," said the boy, emphatically.
"Ask him what kind," said the first cop, to which the boy replied, "I'm making
an Italian policeman."
"Why you doing that?" asked Tony.
"Because I don't have enough shit to make an Irish policeman," he said.

It wasn't until I entered college that I found a piece of black literature
funny. It was unintentional comedy, but nonetheless a start. My crew of
conscious brothers and I were sitting in the student union rehashing books
we hadn't read and dictating laws of governance for countries we'd never
been to when bud-smoking Bernie from Chicago strode by with a copy of
New Black Voices, the revolutionary primer. "Listen to this, fellas," he said
taking a seat and slice of pizza, "Sacred Chant for the Return of Black
Spirit and Power," by Amiri Baraka." His mouth full of molten cheese,
Bernie recited the poem: " 'Ohhh break love with white things . . .' " His
sharp intakes of air between lines failed to cool his burning mouth and his
burning resentment. " 'Evil out. Evilin. Evil.' " I started to snicker. " 'They
die in the streets . . . stab him . . . aggggg . . . OOOOO . . .' " It wasn't
that I thought Baraka's lyrical vituperation funny, but the too guilty joy
that accompanies hubris got to me. The sheer seriousness of the poem was
funny to me. " 'Death music . . . Bring us back our strength.' "

Yet that poem called to me, and I began to explore a black literature
that conveyed a purpose and pride with which I was unfamiliar, despite
having been raised and chaperoned by a village of ex-radicals. I pored
through Sanchez, Lorde, Wright, Toomer, Baldwin, Hansberry, welcoming the rhetoric but over time missing the black bon mot, the snap, the
bag, the whimsy upon which "fuck you" and freedom sail. It was as if the
black writers I'd read didn't have any friends. Where was the Richard
Pryor cynicism? Ms. Keaton's sarcasm? Biz Markie's inanity? Where was
the mumbling Cleveland folklore of Uncle Rufus, whose unintelligible
tales told over the Thanksgiving table must have been hilarious because
everyone who'd known him for the thirty years it took to understand his
cigar-chewing shibboleth dropped their silverware to bust a gut when he
got to the part about the fishing boat crashing into the breakwater. Where
was Toi's fresh-off-the-skateboard tanka-like biracial honesty?

"I'm tellin' you white people are evil."

"How can you say that your own mother is white?"

"Then don't you think I should know what I'm talking about?"

It's always struck me as odd that there has never been a colored Calvin Trillin, Bennett Cerf, or Mark Twain. Hell, I'd settle for a cornball Dave Barry who'd write columns for the rap magazines titled "Snitches Get Stitches," "All Pimps Are Gay and All Lesbians Aren't," "Act Your Age and Not Your Shoe Size," and "Boogers: The Ghetto Sushi."

One can't attend a writer's conference without having to pay penance to the vaunted African-American oral tradition. Ironically, whenever a fellow panelist says to me, "Mr. Beatty, you've been awful quiet, can you say a little something about the African-American oral tradition?" I like to mime a reenactment of a toothless, mute, and gagged African captive asking his slave ship bunkmate to stop stepping on his toes. What is never discussed is the cognitive dissonance created by the perception that African-Americans *write* in a *spoken* tradition. One canon consists of songs, folktales, and insider apothegms that are deeply and invariably funny, whereas the other, as Danzy Senna once pointed out to me over Mexican food, comes out of a tradition of abolitionist "And ain't I an intellect?" activism aimed, then as now at whites. Save for Langston Hughes, Ralph Ellison, George Schuyler, Zora Neale Hurston, and a select group of others, the defining characteristic of the African-American writer is sobriety—moral, corporeal, and prosaic, unless you buy your black literature from the book peddler standing on the street corner next to the black-velvet-painting dealer, next to the burrito truck: then the prevailing theme is the ménage à trois.

Hokum is my chance to recognize and thank the black upper-, middle-, low-, and no-class clown for being more than comic relief. For being scapegoat and sage, unafraid to tell the world, as the Fool told Lear, "Truth's that a dog must to kennel," thus validating our humanity through our madness. This book is not meant be a comprehensive collection of African-American humor but more of a mix-tape narrative dubbed by a trusted, though slightly smarmy, friend. A sampler of underground classics, rare grooves, and timeless summer jams, poetry and prose juxtaposed with the blues, hip-hop, political speeches, and the world's funniest radio sermon, delivered by the Prophet Omega, founder and overseer of the Peaceway Temple. The subtle musings of Toni Cade

Bambara, Henry Dumas, and Harryette Mullen are bracketed by the profane and often loud ruminations of Langston Hughes, Darius James, Wanda Coleman, Tish Benson, and Steve Cannon. In compiling *Hokum*, I tried to focus mostly on literary works, but some of the funniest writers don't write, so also included are selections from well-known yet unliterary wits: Lightnin' Hopkins, Mike Tyson, and the Reverend Al Sharpton. Other selections come from public figures and authors whose humor, although incisive and profound, is often overlooked or rarely on display: Malcolm X, Suzan-Lori Parks, Zora Neale Hurston, Sojourner Truth, and W. E. B. DuBois.

These works, like Godard's films and David Hammon's art, are eccentric, liberating, and savagely comic, and make one appreciate that not everyone has guts and imagination to do the thing and do it well. Ishmael Reed said it best, *Writin' Is Fightin'*, and I hope *Hokum* beats you down like an outclassed club fighter. Each blow plastering that beaten boxer smile on your face, that ear-to-ear grin you flash to the crowd to convince them that if you're laughing, then you ain't hurt.

Jesus

Homeboy went to Westchester and stood marveling at all the beautiful houses. Noticing one in which it appeared no one was home, he gained entrance through a window and began to steal. After a moment he heard a voice saying, "Jesus is watching you!"

Looking around, he saw no one, and, not being particularly religious, he went back to stealing. Then he heard the voice again: "Jesus is watching you!" Again seeing no one, he was about to return to his task when he spied a parrot in a cage. Approaching the cage with much swagger and bravado, he said, "Motherfucker— can you talk?"

"You goddamn right I can talk," said the parrot. "Whaddaya want me to say?"

"Tell me your name," said the homeboy.

"My name is Ralph," said the parrot.

Breaking into paroxysms of laughter, Homeboy asked who had been dumb enough to name a parrot that, to which the parrot replied, "The same one that named the rottweiler!"

"Acculturation," "Quality of Life," and "Jesus" as told by John Farris.

pissed off
to the highest degree
of pisstivity

i n 1977, on a dreary Tuesday evening, Richard Pryor was snatched off a slave galley by John Belushi and, while still in shackles, forced to host a one-hour comedy special on NBC, a fate so horribly cruel that one earlier captive had thrown himself overboard to face the sharks rather than the task of resurrecting the then struggling and career-killing network.

Pryor spends the entire hour battling writer's block. His struggle is understandable; after all, it's a daunting mission for anyone, much less a querulous black comedian, to go on national television and, as he stated in the opening scene, "explain who I am, be American." Dressed in a tuxedo, he wanders the corridors and studio backlots soliciting advice from everyone he meets. Black women in Easter bonnets on the studio tour caution him to be pious. The children want something for them that isn't corny. The NBC shoeshine man, who hipped the corporate suits to his records and feels responsible for Richard's newfound success, wants his just due. Forty minutes into the show the idea-bereft host is accosted by his head writer, a tam-, combat-boots, and, khaki-wearing black nationalist, and his surly band of script-doctoring afro-pick-wielding revolutionaries. The brothers have solved Pryor's writer's block. They have a script, a script that glorifies black unity and brings the message to people. Concerned the teleplay sounds a bit heavy-handed, Pryor asks if there's anything funny in it. Taken aback by his incredulity, one of the writers responds, "Funny? I'm talking about really funny. Dig on this here—in one of the sketches you slap this white broad upside her head and knock her to the floor! Ain't that funny, man?"

"That's funny?" Pryor asks.

"Yeah!"

"I could kick her a little too."

"Yeah!"

No, kicking the white woman when's she down (and when is she not?) isn't funny, but talking about it being funny is. Rarely is African-American humor anxiety displacement. For black Americans, a people Richard Pryor might characterize as being "pissed off to the highest degree of pisstivity," the fears that accompany being born in a country founded on persecution and propelled forward by paranoia are best confronted head on. Oh, there are a few mannered Negro humorists who repress their neuroses with sublimation, but the seething anger is visible beneath the calm façade. Take, for example, Bill Cosby's prime-time alter ego, Dr. Cliff Huxtable. The avuncular Cliff delivered babies of all colors and told wisecracks in every shade but blue, but, if you listen closely, these mush-mouthed quips were always threatening. Laced with rage and contempt for anyone black who earns less than one hundred thousand dollars a year and doesn't own a wine decanter, his jokes loomed over his targets like a father's strap. If one didn't stop annoying his patrician sensibilities, Bill Cosby would browbeat and ridicule one until the onset of appropriate white, I mean human, behavior. In a perverse way, Cosby's funnier now than he's ever been. Dressed in these garish suits looking like an aged pimp on disability, he parades from civic forum to civic forum, a sad, attention-starved clown, oblivious to the hypocrisy that despite his protestations against the supposed glorification of the African-American sociopath, he made a large part of his fortune off what my friend Victoria points out was a cartoon gang of ebonic-talking, perpetually unsupervised, and crazily dressed black males.

African-Americans, like any other Americans, are an angry people with fragile egos. Humor is vengeance. Sometimes you laugh to keep from crying. Sometimes you laugh to keep from shooting. And if you aren't a white woman, don't think you've got getting-hit-upside-the-head amnesty; black folk are mad at everybody, so duck, because you're bound to be in somebody's line of fire.

and a'n't i a woman?

1851

"Well, chilern, whar dar is so much racket dar must be somethin' out o' kilter. I tink dat 'twixt de niggers of de Souf and de womin at de Norf, all talkin' 'bout rights, de white men will be in a fix pretty soon. But what's all dis here talkin' 'bout?

"Dat man ober dar say dat womin needs to be helped into carriages, and lifted ober ditches, and to hab de best place everywhar. Nobody eber helps me into carriages, or ober mud-puddles, or gibs me any best place!" And raising herself to her full height, and her voice to a pitch like rolling thunder, she asked, "And a'n't I a woman? Look at me! Look at my arm! (and she bared her right arm to the shoulder, showing her tremendous muscular power). I have ploughed, and planted, and gathered into barns, and no man could head me! And a'n't I a woman? I could work as much and eat as much as a man—when I could get it—and bear de lash as well! And a'n't I a woman? I have borne thirteen chilern, and seen 'em mos' all sold off to slavery, and when I cried out with my mother's grief, none but Jesus heard me! And a'n't I a woman?

"Den dey talks 'bout dis ting in de head; what dis dey call it?" ("Intellect," whispered some one near.) "Dat's it, honey. What's dat got to do wid womin's rights or nigger's rights? If my cup won't hold but a pint, and yourn holds a quart, wouldn't ye be mean not to let me have my little half-measure full?" And she pointed her significant finger, and set a keen glance at the minister who had made the argument. The cheering was long and loud.

"Den dat little man in black dar, he say women can't have as much rights as men, 'cause Christ wan't a woman! Whar did your Christ come from?" Rolling thunder couldn't have stilled that crowd, as did those deep, wonderful tones, as she stood there with outstretched arms and eyes of fire. Raising her voice still louder, she repeated, "Whar did your Christ come from? From God and a woman! Man had nothin' to do wid Him." Oh, what a rebuke that was to that little man.

Turning again to another objector, she took up the defense of Mother Eve. I can not follow her through it all. It was pointed, and witty, and solemn; eliciting at almost every sentence deafening applause; and she ended by asserting: "If de fust woman God ever made was strong enough to turn de world upside down all alone, dese women togedder (and she glanced her eye over the platform) ought to be able to turn it back, and get it right side up again! And now dey is asking to do it, de men better let 'em." Long-continued cheering greeted this. " 'Bleeged to ye for hearin' on me, and now ole Sojourner han't got nothin' more to say."

W. E. B. DUBOIS

on being crazy
1923

it was one o'clock and I was hungry. I walked into a restaurant, seated myself and reached for the bill-of-fare. My table companion rose.

"Sir," said he, "do you wish to force your company on those who do not want you?"

No, said I, I wish to eat.

"Are you aware, Sir, that this is social equality?"

Nothing of the sort, Sir, it is hunger,—and I ate.

The day's work done, I sought the theatre. As I sank into my seat, the lady shrank and squirmed.

I beg pardon, I said.

"Do you enjoy being where you are not wanted?" she asked coldly.

Oh no, I said.

"Well you are not wanted here."

I was surprised. I fear you are mistaken, I said. I certainly want the music and I like to think the music wants me to listen to it.

"Usher," said the lady, "this is social equality."

No, madame, said the usher, it is the second movement of Beethoven's Fifth Symphony.

After the theatre, I sought the hotel where I had sent my baggage. The clerk scowled.

"What do you want?" he asked.

Rest, I said.

"This is a white hotel," he said.

I looked around. Such a color scheme requires a great deal of cleaning, I said, but I don't know that I object.

"We object," said he.

Then why—, I began, but he interrupted.

"We don't keep 'niggers,'" he said, "we don't want social equality."

Neither do I. I replied gently, I want a bed.

I walked thoughtfully to the train. I'll take a sleeper through Texas. I'm a bit dissatisfied with this town.

"Can't sell you one."

I only want to hire it, said I, for a couple of nights.

"Can't sell you a sleeper in Texas," he maintained. "They consider that social equality."

I consider it barbarism, I said, and I think I'll walk.

Walking, I met a wayfarer who immediately walked to the other side of the road where it was muddy. I asked his reasons.

"'Niggers' is dirty," he said.

So is mud, said I. Moreover I added, I am not as dirty as you—at least, not yet.

"But you're a 'nigger,' ain't you?" he asked.

My grandfather was so-called.

"Well then!" he answered triumphantly.

Do you live in the South? I persisted, pleasantly.

"Sure," he growled, "and starve there."

I should think you and the Negroes might get together and vote out starvation.

"We don't let them vote."

We? Why not? I said in surprise.

"'Niggers' is too ignorant to vote."

But, I said, I am not so ignorant as you.

"But you're a 'nigger.'"

Yes, I'm certainly what you mean by that.

"Well then!" he returned, with that curiously inconsequential note of triumph. "Moreover," he said, "I don't want my sister to marry a nigger."

I had not seen his sister, so I merely murmured, let her say, no.

"By God you shan't marry her, even if she said yes."

But,—but I don't want to marry her, I answered a little perturbed at the personal turn.

"Why not!" he yelled, angrier than ever.

Because I'm already married and I rather like my wife.

"Is she a 'nigger'?" he asked suspiciously.

Well, I said again, her grandmother—was called that.

"*Well then!*" he shouted in that oddly illogical way.

I gave up. Go on, I said, either you are crazy or I am.

"We both are," he said as he trotted along in the mud.

ZORA NEALE HURSTON

'possum or pig?
1926

before freedom there was a house slave very much in the confidence of the Master. But young pigs began to disappear, and for good reasons the faithful house slave fell under suspicion.

One night, after his duties at the "big house" were over, he was sitting before his cabin fire. From a pot was seeping the odor of young pig. There was a knock at the door.

"Who dat?" he asked cautiously.

"It's me, John," came the Master's voice.

"Lawd, now, Massa, whut you want way down heah?"

"I'm cold, John. I want to come in."

"Now, Massa, ah jes' lef' a lovely hot fire at de big house. You aughter gwan up dere an' git warm."

"I want to come in, John."

"Massa, whut you wanta come in po' niggah's house an' you got dat fine big house up yander?"

"John, if you don't open this door, I'll have you whipped tomorrow."

John went to the door grumbling about rich white folks hanging around po' niggahs' cabins.

The white man sat down before the blazing fire. The pot boiled and breathed of delicious things within.

After a while he said, "I'm hungry, John. What have you got in that pot?"

"Lawd, now, Massa, whut you wanter eat mah po' vittles fuh and Mistis got roas' chicken an' ham an' chine-bone pie an' everything up to de house? White folks got de funniest ways."

"What's in that pot, John?"

"It's one lil' measly possum, Massa, ah'm bilin' tuh keep fuh a cold snack."

"I want some of it."

"Naw, Massa, you don't want none uh dat dirty lil' possum."

"Yes I do, and if you don't give me some, I'll have you whipped."

John slowly arose and got a plate, knife and fork and opened the pot.

"Well," he said resignedly before dipping in. "Ah put dis heah critter in heah a possum,—if it comes out a pig, 'tain't mah fault."

Stepped on a tin, mah story ends.

CHESTER HIMES

let me at the enemy—
an' george brown
1944

i t warn't that I minded the twenty-five bucks so much. Twenty-five
bucks ain't gonna break a man. An every cat looks to get hooked some
time or other, even a hustler as slick as me. 'Fore it was done I wished I'da
just give this icky twenty-five bucks and forgot 'bout it.

But even at that if'n it hadn't been for him puttin' all them fancy ideas
in my queen's head he never woulda got me. That jive he was pullin' was
sad. But my queen, she like a lot of those queens 'round L.A. nowdays—
done gone money mad.

We was at the Creole Breakfast Club knockin' ourselves out when this
icky George Brown butts in. Ain't nobody called him an' I hardly knew
the man, just seen him four or five times 'round the pool room where I
worked. He takes a seat at our table an' grabs my glass of licker an' asts,
"Is you mad at anybody?"

I was gettin' mad but I didn't tell him. "Me?" I laughed, tryna be a good
fellow. "Only at the man what put me in 1-A."

The bugler caught a spot for a rift in *Don't Cry Baby* an' blew off my ear.
All down the line the cats latched on, shoulders rocked, heads bobbed, the
joint jumped. My queen 'gan bouncin' out her twelve dollar dress.

George waited for the bugler to blow outa breath then he said, "Thass
what I mean. You ain't mad at nobody yet you gotta go to war. Thass
'cause you's a fool."

I didn't mind the man drinkin' my licker so much, nor even callin' me a
fool. But when I seen my queen, Beulah, give him the eye an' then get
prissy as a sissy, I figured I better get him gone. 'Cause this George Brown
was strictly an icky, drape-shaped in a fine brown zoot with a pancho conk
slicker'n mine. So I said, "State you plan, Charlie Chan—then scram!"

"Don't rush me, man, don't rush me," he said. "You needs me, I don't need you. If'n you was to die tomorrow wouldn't mean nothing to me. Pour me some mo' of that licker."

He come on so fast I done took out my half pint bottle an poured him a shot under the table 'fore I knew what I was doin'. Then I got mad. "This ain't no river, man," I said.

"Thass what I mean," he said. "Here you is strainin' yo'self to keep up a front. You works in the pool room all day an' you makes 'bout ten bucks. Then comes night an' you takes out yo' queen. You pays two bucks to get in this joint, fo' bucks for a half pint grog, two bucks for a coke setup. If'n you get anything to eat you got to fight the man 'bout the bill. For ten bucks a day you drinkin' yo'self in the grave on cheap licker."

"You calls fo' bucks a half pint cheap," I snarled.

He kept drivin' like he didn't hear me. "Then what happen? They put you in 1-A and say you gotta fight. You don't wanna fight 'cause you ain't mad at nobody—not even at the man what charge you fo' bucks for a half pint grog. Ain't got sense 'nough to be mad. So what does you do?"

"What *does* I *do?*" I just looked at that icky.

"Well, what *does* you *do?*" That's my queen talkin'." She's a strictly fine queen, fine as wine. Slender, tender, and tall. But she ain't got brain the first.

What does I do? "I does what everybody else do," I gritted. "I gets ready an' go."

"Thass what I mean," George Brown said. "Thass 'cause you's a fool. I know guys makin' twice as much as you is, workin' half as hard. And does they have to fight? They is deferred 'cause what they doin' means more to Uncle Sam than them in there fightin'."

"Well, tell High C 'bout it." That's my queen again. "I sho don't want him to go to no war. An' he may's well be makin' all that money. Lil enough he's makin' in that pool room."

That's a queen for you; just last week she was talkin' 'bout how rich us was gettin'.

"Money! Make so much money he can't spend it," he said to her. They done left me outen it altogether; I'se just the man what gonna make the money. "W'y in less than no time at all this cat can come back and drape yo' fine shape in silver foxes an' buy you a Packard Clipper to drive up and down the avenue. All he gotta do is go up to Bakersfield and pick a lil cotton—"

I jumped up. "What's your story, morning glory? Me pickin' cotton. I ain't never seen no cotton, don't know what cotton is—"

"All he got to do," he went on talkin' to my queen, "to knock down his double sawbuck is pick a coupla thousand pounds. After that the day is his own."

"Why come he got to stop in the middle of the day," my queen had to ast. "Who do he think he is, Rockefeller or somebody?"

"Thass what I been tryna tell you," George said. "He don't. He keep right on an' pick 'nother ton. Make forty flags. An' does you have to worry 'bout him goin' to the army? You can go to bed ev'y night and dream 'bout them silver foxes."

I had to get them people straight an' get 'em straightened fast. "Yo' mouth may drool and yo' gums may snap—" but my queen cut me off.

"Listen to the man," she shouts. "Don't you want me to have no silver foxes?"

"Ain't like what he thinks," he said. "Litta hustlers up there. Cats say they's goin' East—slip up there an' make them layers; show up in a Clipper. Cats here all wonder where they got their scratch." He turned to me. "I bet you bin wonderin'—"

"Not me!" I said. "All I'se wonderin' is how come you pick on me. I ain't the man. 'Fore I pick anybody's cotton I'll—"

So there I was the next mornin' waitin' for the bus to take me up to Bakersfield. Done give this icky twenty-five bucks to get me the job and all I got is a slip of paper with his name on it I'm supposed to give to the man when I get there. My queen done took what scratch I had left sayin' I wouldn't need nothin' 'cause George said everything I could want would be given to me for nothin'. All I had was the four bits she let me keep.

But by then it had me. Done gone money mad as her. At first I was thinkin' in the C's; knock seven or eight hundred then jump down. But by the time I got to Bakersfield I was way up in the G's; I seen myself with pockets full of thousand dollar bills.

After knockin' the natives cold in my forty-inch frock and my cream colored drapes I looked 'round for the cat George said gonna meet me. Here come a big Uncle Tomish lookin' cat in starched overalls astin' me is I High C.

"What you wanna know for, is you the police?" I came back at him.

"Dey calls me Poke Chops," he said. "I'se de cook at de plantation. I come tuh pick y'all up."

"Well bless my soul if you ain't Mr Cotton Boll," I chirped, givin' him the paper George gimme. Then I ast him, "Is that you parked across the street?"

He looked at the green Lincoln Zephyr then he looked back at me. "Dass me on dis side," he mumbled, pointin' at a battered Model A truck.

Well now that made me mad, them sendin' that loppy for me. But I was so high off'n them dreams I let it pass. I could take my twenty G's and buy me a tank to ride in if'n I wanted; warn't like I just had to ride in that loppy. So I climb in beside old Chops an' he drive off.

After we'd gone aways he come astin' me, " 'Bout how much ken y'all pick, shawty?"

"Don't worry 'bout me, Chops," I told him. "I'll knock out my coupla thousand all ricky. Then if'n I ain't too tired I'll knock out a deuce more."

"Coupla thousan'." He turned in his seat an' looked at me. "Dass uh tun."

"Well now take yo' diploma," I said.

"Wun't tek us long tuh whup de enemy at dat rate," was all he said.

'Bout an hour later we pulled in at a shanty. I got out and went inside. On both sides there was rows of bunks an' in the middle a big long wooden table with benches. Looked like a prison camp where I did six months. I was mad now sure 'nough. "I ain't gonna stay in this dump," I snarled.

"Whatcha gunna do den?" he wanted to know. "Build yo'self a house?"

I'do cut out right then an' there but the bucks had me. I'm a hipcat from way back an' I don't get so mad I don't know how I'm gettin' down. If'n them other hustlers could put up with it, so could I. So when old Chops gimme a bunk down in the corner I didn't want him to know I was mad. I flipped my last half buck at him. "Take good care of me, Chops," I said.

He didn't bat an eye; he caught the half an' stashed it. "Yassuh," he said.

At sundown the pickers came in, threw their sacks on this bunks an' made for the table. If there was any hustlers there, they musta been some mighty hard hustlers 'cause them was some rugged cats. Them cats talked loud as Count Basie's brass an' walked hard as Old Man Mose. By the time I got to the table wasn't nothin' left but one lone pork chop.

Then when us got through eatin' here come Chops from the kitchen. "Folkses, I wants y'all tuh meet High C. High C is a pool shark. He pick uh tun uh cotton ev'y day. Den if'n he ain't tahd he pick unuther'n."

I got up and give 'em the old prize fighter shake.

But them cats just froze. I never seen nothin' like it; ain't nobody moved. Then they turned and looked at me. After that they got up from the table an' went 'bout their business. Ain't nobody said nothin', not one word.

That night Biyo Dad an' Uncle Toliver come down to my bunk. "Whar'd y'all evah pick cotton befo', son?" Biyo Dad ast me.

"Don't start me to lyin' you'll have me cryin'," I said. "I done picked all over. 'Bama to Maine."

Uncle Toliver puffed at his pipe. "Dat Maine cotton is uh killah as de younguns say."

"You ain't just sayin' it," I said.

Somebody shook me in the middle of the night an' I thought the joint was on fire an' jumped up and run outside. By the time I find they was gettin' up for breakfast all the breakfast gone but a spoon of grits. An' the next thing I know there we are out in the cotton patch, darker'n me.

But warn't nobody sayin' nothin' that early in the day. Big cat on the right of me called Thousand Pound Red. 'Nother'n on the left called Long Row Willie. Cats shaped up like Jack Johnson. I hitched up the strap over my shoulder like I seen them do an' threw the long sack out behind me.

"Well, we're off said the rabbit to the snails," I chirped jolly-like, rollin' up the bottoms of my drapes.

An' I warn't lyin' neither. When I looked up them cats was gone. Let me tell you, them cats was grabbin' that cotton so fast you couldn't see the motion of their arms. I looked 'round an' seen all the other cats in the patch watchin' me.

"W'y these cats call themselves racin'," I said to myself. "W'y I'll pick these cats blind deaf an' cripple."

I hauled off and started workin' my arms an' grabbed at the first cotton I saw. Somp'n jumped out an' bit me on the finger an' I jumped six feet. Thought sure I was snake bit. When I found out it was just the sharp point of the cotton boll I felt like a plugged slug. Next time I snuck up on it, got aholt and heaved. Didn't stop fallin' 'til I was flat on my back. Then I got mad. I 'gan grabbin' that cotton with both hands.

In 'bout an hour looked like I'd been in the rain. Hands ain't never been so bruised, look like every bolls musta bit 'em. When I tried to straighten up, got more cramps than Uncle Saul. Looked at my bag. The mouth was full but when I shook it the cotton disappeared. Then I thought 'bout the money; forty bucks a day, maybe fifty since I'd done begun in the middle of the night. Money'll make a man eat kine pepper. I started off again.

By the time I got halfway through my row I couldn't hear nobody. I raised my neck and skinned my glims. Warn't nobody in the whole patch but a man at the end of my row. Thought the rest of them cats musta gone for water so I 'cided to hurry up an' finish my row while they was gone an' be ahead of 'em.

I'd gone ten yards through the weeds pickin' thistledown from dried weeds 'fore it come to me I was at the end of my row.

"Whew!" I blew an' wiped the sweat out my eyes. An' then I seen the walkin' boss. "Howma doin', poppa," I crowed. "Didn't quit when them other cats did; thought I'd knock out my row 'fore I went for a drink."

"You did?" He sounded kinda funny, but I didn't think nothing of it.

"That's my story, Mister Glory; never get my Clipper stoppin' every few minutes for a drink." I shifted my weight an' got groovy. "I ain't like a lotta cats what swear they won't hit a lick at a snake then slip up here an' cop this slave sayin' the goin' east an' come back all lush. I don't care who knows I'm slavin' long as I get my proper layers. Now take when this icky, George Brown, sprung this jive; I got a piece a slave in a pool room and figure I'm settin' solid—"

"This ain't no pool room and the others ain't gone for no water," the man cut in. "They finished out their rows and went over the hump."

"Well, run into me!" I said. "Finished!" But I couldn't see how them cats got finished that quick. "Maybe they didn't have as much to pick as me," I pointed out.

The man stood there lookin' at me an' not sayin' a mumblin' word. Made me nervous just astandin' there. I picked up my sack an' sorta sashayed off. "Which way they go, man?"

"Come back here, you!" he yelled.

"All right, I can hear you, man," I muttered.

"Take a look at that row." He pointed at the row I'd just finished.

I looked. It was white as rice. "Well look at that jive!" I said. "What's that stuff, man?"

"It's cotton," he said. "You know what cotton is, don't you? You heard of it somewhere, ain't you?"

I stepped over an' looked down the other rows. They were bare as Mama Hubbard's cubbard. I came back an' looked at my row again. "Say, man, where did all that jive come from?" I wanted to know.

"It grew," he said.

"You mean since I picked it? You kiddin' man?"

He didn't say nothin'.

"Well then how come it grew on my row an' didn't grow nowhere else?" I pressed him.

He leaned toward me an' put his chops in my face, then he bellowed, "Pick it! You hear me, pick it! Don't stand there looking at me, you—you grasshopper! Pick it! And pick every boll!"

I got out that man's way. "Well all root," I said quickly. "You don't have to do no Joe Louis."

That's where I learned 'bout cotton; I found out what it was all 'bout, you hear me. I shook them stalks down like the F.B.I. shakin' down a slacker. I beat them bolls to a solid pulp. As I dragged that heavy sack I thought, Lord, this cotton must weight a ton—a halfa ton anyway. But when I looked at the sack, didn't look like nothin' was in it. Just a lil old knot at the bottom. Lord, cotton sure is heavy, I thought.

Then it come to me all of a sudden I must be blowin' my lid. Here I is gettin' paid by the pound and beefin' 'cause the stuff is heavy. The more it weigh the more I earn. Couldn't get too heavy. I knowed I'd done picked a thousand pounds if'n I'd picked a ounce. At that rate I could pick at least four thousand 'fore sundown. Maybe five! Fifty flags—in the bag! "Club Alabam, here to you I scram," I rhymed just to pass the time. Them cotton bolls turned into gin fizzes.

At the end of the row I straightened up an' looked into the eyes of the man. "Fifty flags a day would be solid kicks, please believe me," I said. "I could knock me that Clipper an' live on Lennox Avenue." I sat down on my thousand pounds of cotton an' relaxed. "There I was last Friday, just dropped a trey of balls to Thirty NoCount, an' it seemed like I could smell salty pork fryin'. Man, it sure smelt good."

"Turn around," the man said.

I screwed 'round, thinkin' he was gonna tell me what a good job I done. "Look down that row."

I looked. That was some row. Beat as Mussolini. Limp as Joe Limpy. Leaves stripped from stalks. Stalks tromped 'round and 'round. And just as many bolls of cotton as when I first got started. I got mad then sure 'nough. "Lookahere, man," I snarled. "You goin' 'long behind me fillin' up them bolls?"

The man rubbed his hand over his face. He pulled a weed an' bit off the root. Then he blew on the button of his sleeve an' polished it on his shirt. He laughed like a crazy man. "Ice cream and fried salt pork shore would taste good riding down Lennox Avenue in a Clipper. Look, shorty, it's noon. Twelve o'clock. F'stay? Ice cream—" He shook himself. "Listen, go weigh in and go eat. Eat all the fried ice cream and salty clipper you can stand. Then come back and pick this row clean if it takes you all week."

"Well all root, man," I said. "Don't get on your elbows."

I dragged my sack to the scales. Them other cats stopped to watch. I waved at them, then threw my sack on the scales. I stood back. "What does she scan, Charlie Chan?"

"Fifty-five!" the weigher called.

"Fifty-five," I said. "Don't gimme no jive." I started toward the shanty walkin' on air. Fifty-five smackeroos an' the day just half gone. Then I heard somebody laugh. I stopped, batted my eyes. I wheeled 'round. "Fifty-five!" I shouted. "Fifty-five what?"

"Pounds," the weigher said.

I started to assault the man. But first I jumped for the scales. "Lemme see this thing," I snarled.

The weigher got out my way. I weighed the cotton myself. It weighed fifty-five pounds. I swallowed. I went over an' sat down. It was all I could do to keep from cryin'. Central Avenue had never seemed so far away. Right then and there I got suspicious of that icky, George Brown. Then I got mad at my queen. I couldn't wait to get back to L.A. to tell her what a lain she was. I could see my queen on this George Brown. My queen ain't so bright but when she gets mad look out.

When them cats went in for dinner I found the man an' said, "I'm quittin'."

"Quit then," he said.

"I is," I said. "Gimme my pay."

"You ain't got none coming," he said.

I couldn't whip the man, he was big as Turkey Thompson. An' I couldn't cut him 'cause I didn't have no knife. So I found Poke Chops an' said, "I wanna send a tellygraph to my queen in L.A."

"Go 'head an' send it den," he said.

"I want you to go in town an' send it for me," I said.

He said, "Yassuh. Cost yuh two bucks."

"I ain't got no scratch," I pointed out. "That's what I wanna get."

"'Tis?" he said. "Dass too bad."

All I could do was go back out and look them bolls in the face. At sundown I staggered in, beat as Mama Rainey. I didn't even argue with the weigher when he weighed my thirty-five pounds. Then I got left for scoff. Old Chops yelled, "Cum 'n git it!" and nine cats run right over me.

After supper I was gonna wash my face but when I seen my conk was ruint an' my hair was standin' on end like burnt grass I just well in the bed.

There I lay wringin' and twistin'. Dreamt I was jitterbuggin' with a cotton boll. But that boll was some ickeroo 'cause it was doin' some steps I ain't never seen an' I'm a 'gator from way back.

Next day I found myself with a row twixt two old men. Been demoted. But I figured surely I could beat them old cats. One was amoanin': "*Cotton is tall, cotton is shawt, Lawd, Lawd, cotton is tall, cotton is shawt . . . How y'all comin' dare, son? . . . Lawd, Lawd, cotton is tall, cotton is shawt . . .*" The other'n awailin': "*Ah'm gonna pick heah, pick heah a few days longah, 'n den go home. Lawd, Lawd, 'n den go home . . .*"

Singin' them down home songs. I knew I could beat them old cats. But pretty soon they left me. When I come to the end of my row an' seen the man I just turned 'round and started back. Warn't no need 'f arguin'.

All next day I picked twixt them ancient cats. An' they left me at the post. I caught myself singing: "*Cotton is tall, cotton is shawt,*" an' when I seen the man at the end of my row I changed it to: "*Cotton is where you find it.*"

That night I got a letter from my fine queen in L.A. I felt just like hollerin' like a mountain Jack. Here I is wringin' an' twistin' like a solid fool, I told myself, an' I got a fine queen waitin' for me to come back to her everlovin' heart. A good soft slave in the pool room. An' some scratch stashed away. What is I got to worry 'bout.

Then I read the letter.

"Dear High C daddy mine:

"I know you is up there making all that money and ain't hardly thinking none about poor little me I bet but just the same I is your sweet little sugar pie and you better not forget to mail me your check Saturday. But don't think I is jealous cause I aint. I hates a jealous woman worsen anything I know of. You just go head and have your fun and I will go head and have mine.

"I promised him I wouldn' say nothing to you 'bout him but he just stay on my mind. Didn you think he was awful sweet the way he thought bout me wanting some silver foxes. Mr Brown I mean. And it was so nice of him getting you that fine job where you can improve your health and keep out the army at the same time. And then you can make all that money.

"He been awful nice to me since you been gone. I just dont know rightly how to thank him. He been taking care of everything for you so nice. He wont let me worry none at all you being away up there mong all those fine fellows and me being here all by my lonely self. He say you must be gained five pounds already cause you getting plenty fresh air and exercise and is eating and sleeping regular. He say I the one what need taking care of (aint he cute). He been taking me out to keep me from getting so lonesome and when I get after him bout spending all his time with me he say dont I to worry none cause youd want me to have a little fun too (smile). Here he come now so I wont take up no more of your time.

"I know this will be a happy surprise hearing from me this way when I dont even write my own folks in Texas.

"xxxxxxxx them is kisses.

"Your everloving sugar pie,
"Beulah

"P.S. Georgie say for me to send you his love (smile) and to tell you not to make all the money save him some."

There I was splittin' my sides, rollin' on the ground, laffin' myself to death I'se so happy. Havin' my fun. Makin' plenty money, just too much money. With tears in my eyes as big as dill pickles. I couldn't hardly wait to get my pay. Just wait 'til I roll into L.A. an' tell her how much fun I been havin'.

Then come Sat'day night. There we was all gathered in the shanty an' the man callin' names. When he call mine everybody got quiet but I didn't think nothin' of it. I went up an' said, "Well, that's a good deal. Just presh the flesh with the cesh."

But the man give my money to old Chops an' Chops start to figurin'. "Now lemme see, y'all owes me thirteen dollahs. Uh dollah fuh haulin' yuh from de depo. Nine dollahs fuh board countin' suppah. Three dollahs fuh sleepin'." He counted the money. He counted it again. "Is dis all dat boy is earned?" he ast the man.

The man said, "That's all."

"Does y'all mean tuh say dat dis w'ut y'all give George Brown twenty-five dollahs fuh sendin' up heah fuh help?"

The man rubbed his chin. "We got to take the bad ones with the good ones. George has sent us some mighty good boys."

My eyes bucked out like skinned bananas. Sellin' me like a slave! Slicin' me off both ends. Wait 'til my queen hears 'bout this, I thought. Then I yelled at Chops, "Gimme my scratch! I gotta throat to cut!"

Chops put his fists on his hips and looked at me. "W't is y'all reachin' fuh?" he ast. "Now jes tell me, w'ut is y'all reachin' fuh?"

"Lookahere men—" I began.

But he cut me off. "Wharis mah nine dollahs? All y'all is got heah is three dollahs 'n ninety-nine cents."

"Say don't play no games, Jesse James," I snarled. "If'n I ain't got no more dough 'n that—"

But 'fore I could get through he'd done grabbed me by the pants an' heaved me out the door. "An' doan y'all come back t' y'all gits mah nine dollahs t'gethah," he shouted.

I knew right then and there is where I shoulda fit. But a man with all on his mind what I had on mine just don't feel like fightin'. All he fell like doin' is lyin' down an' grievin'. But he gotta have some place to lay an' all I got is the hard, cold ground.

A old cat took pity on me an' give me some writin' paper an' I writ my queen an' he say he take it in to church with him next day an' get the preacher to mail it. That night an' the next I slept on the ground. Some other old cats brung me some grub from the table or I'da starved.

Come Monday I found myself 'mongst the old queens an' chillun. They men work in the mill and they pick a lil now an' then. I know I'da beat them six year olds if'n I hadn't got so stiffened sleepin' on the ground. But I couldn't even stand up straight no more. I had to crawl down the row an' tree the cotton like a cotton dog. I was beat, please believe me. But I warn't worried none. I'd got word to my queen an' looked any minute to get a money tellgraph.

'Stead I got letter come Wednesday. Couldn't hardly wait to open it.

"High C:

"I is as mad as mad can be. I been setting here waiting for your check and all I get is a letter from somebody signing your name and writing in your handwriting to send them some money and talking all bad bout that nice man Mr Brown. You better tell those hustlers up there that I aint nobodys lain.

"Georgie say he cant understand it you must of got paid Saturday. If you think I is the kind of girl you can hold out on you better get your thinking cap on cause aint no man going to hold out on this fine queen.

"Your mad sugar pie,
"Beulah

"P.S. George bought a Clipper yesterday. We been driving up and down the Avenue. I been hoping you hurry up and come on home and buy me one just like isn."

"Lord, what is I done?" I moaned. "If'n I done somep'n I don't know of please forgive me, Lord. I'd forgive you if you was in my shape."

The first thing I did was found that old cat an' got some more writin' paper. I had to gat that queen straight.

"Dear Sugar pie:
"You doesn understand. I aint made dollar the first. Cotton aint what you think. Ifn you got any cotton dresses burn em. I is stranded without funds. Does you understand that. Aint got one white quarter not even a blip. That was me writing in my handwriting. George Brown is a lowdown dog. I is cold and hungry. Aint got no place to stay. When I get back I going to carve out his heart. Ifn you ever loved your everloving papa send me ten bucks (dollars) by tellgraph.
"Lots of love and kisses. I cant hardly wait.
          "Your stranded papa
              "High C"

Come Friday I ain't got no tellygram. Come Sat'day I ain't got none neither. The man say I earned five dollars an' eighty-three cents an' Chops kept that. Come Sunday, Monday, Tuesday, Wednesday, I ain't got word one.

I was desperate, so he'p me. I said to myself, I gotta beat this rap, more way to skin a cat than grabbing to his tail. So I got to thinkin'.

At night after everybody weighed in an' the weigher left, lots of them cats went back to the field and picked some more cotton so they'd have a head start next day. They kept it in their bags overnight. But them cats slept on them bags for pillows.

Well I figured a cat what done picked all day an' then pick half the night just got to sleep sound. So Thursday night I slipped into the shanty after everybody gone to sleep an' stole them cats' cotton. Warn't hard, I just lifted their heads, tuk out their bags an' emptied 'em into mine an' put the empty bags back. Next day at noon I weighed in three hundred pounds.

Ain't got no word that night. But I got somep'n else. When I slipped into the shanty an' lifted one of them cats head he rolled over an' grabbed me. Them other cats jumped up an' I got the worse beatin' I ever got.

Come Sat'day I couldn't walk attall. Old Chops taken pity on me an' let me come back to my bunk. There I lay amoanin' an' agroanin' when the letter come. It was a big fat letter an' I figured it sure must be filled with bills. But when I opened it all dropped out was 'nother letter. I didn't look at it then, I read hers'n first.

"High C:

"I believe now its been you writing me all these funny letters in your handwriting. So thats the kind of fellow you turned out to be. Aint man enough to come out in the open got to make out like you broke. You the kind of a man let a little money go to his head. But that dont worry me none cause I done put you down first.

"Me and George Brown is getting married. He bought me a fur coat yesterday. Aint no silver foxes but it bettern you done and it cost $79.99. So you just hang on to your little money and see ifn you can fine nother queen as fine as me.

"Your used to be sugar pie,
"Beulah

"P.S. Here is your induction papers come to your room while you have been gone. I hope the army likes you bettern I does."

That's how I got back to L.A. The man bought me a ticket when he seen the army wanted me. But I warn't the same cat what left tryna dodge the draft. I'se mad now sure 'nough. Done lost my queen, lost my soft slave, an' the man got me. Now why them dirty rotten Japs and Jerries start all this cuttin' an' shootin' in the first place you just tell me. They know they couldn't win. Just like me takin' a punch at Joe Louis. Either I done gone crazy or else I done got tired of livin'. That's what make me so mad.

Warn't but one thing I want'd to do worse'n fightin' them stinkin' enemies; that was fightin' George Brown.

The Lord musta heard my prayer 'cause the man got him less'n two weeks after he got me. An' they put him in the same camp. That's me you see grinnin'. *Yes suh!* Sure gonna be a happy war.

message to the grass roots
1963

When you want a nation, that's called nationalism. When the white man became involved in a revolution in this country against England, what was it for? He wanted this land so he could set up another white nation. That's white nationalism. The American Revolution was white nationalism. The French Revolution was white nationalism. The Russian Revolution too—yes, it was—white nationalism. You don't think so? Why do you think Khrushchev and Mao can't get their heads together? White nationalism. All the revolutions that are going on in Asia and Africa today are based on what?—black nationalism. A revolutionary is a black nationalist. He wants a nation. I was reading some beautiful words by Rev. Cleage, pointing out why he couldn't get together with someone else in the city because all of them were afraid of being identified with black nationalism. If you're afraid of black nationalism, you're afraid of revolution. And if you love revolution, you love black nationalism.

To understand this, you have to go back to what the young brother here referred to as the house Negro and the field Negro back during slavery. There were two kinds of slaves, the house Negro and the field Negro. The house Negroes—they lived in the house with master, they dressed pretty good, they ate good because they ate his food—what he left. They lived in the attic or the basement, but still they lived near the master; and they loved the master more than the master loved himself. They would give their life to save the master's house—quicker than the master would. If the master said, "We got a good house here," the house Negro would say, "Yeah, we got a good house here." Whenever the master said "we," he said "we." That's how you can tell a house Negro.

If the master's house caught on fire, the house Negro would fight harder to put the blaze out than the master would. If the master got sick, the house Negro would say, "What's the matter, boss, *we* sick?" *We* sick! He identified himself with his master, more than his master identified with himself. And if you came to the house Negro and said, "Let's run away, let's escape, let's separate," the house Negro would look at you and say, "Man, you crazy. What you mean, separate? Where is there a better house than this? Where can I wear better clothes than this? Where can I eat better food than this?" That was that house Negro. In those days he was called a "house nigger." And that's what we call them today, because we've still got some house niggers running around here.

This modern house Negro loves his master. He wants to live near him. He'll pay three times as much as the house is worth just to live near his master, and then brag about "I'm the only Negro out here." "I'm the only one on my job." "I'm the only one in this school." You're nothing but a house Negro. And if someone comes to you right now and says, "Let's separate," you say the same thing that the house Negro said on the plantation. "What you mean, separate? From America, this good white man? Where you going to get a better job than you get here?" I mean, this is what you say. "I ain't left nothing in Africa," that's what you say. Why, you left your mind in Africa.

On that same plantation, there was the field Negro. The field Negroes—those were the masses. There were always more Negroes in the field than there were Negroes in the house. The Negro in the field caught hell. He ate leftovers. In the house they ate high up on the hog. The Negro in the field didn't get anything but what was left of the insides of the hog. They call it "chitt'lings" nowadays. In those days they called them what they were—guts. That's what you were—gut-eaters. And some of you are still gut-eaters.

The field Negro was beaten from morning to night; he lived in a shack, in a hut; he wore old, castoff clothes. He hated his master. I say he hated his master. He was intelligent. That house Negro loved his master, but that field Negro—remember, they were in the majority, and they hated the master. When the house caught on fire, he didn't try to put it out; that field Negro prayed for a wind, for a breeze. When the master got sick, the field Negro prayed that he'd die. If someone came to the field Negro and said, "Let's separate, let's run," he didn't say "Where we going?" He'd say, "Any place is better than here." You've got field Negroes in America today. I'm a field Negro. The masses are the field Negroes. When they see this man's house on fire, you don't hear the little Negroes talking about "*our* government is in trouble." They say, "*The* government is in trouble."

Imagine a Negro: "*Our* government"! I even heard one say "*our* astronauts." They won't even let him near the plant—and "*our* astronauts"! "*Our* Navy"—that's a Negro that is out of his mind, a Negro that is out of his mind.

because America has gone bad with us, can't say our.

Field negro wants that nation doesn't love his master.

House negro didn't want black nation / love ol master

masses the common people.

pose-outs
1965

"Sit-ins and such, picketings and such, for civil rights has been so common," said Simple, "that they no longer attracts attention. A lot of demonstrations nowadays do not even get in the papers any more. There has been too many, so I thought up something new."

"What?" I asked.

"Pose-ins," said Simple, "or pose-outs."

"What do you mean, 'pose-outs'?"

"Statues is often naked, are they not?" said Simple.

"Yes."

"Well, by pose-outs," said Simple, "I mean Negroes undressing down to their bare skin and posing naked as statues for freedom's sake. Twenty million Negroes taking off every stitch—stepping out of pants, dress, and drawers in public places and posing in the nude until civil rights have come to pass."

"You are demented," I declared.

"No," said Simple. "Nothing would attract as much attention to segregation, integration, desegregation, and ratiocination than if every Negro in this American country would just stand naked until Jim Crow goes."

"Fantastic!" I said. "Mad! Completely absurd!"

"Yes," said Simple, "at a certain time on a certain day let even those Negroes that be in Congress—Dawson, Diggs, Adam Powell—like that first Adam in the Garden—rise naked to answer the roll call. Ordinary people, if at work in factories, foundries, offices, or homes, will establish a nude-in. If on the streets, a nude-out. Black waiters at the Union League Club, a nude-in. Colored boys pushing racks in the streets of the garment district, a nude-out. Black cooks could pose in white kitchens naked. Maids could pose dusting the parlor with nothing on but a dust cap.

Pullman porters on trains in the raw. Redcaps at stations bare except for badge numbers. Ralph Bunche at the United Nations, naked as a bird. At home, a nude-in. On the street, a nude-out. Until all Negroes get our rights, we pose. You know that statue 'The Thinker'?"

"By Rodin," I said.

"Setting on a stone with nothing on in God's world—'The Thinker'— with his chin in his hand, just setting lost in thought. Imagine James Farmer demonstrating for CORE at City Hall, posing at high noon naked, making like 'The Thinker,' chin in hand! Also on the same day at the same time Roy Wilkins upholding the NAACP, buck-naked between them two lions on the steps of the New York Public Library, with nothing on but his nose glasses. At the back of the library, on the terrace facing Bryant Park, Borough President Constance Baker Motley just as she came in this world, whilst at Fiftieth and Broadway where the theatres is, Miss Lena Horne, bare as Venus. Down the way a piece, in front of the Metropolitan Opera, Leontyne Price in all her glory on a podium, not a stitch to her name. The traffic tie-up on Broadway would be terrific. We would not need a stall-in. Nude-outs would be enough. In Central Park, Willie Mays, on Sugar Hill, Jackie Robinson. And uptown in Harlem at 125th and Lenox I would place on a pedestal Miss Pearl Bailey."

"Unclothed?"

"Except by nature," said Simple. "With Negroes posing like statues all over town, traffic would jam. On Wall Street tickers would stop running. In Washington at the sight of Adam Powell in his birthday suit, filibusters would cease to be. In Atlanta, Rev. Martin Luther King, with not even a wrist watch on, would preach his Sunday-morning sermon. In New York colored subway conductors would report for duty in the all-together. Every waitress in Chock full o' Nuts would look like Eve before the Fall. In Harlem, Black Muslims would turn to Black Nudists. And at the Apollo, Jackie Mabley would break up the show. Oh, if every Negro in America, big and small, great and not so great, would just take his clothes off and keep them off for the sake of civil rights, America would be forced to scrutinize our cause."

"How shocking!" I said.

"Which is what we would mean it to be," declared Simple. "A nude-out to shock America into clothing us in the garments of equality, not the rags of segregation. And when Negroes got dressed again, we could vote in Mississippi."

"That would be when hell freezes over," I said. "Besides, by that time the Legion of Decency would have all of you in jail for indecent exposure."

"Not me," said Simple, "because I would be in Harlem. The colored cops in Harlem would be naked, too, so how would I know, without his uniform, that he were a cop?"

"Considering all the dangers involved, would you be the first to volunteer for a nude-out?" I asked.

"That honor I would leave you," said Simple.

cadillac blues
performed 1968

Wooo! excuse me miss, from asking you this, but who may your good man be? Sugar, I know I'm a funny lookin' fella. Wooo, but if I clean up won't you have a little pity on me? That's what I'm talkin' about.

I'm the man that is the Lightnin' Hopkins, tell you what I done. I rode an old T Model Ford until I decided I would buy me a Cadillac. Look'a here, I went a long way in that T Model; I saved pennies by pennies to get to pay a down payment on me a Cadillac. Nobody liked poor Lightnin' when he drive up in that T Model, you know they act? Look at me and look off. I get me my two bits worth of gasoline and I'd drive on. Yeah, I'd drive on.

But you know I don't know how it happened, but one day I got lucky. I got me a Cadillac—black Cadillac with white-walled tires. I'm sittin' up there I'm black, white teeth and white eyed. Yes, I did. I decided I'm goin' drive my Cadillac.

They say, "Who . . . ? Uh-uh, that ain't Lightnin'."

I said, "*Toot-toot.*" I'd hear 'em, but I just blow back at 'em, let 'em know it *is* me.

Every stop sign I get to I wanted somebody to be standing there to see that I had changed that T Model into a Cadillac. So, last Monday I drove up to an old stop sign and it was a pretty, *beautiful* little girl standing up there talkin' to one of them slick cats, y'know. He was twirlin' a little chain around his finger. He was telling her something at the time and when she see that pretty Cadillac I squatted down. He looked over and he'd seen that it was . . . you understand what I might say to myself, "That's a fish for her."

He turned his back and went to whistlin'.

She say, "Hey, mister. How far you goin'?"

I say, "Aww, kid, I'm goin' a pretty good piece. Why?"

"Could I ride with you just about, y' know, another block or two? I would like to."

I said, "Aww, get in!" I asked him, "You goin' mister?"

"No, nooo. pardner. Nooo."

I left him standin' there. I'm glad of my Cadillac. I drove up to a coffeehouse. I said, "Now, I want me a cup of coffee."

I pulled over to the side. I said, "Darling, come on in here and let's drink a cup of coffee. And what's next is, where you go—I go."

She said, "Well, wait a minute. It's such a beautiful car and you such a nice person, let me show you something."

She pulled out her driving license. She said, "Now, I got my driving license and I know you not scared to trust me. I just want to make *one* block. Just about the time you drink that coffee, why I'll be right back."

And you know what? That made me feel good, because it looked like I been knowing her a long time and could trust her, y' know? "That's okay," I say, "Go 'head."

She slide down to the wheel and I got out. So, she made that block and went right back to where that boy was whistlin'. Just as she got there I thought about it when I ordered my coffee. I said, "Uh-unh." I said, "Wait a minute." I said, "Now, when a man trust that much money in a woman and don't know nothin' about her she liable to be feelin' it."

I run down there. I'm goin' make that block, y' understand, and catch her before she leave.

I said, "Now, she could be goin' to pick up that guy."

There she was he gettin' in.

I said, "Hold it!"

Y' know, rubber on wheels is faster than rubber on heels. So, I'm . . . yeah . . . I'm sure is puttin' 'em down. I'm tryin' to catch this guy, y' know, and the girl. But what hurt me so bad is that she done slide over and he get on the wheel. And when I got up to the scene just about close enough I could holler at 'em, I hollered . . .

(song begins)

Whoa, baby,

Please come on back,
For you've got something of mine,

I sure do like and that's black Cadillac this morning,
My black Cadillac this morning,

Yeah, my black Cadillac,
With them white-wall tires,

Y'know, she was sittin' glad that 'cause he could sure drive,

She said, step on it,
Is this as fast as it's running?
He said, I don't know,
I don't want to get no ticket,

She said, step on this thing!
If that's as fast as it go,
I don't want to ride this Cadillac no more,
He said, well I'm gonna let the hammer down,
She said, well, if you see a red light,
Run over it and get a ticket,
He said, no I aint gonna get no ticket,

If I can make a breathe
That thing was wide open man,

My black Cadillac,
They left me and that was somethin' I sure didn't like,

It run alright,

Whoa, baby,
Will you come on back,
Got something that I sure do like,
And that's my black Cadillac,
My black Cadillac this morning,

Yeah, my black Cadillac,
With them white-wall tires,

And hear what she told me,
I know your Cadillac,
Is really black,
I know you got them white-wall tires,
But I got a black man on beside me,
White eyes and white teeth,

Woo, Lightnin'—you can't catch me,
No, Lightnin'—you can't catch me,
Well, it's obvious still now
Wonder where can they be,

I stopped in the parking lot,
They done parked in the busted block,
I caught him,
But what good would it do,

That Cadillac wouldn't run for me,
And it wouldn't run for you.

H. RAP BROWN

from die, nigger, die!
1969

i was born into a family of dark-skinned negroes, but I'm what many consider a red nigger. My mother, my father, my brother Ed and my sister are all darker than I am. Because I was lighter, it meant that I was supposed to get ahead. So my mother gave me what I would call preferential treatment. Because of this there was a lot of rivalry between my brother Ed and myself. He and I weren't "tight" when we were young. He thought that our mother treated me better than she did him. In negro america the more you look like buttermilk, the prettier you're supposed to be. This is color prejudice. I don't think that my mother was conscious of all this, but it happened a lot of times. So Ed and I used to have a lot of conflicts. I didn't want it that way. Ed was my older brother and I looked up to him. But he didn't want me hanging around him.

Ed and I are very close now and that color thing doesn't come between us anymore. But it's a thing which could really damage the Black community if people don't begin to understand it. There are nationalist groups that won't accept light-complexioned Blacks. What they're doing is helping the white man, because they're creating the potential for a divisive fight inside the Black community. And it's totally unnecessary and damaging. The government is doing enough to try and divide the Black community. We shouldn't be helping them. We must learn that Black is not a color but the way you think.

If we are to succeed in the struggle we must eliminate the significance that we have assigned to color in our community. The range of Black runs from the brother who is Black enough to poot smoke, to the blood who is pale with the rape of Mothers. Among Black people color can have no value, no significance. Commitment will determine the value of individuals. If I had identified with the attitudes of white-minded negroes and then come home to my dark-skinned brother and family, I wouldn't have been able to accept them. But that wasn't a problem for me, because I knew who I wanted to identify with. It was the bloods in my neighborhood, the guys who hung out down on the corner. The Black community, in other words. I always hung out with cats who had made hanging out a profession. I found that it took special skills to hang out 14 hours just laying and playing.

My first institutionalized schooling came in an orphanage —Blundon Orphanage Home. It was operated by white missionaries whose role was similar to that of whites in Africa. Civilize the savage through Christianity. Savages in this case being Black kids from families too poor to support them. The school had the look of a huge plantation with two big shabby old buildings located near the bottom of the hill and a relatively well-kept building at the top. The grounds around the building at the top of the hill were also well-kept with trees and shrubs and Keep-Off signs. More attention, in fact, was paid to the grounds on the "hill" than was paid to the two buildings in the "Bottom." Each of the "Big Houses," as they were called, had classrooms on the bottom floors and living quarters above. All of the teachers and students in the school were Black. The Black residents were of all ages and basically responsible for each other. The older children attended to the needs of the smaller children. Children of all ages were expected to work and were assigned jobs.

This was my first real contact with a world bigger and badder than that of my street. You had to excel in either fighting, running or tomming; I integrated the three. In this world, the heroes were bloods who will never be remembered outside our Black community. Cats like Pie-man, Ig, Yank, Smokey, Hawk, Lil Nel—all bad muthafuckas. Young bloods wanted to be like these brothers. They were the men in our community. They had all the women and had made their way to the top through sports and knowing the streets. So to us, the most important thing was to excel in athletics. Recess was the most essential part of the school day, for we could practice our skills. One play could make or break you. We all lived for the big play. For many it never came.

Once I'd established my reputation, cats respected it. "You don't mess with Rap, cause he's our man." If I went out of my neighborhood, though, it was another story. I'd be on somebody else's turf and would have to make it or take it over there. So there was always a lot of fighting and competition among the young brothers.

It really gets bad when you get to high school. In high school there's always rivalry between the football teams of the two high schools in town or something like that. But it's more than athletic rivalry. It may start on the football field, but it's carried to the street. In Baton Rouge there was a rivalry between McKinley High and Capitol High. You'd think the students were two totally different races. People were perpetually at war. I mean they were really at war. Gangs from South Baton Rouge would be expected to fight dudes from the Park. Dudes from the Park couldn't come to South Baton Rouge and vice-versa unless they were *bad* muthafuckas. And if they were caught, being bad didn't make no difference.

That type of rivalry still exists. It's perpetuated by the schools, by the negroes in authority who pretend they're handling it, but don't. The whole fever pitch which builds up in those gangs is transferred from the people who are being "educated" to the cats who hang around the streets.

But when most of us rivals went on to college, then college made a kind of bond between us. The athletes who had scholarships and the cats who worked during the summer to get that tuition came to college and then they became allies against dudes from other cities. Like, "you my home-boy, and the dude who ain't from around here, he ain't one of us." Yeah, well that's part of that whole primitive thing and it's very dangerous. Given the destruction by slavery of both tribe and culture, negroes created a new kind of american tribalism. A tribalism based on the exclusion of certain types. A deliberate attempt to make race a secondary consideration. There are tribes and tribes of negroes. The A.K.A. tribe, Kappa tribe, Doctor tribe, Teacher tribe, Entertainer tribe, High School tribe, College tribe, etc. This tribalism has extended into what is called the "Movement." "Militant" tribes compete against other "militant" tribes and "moderate" tribes, to promote tribal interests and not the interests of the race or the masses. We treat revolution as if it is an historic process rather than an evolutionary movement. In other words, we all got a monopoly on truth. Whites who consider themselves allies add to this by deciding which tribe is "correct" and which is "incorrect." In other words, the one which best fits their needs. As a result of this kind of external control, tribes engage in fratricide (unknowingly in most cases) to gain the favor of the white "ally." Tribe is placed above race. It is not uncommon to hear negroes say, "My loyalty is to my Frat., God, and my country, in that order."

When a race of people is oppressed within a system that fosters the idea of competitive individualism, the political polarization around individual interests prevents group interests. Each negro prides himself on his ability to reason or think as an individual. Therefore, any gains are to the individual and not to the group. So individuals join tribes or groups to further their own personal ambitions. It's one of the things that keeps us fighting ourselves instead of the enemy. Black people have always been ready to shoot and cut each other up. The weekend is always wartime in the Black community. Every week when Friday rolls around, you know that somebody is gon' get killed before church time Sunday morning. But let one white man come down the street acting bad and all he got in his pocket is a toothpick, all of them bad niggers, niggers ready to kill in a minute, be hiding in the alleys or be grinning and bowing. "Yassuh, Mr. White Man." White bleeds just as red as Black does, but you can only prove it by hearsay. And the press has done a job on negroes and whites, because it makes you think that Black people are killing 14 white folks a day. But even J. Edgar Hoover, with his faggot ass, admits that more Black folks kill Black folks than Blacks kill whites. But everybody thinks that we're killing white folks. Uh-uh. We're still killing off each other. Even a lot of these so-called "militants" go around pulling their 22's on Black people and "tomming" when the white man comes around. And they supposed to be so muthafucking bad. Yeah, we are bad when it comes to us. And the white man sits back and laughs 'cause niggers ain't got no better sense than to be fighting one another.

However, we must understand the many ways in which the white man brainwashes people into acting and thinking like he wants them to so he can continue to control them.

You grow up in Black america and it's like living in a pressure cooker. Babies become men without going through childhood. And when you become a man, you got nothing to look forward to and nothing to look back on. So what do you make it on? The wine bottle, the reefer or Jesus. A taste of grape, the weed or the cross. These are our painkillers.

I knew dudes who were old men by the time they were seven. That's the age when little white kids are dreaming about fairy princesses and Cinderella and playing in tree houses and wondering whether they want two cars or four cars when they grow up. We didn't have time for all that. Didn't even have time for childhood. If you acted like a child, you didn't survive and that's all there was to it. Hell, you be walking home from school and up come some high school dudes who'd jack you up and take the little dime your mama had given you to buy some candy with. So

what'd you do? Jump some dude who was younger and littler than you
and take his dime. And pretty soon you started carrying a razor blade, a
switch blade or just a pocketful of rocks so you could protect yourself as a
man. You had to if you were going to survive.

White folks get all righteous and wonder why Black people steal and
gamble. Same reason white folks do. We need money, because the society
says you must have it to keep from starving. If you got it, you eat. If you
don't, tough. But white people are able to make their stealing and
gambling legitimate. White man'll sell you a $20 suit for $50 and call
it good business. What he actually did was steal $30. White man'll buy a
watch for $5.00 sell it for $49.95 and call the difference, profit. Profit is a
nice word for stealing which the society has legitimatized. Catholics go to
church every week and gamble, but they call it Bingo. The Pope blesses
'em, so it's all right. The state of Nevada is built on a deck of cards and a
roulette wheel, but that's okay, 'cause it's white folks that passed the law
saying it was okay. But you let us get over in the corner of the alley with
some dice and try to make a little profit and here come the police, the
judge, the jailer and the sociology student. We get thrown into jail for
gambling or stealing. White folks go to Congress for stealing and they call
that democracy.

America is a country that makes you want things, but doesn't give you
the means to get those things. Little Black children sit in front of the t.v. set
and all they see are fine cars, perfumes, clothes and everything else they
ain't got. They sit there and watch it, telling the rats to sit down and stop
blocking their view. Ain't nobody told them, though, that they don't have
any way of getting any of that stuff. They couldn't even get full at supper,
but that don't matter. They want an Oldsmobile. So next day during
recess, they go off in a corner of the schoolyard and pitch pennies, play
Odd Man Wins, Heads-up Basketball for a quarter, Pitty-Pat for a nickel,
Old Maid for a penny. Once they become pros at that, they move on up to
Tonk, Black Jack and Craps. After school, there's the pinball machines.
Some of them little dudes could barely see the game board, but they
would be there, jim, shoving nickels in the machine, trying to manipulate
the lights into a straight line. You could win 50 cents or a dollar and if you
were lucky, $5.00. Once you graduated from the pinball machine, you
entered the poolroom.

America's a bitch. Being Black in this country is like somebody asking
you to play white Russian roulette and giving you a gun with bullets in all

the chambers. Any way you go, jim, that's your ass. America says you got to have money to live and to get money you got to have a job. To get a job, you got to have an education. So along comes a Black man and he gets a worse than inferior education so he can't qualify for a job he couldn't get because he was Black to begin with and still he's supposed to eat, keep his family together, pay the rent and buy an Oldsmobile. And white folks wonder why niggers steal and gamble. I only wish we would stop this petty stealing and take care of Chase Manhattan Bank, Fort Knox or some armories.

There was this blood I grew up with named J.S. He was a smart dude, particularly in math. Dude would have given a computer competition. He lived with his aunt, who worked as a maid, and three sisters. 'Cause his aunt was a maid, she didn't make hardly nothing. White folks love to pay their niggers in old clothes and leftovers. So he couldn't dress like some of the other students whose parents were making it in negro america. The teachers were all trying to make it in negro america too. They took a bath once a day and wiped under their arms and between their legs twice a day and always tried to smell like they lived in perfume bottles. Well, I know how my man must've felt sitting in class in front of some bitch like this. He felt like a piece of shit, particularly when the teacher would stand up in front of the class and talk about him 'cause his clothes were dirty. You damned right his clothes were dirty! His aunt worked from can to can't, and by the time she got home at night she was too tired to bend over the scrub board to wash out some clothes for J.S. to wear every day. She did the best she could.

J.S. was as smart as anybody in school and he showed it, too, but in negro america if you didn't have the right color, the right clothes, and the right manners, sorry for you. Them teachers were slick, though, when it came to telling a kid he wasn't shit. They were always going out of the room to stand in the hall and gossip with the other teachers. When they did, they'd leave a student in charge to sit behind the desk and take the names of the students who talked or cut up. And always, the one left in charge was light, bright and almost white. If a light-skinned student was reciting in class, the teacher had the patience of Job, the understanding of Solomon and the expectations of God Almighty himself. But you let a sho-nuf blood just pause when he was reciting and the teacher told him to sit down in a voice filled with hatred. "I didn't expect you to know it anyway," the teacher would sometimes say, meaning, you're black. You're black! You're black!

The teachers had to tell J.S. he was smart, 'cause it was so obvious. But they made a point of letting him know that being smart wasn't enough if your hair was uncombed, your clothes a little dirty, your skin a little ashy and your manners not the best. In other words, you may be smart, but you black! So J.S. learned pretty quick that there wasn't no reward in being smart and that it didn't have a damned thing to do with surviving.

But this is the kind of education we were subjected to. Education ain't just what comes out of the books, but it's everything that goes on in the school. And if you leave school hating yourself, then it doesn't matter how much you know. Education in america has to be viewed as propaganda machinery. All educational systems are propaganda machines, but for Black people, the american educational system is a propaganda machine we don't need. It propagandizes against us. It makes us hate ourselves.

I began realizing this when I was in high school. I saw no sense in reading Shakespeare. After I read Othello, it was obvious that Shakespeare was a racist. From reading his poetry, I gathered that he was a faggot. But we never discussed the racist attitude expressed in his works. This was when I really began to raise questions. I was in constant conflict with my teachers in high school. I would interpret the thing one way and they would say it's wrong. Well, how could they tell me what Shakespeare was thinking. I knew then that something was wrong, unless the teachers had a monopoly on truth or were communicating with the dead.

Part of my mother's whole attempt to make us a part of negro america was that she took us out of McKinley High and sent us to Southern High. Anybody who could pay $12 a year could go and that was for the activities card. So, you see how jive the thing was. It was connected with the negro college in Baton Rouge, Southern University, and it was really set up so the teachers at Southern wouldn't have to send their children to school with Black kids. It was a crock of shit, but it had an air of "respectability." This was where all the bourgeois negroes were supposed to go.

It could've created problems for me, because if I had identified with most of the white-minded negroes at school, I wouldn't have been able to relate to brothers on the block. Worse than that, I would've thought that I was better than them. It's like the whole school busing thing now. Busing Black children to schools outside the Black community is nothing but a move to divide the community. If integration is what's wanted, then bus the whole community. But to take individuals out of the community is a very dangerous and immoral thing. The "brightest" students are taken, students who can fit into the white man's program best, and they're bused out of the community so they can come back and articulate the white man's program. That splits the community. Parents who sent their children to white schools in the South made a mistake. They injured those students mentally for life. To send a Black kid to a school full of howling maniacs. Madmen! Wildmen! Animals! And those Black kids got their minds messed up. You send a student to a white school and he has to come home to a Black family and a Black community. It messes him up and it messes the community up. This is a deliberate part of "the man's" game.

I could've gotten messed up like that at Southern High if I hadn't known where it was at and what was happening. But I didn't change myself to fit that phony-ass atmosphere and try to be respectable and all that shit. Me and Southern High had quite a few conflicts. One time I got put out of school for wearing my shirt out of my pants. Another time I got put out for cursing out a teacher.

Ed and my sister, who're both older than I, went to the same school. So when I came along, I had to go through the same teachers they'd gone through. The teachers said I should be just like them. I should open doors for them and shit like that. Just like my family had always said I should do things like Ed. So when I wouldn't do all these things and started raising hell, my homeroom teacher started criticizing me. One day I got sick of that shit and I cussed her out. I got put out of school for that.

I was always at odds with teachers. There are certain things in negro institutions that you have to do if you expect to make good grades and certain things you don't do. One of those things is you don't talk back. You don't challenge the existing order. Well, I challenge anything that doesn't make good sense.

Another time in high school they called my mother in about me because I got into it with one of the dudes teaching shop. I knew he was screwing my homeroom teacher, so I didn't have no respect for him, especially since I knew his wife. Us young dudes in the Black community directed our aggression against negroes who had these positions because there was a failure on their part to take out their aggression against white people. But, these negroes in position would always direct their grievances toward Black students. They got mad at us 'cause the white man was mistreating them, and we got mad at them 'cause they let the white man mistreat 'em and then turned around and mistreated us, on top of the white man mistreating all of us.

But I stayed in school, 'cause I wasn't willing to get caught in another trick that eventually led to long sentences in jail or ending up in the gutter one night with a knife in your back. A lot of bloods, though, couldn't cut school. When they came, it was to practice the education they'd been getting out in the street. While we were still in elementary school, J.S. would wait for recess to get out to the playground where he'd sneak a deck of cards out of his pocket, get way off in a corner and start gambling. After school, we'd go home and J.S. would go on down to the pool hall. By the time he was fourteen, he was dealing in a gambling club in West Baton Rouge. After a while he quit school. Working at the club like he was, he was ready to go to bed when the rest of us were getting up to go to classes. We used to see him in the afternoon, though. He'd drop by the school and be vined down. He was clean, jim. Had him a conk then and he knew he was ready.

After a while the state police started cracking down on gambling and J.S. cut out of Baton Rouge and started following the action from Biloxi, Mississippi, over to Houston, Texas, and back again. He was sixteen.

It was a couple of years later when I saw him again. I'd just entered college. I was thumbing my way to school when who should I see hanging out on the corner but J.S., looking clean. I went up to him. We greeted each other like we were ol' cut-buddies, but after all the greeting and slapping hands, we found it hard to talk to each other. Too many different kinds of experience had come between us. He was my nigger, but J.S. had made a way of life on the block which I just figured had aged him. It was a rough life. Drinking, fighting, dodging the police, gambling—it can wear a man down fast. I looked at J.S. and it was beginning to show on him. His eyes once used to shine, but they'd gotten dull and red. His face was getting tight and there were wrinkles starting to crawl across his forehead. He told me that he'd just gotten out of the joint on a concealed weapons charge. Plus he told me that when gambling and living off women wasn't enough to survive, he'd become a cat burglar and a fence on the side. But he definitely wasn't feeling sorry for himself. Only thing he was unhappy about was that his luck in gambling was off. We went and got some "pluck" (wine) and I told him I was in college. He asked what I wanted to be. I told him rich. He looked up at the ceiling and paused for a minute before he said, "You know, I've never given any thought to what I want to become." I told him he should think about it, but I knew I was shuckin' and jivin'. Hell, hardly any of us had ever thought about what we wanted to become. What was the future? That was something white folks had. We just lived from day to day, expecting whatever life put on us and dealing with it the best way we knew how when it came. I had accepted the big lie of a Black man succeeding.

I remembered that J.S. was always good with math. I knew how to count money and always figured I didn't need to know no more about numbers, but I had to take math in college. So I showed J.S. some of the math problems I had been having trouble with and he looked 'em over for a short while and knocked 'em out in no time. He said he'd tutor me in math. I told him that was cool. But that was the last time I saw him. A couple of weeks later he shot and killed some dude and the judge gave him life. He was eighteen.

That's the way the deal goes down for a lot of bloods. Wiped out by the time they're eighteen and don't ever really know why. He was rebelling against the way the cards were stacked against him and even his rebellion was a stacked deck. He lived his life the way he saw it, made his own laws, but what was legal in our world wasn't "legal" in the white world and eventually he went down.

My ol' lady wanted to keep all that away from me. Didn't want me to know anything about it. I guess she called it protecting me, but I had to be out there where the action was. She thought I should be in the house reading books like Ed so I could make my way in negro america, but I wasn't hearing that. I never was one for too much reading anyway. Too, how was I supposed to stay on top of what was going down if I was sitting up in the house with a book. If you were going to stay in control, you had to be in the street.

The street is where young bloods get their education. I learned how to talk in the street, not from reading about Dick and Jane going to the zoo and all that simple shit. The teacher would test our vocabulary each week, but we knew the vocabulary we needed. They'd give us arithmetic to exercise our minds. Hell, we exercised our minds by playing the Dozens.

> I fucked your mama
> Till she went blind.
> Her breath smells bad,
> But she sure can grind.

I fucked your mama
For a solid hour.
Baby came out
Screaming, Black Power.

Elephant and the Baboon
Learning to screw.
Baby came out looking
Like Spiro Agnew.

And the teacher expected me to sit up in class and study poetry after I could run down shit like that. If anybody needed to study poetry, she needed to study mine. We played the Dozens for recreation, like white folks play Scrabble.

In many ways, though, the Dozens is a mean game because what you try to do is totally destroy somebody else with words. It's that whole competition thing again, fighting each other. There'd be sometimes 40 or 50 dudes standing around and the winner was determined by the way they responded to what was said. If you fell all over each other laughing, then you knew you'd scored. It was a bad scene for the dude that was getting humiliated. I seldom was. That's why they call me Rap, 'cause I could rap. (The name stuck because Ed would always say, "That my nigger Rap," "Rap my nigger.") But for dudes who couldn't, it was like they were humiliated because they were born Black and then they turned around and got humiliated by their own people, which was really all they had left. But that's the way it is. Those that feel most humiliated humiliate others. The real aim of the Dozens was to get a dude so mad that he'd cry or get mad enough to fight. You'd say shit like, "Man, tell your mama to stop coming around my house all the time. I'm tired of fucking her and I think you should know that it ain't no accident you look like me." And it could go on for hours sometimes. Some of the best Dozens players were girls.

Signifying is more humane. Instead of coming down on somebody's mother, you come down on them. But, before you can signify you got to be able to rap. A session would start maybe by a brother saying, "Man, before you mess with me you'd rather run rabbits, eat shit and bark at the moon." Then, if he was talking to me, I'd tell him:

Man, you must don't know who I am.

I'm sweet peeter jeeter the womb beater

The baby maker the cradle shaker

The deerslayer the buckbinder the women finder

Known from the Gold Coast to the rocky shores of Maine

Rap is my name and love is my game.

I'm the bed tucker the cock plucker the motherfucker

The milkshaker the record breaker the population maker

The gun-slinger the baby bringer

The hum-dinger the pussy ringer

The man with the terrible middle finger.

The hard hitter the bullshitter the poly-nussy getter

The beast from the East the Judge the sludge

The women's pet the men's fret and the punks' pin-up boy.

They call me Rap the dicker the ass kicker

The cherry picker the city slicker the titty licker

And I ain't giving up nothing but bubble gum and hard times and I'm
    fresh out of bubble gum.

I'm giving up wooden nickels 'cause I know they won't spend

And I got a pocketful of splinter change.

I'm a member of the bathtub club: I'm seeing a whole lot of ass but
    I ain't taking no shit.

I'm the man who walked the water and tied the whale's tail in a knot

Taught the little fishes how to swim

Crossed the burning sands and shook the devil's hand

Rode round the world on the back of a snail carrying a sack saying
    AIR MAIL.

Walked 49 miles of barbwire and used a Cobra snake for a necktie

And got a brand new house on the roadside made from a cracker's hide,

Got a brand new chimney setting on top made from the cracker's
    skull

Took a hammer and nail and built the world and calls it
    "THE BUCKET OF BLOOD."

Yes, I'm hemp the demp the women's pimp

Women fight for my delight.

I'm a bad motherfucker. Rap the rip-saw the devil's brother 'n law.

I roam the world I'm known to wander and this .45 is where I get
    my thunder.

I'm the only man in the world who knows why white milk makes
  yellow butter.
I know where the lights go when you cut the switch off.
I might not be the best in the world, but I'm in the top two and my
  brother's getting old.
And ain't nothing bad 'bout you but your breath.

Now, if the brother couldn't come back behind that, I usually cut him
some slack (depending on time, place and his attitude). We learned what
the white folks call verbal skills. We learned how to throw them words
together. America, however, has Black folk in a serious game of the
Dozens. (The dirty muthafucka.) Signifying allowed you a choice—you
could either make a cat feel good or bad. If you had just destroyed
someone or if they were just down already, signifying could help them
over. Signifying was also a way of expressing your own feelings:

Man, I can't win for losing.
If it wasn't for bad luck, I wouldn't have no luck at all.
I been having buzzard luck
Can't kill nothing and won't nothing die
I'm living on the welfare and things is stormy
They borrowing their shit from the Salvation Army
But things bound to get better 'cause they can't get no worse
I'm just like the blind man, standing by a broken window
I don't feel no pain.
But it's your world
You the man I pay rent to
If I had your hands I'd give 'way both my arms.

SAM GREENLEE

from the spook who sat by the door
1969

freeman watched the class reunion from a corner of the common room of the CIA training barracks. It was a black middle-class reunion. They were black bourgeoisie to a man, black nepotism personified. In addition to those who had recruited themselves upon receiving notice that the CIA was now interested in at least token integration, five were relatives or in-laws of civil rights leaders, four others of Negro politicians. Only Freeman was not middle class, and the others knew it. Even had he not dressed as he did, not used the speech patterns and mannerisms of the Chicago ghetto slums, they would have known. His presence made them uneasy and insecure; they were members of the black élite, and a product of the ghetto streets did not belong among them.

They carefully ignored Freeman and it was as he wished; he had no more love for the black middle class than they for him. He watched them establishing the pecking order as he sat sipping a scotch highball. It was their first day in the training camp after months of exhaustive screening, testing, security checks. Of the hundreds considered, only the twenty-three present in the room had survived and been selected for preliminary training and, constantly reminded of it since they had reported, they pranced, posed and preened in mutual and self-admiration. To be a "Negro Firster" was considered a big thing, but Freeman didn't think so.

"Man, you know how much this twelve-year-old scotch cost me in the commissary? Three bills and a little change! Chiv-head Regal! As long as I can put my mouth around this kind of whisky at that price, I'm in love with being a spy."

"You know they call CIA agents spooks? First time we'll ever get paid for that title."

"Man, the fringe benefits—they just don't stop coming in! Nothing to say of the base pay and stuff. We got it made."

"Say, baby, didn't we meet at the Penn Relays a couple of years ago? In that motel on the edge of Philly? You remember that chick you was with, Lurlean? Well, she's teaching school in Camden now and I get a little bit of that from time to time. Now, man, don't freeze on me. I'm married, too, and you know Lurlean don't give a damn. I'll tell her I saw you when we get out of here."

Where'd you go to school, man? Fisk? I went to Morris Brown. You frat? Q? You got a couple brothers here, those two cats over there. What you major in? What your father do? Your mother working, too? Where your wife go to school? What sorority? What kind of work you do before you made this scene? How much bread you make? Where's your home? What kind of car you got? How much you pay for that suit? You got your own pad, or you live in an apartment? Co-op apartment? Tell me that's the new thing nowadays. Clue me in. You got colour TV? Component stereo, or console?

Drop those names: doctors I have known, lawyers, judges, businessmen, dentists, politicians, and Great Negro Leaders I have known. Drop those brand names: GE, Magnavox, Ford, GM, Chrysler, Zenith, Brooks Brothers, Florsheim. Johnnie Walker, Chivas Regal, Jack Daniel's. Imported beer. Du Pont carpeting, wall-to-wall. Wall-to-wall drags with split-level minds, remote-control colour TV souls and credit-card hearts.

Play who-do-you-know and who-have-you-screwed. Blow your bourgeois blues, your nigger soul sold for a mess of materialistic pottage. You can't ever catch Charlie, but you can ape him and keep the gap widening between you and those other niggers. You have a ceiling on you and yours, your ambitions; but the others are in the basement and you will help Mr. Charlie keep them there. If they get out and move up to your level, then what will you have?

They eyed Freeman uneasily; he was an alien in this crowd. Somehow, he had escaped the basement. He had moved up to their level and he was a threat. He must be put in his place. He would not last, breeding told, but he should know that he was among his betters.

The tall, good-looking one with the curly black hair and light skin approached Freeman. He was from Howard and wore his clothes Howard-style, the cuffless pants stopping at his ankles. His tie was very skinny and the knot almost unnoticeable, his shoulder-padding non-existent. He had known these arrogant, Chicago niggers like Freeman before, thinking they owned Howard's campus, moving in with their down-home ways, their Mississippi mannerisms, loud laughter, no manners, elbowing their way into the fraternities, trying to steal the women, making more noise than anyone else at the football games and rallies. One of those diddy-bop niggers from Chicago had almost stolen his present wife.

"Where you from, man? You don't seem to talk much."

"No, I don't."

"Don't what?"

"Don't talk much. I'm from Chicago."

"Chicago? Where you from before that? Wayback, Georgia, Snatch-back, Mississippi? You look like you just got off the train, man. Where's the paper bag with your sack of fried chicken?"

Freeman looked at him and sipped his drink.

"No, seriously, my man, where you from? Lot of boys here from the south; how come you got to pretend? I bet you don't even know where State Street and the Loop is. How you sneak into this group? This is supposed to be the cream, man. You sure you don't clean up around here?"

Freeman stood up slowly, still holding his drink. The tall one was standing very close to his armchair and had to step back when Freeman rose.

"Baby, I will kick your ass. Go away and leave me to hell alone."

The tall one opened his mouth to speak; a fraternity brother sidled up, took his arm and led him away. Freeman freshened his drink and sat down in front of the television set. After a lull, the black middle-class reunion resumed.

He had not made a mistake, he thought. All niggers looked alike to whites and he had thought it to his advantage to set himself apart from this group in a way that would make the whites overlook him until too late. They would automatically assume that the others—who looked and acted so much like their black representatives and spokesmen who appeared on the television panels, spoke in the halls of congress, made the covers of *Time* and *Life* and ran the Negro newspapers and magazines, who formed the only link with the white world—would threaten to survive this test. Both the whites and these saddity niggers, Freeman thought, would ignore him until too late. And, he thought, Whitey will be more likely to ignore a nigger who approaches the stereotype than these others who think imitation the sincerest form of flattery.

He smiled when he thought about walking into his friend's dental office that day.

"Hey, Freebee, what's happening, baby? Ain't seen you in the Boulevard Lounge lately. Where you been hiding? Got something new on the string?"

"No, been working. Look, you know the cap you put on after I got hung up in the Iowa game? I want a new one. With an edge of gold around it."

"Gold? You must be kidding. And where you get that refugee from Robert Hall suit?"

"That's where I bought it. I'm going out to Washington for a final interview panel and I want to please the crackers." His friend nodded. He understood.

Freeman did not spend much time socialising with the rest of the Negro pioneers, those chosen to be the first to integrate a segregated institution. He felt none of the gratitude, awe, pride and arrogance of the Negro "firsts" and he did not think after the first few days that many of them would be around very long; and Freeman had come to stay.

They had calisthenics in the morning and then six hours of classes. Exams were scheduled for each Saturday morning. They were not allowed to leave the area, but there was a different movie screened each night in a plush, small theatre. There was a small PX, a swimming pool, a bar and a soda fountain. There was a social area at each end of the building in which they lived that included pool tables, ping-pong, a television room with colour TV, chess and checker sets. There was a small library, containing technical material related to their classes and light fiction, magazines and periodicals. There was a music room with a stereo console containing an AM-FM receiver and with records consisting mostly of show tunes from Broadway hits of the last decade. There were coke machines. It was like a very plush Bachelor Officer's Quarter.

There were basketball courts, badminton courts, a nine-hole golf course, squash courts, a gym, a 220-yard rubberised track, a touch-football field. After the intensive screening which they had undergone prior to their selection, none of the rest thought that the classes and examinations were anything more than window dressing. They settled down to enjoy their plush confinement during the training period after which they would be given offices in the vast building in Langley Virginia down by the river.

Freeman combined a programme of calisthenics, weight training, isometrics, running and swimming, which never took more than an hour, usually less than half that time. He would watch television or read until dinner, take an hour's nap and then study until midnight.

No one at the training camp, white or coloured, thought it strange that Freeman, a product of the Chicago ghetto, where Negroes spend more time, money and care in the selection of their wardrobe than even in Harlem, should be so badly dressed. Or that, although he had attended two first-rate educational institutions, he should speak with so limited a vocabulary, so pronounced an accent and such Uncle Tom humour. They put it down to the fact that he had been an athlete who had skated through college on his fame. Freeman did not worry about the whites because he was being exactly what they wished. The Negroes of the class would be ashamed of him, yet flattered by the contrast; but there might be a shrewd one among them.

There was only one. He approached Freeman several times with penetrating questions. The fraternity thing put him off.

"You a fraternity man, Freeman?" he asked once over lunch.

"Naw. I was once because of the chicks. You had to have that pin, you know. Almost as good as a letter in football. But I thought that kinda stuff was silly. I used to be a Kappa."

He looked at Freeman coldly. "I'm still a Kappa," he said. He finished lunch and never spoke to Freeman again.

Mid-way through the fourth week, three of the group were cut. They were called into the front office and informed that their grades were not up to standard, and that same evening they were gone. Panic hit the group and there were several conferences concerning what should be done. Several long-distance phone calls were made, three to politicians, five to civil rights bureaucrats. The group was informed that they were on their own and that after the time, energy, money and effort that had gone into their integration, they should feel obligated to perform up to the highest standards. Freeman had received the best grades in each of the exams, but no one was concerned with that fact.

Two others left the following weekend, although their grades were among the highest in the group. Freeman guessed correctly that it was for homosexuality and became convinced that in addition to being bugged for sound, the rooms were monitored by closed-circuit TV. He was right. The telephones, even the ones in the booths with coin boxes, were bugged as well. The General received a weekly report regarding the progress of the group. It appeared that those intellectually qualified could be cut on physical grounds. They were already lagging at the increasing demands of the morning calisthenics and were not likely to survive the rigours of hand-to-hand combat. The Director of the school confidently predicted that not one of the Negroes would survive the ten weeks of the school, which would then be completely free for a new group of recruits presently going through preliminary screening. It was to the credit of Freeman's unobtrusive demeanour that the school's Director did not even think of him, in spite of his excellent grades and physical condition, when making his report to the General. If he had, he might have qualified his report somewhat.

The General instructed his school's Director to forward complete reports to the full Senatorial Committee. He intended to head off any possible criticism from Senator Hennington. He could not know that the Senator was not in the least concerned with the success or failure of the Negro pioneers to integrate the Central Intelligence Agency. He had won his election and for another six years he was safe.

"When this group is finished, I want you to begin screening another. Don't bother to select Negroes who are obviously not competent; they have already demonstrated their inability to close the cultural gap and no one is in a position seriously to challenge our insistence not to lower standards for anyone. It will cost us a bit to flunk out six or eight a year, but we needn't worry about harassment on this race thing again in the future if we do. It's a sound investment," said the General. He was pleased and again convinced that he was not personally prejudiced. Social and scientific facts were social and scientific facts. He ate a pleasant meal in his club that evening and noted that there were both white and coloured present. The whites were members and guests; the Negroes served them. The General did not reflect that this was the proper order of things. He seldom approved of the rising of the sun, either.

Two more were cut for poor marksmanship. Freeman had obtained an ROTC commission at college and had served in Korea during the police action. He was familiar with all of the weapons except the foreign ones, and a weapon is a weapon. Only the extremely high cyclic rate of the Schmeisser machine pistol bothered him and that did not last very long.

"Mr. Freeman," the retired Marine Gunnery Sergeant said, "that is an automatic weapon and designed to be fired in bursts. Why are you firing it single-shot?"

"It's to get its rhythm, Sergeant. I couldn't control the length of the bursts at first and I was wasting ammo, but I think I have it now."

The Sergeant knew that Freeman had been an infantryman, and Marines, in spite of what they claim, have at least a modicum of respect for any fighting man. "OK, Mr. Freeman. Show me what you mean. Targets one through five, and use only one clip."

"Call the bursts, Sergeant."

"Three. Five. Five . . ." He called the number of rounds he wanted in rapid succession, as fast as Freeman could fire them. There were rounds left for the final target and, on inspection, they found that one five-round burst had been six instead.

"That is very good shooting, Mr. Freeman. Were you a machine gunner in Korea?"

"No. I was in a Heavy Weapons company for a while and got to know MG's fairly well, but I spent most of my time in a line infantry company. I like automatic weapons, though. I learned it's not marksmanship, but fire-power that wins a fire fight. I want to know as much as I can about these things."

"All right, Mr. Freeman, I'll teach you what I know. You can have all the extra practice and ammo you want. Just let me know a day ahead of time and I'll set it up. We'll leave the Schmeisser for a while and start with the simpler jobs, and then work up. Pistols, too?"

"Yes, I'd like that, Sergeant. And I'd rather your maintenance section didn't clean them for me. I'd rather do it myself. No better way I know of to learn a weapon than to break it down, clean and re-assemble it."

The Gunnery Sergeant nodded his head and something rather like a smile crossed his face.

Freeman read everything in the library on gunnery, demolition, sub-version, sabotage and terrorism. He continued to head the class in examination results. There was much more study among the group now and they eyed one another uneasily, wondering who would be the next to go. They had no taste for returning to the jobs they had left: civil rights bureaucracies, social welfare agencies, selling insurance, heading a playground in the ghetto, teaching school—all of the grinding little jobs open to a non-professional, middle-class Negro with a college degree. Long after Freeman retired, between midnight and one, his programme not varying from the schedule he had established during the first week, the rest of the class studied far into the night. The group was given the Army physical aptitude test, consisting of squat jumps, push-ups, pull-ups, sit-ups and a 300-yard run.

Freeman headed the group with a score of 482 out of a possible 500. The men finishing second and third to him in academics were released when they scored less than 300 points. There were only two other athletes in the group, one a former star end at Florida A & M, the other a sprinter from Texas Southern. They were far down on the list academically, although they studied each night until dawn. It was just a matter of time before they left. In two months there were five of the group left, including Freeman. Hand-to-hand combat rid them of two more.

The instructor was a Korean named Soo, but Calhoun, his supervisor, was an American from North Carolina. The niggers would leave or Calhoun would break their necks. He broke no necks, but he did break one man's leg and dislocated another's shoulder. He was surprised and angered to find that Freeman had studied both judo and jiu-jitsu and had a brown belt in the former and a blue stripe in the latter. He would throw Freeman with all the fury and strength he could muster, each time Freeman took the fall expertly. He dismissed the rest of the class one day and asked Freeman to remain.

"Freeman, I'm going to be honest with you. I don't think your people belong in our outfit. I don't have anything against the rest of the group; I just don't think they belong. But you I don't like."

"Well, I guess that's your hang-up."

"I don't like your goddamn phony humility and I don't like your style. This is a team for men, not for misplaced cotton-pickers. I'm going to give you a chance. You just walk up to the head office and resign and that will be it. Otherwise, we fight until you do. And you will not leave this room until I have whipped you and you walk out of here, or crawl out of here, or are carried out of here and resign. Do I make myself clear?"

"Yes, Whitey, you make yourself clear. But you ain't running me nowhere. You're not man enough for that." Freeman felt the adrenaline begin coursing through his body and he began to get that limp, drowsy feeling, his mouth turning dry. I can't back away from this one, he thought.

"Mr. Soo will referee. International judo rules. No chops, kicks or hand blows. Falls and choke holds only. After a fall, you get three minutes' rest and we fight again and I keep throwing you, Freeman, until you walk out of this outfit for good."

"Mr. Soo?"

They bowed formally and circled one another, each reaching gingerly for handholds on the other's jacket. He had fifteen pounds on Freeman and wore a black belt; but a black belt signifies only that the wearer has studied judo techniques enough to instruct others. The highest degree for actual combat is the brown belt Freeman wore. Calhoun was not a natural athlete and had learned his technique through relentless and painstaking practice. His balance was not impressive and he compensated with a wide stance. Freeman figured his edge in speed all but nullified his weight disadvantage. He had studied Calhoun throughout the courses; he had watched him when he demonstrated throws and when he fought exhibition performances with Soo. Freeman was familiar with his technique and habits and knew that he favoured two throws above all others, a hip throw and a shoulder throw, both right-handed.

He came immediately to the attack. Freeman avoided him easily, feeling him out, testing his strength. Calhoun was very strong in the shoulders and arms, but as slow as Freeman had anticipated. He compensated by bulling his opponent and keeping him on the defensive.

Calhoun tried a foot sweep to Freeman's left calf, a feint, then immediately swung full around for the right-handed hip throw. Freeman moved to his right to avoid the sweep, as the North Carolinian had wanted, then, when Calhoun swung into position for the hip throw, his back to Freeman, Freeman simply placed his hand on his back and, before he could be pulled off balance and onto the fulcrum of Calhoun's hip, pushed hard with his left hand, breaking contact. It had been a simple and effective defensive move, requiring speed and expert timing. They circled and regained their handholds on each other's jackets. After a few minutes of fighting, realising that he was out-sped, Calhoun began bulling Freeman in an effort to exhaust him.

Soo signalled the end of the first five-minute period. They would take a three-minute rest. By now, Freeman knew his opponent.

You'd be dangerous in an alley, thought Freeman, but you hung yourself up with judo. Karate, or jiu-jitsu, maybe, to slow me down with the chops and kicks. But there is just no way you can throw me in judo, white boy. He wondered whether to fight, or to continue on the defence. He looked at Calhoun, squatting Japanese-style on the other side of the mat, the hatred and contempt naked on his face. No, he thought, even if I blow my scene, I got to kick this ofay's ass. When you grab me again,

Whitey, you are going to have two handfuls of one hundred and sixty-eight pounds of pure black hell. He took slow, deep breaths and waited for the three minutes to end.

Soo nodded to them, they strode to the centre of the mat, bowed and reached for one another.

Freeman changed from the standard judo stance, with feet parallel, body squared away and facing the opponent, to a variation; right foot and hand advanced, identical to a south-paw boxing stance. It is an attacker's stance, the entire right side being exposed to attack and counter from the opponent. Freeman relied on speed, aggressiveness, natural reflexes and defensive ability to protect himself in the less defensive position. He wanted only one thing: to throw this white man. He moved immediately to the attack.

Freeman tried a foot sweep, his right foot to Calhoun's left, followed up with a leg throw, *osoto-gare*, then switched from right to left, turning his back completely to his opponent, whose rhythm he had timed, and threw him savagely with a right-handed hip throw.

Calhoun lay there and looked at Freeman in surprise. He got slowly to his feet, rearranging his judo jacket and re-tying his belt. Freeman did the same, then, facing him, he bowed as is the tradition. Calhoun remained erect, staring at Freeman coldly. Freeman maintained the position of the bow, hands on thighs, torso lowered from the hips.

"Calhoun-san. You a judokan. You will return bow of Freeman-san," hissed Soo. Reluctantly, Calhoun bowed. They returned to their places on the mat, squatting Japanese style, waiting for the three minutes to end. Freeman wondered if he could keep from killing this white man. No, he thought, he's not worth it and it would really blow the scene. But he does have an ass-kicking coming and he can't handle it. This cat can't believe a nigger can whip him. Well, he'll believe it when I'm through . . .

Soo signalled them to the centre of the mat.

Freeman methodically chopped Calhoun down. He threw him with a right-foot sweep, a left-handed leg throw, another hip throw and finally a right-handed shoulder throw. Calhoun, exhausted by now, but refusing to quit, reacted too slowly and landed heavily on his right shoulder, dislocating it. Soo forced the shoulder back into the socket and the contest was finished. Saying nothing, they bowed formally and Freeman walked slowly to the locker room. It was the end of the day, Friday, and he would have the weekend to recuperate. He would need it.

Calhoun asked for an overseas assignment. Within three days he left for leave at his family home in North Carolina, then disappeared into the Middle East.

Freeman would have to be more careful; there were holes in his mask. He would have to repair them.

WANDA COLEMAN

april 15th 1985

c. 1985

it's been a wonderful trip and I'm feeling great! But fun costs and I've overspent on my trip to San Francisco and go to the bank to cash a check. There's an old white woman damn near eighty in front of me. She needs a deposit/withdrawal slip from the counter across the room, but hesitates to leave the long Monday A.M. line because she might lose her place. Rather than ask me to hold it for her, which I don't mind doing, she talks *around* me, as if I'm not standing there, to a white woman in her sixties directly *behind* me. (I'm 6′2″ in my brown leather boots and have the darkest skin in the place.) When the woman in her sixties reassures her, she leaves the line. When the line moves up I move up a step, leaving enough room for the eighty-year-old's return. Suddenly, the sixty-year-old addresses me boldly: "She wants her place back when she returns!"

"I heard. I got ears," I say extremely rude and loud.

"You don't have to talk to me like that!" she says—half whine and half revulsion.

"Fuck off lady!" I say loud enough to silence her and the entire bank. Then I allow the eighty-year-old to re-enter the line ahead of me.

I'm satisfied my behavior will puzzle the sixty-year-old for time to come; wondering what she did to evoke such nastiness. Or perhaps she'll dismiss me as just another hostile young nigger wench. I'm not feeling so great any more.

Save me from bigoted old white bitches.

identifying marks
c. 1985

raised
black mole $\frac{1}{4}$ inch in diameter on nape of left cocoa breast
birthmark

callus on first joint of second finger, right hand
continual rubbings of pencils & pens held too firmly

assorted dark splotches
and patches on hands, neck, arms and backs of legs
stasis dermatitis since birth erupting under acute and/or
chronic stress

tiny dark spot on right back five inches below shoulder blade
where lung was pierced by needle to remove fluid
when hospitalized for walking pneumonia

green-black freckle left upper nose, flat mole

tigerish striping/striae of skin from navel to pubic area
six pregnancies and three-hundred pound weight loss
over sixteen year period

oval indentation two cm in diameter on right eye
residual from black eye received in fight with first husband
over which late night television program to watch

slightly puffy right lip with scar on inner tissue
busted following duke-out with drunk louisianan boyfriend
who stole ten dollars from purse

triangular indentation on right pinky, healed scars
from cuts received when jumping thru a
plate glass window following lover's quarrel

beige scar where skin was torn off dorsum of left foot
remainder of fist fight which ensued after
discovering lover in bed with best friend girl

dark spot three inches below left eye, healed
severe skin eruption following employer's threat to fire
& sudden unexpected return of estranged second husband

light band of skin around third finger, left hand
recent removal of wedding band

shadows circling eyes

on that stuff that ain't nevah been long enuff for no damn body
c. 1985

"say—when i'm gonna see you wear your hair down?"
went the taunt

i keep it under caps and raps
so fine
and i ain't no beautician

    watch close
    back it will shrink
    to its original kink

Mama Pauline used to burn my neck trying to get
the edges straight. she gave me
chinese bangs and my first and last pony tail
it broke off and never grew back

could never never hold a press more'n five days

time i sweated "back home" during gym
and had to go to chemistry class with my naps
gone all the way back to Africa
and Mr. Cord the nice white teacher who couldn't see good
without his glasses
had never seen black woman hair in its nigger state
i came thru the door last to our all black class
everybody held their breath when his unfocused eyes
landed on my head

he reached for his glasses, adjusted them scientifically
and made careful observation
he said nothing but his astonishment
made the class so angry they didn't speak to me
the rest of the semester
(any wonder at my sedentary life—to sweat is to betray
the shame of a race)

i feel kinship to Van Gogh
'cept only a piece of my left ear is missing
burned off by generations of
hot iron

young love ran passionate hand tenderly
thru my freshly primped bush
cried, "Ugh!
What does you put on yo head, woman?"
and hastily wiped his hand against his jeans

pine tar mange beer raw eggs & honey soaks
steams creams lanolin gels
a head given hell

at 19 i had bald spots from yrs of hard press
& curling rods
saw two girls struttin' up the avenue sportin'
the first afro dos i'd seen
in great ceremony i washed my hair and threw all
that heavy metal into the trash

Richard Burton once politely asked permission to
touch my hair
during a motion picture press party
for *The Klansman*
i was kind enuff to say yes
"it's soft!" he said
"of course," said i

i've always gotten compliments on my loose scalp
occasionally when i have my backside to them
store clerks address me as "Sir"

HATTIE GOSSETT

yo daddy
an 80s version of the dozens
1988

for carolyn j. and calvin h.

1.

yo daddy

yo daddys daddy

his daddy

his great granddaddys great great granddaddys daddy

yo daddy look like death ridin radar wings

yo daddy walk like a broke dick dog

yo daddys breath smell like chemical fallout and industrial waste and he always up in somebodys face

yo daddy deals coke outta platinumplated minklined deluxe rolls royce van with 16track quad deck and 3d color tv yet he got all 13 of yall livin in a furnished room the size of a mosquitoes tweeter cookin hamhocks on a hotplate and you got to go downstairs to the greasyspoon to go to the bathroom

yo daddy dips snuff wears a bowler hat and walks pintoed with a cane

yo daddys daddys daddys daddy was the slave who stayed behind when everyone else escaped to freedom talkin bout i aint gonna leave ma massa cuz he been so good to me

2.

pierre cardin daddy
eleganza daddy
robert hall daddy
robe wearin daddy
joggin suit runnin shoes daddy
surplus store daddy
skullcap earring daddy
greasy do rag daddy
pinhead beanhead footballhead beadyhead dad
earwax toejam daddy
frogeyed redeyed crosseyed daddy
bucktooth snaggletooth gaptooth notooth daddy
highbehind bigbelly daddy
knockkneed slewfooted pigeontoed daddy
liverlip talkinshit tonguetied daddy
sugardaddy with a chippies playground the size of central park

3.

the employer who wants to pinch my ass and pay me less money than he
     would a man? his daddy

the wifebeaters daddy

the rapists daddy

the childmolesters daddy

the socialworkers and judges who say lesbians aint fit mothers? their
     daddies

the lowlifed protoplasm that steals old peoples welfare and
     social-security checks outta they mailboxes and mugs they money
     outta they pockets? his daddy

the groceryman who raises the prices on them rotten greens and that
     rancid meat on check day? his daddy

the healthfood storeman who keeps his prices high all the time? his daddy

the insuranceman who comes round everyweek beatin poorfolks outta they nickles and dimes for some jive insurancepolicies that dont never pay off? his daddy

the slumlords daddy

the industrial polluters? their daddies

the committee in charge of cuttin back social services? their daddies

the stepup nuclear power production committee? their daddies

all the bigtime capitalist daddies

and their smalltime neocolonial overseer daddies too

4.

if you white you allright if you black git back daddy

i dont haul no coal daddy

all a blackbitch can do for me is drive me in my whiteonwhitein-white cadillac to see a white lady daddy

i dont want nothin black but a cadillac daddy

talkin black sleepin white daddy

makin babies for the revolution he doesnt take care of daddy

the womans position in the revolution is prone daddy

speakin out about womans oppression in public but insistin on his patriarchal privileges in private daddy

no foreplay daddy

all technique and no feelins daddy

yes i enjoy oral sex but i think cunnilingus is abhorrent and repulsive daddy yeah i want some head and naw i aint gonna eat no pussy daddy

no stayin power daddy

if i give you some money and some coke can i watch you and your
   girlfriend freak off daddy

do you want to tie me up and beat me daddy

can i tie you up and beat you daddy

group sex at the singles club daddy

find em feel em fuck em forget em daddy

seen at the gaybaths after talkin long and loud bout faggots this and
   faggots the other daddy

no technique daddy

no warmth sensitivity gentleness tenderness affection either daddy

60second daddy

did you come did you come did you come daddy

roll over and go to sleep daddy

5.

soldier sailor green beret daddy
executive suite daddy
maintenance man daddy
hotshot athlete daddy
porno star daddy
ebony bachelor daddy
reefer smokin guntotin asskickin gorilla revolutionary daddy
rushin off to africa where the real struggle is daddy
blissfully ignorant about whats goin on right here daddy
incense sellin daddy
loose joints king daddy
bigtime politico daddy
assembly line daddy

secretary nurse homecompanion daddy

coldbeer fishnchips place daddy

rags and old iron daddy

highclass houseniggah daddy

noclass fieldniggah daddy

passin out poorly printed religious tracts in the busstation daddy

shoppingbagman daddy

pimp pusher daddy

hoodoo voodoo poet daddy

parttime prophet and guru daddy

parttime nonskilled unemployed daddy

wont get no job daddy

wont wash no dishes daddy

wont take care of no babies daddy

how come my dinner aint ready daddy

what you mean you tired daddy

seen at the hotel notell with yo wifes best friend daddy

what you mean you goin out with the sisters daddy

seen at the hotel notell with yo best friends wife daddy

but baby i didnt mean to hurt yo feelins daddy

wont use no protection daddy

wont let yo woman use no birthcontrol daddy

beat yo woman cuz she had an abortion daddy

it aint none of my baby daddy

strip your woman naked mutilate her body kick her out in the snow
    daddy

chastity belt daddy

harlot branding daddy

drawing&quartering bonebreaking burning at the stake daddy

madonna in a crisscross on the cross daddy

polygamy daddy

clitoridectomy daddy

hysterectomy daddy

foot binding daddy

child bride daddy

chador and veil daddy

we will not have our women wearing those decadent western bluejeans
    daddy

if a woman is not a profit to me shes a pain in my ass daddy

i dont want no woman with no hair shorter than mine daddy

a woman is like a pipe you gotta break em in daddy

a menstruating or lactating woman cant touch food enter holy places
sleep in the house or touch men daddy

women are childlike sickly neurotic helpless incapable of serious
thought son they will throw lye and cocacola on you while you sleep
take you money and make a fool outta you barbeque yo clothes slash
yo tires put things in yo food bleed every month blow yo mind live
longer than you daddy

shes cute when shes mad daddy

little girls should wear bouncy curls play passively with pink-pastyfaced
dolls and with all their hearts and soul hope to die sho nuff cross yo
heart and open yo legs love their daddies daddy

yo daddy

my daddy

they all got little bitty peanut dicks

AMIRI BARAKA

wise 1
1995

WHY's (Nobody Knows The Trouble I Seen) Trad.

If you ever find
yourself, some where
lost and surrounded
by enemies
who won't let you
speak in your own language
who destroy your statues
& instruments, who ban
your oom boom ba boom
then you are in trouble
deep trouble
they ban your
oom boom ba boom
you in deep deep
trouble

humph!

probably take you several hundred years
to get
out!

CORNELIUS EADY

the cab driver who ripped me off
1997

That's right, said the cab driver,
Turning the corner to the
Round-a-bout way,
Those stupid, fuckin' beggars,
You know the guys who
Walk up to my cab
With their hands extended
And their little cups?
You know their problem?
You know what's wrong with them?
They ain't got no brains.
I mean, they don't know nothin'
'cause if they had brains
They'd think of a way
To find a job.
You know what one of 'em told me once?
He said what he did,
Begging
He said it was work.
Begging
Was work.
And I told him
Straight to his face:
That ain't work.
You think that's work?
Let me tell you what work is:
Work is something that you do
That's of value

To someone else.
Now you take me.
It takes brains to do
What I do.
You know what I think?
I think they ought to send
All these beggars over
To some other country,
Any country,
It don't matter which,
For 3, 4, years,
Let them wander around
Some other country,
See how they like that.
We ought to make a
National program
Sending them off
To wander about
Some other country
For a few years,
Let 'em beg over there,
See how far it gets them.
I mean, look at that guy
You know, who was big
In the sixties,
That drug guy,
Timothy Leary?
Yeah, he went underground,
Lived overseas.
You know what?
A few years abroad
And he was ready to
Come back
On any terms.
He didn't care if
They arrested him.
He said
The U.S. is better

Than any country
In the world.
Send them over there
For a few years.
They'd be just like him.
This is the greatest country
In the whole world.
Timothy Leary
Was damn happy
To get back here,
And he's doing fine.
Look at me.
I used to be like that.
I used to live underground.
I came back.
I think all those beggars got a mental block.
I think you should do something.
I mean, you ought to like what you do,
But you should do something.
Something of use
To the community.
All those people,
Those bums,
Those scam artists,
Those hustlers,
Those drug addicts,
Those welfare cheats,
Those sponges.
Other than that
I don't hold nothin'
Against no one.
Hey, I picked you up.

TISH BENSON

fifth-ward e-mail
2003

memo to the bitch tryin to cause disharmony between me and my husband

Greetings ho—

this is kwanzal jahritareneeJackson@yahoo.com
aka: ms. prim n proper@blackplanets.com
aka: #1 RoosBoo@aol.com
aka: lovetunnel@search.net
aka: mamaspearl@soulsurvivor.net
aka:juicyfruit69@socialserve.net
aka:the1whowill
aka:marriedfuhreal

It's 3:30 p.m. Saturday. Roo—my man who put the ring of eternal life on my 3rd finger left hand bended knee at the big water sprinkler fountain thang in the park when it was lit up with folks and kids and everybody clapped and somebody asked us to join them havin a cook out—we said no cause we had our own 'que set up cause my Uncle Lemmo and Aunt Patrice brought down two of they smokers . . .
He is somewhere workin on somethin for my momma—that part is none of yo' damn business . . . leavin me here to use his computer he won at the Library Friends Celebrate Us . . .
I go to check my business and all his e-mail pops up . . .

Long story short I chance upon correspondences
(e mails—you silly bitch)

between you and my Husband . . .
not my boyfriend
or playmate just chillin on the lo
or my off and on again
or we serious—but . . .
not even
we common-law
Naw naw naw
MY FUCKIN HUSBAND!
LEGAL like taxes and my foot up yo' ass
cause we went down to the court house
stood in that long freakin line that wrapped out the door
and halfway down the stairs—got the papers signed
then had to go back through a whole lotta traffic
cause we forgot two forms of i.d.
had the weddin which you were not invited to cause of your ho-ish
ways and yes I do know how to spell whore
but that's too dignified for yo' slutty ho-ish ways
5 bridesmaids—all of 'um wearin fierce dresses looked like Beyoncé's
momma made 'um but I ain't sayin who made 'um
since we both know you like to bite every damn thang I got
Scooped out backs
Blue sequins on baby-blue satin handkerchief knee length hems
White mums sprinkled with silver glitter on the sides of they hair
3 flower girls—yeah Silia and Nay-Nay was in it
even though they yo cousins I am not the kind
to allow the sins of kin to interfere with my love show
150 people total—all bearin good gifts
which you will never see or even experience
in no kinda way . . . not when I make some waffles
on my waffle iron Bertese got me or fix a cake
and have it sit up under
this bad ass chandelier lookin cake plate my auntie got me
Cause you will always be the other woman
and not the woman—and Roo don't need no other woman
cause he got me
which is plenty enough for his ass

35 of Roos's family came from outta town—five from California
stayed at the Marriott . . . big sky-high butter rum cake with butter rum
frostin . . . rainbow streamers and bells lacin the whole damn church
grounds

Rev. Welch preached so hard he sweated his curl back
and gave my momma a place to lay her tears
and she don't be cryin at no weddin's
even my Uncle Cordell and some of the other men were dabbin

Rev. said love like ours is what the world needs
What the world needs
Did you hear me bitch?
Love Like Ours Is What The World Needs!
These are terrible times we livin in
Do you hear me!
Yeah yeah it was real
And now 3 months after my glory day
rockin rollin big time all the time
suspended time
cause that's just the way it is with me and Roo
day in day out
we make the bed dance across the floor
make the light socket loose up
if you thought you heard thunder
that be us bitch
that be us
But
now my heart pitter patters
races
wonderin what it all means . . . where is truth really?

Then I stop wonderin . . . I begin to know

Cause I know you
knew you when I was tryin to help you crawl
out from under the rock
you like to lay

Yes I know that married men are
your specialty . . .
Knew that from the giddy up go
you never respected me when I was tryin
to help you get it together
so why should you now . . .
I ain't never gonna forget how you came up
ovah when I was livin in them apartments by the ferris wheel park
—that time you was
playin mo' drunk than yo' ass was—rubbin up and down yo leg
playin with the hairs on'um—sayin you sho' need to shave
brushin up and down talkin bout—"it's likea forest-seeee"
So Roo could tell you that you ought not shave
cause his daddy always tole him a
hairy legged woman mean she got rich hot blood
that can make a man dream winnin numbers
and have a lotta superbowl winnin sons . . .
and you laughin
rarin back
talkin bout—"really? really? you think?"
I forgave you for that
cause I knew you always had low self esteem
and I forgave him cause I figured he knew you had it too
He got that Jesus with a hard dick complex
wanna save every bitch that's got hoe DNA
he just lucked up with me
cause if he wasn't with me he'd probably been part of yo fool collection
suckin niggahs dry
crushin they bones for face scrub
But that taught me a valuable lesson—any bitch come ovah to my crib
discussin they personals, rubbin up on they self—ovah posin in my foyer
full length mirror—any thang while my husband is around will immediately get a door slammed hard . . .
let the do' knob hitcha where the good Lord splitcha

Anyway this is all to say that
I suggest you be clear
to your self about how much

you wanna—as you said in that silly ass email of yours: "just stay friends
like always;)"

with My HUSBAND

Because if you rollin like a tramp down a truckstop diner on payday
then know that with all actions there is an equal opposite reaction . . .
Don't think this is about some jealous shit—naw this is about respect
There is a difference
Learn it and live
In case you too stupid to know what I'm talkin about
then go rent the Godfather bitch
or tape it between them ham hock thighs of yours
five finger discount style that you know so well how to do—
Watch it—think of ya self when you see that horse head
bloodied up in that bed
What go around will be dealt with by #1RoosBoo . . .
Connect the dots bitch cause I know you goin "huh? what?"
ooo see I know you with that fake baby voice will never fool the
1 who will stir that shit up and eat it for breakfast like nothin
Don't think I'm checkin on a one sided tip . . . I see Roo wrote you first
to say we got married
I guess that's something yall share in common . . . neither of yall is too
bright so
knowin you sucha dumb heifer from hell
lemme break it down in this way:
I'm like Solomon
gettin to the bottom
truth at the top
all that I seek
third eye fabreal blazed heated steel . . . on fire
Usin my sword in judgement
deception means destruction . . . yeah he'll feel it
my wrath and vengence . . . I don't know no way
just crazy some say . . .
so if it comes to that
a time bomb set off cause of you
tryin to come between 2

doin the do . . .
just gone have to be yo head
laid up at the foot
hung up by a tree
cut off by a guillotine . . . Roo got it comin too
peace to yall both
knotted up like a soap on a rope
yeah I'll do the time if it comes to that
probably won't
I'll be free to go
get a lawyer who knows the loops
like a Cochran with a suit of gold
or a judge needin his back scratched
get a juror with a tear in eye seein me and identyfyin
jet to France call it—passion crime
Saint
Untainted

yeah I got it like that and you should hear the beat that goes behind it
snatchin yo mug off into a thousand particles

One final word to you:
all you really wanna do is suck ya daddy's dick cause he wasn't there for
you
in a real way
From me: who don't give a rat's asshole
Know that you have met your match
cause an ass whuppin ain't but a blink away . . .
all done with out ever lookin at your troll ass mug

To you and your future if you thank you have one don't fuck with me

presidential campaign speech delivered to the san francisco commonwealth club

december 11, 2003

We are witnessing on a domestic front a non-military civil war led by the right wing. It began with the recount in Florida; it went from there to redistricting in Texas; and it went from there to the recall in California. It all spells undermining the right of voters in America to be heard.

I've been involved in public policy for over a quarter of a century. They say, You've never been elected. (I would argue that many people elected have never been of public service, they've just been on the public payroll, but it's interesting that the right wing would question my public service and then turn around and elect someone who never had a serious thought to be the governor of California. Aside from our politics, the difference between Governor Schwarzenegger and I is that I never had a stuntman do my dirty work; I did it all myself.)

Florida: I did not think that the party stood enough, and strongly enough, for the people and the arguments that could have been used. We should have argued the denial of voter rights, which was clearly established in Duval County; and that *we* do have a constitutional right against being discriminated against in terms of our vote. That was not the argument we used in the Supreme Court. We handed five members of the Supreme Court an easy way out to *select* George Bush.

The first year of Bush's administration: by all accounts it was lackluster. But in the post-9/11 period everyone united; we had an unusual opportunity of having the sympathy and the alliance and the sense of comradeship from around the world. George Bush had an opportunity to unite the world in a common fight against terrorism, senseless murder and ruthlessness. He unraveled that in a way that history will not be kind to him. Rather than pursue new alliances, new arrangements that would have protected American citizens and set a new paradigm in human rights standards, he decided to go after Saddam Hussein and Iraq. Now, I am not a sympathizer of Saddam Hussein, but I do not understand how we are attacked by Al Qaeda and Osama bin Laden and end up going after Saddam Hussein.

I was born in the 'hood in Brooklyn. In the 'hood, unfortunately there is crime, and people break into your house. If they break into your house and you call the police and the police come, you don't send the police after a guy around the corner that offended your daddy 20 years ago. To add insult to injury, he did it in a unilateral way. The only power that agreed was his friend in England, Tony Blair. George Bush and Tony Blair have a meeting and act like the whole world met—two guys in a phone booth call it a world summit. And they come out with a world manifesto: *We go into Iraq and we tell the American people that we have to go in because there are weapons of mass destruction. And we are in imminent danger.*

Where I went to school *imminent* means "immediate," not "they *may* have" or "they are *preparing* to have weapons." *Imminent* means "we need to go because we are in immediate danger." That was the premise of the war, the basis of the support he got from the American people that did support it. The language changed from *they had weapons* to *they were planning to have weapons* to *they may have been developing weapons.* When people began raising their voices—and there were huge marches of just regular citizens, no leaders, people just coming with common sense—he brings Tony Blair over to talk to the U.S. Congress. (As you know, it's difficult for him to speak at the joint Parliament in England, where every time he gets up they were throwing shoes at him.) And he had the audacity to say, It doesn't matter whether it was weapons or not, Saddam Hussein was a bad guy and it was the right thing to do.

It does matter, because telling the truth to people who are going to give their lives, who are going to see the lives of their children, relatives, friends, neighbors lost; it matters that you tell them the real reason we are doing this. That's like me coming to The Commonwealth Club and saying that we all must get out of the building, we are in immediate danger. And we all get outside on Market and you say, "Reverend Al, where's the danger?" "Ahh, it doesn't matter; you all needed some fresh air anyhow." The deception of the American people is something we should not tolerate.

We forget the human side this war has cost, and then we look at oil companies that are getting unusual prices per gallon for oil in Iraq. We are seeing kids dying while oil companies are making profits at an unusually marked-up price, and we are called unpatriotic if we question it; we are unpatriotic if we *don't* question it. If you really love America then you don't have Americans in danger's way unnecessarily. If you really love America, you do not open America to danger and ignore those that continue to have terrorist cells even in this country while you pursue other policies. If you really are patriotic, you do not take billions of dollars for an adventure in Iraq when we need billions to cover state budgets all over the United States. They want to know how we can get the money to rebuild Iraq, because Iraq needs to be supported, and yet we don't have the money for the fifty states we already occupy. It's amazing that Bush believes in public education in Iraq but he doesn't believe in public education in Oakland. He believes in universal health care in Iraq, but he doesn't believe in it in the United States. He believes in the democratic vote in Baghdad, but he doesn't believe in the democratic vote on a federal level in the capital of the United States in Washington, D.C. It would seem to me that Bush is a progressive on an international level and a conservative at home. We need to have a progressive at home and be more conservative in our trying to pursue things that are not directly provable and directly clear to us.

I challenged my own party, some of whom voted for the war, who have said that we must continue occupation. We must say, one: the philosophy of unilateral invasion is wrong. The philosophy of unilateral occupation is wrong. We must go to the UN and say, We will submit to a multilateral withdrawal and multilateral engagement for reconstruction. We will not talk about how people cannot do business with the U.S. if they are opposed to our policies.

We must have a commitment to public education. Government's job is to guarantee quality education for *all* students, not set up schemes that will select *some* students. Vouchers, at best, will still only have some students selected at the expense of other students left behind. We must put money back into Title I, we must bring public schools up to a level of technology that is equivalent with the times in which we live, and we must pay teachers salaries that would make young people want to become teachers and give them college debt forgiveness in order to achieve that.

I've advocated for the last decade for a universal health plan, a single-payer plan. If we can see Canada guarantee its citizens a single-payer plan, and other nations that do not have the strong economy we do, certainly the U.S. can do the same. Health care ought to be guaranteed for every American citizen. A lot of the money spent on health care today would be unnecessary if we had a guaranteed government plan. Some studies say fifteen percent of what we spend on health care today is on advertising. Some studies say twenty-seven percent is on administrative overrun. If we put that money into a single-payer system that the government would be responsible for, we could afford to move forward with universal health-plan coverage.

I also am opposed to the death penalty. We have liberals who believe in the death penalty—in light of so many cases that have been proven wrong, and that have been proven to have been adjudicated in a way that was not just for the defendant. How can we therefore continue to take lives if we know we can't refund their lives if a further study shows that is wrong?

I believe also that we face a serious threat to civil liberties and civil rights in this country. I sat almost in shock at the hearings in the Senate Judiciary Committee about the Patriot Act when they were arguing it and ultimately passed it. Attorney General Ashcroft said, "Are you with them or us?"—never clearly defining who *them* was and who *us* was—and used that to justify the invasion of the civil liberties and privacy of American citizens in the name of terrorism. It was like McCarthyism in the twenty-first century. Mind you, this in an administration that the vice president says, "I'm not going to tell you what I was meeting with Enron about in the executive office of the White House, but I want the right to know what your librarian gives you as a book to go to your home. We want the right to eavesdrop on lawyer-client conversations; we want the right to do anything we want to invade your privacy, in the name of terrorism." We cannot say to the world to join us, we are the land of the free and the home of the brave, and then say we are going to suspend freedom and you better not be brave enough to question us.

This administration has had a no-dissent policy. Before 2001, I protested the Navy bombings in Vieques with Robert Kennedy Jr. and others. I had to go to jail ninety days and Robert Kennedy Jr. went thirty days—as a result of the personal call of John Ashcroft and this administration. This was before 9/11, so this is the tone of this administration.

There are those that have said to me as I've traveled, "Reverend

Sharpton, I agree with you on issues—on health care, education, the war—I agree with you that we must be progressive again. But I don't know if you can win." Let me tell you a secret: There are nine of us running, eight of us gonna lose. Don't let nobody tell you Al Sharpton is the only one who may lose. The issue is not trying to pick a winner. I respectfully suggest that if you're looking for winners, go to the racetrack and make money. Politics is about standing with who represents what you believe in. If enough of us vote I can win, but the worst that can happen is that we go to the convention and stop this drift to the right that the Democratic Party has had, where we have imitated Republicans and said the only way to win is to act like elephants in donkey jackets. By running that way we have turned off a lot of our base supporters; a lot of young people are not registered because they don't feel this party speaks to their needs and to their grievances. If we become the Democratic Party again, for working-class people and middle-class people and blacks and Latinos and gays and lesbians, they will come out. But why should they come out if we are not going to represent them?

They say, "Reverend Sharpton, moving to the left will hurt the party." I hate to tell you this, but the party is already in disarray. We've lost the Congress, the Senate, the White House and the Supreme Court. How could I kill a dead body? The answer is to go back to our roots and to stand for something. My mother advised me at eighteen, when I was registering to vote: "We're Democrats." We knew what a Democrat meant then. We don't know what a Democrat means today; we don't know what it stands for. I hope in my running not to win the nomination but to define the party. I hope to be the one that says, "We don't have to apologize for standing up for social justice, for those that are discriminated against, those that need jobs."

We are being told we're in an economic recovery while unemployment is at 6 percent and people right in the Bay Area are losing jobs or are in low-wage jobs. More offensive than being sick is for somebody to tell you that you are well when you know you're not well. So it is my intention to challenge the party to be the party that it's supposed to be.

My grandmother and mother come from Dothan, Alabama. I used to go to see my grandmother when I was a little boy. She had a farm and would show me what the pigs and cows and chickens did. (I was known for eating a lot of chicken, so the chickens usually ran away when I visited.) One animal I never understood was the donkey, because it was a stubborn, and to me, useless animal. My grandmother said, "The only way you get the donkey to do something is you gotta slap the donkey; you can't entice it, you can't bribe it; you have to slap the donkey." Well, many people think that I'm not right to challenge this party, but I'm doing what Grandma taught me. I'm trying to slap this donkey, and I intend to slap this donkey until this donkey kicks George Bush out of the White House in 2004.

MIKE TYSON

the wit and wisdom of mike tyson
1987–2004

Pre-fight hype and Post-fight Hubris

"Lennox Lewis, I'm coming for you man. My style is impetuous. My defense is impregnable, and I'm just ferocious. I want your heart. I want to eat his children. Praise be to Allah!"

"My main objective is to be professional but to kill him [Lennox Lewis]."

"I may have smoked too much weed, but I wasn't taking drugs or anything."—after losing to Lennox Lewis

"You're [Razor Ruddock] sweet. I'm going to make sure you kiss me good with those big lips. I'm gonna make you my girlfriend."

Family

"Her mother is beautiful, but she [daughter Rayna] is so gorgeous she makes her mother look like a junkyard dog."

"No one gives a fuck about me. No one cares if my children starve, if they're on welfare. I have to support my children. I need more money."—commenting on purse for Frank Bruno fight

The Public

"I don't feel love from them because there's no love. They don't know me as an individual; they know me for what I actually do. Because they pay to see me smash anybody. If they're white they pay, [it's] because the only thing they have respect for is my ability as an athlete. But if I was in court and I had to use them to testify against me on my character, they wouldn't testify positively against me and they would think I'm a cad . . ."

"There are nine million people who see me in the ring and hate my guts. Most of them are white. That's okay. Just spell my name right."

"I think the average person thinks I'm a fucking nut and I deserve whatever happens to me. That's what I believe."

"When you see me smash somebody's skull, you enjoy it."

The Competition

"You have to understand, Frank Bruno would not have been champion if I had not been in prison. Oliver McCall would not have been champion if I had not been in prison. A lot of these guys would not have been champion. Michael Moorer would not have been champion. Those guys would not have been champion if I had been around. They would have had no legacy. None of those guys would have had a legacy . . . But you really have to look at the science of the situation. You guys come here to talk and report but you don't actually look at the facts of what this business is all about. The best thing that happened to those guys and they should stand on their mother's shoulders and kiss my ass because I went to prison or they would not be existing right now. They'd be a flash in the pan and would have made some money and opened up a restaurant or bar somewhere where they live at."

The Sweet Science

"They all have a plan until they get hit."

"How dare these boxers challenge me with their primitive skills?"— after a fifth round KO of Frank Bruno

"My power is discombobulatingly devastating. I could feel his muscle tissues collapse under my force. It's ludicrous these mortals even attempt to enter my realm."

"I try to catch him right on the tip of the nose, because I try to push the bone into the brain."

"It's interesting that you put me in the league with those illustrious fighters [Muhammad Ali, Joe Louis, Jack Johnson], but I've proved since my career I've surpassed them as far as my popularity. I'm the biggest fighter in the history of the sport. If you don't believe it, check the cash register."

"The knee feels fine, I've been training Confuciously."

The Media

"I wish that you guys had children so I could kick them in the fucking head or stomp on their testicles so you could feel my pain because that's the pain I have waking up every day."

[Addressing a female reporter] "It's no doubt I am going to win this fight and I feel confident about winning this fight. I normally don't do interviews with women unless I fornicate with them. So you shouldn't talk anymore . . . unless you want to, you know."

"[He] called me a 'rapist' and a 'recluse.' I'm not a recluse."—referring to *New York Post* sports writer Wallace Matthews

"Sometimes you guys have no pride, so no matter what I say, you guys . . . it doesn't affect you because you don't care about nothing but money. So every now and then I kick your fucking ass and stomp on you and put some kind of pain and inflict some of the pain on you because you deserve to feel the pain that I feel."—ESPN interview, Maui, Hawaii

"If I take this camera and put it in your face for twenty years, I don't know what you might be. You might be a homosexual if I put that camera on you since you were thirteen years old. I've been on that camera since I was thirteen years old."

Religion

"All praise is to Allah, I'll fight any man, any animal, if Jesus were here I'd fight him too."

"I feel like sometimes that I was born, that I'm not meant for this society because everyone here is a fucking hypocrite. Everybody says they believe in God but they don't do God's work. Everybody counteracts what God is really about. If Jesus was here, do you think Jesus would show me any love? Do you think Jesus would love me? I'm a Muslim, but do you think Jesus would love me . . . I think Jesus would have a drink with me and discuss . . . why you acting like that?"

"Now, he would be cool. He would talk to me. No Christian ever did that and said in the name of Jesus even . . . They'd throw me in jail and write bad articles about me and then go to church on Sunday and say Jesus is a wonderful man and he's coming back to save us. But they don't understand that when he comes back, that these crazy greedy capitalistic men are gonna kill him again."

Mike Tyson on Mike Tyson

"The one thing I know, everyone respects the true person and everyone's not true with themselves. All of these people who are heroes, these guys who have been lily white and clean all their lives, if they went through what I went through, they would commit suicide. They don't have the heart that I have. I've lived places they can't defecate in."

"I'm not Mother Teresa and I'm not Charles Manson."—Testifying before the Nevada State Athletic Commission

"Fear is your best friend or your worst enemy. It's like fire. If you can control it, it can cook for you; it can heat your house. If you can't control it, it will burn everything around you and destroy you. If you can control your fear, it makes you more alert, like a deer coming across the lawn."

"I'm just like you. I enjoy the forbidden fruits in life, too. I think it's un-American not to go out with a woman, not to be with a beautiful woman, not to get my dick sucked . . . It's just what I said before, everybody in this country is a big fucking liar. [The media] tells people . . . that this person did this and this person did that and then we find out that we're just human and we find out that Michael Jordan cheats on his wife just like everybody else and that we all cheat on our fucking wife in one way or another either emotionally, physically or sexually or one way."

"There's no one perfect. We're always gonna do that. Jimmy Swaggart is lascivious, Mike Tyson is lascivious—but we're not criminally, at least I'm not, criminally lascivious. You know what I mean. I may like to fornicate more than other people—it's just who I am. I sacrifice so much of my life, can I at least get laid? I mean, I been robbed of most of my money, can I at least get [oral sex] without the people wanting to harass me and wanting to throw me in jail?"

"That's just who I am. I want to have a nice career for my children. I want them to have a great education. I want to fly my birds. I want to live my life. I want to have a drink every now and then. I want to have a charity event every now and then. And every now and then, I want to fornicate and that's just being a human being."

"At times, I come across as crude or crass. That irritates you when I come across like a Neanderthal or a babbling idiot, but I like to be that person. I like to show you all that person, because that's who you come to see."—press conference, Maui, Hawaii

"I'm the most irresponsible person in the world. The reason I'm like that is because, at twenty-one, you all gave me fifty or a hundred million dollars and I didn't know what to do. I'm from the ghetto. I don't know how to act. One day I'm in a dope house robbing somebody. The next thing I know, 'You're the heavyweight champion of the world.' I'm twenty years old. I'm the heavyweight champion of the world. Most of my girlfriends are fifteen, sixteen years old. I'm twenty years old with a lot of money. Who am I? What am I? I don't even know who I am. I'm just a dumb child. I'm being abused. I'm being robbed by lawyers. I think I have more money than I do. I'm just a dumb pugnacious fool. I'm just a fool who thinks I'm someone. And you tell me I should be responsible?"

"Well, that feeling [suicide] goes through everyone's mind, I'm sure, and if it doesn't I really must be crazy. Everyone thinks about that because sometimes, you know what I mean, it's just tough being a nigger and it's tough being a bad nigger."

"I'm just a dark guy from a den of iniquity. A dark shadowy figure from the bowels of iniquity. I wish I could be Mike who gets an endorsement deal. But you can't make a lie and a truth go together."

"I guess I'm gonna fade into Bolivian."

"Look at my life, I've been embarrassed, humiliation, degradation and other t-i-o-n you can name."

(nothing serious) just buggin'

b ack in the day before people said "back in the day," before "def" was in the dictionary and only vegetables, ideas, and office managers were "fresh," it was hard to be black. These days, all you have to do is put on a baseball cap, slide the bill over one ear, and wah-la, you're black. Having renounced my blackness after Toni Morrison announced Bill Clinton's, I can only suppose being black is as hard now as it was then. However, reliable sources (black folk whose renouncement paperwork hasn't come through) inform me people don't talk about black hardship as much as they used to. Whites know better than to approach them at the company Christmas party asking "So is it hard being black?" which lessens the oppressed Negro's workload appreciably. This "progress" leaves more social heavy lifting for the Asians, of course: "No, I mean where are you from originally?"

Growing up, there used to be lots of pressure to take blackness seriously. Public blackness had to be kept groomed, polished, well creased, and well greased. The risk of running into a white person, police officer, member of Grandma's parish, or one of the paragons of good blackness, Sidney Potier, Rosa Parks, and Frederick Douglass, was not to be taken lightly, even if Frederick had been dead for hundred years.

Being black then was like growing up in East Germany. The sloganeering. The uplifting songs. No electricity. No long-distance phone service. The insufferable, hopelessly vague daily admonishments to "grow up and be somebody." Any youth with the temerity to stand up and say, "But according the almighty irrefutable Führer of furor the Reverend Jesse Jackson, I am somebody," was sent to the DAP, work camp (the Deputy Auxiliary Police—an urban Young Pioneers), given a blue windbreaker and a list of things not be. Though the What Not to Be list tended to accentuate the negative, its specifics were most welcome. Don't be no nigger. Don't be a junkie. Don't be talkin' about my mama. And, first and foremost, don't be no fool. "But if it's first and foremost, shouldn't 'Don't be no fool' come at the beginning of the list?" Unfortunately, I was an inveterate fool, and a wry one at that. While admittedly there was some leeway for foolishness in the black community, there was no room for wryness.

Despite numerous beatings, detentions, and dunce-capped public self-criticisms, my ign'ant foolhardy ways proved to be incurable and I suffered in private, never quite able to snuff out my snide castigations with a loud and crisp "Yes, sir" or "No, ma'am." Then, in the mid-eighties, when deconstruction reached its apotheosis and revisionist histories abounded, the fool—along with segregation, pornography, child molesters, and unabashed corporate greed—received a quasi-reprieve. Fools were cool.

I'd attend readings where, between poems, Amiri Baraka would cite the Stepin Fetchits, Mantan Morelands, and Lightnings for wartime heroics, explaining how these slow-moving, slow-thinking show business coons were in actuality subversives, members of a colored resistance, because only an insane person would hop to and up 'n' at 'em for a heartless bossman who paid them little heed, no money, and even less respect. Shit, according to Baraka and Derrida, I was a revolutionary.

With the advent of rap, my joker antics garnered street credibility. From the West Coast the thuggish King Tee was fittin' to "Act a Fool" and "Just Clownin'." On the Eastern Seaboard, Whistle released the single that serves as the namesake for this section, "(Nothing Serious) Just Buggin'." I finally had a diagnosis. I was buggin'. Folks used to say I was trippin', but trippin' had drug and schizophrenic connotations. Trip out and you might never come back. Bug out and, well, aren't we all entitled to a moment of frivolity? Who knows, maybe the real purpose of the trickster's public histrionics is to clear enough head space to allow for some wry, American, backstage blackness.

PAUL LAURENCE DUNBAR

when de co'n pone's hot
1895

Dey is times in life when Nature
   Seems to slip a cog an' go,
Jes' a-rattlin' down creation,
   Lak an ocean's overflow;
When de worl' jes' stahts a-spinnin'
   Lak a picaninny's top,
An' yo' cup o' joy is brimmin'
   Twell it seems about to slop,
An' you feel jes' lak a racah,
   Dat is trainin' fu' to trot—
When yo' mammy says de blessin',
   An' de co'n pone's hot.

When you set down at de table,
   Kin' o' weary lak an' sad,
An' you 'se jes' a little tiahed
   An' purhaps a little mad;
How yo' gloom tu'ns into gladness,
   How yo' joy drives out de
     doubt
When de oven do' is opened,
   An' de smell comes po'in' out;
Why, de 'lectric light o' Heaven
   Seems to settle on de spot,
When yo' mammy says de blessin'
   An' de co'n pone's hot.

When de cabbage pot is steamin'
  An' de bacon good an' fat,
When de chittlins is a-sputter'n'
  So's to show you whah dey's at;
Tek away yo' sody biscuit,
  Tek away yo' cake an' pie,
Fu' de glory time is comin',
  An' it's 'proachin' mighty nigh,
An' you want to jump an' hollah,
  Dough you know you'd bettah not,
When yo' mammy says de blessin'
  An' de co'n pone's hot.

I have hyeahd o' lots o' sermons,
  An' I've hyeahd o' lots o'
     prayers,
An' I've listened to some singin'
  Dat has tuck me up de stairs
Of de Glory-Lan' an' set me
  Jes' below de Mastah's th'one,
An' have lef' my hea't a-singin'
  In a happy aftah tone;
But dem wu'ds so sweetly murmured
  Seem to tech de softes' spot,
When my mammy says de blessin',
  An' de co'n pone's hot.

how fried?

1913

Uncle benjamin, who lived right close to us, had the most marvelous memory of any man I'd ever seen in my life. Never seen a man who could remember so much, no matter what happened, anytime, anyplace, he knew all about it.

One day he sittin' down out on his porch and I asked him how he come to have such a memory, and he told us this, says, "Well," he says, "see my great-great-grandfather had the most marvelous memory of any man in the state of Kentucky. And the Colonel who owned him used to carry him with him to court and put him in the chair in back of him and he would remember *so good* that six months . . . a year after that time he could ask you, 'What did so and so say, Sam?' Sam could tell him! That's how I comes to have my memory. Why, don't you know my great-great-grandfather had such a marvelous memory they had a fuss ovah him? The devil comes to his master and says, 'Colonel, I want that coon.'

"Master says, 'Well I'm very sorry, but you can't have him. 'Cuz I ain't got nobody to help me out, I ain't got nobody to write my reports or nuthin' and I have to depend on him all the time.'

"They argued for over an hour about it. At the finish of the argument the Colonel says, 'Well, if you can catch Sam where he don't remember, why, take him!'

"Well, suh, of course you know Sam didn't have nuthin' to do around the plantation, he was one of the favored few. 'Cept go out every mornin' and rake the dead offen the lawn where the gentle zephyrs had blowed 'em the evening befo'. He was out raking the leaves off the lawn one mornin' when all of sudden the devil appeared before him . . . sudden, like *that*, in the guise of a man. Well, the devil asked him, 'Do you like eggs?'

"Sam looked at him for a minute and said, 'Yes, suh!'

"'Hmm mmm,' and the devil was gone.

"Well, lemme see now that was . . . ten years *befo'* the war! Well, after the war, let me see, 'bout twenty years after the war, why, Uncle Samuel was out plowing a little field the Colonel had give him so he could take care of his family. He was out plowin' amongst his corn on this mornin', now, remember now, this is *thirty* years since the war, while he was plowing along singin' his favorite hymn, 'Didn't de Walls of Jericho Fall When de Bugle Sounded?'

"*Didn't de wa-a-l-l-s of Jericho, didn't de wa-a-l-l-s of Jericho . . . giddiyup Sukey . . . Didn't de wa-a-l-l-s of Jericho fall when de bugle sounded?*"

"And just like that the devil appeared before him again and said, 'How?'

"Uncle Sam said, 'Fried!'

"Ha-ha yaaa ha."

assorted jokes compiled by alex rogers
1918

I remember the first time I went on visit to a big city. It was Chattanoogy. I sported 'round and spent money so fast that when I got ready to go back home I found myself with one lone two-dollar bill. The railroad fare back home was three dollars. Well, I figgered and worried and worried and figgered and finally somehow or 'nother a thought come to me, so I takes the two-dollar bill 'round to a pawn shop and pawns it for a dollar and a half. Then I takes and sells the pawn ticket to a man for a dollar and a half and that made me have the three dollars I needed. Now the question in my mind is: who loses that dollar?

"Look here, Spruce," I said to him recently, "what's this I see in the paper about your advertising to give a reward of fifteen dollars for that cat of yours?"

"I jes done dat to please my ole ooman," answered Spruce.

"Why, man," says I, "I thought you told me that you fairly hated the cat. Don't you know that fifteen-dollar reward is liable to bring the cat back?"

"I is quite sho dat it won't," replied Spruce. "You see *I* drowned dat cat my *own* se'f."

"Pas de 'lasses."

"Don't say 'lasses. Say mo-lasses."

"How come I got to say mo'—I ain't had none yit."

An old colored man was leadin' a sad-lookin' horse into a blacksmith shop. Somebody asked him, "What's the speed of that horse?"

"Which way?"

"Why I can't see what difference it makes which way he's headed."

"That's kase you don't own him. Whenever he's goin' todes home his speed compares putty favable wid a Ford Runabout; but when he's comin' 'way frum de barn, you kin ketch his time wid a terbacker box."

Speakin' 'bout horses always put me in mind of a circus. One time I was stranded in a town an' a circus come along so I went an' told the manager that I was desperate and jus' *had* to have work. He said, "Well, one of our best lions died last week and as we saved the skin, if you want you can git in it and be a lion till something better comes along."

Naturally I grabbed it and that same afternoon I made my first 'pearance as "The King of the Jungles." Then here comes the man what does the stunts inside of the animals' cages. He come in my cage first an' after 'splainin' 'bout what a fine specimen I was and how much trouble they had ketchin' me in Africa, he say, "Now ladies and gent'men, to show much we have tamed and trained him; I am goin' to turn him into this next cage with this large an' f'rocious Bengal Tagger."

I *imeegitly* backed into the furtherst corner of my cage. The man opened up the door between the two cages, drawed out a big pistol an' say, "Git in thare or I'll blow yo' head off." An' kinder under his breath he say to me, "And that *goes* too." Then he took and fired the gun off once over his head to show me that it would shoot and I looked up and seen the hole made in the roof of the cage so jus' went on in the nex' cage and got right down on my knees and commence prayin'. And this big Bengal Tagger leaped todes me and jus' as my heart was gittin' ready to stop for good, that Tagger took and leaned over and I heard him whisper right in my ear, "Don't be skeered, pal; I'm colored same as you."

It certainly was too bad about Jim Towels and Joe Madison. Both of 'em good friends of mine. They was shootin' a little friendly craps here not long ago and they got in an argument and Joe hit Jim over the head with a club and killed him. Yes sir, broke his skull. But at the trial it was shown that Jim had an unusually thin skull. 'Cose I never knowed much 'bout Jim's skull but I know his hair was mighty hard an' nappy. They used to have to chloroform him ev'ry time they to comb it. But anyhow at the trial they claimed that his skull was very thin indeed but thin as they claimed it was it didn't seem to have much 'fect on the judge, 'cause he gave Joe twenty-three years. Think of it!! Twenty-three years! Well, all I got to say is—it ain't right. Naw sir. It ain't right.

No man ain't got no bizness being allowed to bring that kind of skull to a crap game. Naw sir!!!

The Easiest Way

He was colored and he said he was a carpenter.

"Do you thoroughly understand carpentry?" he was asked.

"Yas suh."

"You can make doors, windows and blinds?"

"Oh, sho'. Yas suh."

"How would you make a Venetian blind?"

He scratched his head and thought for a few seconds, then finally replied, "Well, I reck'n 'bout de easiest way would be to poke him in de eye."

A new collector called at a man's house and asked if the man was in. The woman that came to the door said, "Naw suh."

"Can you tell me where he is?" asked the man.

"Naw suh, I kinnot," said the woman.

"When did you see him last?" asked the man.

"At his fun'ral," she replied.

Then the man asked, "And who may you be?"

"I'm his remains," she said, as she slammed the door.

The family Susie cooked for moved out to the Pacific Coast to live. They took Susie with them. After they had been there some months she said to her madam, "I don't 'spec' I'm goin' to able to stay out here, Miss Em'ly. You see the colored folk out here, Miss Em'ly, ain't de same. They more like de Hawaiians or de Indians an' you see I'se always ben used to de puah Anglo-Saxon type.

Mom Toles

Old Mom Toles is a funny old soul. She was in a shoe store tryin' on some new shoes. The clerk asked, "How does that shoe feel?"

Mom says, "Lord knows. But if that shoe feels half as bad as my foot feels, it sho has my sympathy."

Mom runs a boarding house and she always has an answer or an excuse for everything that goes wrong. The other day one of her boarders yelled right out at the table, "Say, look a here. What's dis collar button doin' in my soup?"

Mom says, "It jes means that you is de lucky man. Dat's all. We has prize soup ev'ry Monday an' Wensday. Dare is a gift in ever tenth bowl. You gits de prize to-day. You sho is lucky."

During the same meal another fellow says to her, "Missus Toles, dis mutton you has heah fuh dinner certny aint da kine a meat dat I ben use to."

Mom says, "I don't doubt it 'tall, 'cause I always gits de bes'."

One fellow at de table asked another, "How long has she kept boarders?"

The other fellow answers, "Sometime she has kept 'em as long as three days."

One day she caught one of the boarders putting butter in his coffee. Mom yelled, "Whut in de worl' you mean puttin' butter in yo' coffee?"

He say, "Madam, I always bleeves it is de duty a de strong to he'p de weak."

Providing

Something caused the lady of the house to ask her colored servant, A'nt Malinda, the other day, "Is your husband much of a provider, Malinda?"

"Yassum," replied Malinda, "he sho' is. He's gwine to git me some new funnicher pervidin' he gits de money; he's gwine to git de money pervidin' he goes to work an' he's gwine to work pervidin' de job suits him. He's de most pervidines' man ever I did see."

Rasmus Bigby used to play with a little white boy about his age. One day the little pale one was crying bitterly and his mother says to Rasmus, "What's the matter with Ronald, Erasmus?"

"He's cryin' 'cause I'm eatin' my cake an' won't gib him none."

"Is his own cake finished?"

"Yassum. An' he cried while I'se eatin' dat too."

RUDOLPH FISHER

the city of refuge
1925

I

Confronted suddenly by daylight, King Solomon Gillis stood
dazed and blinking. The railroad station, the long, white-walled
corridor, the impassable slot-machine, the terrifying subway train—he felt
as if he had been caught up in the jaws of a steam-shovel, jammed together
with other helpless lumps of dirt, swept blindly along for a time, and at last
abruptly dumped.

There had been strange and terrible sounds: "New York! Penn
Terminal—all change!" "Pohter, hyer, pohter, suh?" Shuffle of a thousand
soles, clatter of a thousand heels, innumerable echoes. Cracking rifle-
shots—no, snapping turnstiles. "Put a nickel in!" "Harlem? Sure. This
side—next train." Distant thunder, nearing. The screeching onslaught of
the fiery hosts of hell, headlong, breathtaking. Car doors rattling, sliding,
banging open. "Say, wha' d'ye think this is, a baggage car?" Heat,
oppression, suffocation—eternity—"Hundred 'n turdy-fif' next!" More
turnstiles. Jonah emerging from the whale.

Clean air, blue sky, bright sunlight.

Gillis set down his tan cardboard extension case and wiped his black,
shining brow. Then slowly, spreadingly, he grinned at what he saw:
Negroes at every turn; up and down Lenox Avenue, up and down 135th
Street; big, lanky Negroes, short, squat Negroes; black ones, brown ones,
yellow ones; men standing idle on the curb, women, bundle-laden,
trudging reluctantly homeward, children rattle-trapping about the side-
walks; here and there a white face drifting along, but Negroes predomi-
nantly, overwhelmingly everywhere. There was assuredly no doubt of his
whereabouts. This was Negro Harlem.

Back in North Carolina Gillis had shot a white man and, with the aid of prayer and an automobile, probably escaped a lynching. Carefully avoiding the railroads, he had reached Washington in safety. For his car a Southwest bootlegger had given him a hundred dollars and directions to Harlem; and so he had come to Harlem.

Ever since a traveling preacher had first told him of the place, King Solomon Gillis had longed to come to Harlem. The Uggams were always talking about it; one of their boys had gone to France in the draft and, returning, had never got any nearer home than Harlem. And there were occasional "colored" newspapers from New York: newspapers that mentioned Negroes without comment, but always spoke of a white person as "So-and-so, white." That was the point. In Harlem, black was white. You had rights that could not be denied you; you had privileges, protected by law. And you had money. Everybody in Harlem had money. It was a land of plenty. Why, had not Mouse Uggam sent back as much as fifty dollars at a time to his people in Waxhaw?

The shooting, therefore, simply catalyzed whatever sluggish mental reaction had been already directing King Solomon's fortunes toward Harlem. The land of plenty was more than that now; it was also the city of refuge.

Casting about for direction, the tall newcomer's glance caught inevitably on the most conspicuous thing in sight, a magnificent figure in blue that stood in the middle of the crossing and blew a whistle and waved great white-gloved hands. The Southern Negro's eyes opened wide; his mouth opened wider. If the inside of New York had mystified him, the outside was amazing him. For there stood a handsome brass-buttoned giant directing the heaviest traffic Gillis had ever seen; halting unnumbered tons of automobiles and trucks and wagons and pushcarts and streetcars; holding them at bay with one hand while he swept similar tons peremptorily on with the other; ruling the wide crossing with supreme self-assurance. And he, too, was a Negro!

Yet most of the vehicles that leaped or crouched at his bidding carried white passengers. One of these overdrove bounds a few feet, and Gillis heard the officer's shrill whistle and gruff reproof, saw the driver's face turn red and his car draw back like a threatened pup. It was beyond belief—impossible. Black might be white, but it could n't be that white!

"Done died an' woke up in Heaven," thought King Solomon, watching, fascinated; and after a while, as if the wonder of it were too great to believe simply by seeing, "Cullud policemans!" he said, half aloud; then repeated over and over, with greater and greater conviction, "Even got cullud policemans—even got cullud—"

"Where y' want to go, big boy?"

Gillis turned. A little, sharp-faced yellow man was addressing him.

"Saw you was a stranger. Thought maybe I could help y' out."

King Solomon located and gratefully extended a slip of paper. "Wha' dis hyeh at, please, suh?"

The other studied it a moment, pushing back his hat and scratching his head. The hat was tall-crowned, unindented brown felt; the head was brown patent-leather, its glistening brush-back flawless save for a suspicious crimpiness near the clean-grazed edges.

"See that second corner? Turn to the left when you get there. Number forty-five's about halfway [down] the block."

"Thank y', suh."

"You from—Massachusetts?"

"No, suh, Nawth Ca'lina."

"Is 'at so? You look like a Northerner. Be with us long?"

"Till I die," grinned the flattered King Solomon.

"Stoppin' there?"

"Reckon I is. Man in Washin'ton 'lowed I'd find lodgin' at dis address."

"Good enough. If y' don't maybe I can fix y' up. Harlem's pretty crowded. This is me." He proffered a card.

"Thank y', suh," said Gillis, and put the card in his pocket.

The little yellow man watched him plod flat-footedly on down the street, long awkward legs never quite straightened, shouldered extension-case bending him sidewise, wonder upon wonder halting or turning him about. Presently, as he proceeded, a pair of bright green stockings caught and held his attention. Tony, the storekeeper, was crossing the sidewalk with a bushel basket of apples. There was a collision; the apples rolled; Tony exploded; King Solomon apologized. The little yellow man laughed shortly, took out a notebook, and put down the address he had seen on King Solomon's slip of paper.

"Guess you're the shine I been waitin' for," he surmised.

As Gillis, approaching his destination, stopped to rest, a haunting notion grew into an insistent idea. "Dat li'l yaller nigger was a sho' 'nuff gen'man to show me de road. Seem lak I knowed him befo'—" He pondered. That receding brow, that sharp-ridged, spreading nose, that tight upper lip over the two big front teeth, that chinless jaw—He fumbled hurriedly for the card he had not looked at and eagerly made out the name.

"Mouse Uggam, sho' 'nuff! Well, dog-gone!"

II

Uggam sought out Tom Edwards, once a Pullman porter, now prosperous proprietor of a cabaret, and told him:

"Chief, I got him: a baby jess in from the land o'cotton and so dumb he thinks ante bellum's an old woman."

"Where'd you find him?"

"Where you find all the jaybirds when they first hit Harlem—at the subway entrance. This one come up the stairs, batted his eyes once or twice, an' froze to the spot—with his mouth wide open. Sure sign he's from 'way down behind the sun and ripe f' the pluckin'."

Edwards grinned a gold-studded, fat-jowled grin. "Gave him the usual line, I suppose?"

"Did n't miss. An' he fell like a ton o' bricks. 'Course I've got him spotted, but damn 'f I know jess how to switch 'em on to him."

"Get him a job around a store somewhere. Make out you're befriendin' him. Get his confidence."

"Sounds good. Ought to be easy. He's from my state. Maybe I know him or some of his people."

"Make out you do, anyhow. Then tell him some fairy tale that'll switch your trade to him. The cops'll follow the trade. We could even let Froggy flop into some dumb white cop's hands and 'confess' where he got it. See?"

"Chief, you got a head, no lie."

"Don't lose no time. And remember, hereafter, it's better to sacrifice a little than to get squealed on. Never refuse a customer. Give him a little credit. Humor him along till you can get rid of him safe. You don't know what that guy that died may have said; you don't know who's on to you now. And if they get you—I don't know you."

"They won't get *me*," said Uggam.

King Solomon Gillis sat meditating in a room half the size of his hencoop back home, with a single window opening for an airshaft.

An airshaft: cabbage and chitterlings cooking; liver and onions sizzling, sputtering; three player-pianos out-plunking each other; a man and a woman calling each other vile things; a sick, neglected baby wailing; a phonograph broadcasting blues; dishes clacking; a girl crying heartbrokenly; waste noises, waste odors of a score of families, seeking issue through a common channel; pollution from bottom to top—a sewer of sounds and smells.

Contemplating this, King Solomon grinned and breathed, "Doggone!" A little later, still gazing into the sewer, he grinned again. "Green stockin's," he said; "loud green!" The sewer gradually grew darker. A window lighted up opposite, revealing a woman in camisole and petticoat, arranging her hair. King Solomon, staring vacantly, shook his head and grinned yet again. "Even got cullud policemans!" he mumbled softly.

III

Uggam leaned out of the room's one window and spat maliciously into the dinginess of the airshaft. "Damn glad you got him," he commented as Gillis finished his story. "They's a thousand shines in Harlem would change places with you in a minute jess f' the honor of killin' a cracker."

"But I did n't go to do it. 'T was a accident."

"That's the only part to keep secret."

"Know whut dey done? Dey killed five o' Mose Joplin's hawses 'fo he lef'. Put groun' glass in de feed-trough. Sam Cheevers come up on three of 'em one night pizenin' his well. Bleesom beat Crinshaw out o' sixty acres o' lan' an' a year's crops. Dass jess how 't is. Soon 's a nigger make a li'l sump'n he better git to leavin'. An' 'fo long ev'ybody's goin' be lef'!"

"Hope to hell they don't all come here."

The doorbell of the apartment rang. A crescendo of footfalls in the hallway culminated in a sharp rap on Gillis's door. Gillis jumped. Nobody but a policeman would rap like that. Maybe the landlady had been listening and had called the law. It came again, loud, quick, angry. King Solomon prayed that the policeman would be a Negro.

Uggam stepped over and opened the door. King Solomon's apprehensive eyes saw framed therein, instead of a gigantic officer, calling for him, a little blot of a creature, quite black against even the darkness of the hallway, except for a dirty wide-striped silk shirt, collarless, with the sleeves rolled up.

"Ah hahve bill fo' Mr. Gillis." A high, strongly accented Jamaican voice, with its characteristic singsong intonation, interrupted King Solomon's sigh of relief.

"Bill? Bill fo' me? What kin' o' bill?"

"Wan bushel appels. T'ree seventy-fife."

"Apples? I ain' bought no apples." He took the paper and read aloud, laboriously, "Antonio Gabrielli to K. S. Gillis, Doctor—"

"Mr. Gabrielli say, you not pays him, he send policemon."

"What I had to do wid 'is apples?"

"You bumps into him yesterday, no? Scatter appels everywhere—on the sidewalk, in de gutter. Kids pick up an' run away. Others all spoil. So you pays."

Gillis appealed to Uggam. "How 'bout it, Mouse?"

"He's a damn liar. Tony picked up most of 'em; I seen him. Lemme look at that bill—Tony never wrote this thing. This baby's jess playin' you for a sucker."

"Ain' had no apples, ain' payin' fo' none," announced King Solomon, thus prompted. "Did n't have to come to Harlem to git cheated. Plenty o' dat right wha' I come fum."

But the West Indian warmly insisted. "You cahn't do daht, mon. Whaht you t'ink, 'ey? Dis mon loose 'is appels an' 'is money too?"

"What diff'ence it make to you, nigger?"

"Who you call nigger, mon? Ah hahve you understahn'—"

"Oh, well, white folks, den. What all you got t' do wid dis hyeh, anyhow?"

"Mr. Gabrielli send me to collect bill!"

"How I know dat?"

"Do Ah not bring bill? You t'ink Ah steal t'ree dollar, 'ey?"

"Three dollars an' sebenty-fi' cent," corrected Gillis. "Nuther thing: wha' you ever see me befo'? How you know dis is me?"

"Ah see you, sure. Ah help Mr. Gabrielli in de store. When you knocks down de baskette appels, Ah see. Ah follow you. Ah know you comes in dis house."

"Oh, you does? An' how come you know my name an' flat an' room so good? How come dat?"

"Ah fin' out. Sometime Ah brings up here vegetables from de store."

"Humph! Mus' be workin' on shares."

"You pays, 'ey? You pays me or de policemon?"

"Wait a minute," broke in Uggam, who had been thoughtfully contemplating the bill. "Now listen, big shorty. You haul hips on back to Tony. We got your menu all right"—he waved the bill—"but we don't eat your kind o' cookin', see?"

The West Indian flared. "Whaht it is to you, 'ey? You can not mind your own business? Ah hahve not spik to you!"

"No, brother. But this is my friend, an' I'll be john-browned if there's a monkey-chaser in Harlem can gyp him if I know it, see? Bes' think f' you to do is to catch air, toot sweet."

Sensing frustration, the little islander demanded the bill back. Uggam figured he could use the bill himself, maybe. The West Indian hotly persisted; he even menaced. Uggam pocketed the paper and invited him to take it. Wisely enough, the caller preferred to catch air.

When he had gone, King Solomon sought words of thanks.

"Bottle it," said Uggam. "The point is this: I figger you got a job."

"Job? No I ain't! Wha' at?"

"When you show Tony this bill, he'll hit the roof and fire that monk."

"What ef he do?"

"Then you up 'n ask f' the job. He'll be too grateful to refuse. I know Tony some, an' I'll be there to put in a good word. See?"

King Solomon considered this. "Sho' needs a job, but ain' after stealin' none."

"Stealin'? 'T would n't be stealin'. Stealin' 's what that damn monkey-chaser tried to do from you. This would be doin' Tony a favor an' gettin' y'self out o' the barrel. What's the holdback?"

"What make you keep callin' him monkey-chaser?"

"West Indian. That's another thing. Any time y' can knife a monk, do it. They's too damn many of 'em here. They're an achin' pain."

"Jess de way white folks feels 'bout niggers."

"Damn that. How 'bout it? Y' want the job?"

"Hm—well—I'd ruther be a policeman."

"Policeman?" Uggam gasped.

"M-hm. Dass all I wants to be, a policeman, so I kin police all the white folks right plumb in jail!"

Uggam said seriously, "Well, y' might work up to that. But it takes time. An' y've got to eat while y're waitin'." He paused to let this penetrate. "Now how 'bout this job at Tony's in the meantime? I should think y'd jump at it."

King Solomon was persuaded.

"Hm—well—reckon I does," he said slowly.

"Now y're tootin'!" Uggam's two big front teeth popped out in a grin of genuine pleasure. "Come on. Let's go."

IV

Spitting blood and crying with rage, the West Indian scrambled to his feet. For a moment he stood in front of the store gesticulating furiously and jabbering shrill threats and unintelligible curses. Then abruptly he stopped and took himself off.

King Solomon Gillis, mildly puzzled, watched him from Tony's doorway. "I jess give him a li'l shove," he said to himself, "an' he roll' clean 'cross de sidewalk." And a little later, disgustedly, "Monkey-chaser!" he grunted, and went back to his sweeping.

"Well, big boy, how y' comin' on?"

Gillis dropped his broom. "Hay-o, Mouse. Wha' you been las' two-three days?"

"Oh, around. Gettin' on all right here? Had any trouble?"

"Deed I ain't—ceptin' jess now I had to throw 'at li'l jigger out."

"Who? The monk?"

"M-hm. He sho' Lawd doan like me in his job. Look like he think I stole it from him, stiddy him tryin' to steal from me. Had to push him down sho' nuff 'fo I could get rid of 'im. Den he run off talkin' Wes' Indi'man an' shakin' his fis' at me."

"Ferget it." Uggam glanced about. "Where's Tony?"

"Boss man? He be back direckly."

"Listen—like to make two or three bucks a day extra?"

"Huh?"

"Two or three dollars a day more 'n what you're gettin' already?"

"Ain' I near 'nuff in jail now?"

"Listen." King Solomon listened. Uggam had n't been in France for nothing. Fact was, in France he'd learned about some valuable French medicine. He'd brought some back with him,—little white pills,—and while in Harlem had found a certain druggist who knew what they were and could supply all he could use. Now there were any number of people who would buy and pay well for as much of this French medicine as

Uggam could get. It was good for what ailed them, and they did n't know how to get it except through him. But he had no store in which to set up an agency and hence no single place where his customers could go to get what they wanted. If he had, he could sell three or four times as much as he did.

King Solomon was in a position to help him now, same as he had helped King Solomon. He would leave a dozen packages of the medicine—just small envelopes that could all be carried in a coat pocket—with King Solomon every day. Then he could simply send his customers to King Solomon at Tony's store. They'd make some trifling purchase, slip him a certain coupon which Uggam had given them, and King Solomon would wrap the little envelope of medicine with their purchase. Must n't let Tony catch on, because he might object, and then the whole scheme would go gaflooey. Of course it would n't really be hurting Tony any. Would n't it increase the number of his customers?

Finally, at the end of each day, Uggam would meet King Solomon some place and give him a quarter for each coupon he held. There'd be at least ten or twelve a day—two and a half or three dollars plumb extra! Eighteen or twenty dollars a week.

"Dog-gone!" breathed Gillis.

"Does Tony ever leave you heer alone?"

"M-hm. Jess started dis mawnin'. Doan nobody much come round 'tween ten an' twelve, so he done took to doin' his buyin' right 'long 'bout dat time. Nobody hyeh but me fo' 'n hour or so."

"Good. I'll try to get my folks to come 'round here mostly while Tony's out, see?"

"I doan miss."

"Sure y' get the idea, now?" Uggam carefully explained it all again. By the time he had finished, King Solomon was wallowing in gratitude.

"Mouse, you sho' is been a friend to me. Why, 'f 't had n' been fo' you—"

"Bottle it," said Uggam. "I'll be round to your room tonight with enough stuff for tomorrer, see? Be sure 'n be there."

"Won't be nowha' else."

"An' remember, this is all jess between you 'n me."

"Nobody else but," vowed King Solomon.

Uggam grinned to himself as he went on his way. "Dumb Oscar!

Wonder how much can we make before the cops nab him? French medicine—Humph!"

V

Tony Gabrielli, an oblate Neopolitan of enormous equator, wobbled heavily out of his store and settled himself over a soapbox.

Usually Tony enjoyed sitting out front thus in the evening, when his helper had gone home and his trade was slackest. He liked to watch the little Gabriellis playing over the sidewalk with the little Levys and Johnsons; the trios and quartettes of brightly dressed dark-skinned girls merrily out for a stroll; the slovenly gaited, darker men, who eyed them up and down and commented to each other with an unsuppressed "Hot damn!" or "Oh no, now!"

But tonight Tony was troubled. Something was wrong in the store; something was different since the arrival of King Solomon Gillis. The new man had seemed to prove himself honest and trustworthy, it was true. Tony had tested him, as he always tested a new man, by apparently leaving him alone in charge for two or three mornings. As a matter of fact, the new man was never under more vigilant observation than during these two or three mornings. Tony's store was a modification of the front rooms of his flat and was in direct communication with it by way of a glass-windowed door in the rear. Tony always managed to get back into his flat via the side-street entrance and watch the new man through this unobtrusive glass-windowed door. If anything excited his suspicion, like unwarranted interest in the cash register, he walked unexpectedly out of this door to surprise the offender in the act. Thereafter he would have no more such trouble. But he had not succeeded in seeing King Solomon steal even an apple.

What he had observed, however, was that the number of customers that came into the store during the morning's slack hour had pronouncedly increased in the last few days. Before, there had been three or four. Now there were twelve or fifteen. The mysterious thing about it was that their purchases totaled little more than those of the original three or four.

Yesterday and today Tony had elected to be in the store at the time when, on the other days, he had been out. But Gillis had not been overcharging or short-changing; for when Tony waited on the customers himself—strange faces all—he found that they bought something like a yeast cake or a five-cent loaf of bread. Why should strangers leave their own neighborhoods and repeatedly come to him for a yeast cake or a loaf of bread? They were not new neighbors. New neighbors would have bought more variously and extensively and at different times of day. Living nearby, they would have come in, the men often in shirtsleeves and slippers, the women in kimonos, with boudoir caps covering their lumpy heads. They would have sent in strange children for things like yeast cakes and loaves of bread. And why did not some of them come in at night, when the new helper was off duty?

As for accosting Gillis on suspicion, Tony was too wise for that. Patronage had a queer way of shifting itself in Harlem. You lost your temper and let slip a single "*nègre!*" A week later you sold your business.

Spread over his soapbox, with his pudgy hands clasped on his preposterous paunch, Tony sat and wondered. Two men came up, conspicuous for no other reason than that they were white. They displayed extreme nervousness, looking about as if afraid of being seen; and when one of them spoke to Tony, it was in a husky, toneless, blowing voice, like the sound of a dirty phonograph record.

"Are you Antonio Gabrielli?"

"Yes, sure." Strange behavior for such lusty-looking fellows. He who had spoken unsmilingly winked first one eye then the other, and indicated by a gesture of his head that they should enter the store. His companion looked cautiously up and down the Avenue, while Tony, wondering what ailed them, rolled to his feet and puffingly led the way.

Inside, the spokesman snuffled, gave his shoulder a queer little hunch, and asked, "Can you fix us up, buddy?" The other glanced restlessly about the place as if he were constantly hearing unaccountable noises.

Tony thought he understood clearly now. "Booze, 'ey?" he smiled. "Sorry—I no got."

"Booze? Hell, no!" The voice dwindled to a throaty whisper. "Dope. Coke, milk, dice—anything. Name your price. Got to have it."

"Dope?" Tony was entirely at a loss. "What's a dis, dope?"

"Aw, lay off, brother. We're in on this. Here." He handed Tony a piece of paper. "Froggy gave us a coupon. Come on. You can't go wrong."

"I no got," insisted the perplexed Tony; nor could he be budged on that point.

Quite suddenly the manner of both men changed. "All right," said the first angrily, in a voice as robust as his body. "All right, you're clever. You no got. Well, you will get. You'll get twenty years!"

"Twenty year? Whadda you talk?"

"Wait a minute, Mac," said the second caller. "Maybe the wop's on the level. Look here, Tony, we're officers, see? Policemen." He produced a badge. "A couple of weeks ago a guy was brought in dying for the want of a shot, see? Dope—he needed some dope—like this—in his arm. See? Well, we tried to make him tell us where he'd been getting it, but he was too weak. He croaked next day. Evidently he hadn't had money enough to buy any more.

"Well, this morning a little nigger that goes by the name of Froggy was brought into the precinct pretty well doped up. When he finally came to, he swore he got the stuff here at your store. Of course, we've just been trying to trick you into giving yourself away, but you don't bite. Now what's your game? Know anything about this?"

Tony understood. "I dunno," he said slowly; and then his own problem, whose contemplation his callers had interrupted, occurred to him. "Sure!" he exclaimed. "Wait. Maybeso I know somet'ing."

"All right. Spill it."

"I got a new man, work-a for me." And he told them what he had noted since King Solomon Gillis came.

"Sounds interesting. Where is this guy?"

"Here in da store—all day."

"Be here to-morrow?"

"Sure. All day."

"All right. We'll drop in tomorrow and give him the eye. Maybe he's our man."

"Sure. Come ten o'clock. I show you," promised Tony.

VI

Even the oldest and rattiest cabarets in Harlem have sense of shame enough to hide themselves under the ground—for instance, Edwards's. To get into Edwards's you casually enter a dimly lighted corner saloon, apparently—only apparently—a subdued memory of brighter days. What was once the family entrance is now a side entrance for ladies. Supporting yourself against close walls, you crouchingly descend a narrow, twisted staircase until, with a final turn, you find yourself in a glaring, long, low basement. In a moment your eyes become accustomed to the haze of tobacco smoke. You see men and women seated at wire-legged, white-topped tables, which are covered with half-empty bottles and glasses; you trace the slow jazz accompaniment you heard as you came down the stairs to a pianist, a cornetist, and a drummer on a little platform at the far end of the room. There is a cleared space from the foot of the stairs, where you are standing, to the platform where this orchestra is mounted, and in it a tall brown girl is swaying from side to side and rhythmically proclaiming that she has the world in a jug and the stopper in her hand. Behind a counter at your left sits a fat, bald, tea-colored Negro, and you wonder if this is Edwards—Edwards, who stands in with the police, with the political bosses, with the importers of wines and worse. A white-vested waiter hustles you to a seat and takes your order. The song's tempo becomes quicker; the drum and the cornet rip out a fanfare, almost drowning the piano; the girl catches up her dress and begins to dance . . .

Gillis's wondering eyes had been roaming about. They stopped.

"Look, Mouse!" he whispered, "Look a yonder!"

"Look at what?"

"Dog-gone if it ain' de self-same girl?"

"Wha' d' ye mean, self-same girl!"

"Over yonder, wi' de green stockin's. Dass de gal made me knock over dem apples fust day I come to town. 'Member? Been wishin' I could see her ev'y sence."

"What for?" Uggam wondered.

King Solomon grew confidential. "Ain' but two things in dis world, Mouse, I really wants. One is to be a policeman. Been wantin' dat ev'y sence I seen dat cullud traffic cop dat day. Other is to get myse'f a gal lak dat one over yonder!"

"You'll do it," laughed Uggam, "if you live long enough."

"Who dat wid her?"

"How 'n hell do I know?"

"He cullud?"

"Don't look like it. Why? What of it?"

"Hm—nuthin'—"

"How many coupons y' got to-night?"

"Ten." King Solomon handed them over.

"Y' ought to've slipt 'em to me under the table, but it's all right now, long as we got this table to ourselves. Here's y' medicine for to-morrer."

"Wha'?"

"Reach under the table."

Gillis secured and pocketed the medicine.

"An' here's two-fifty for a good day's work." Uggam passed the money over. Perhaps he grew careless; certainly the passing this time was above the table, in plain sight.

"Thanks, Mouse."

Two white men had been watching Gillis and Uggam from a table nearby. In the tumult of merriment that rewarded the entertainer's most recent and daring effort, one of these men, with a word to the other, came over and took the vacant chair beside Gillis.

"Is your name Gillis?"

"'T ain' nuthin' else."

Uggam's eyes narrowed.

The white man showed King Solomon a police officer's badge.

"You're wanted for dope-peddling. Will you come along without trouble?"

"Fo' what?"

"Violation of the narcotic law—dope-selling."

"Who—me?"

"Come on, now, lay off that stuff. I saw what happened just now myself." He addressed Uggam. "Do you know this fellow?"

"Nope. Never saw him before tonight."

"Did n't I just see him sell you something?"

"Guess you did. We happened to be sittin' here at the same table and got to talkin'. After a while I says I can't seem to sleep nights, so he offers me sump'n he says 'll make me sleep, all right. I don't know what it is, but he says he uses it himself an' I offers to pay him what it cost him. That's how I come to take it. Guess he's got more in his pocket there now."

The detective reached deftly into the coat pocket of the dumfounded King Solomon and withdrew a packet of envelopes. He tore off a corner of one, emptied a half-dozen tiny white tablets into his palm, and sneered triumphantly. "You'll make a good witness," he told Uggam.

The entertainer was issuing an ultimatum to all sweet mammas who dared to monkey around her loving man. Her audience was absorbed and delighted, with the exception of one couple—the girl with the green stockings and her escort. They sat directly in the line of vision of King

Solomon's wide eyes, which, in the calamity that had descended upon him, for the moment saw nothing.

"Are you coming without trouble?"

Mouse Uggam, his friend. Harlem. Land of plenty. City of refuge—city of refuge. If you live long enough—

Consciousness of what was happening between the pair across the room suddenly broke through Gillis's daze like flame through smoke. The man was trying to kiss the girl and she was resisting. Gillis jumped up. The detective, taking the act for an attempt to escape, jumped with him and was quick enough to intercept him. The second officer came at once to his partner's aid, blowing his whistle several times as he came.

People overturned chairs getting out of the way, but nobody ran for the door. It was an old crowd. A fight was a treat; and the tall Negro could fight.

"Judas Priest!"

"Did you see that?"

"Damn!"

White—both white. Five of Mose Joplin's horses. Poisoning a well. A year's crops. Green stockings—white—white—

"That's the time, papa!"

"Do it, big boy!"

"Good night!"

Uggam watchéd tensely, with one eye on the door. The second cop had blown for help—

Downing one of the detectives a third time and turning to grapple again with the other, Gillis found himself face to face with a uniformed black policeman.

He stopped as if stunned. For a moment he simply stared. Into his mind swept his own words, like a forgotten song suddenly recalled:

"Cullud policemans!"

The officer stood ready, awaiting his rush.

"Even—got—cullud—policemans—"

Very slowly King Solomon's arms relaxed; very slowly he stood erect; and the grin that came over his features had something exultant about it.

ZORA NEALE HURSTON

the bone of contention

c. 1929

I

eatonville, florida is a colored town and has its colored interests. It has not now, nor ever has had anything to rank Brazzle's yellow mule. His Yaller Highness was always mentioned before the weather, the misery of the back or leg, or the hard times.

The mule was old, rawbony and mean. He was so rawbony that he creaked as he ambled about the village street with his meanness shining out through every chink and cranny in his rattling anatomy. He worked little, ate heartily, fought every inch of the way before the plow and even disputed with Brazzle when he approached to feed him. Sale, exchange or barter was out of the question, for everybody in the county knew him.

But one day he died. Everybody was glad, including Brazzle. His death was one of those pleasant surprises that people hope for, but never expect to happen.

The city had no refuse plant so H.Y.H. went the way of all other domestic beasts who died among us. Brazzle borrowed Watson's two grey plugs and dragged the remains out to the edge of the cypress swamp, three miles beyond the city limits and abandoned them to the natural scavengers. The town attended the dragging out to a man. The fallen gladiator was borne from the arena on his sharp back, his feet stiffly raised as if in a parting gesture of defiance. We left him to the village. Satisfied that the only piece of unadulterated meanness that the Lord had ever made was gone from among us forever.

Three years passed and his bones were clean and white. They were scattered along the swamp edge. The children still found them sufficiently interesting to tramp out to gaze upon them on Sunday afternoons. The elders neglected his bones, but the mule remained with them in song and story as a simile, as a metaphor, to point a moral or adorn a tale. But as the mean old trouble-making cuss, they considered him gone for good.

II

It was early night in the village. Joe Clarke's store porch was full of chewing men. Some chewed tobacco, some chewed cane, some chewed straws, for the villager is a ruminant in his leisure. They sat thus every evening ostensibly waiting for the mail from Number 38, the south-bound express. It was seldom that any of them got any but it gave them a good excuse to gather. They all talked a great deal, and every man jack of them talked about himself. Heroes all, they were, of one thing or another.

Ike Pearson had killed a six-foot rattler in a mighty battle that grew mightier every time Ike told about it; Walter Thomas had chinned the bar twenty times without stopping; Elijah Moseley had licked a "cracker"; Brazzle had captured a live catamount; Hiram Lester had killed a bear; Sykes Jones had won the soda-cracker eating contest; AND JOE CLARKE HAD STARTED THE TOWN!

Reverend Simms, the Methodist preacher, a resident of less than a year, had done nothing to boast of, but it was generally known that he aspired to the seat of Joe Clarke. He wanted to be the mayor. He had observed to some of his members that it wasnt no sense in one man staying in office all the time.

"Looka heah," Clarke cut across whoever it was that was talking at the time, "when Ah started dis town, Ah walked right up to de white folks an' laid down TWO HUN'DED DOLLAHS WID DIS RIGHT HAND YOU SEE BEFO' YOU AN' GOT MAH PAPERS AN' PUT DIS TOWN ON DE MAP! It takes uh powerful lot uh sense an' grit tuh start uh town, yessirree!"

"Whut map did you put it on, Joe?" Lindsay disrespectfully asked. "Ah aint seed it on no map."

Seeing Clarke gored to his liver, Rev. Simms let out a gloating snicker and tossed a cane knot to Tippy, the Lewis' dejected dog frame hovering about the group hoping for something more tempting to a dog's palate than cane chews and peanut shells might drop. He tossed the knot and waited for Clarke to answer. His Honor ignored the thrust as being too low for him to stoop, and talked on. Was he not mayor, postmaster, storekeeper and Pooh Bah general? Insults must come to him from at least the county seat.

"Nother thing," Clarke continued, giving Simms a meaning look, "there's a heap goin' on 'round heah under the cover dat Ahm gointer put a stop to. Jim Weston done proaged through mah hen house enough. Last Sat'day Ah missed three uh mah bes' layin' hens, an' Ah been tol' he buried feathers in his backyard the very next day. Cose Ah caint prove nothin', but de minute he crooks his little finger, he goes 'way from mah town. He aint de onliest one Ah got mah eye on neither."

Simms accepted the challenge thrown at him.

"Fact is, the town aint run lak it might be. We oughta stop dat foolishness of runnin' folks outa town. We oughta jail 'em. They's got jails in all de other towns, an' we oughta bring ours up to date."

"Ah'll be henfired! Simms, you tries to know mo' 'bout runnin' de town than me! Dont you reckon a man thats got sense enough to start uh town, knows how tuh run it. Dont you reckon if de place had uh needed uh jailhouse Ah would have got one built long befo' you come heah?"

"We do so need a jail," Lindsay contended. "Jus' cause you stahted the town, dat dont make yo' mouf no prayer book nor neither yo' lips no Bible. They dont flap lak none tuh *me*."

Lindsay was a little shriveled up man with grey hair and bowlegs. He was the smallest man in the village, who nevertheless did the most talk of fighting. That was because the others felt he was too small for them to hit. He was harmless, but known to be the nastiest threatener in the county.

Clarke merely snorted contemptuously at his sally and remarked dryly that the road was right there for all those who were not satisfied with the way he was running the town.

"Meaning to insult me?" Lindsay asked belligerently.

"Ah dont keer HOW yuh take it. Jus' take yo' rawbony cow an' gwan tuh de woods, fuh all I keer," Clarke answered.

Lindsay leaped from the porch and struck his fighting pose. "Jus' hit de ground an' Ah'll strow yuh all over Orange County! Aw, come on! Come on! Youse a big seegar, but Ah kin smoke yuh!"

Clarke looked at the little man, old, and less than half his size and laughed. Walter Thomas and 'Lige Moseley rushed to Lindsay and pretended to restrain him.

"That's right," Lindsay panted, "you better hold me offen him. Cause if I lay de weight uh dis right hand on him, he wont forget it long as he live."

"Aw, shet up, Lin'say, an' set down. If you could fight as good as you kin threaten, you'd be world's champeen'stead uh Jack Dempsey. Some uh dese days when youse hollerin' tuh be let loose, somebody's gointer take you at yo' word, then it will be jus' too bad about yuh," Lester admonished.

"Who?—"

The war was about to begin all over on another front when Dave Carter, the local Nimrod, walked, almost ran up the steps of the porch. He was bareheaded, excited and even in the poor light that seeped to the porch from the oil lamps within, it was seen that he was bruised and otherwise unusually mussed up.

"Mist' Clarke, Ah wants tuh see yuh," he said. "Come on inside."

"Sholy, Dave, sholy." The mayor responded and followed the young man into the store and the corner reserved for City Administration. The crowd from the porch followed to a man.

Dave wiped a bruise spot on his head. "Mist' Clarke, Ah wants uh warrant took out fuh Jim Weston. Ahm gointer law him outa dis town. He caint lam me over mah head wid no mule bone and steal mah turkey and go braggin' about it!"

Under the encouraging quiz of the mayor, Dave told his story. He was a hunter and fisherman, as everybody knew. He had discovered a drove of wild turkeys roosting in the trees along the edge of the cypress swamp near the spot where Brazzle's old mule had been left. He had watched them for weeks, had seen the huge gobbler that headed the flock and resolved to get him.

"Yes," agreed Clarke, "you said something to me about it yesterday when you bought some shells."

"Yes, and thats how Jim knowed Ah was goin' turkey huntin'. He was settin' on de store porch and heard me talkin' to you. Today when Ah started out, jes 'bout sundown—dats de bes' time tuh get turkeys, when they goes tuh roost—he ups and says he's goin' long. Ah didnt keer 'bout dat, but when them birds goes tuh roost, he aint even loaded, so Ah had shot dat gobbler befo' he took aim. When he see dat great big gobbler fallin' he fires off his gun and tries tuh grab him. But Ah helt on. We got tuh pushin' and shovin' and tusslin' 'till we got to fightin'. Jim's a bully, but

Ah wuz beatin' his socks offa him till he retched down and picked up de hock-bone of Brazzle's ol' mule and lammed me ovah mah head wid it and knocked me out. When Ah come to, he had done took mah turkey and gone. Ah wants uh warrant, Mist' Clarke. Ahm gointer law him outa dis town."

"An' you sho gointer get, Dave. He oughter be run out. Comes from bad stock. Every last one of his brothers been run out as fast as they grow up. Daddy hung for murder."

Clarke busied himself with the papers. The crowd looking on and commenting.

"See whut you Meth'dis' niggahs will do?" asked Brazzle, a true Baptist. "Goin' round lammin' folks ovah the head an' stealin' they turkeys."

"Cose everybody knows dem Westons is a set uh bullies, but you Baptists aint such a much," Elijah Moseley retorted.

"Yas, but Ah know yuh know," put in Lindsay. "No Baptis' aint never done nothin' bad as dat. Joe Clarke is right. Jail is too good fuh 'em. The last one uh these heah half-washed christians oughta be run 'way from heah."

"When it comes tuh dat, theres jus' as many no count Baptists as anybody else. Jus' aint caught 'em," Thomas said, joining the fray.

"Yas," Lindsay retorted, "but we done kotched yo' Meth'dis' niggah. Kotched him knockin' people ovah de head wid mule bones an' stealin' they turkeys, an' wese gointer run him slap outa town sure as gun's iron. The dirty onion!"

"We dont know whether you will or no, Joe Lindsay. You Baptists aint runnin' this town exactly."

"Trial set for three oclock tomorrow at de Baptis' church, that being the largest meetin' place in town," Clarke announced with a satisfied smile and persuaded the men to go back to the porch to argue.

Clarke himself was a Methodist, but in this case, his interests lay with the other side. If he could get Jim to taste the air of another town, chicken mortality of the sudden and unexplained variety would drop considerably, he was certain. He was equally certain that the ambitious Simms would champion Jim's cause and losing the fight, lose prestige. Besides, Jim was a troublesome character. A constant disturber of the village peace.

III

It was evident to the simplest person in the village long before three oclock that this was to be a religious and political fight. The assault and the gobbler were unimportant. Dave was a Baptist, Jim a Methodist, only two churches in the town and the respective congregations had lined up solidly.

At three the house was full. The defendant had been led in and seated in the amen corner to the left of the pulpit. Rev. Simms had taken his place beside the prisoner in the role of defense counsel. The plaintiff, with Elder Long, shepherd of the Baptist flock in the capacity of prosecution, was seated at the right. The respective congregations were lined up behind their leaders.

Mutual glances of despisement and gloating are exchanged across the aisle. Not a few verbal sorties were made during this waiting period as if they were getting up steam for the real struggle.

Wize Anderson (Meth.) Look at ole Dave tryin' to make out how Jim hurt his head! Yuh couldnt hurt a Baptist head wid a hammer—they're that hard.

Brother Poke (Bapt.) Well, anyhow we dont lie an' steal an' git run outa town lak de softhead Meth'dis' niggahs.

Some Baptist wag looked over at Jim and crowed like a rooster, the others took it up immediately and the place was full of hencackling and barnyard sounds. The implication was obvious. Jim stood up and said, "If I had dat mule bone heah, Ahd teach a few mo' uh you mud-turtles something." Enter His Honor at this moment. Lum Boger pompously conducted him to his place, the pulpit, which was doing duty as the bench for the occasion. The assembly unconsciously moderated its tone. But from the outside could still be heard the voices of the children engaged in fisticuffy trials of the case.

The mayor began rapping for order at once. "Cote is set. Cote is set! Looka heah, DIS COTE IS DONE SET! Ah wants you folks tuh dry up."

The courtroom grew perfectly still. The mayor prepared to read the charge to the prisoner, when Brother Stringer (Meth.) entered, hot and perspiring with coat over his arm. He found a seat near the middle of the house against the wall. To reach it, he must climb over the knees of a bench length of people. Before seating himself, he hung his coat upon an empty lamp bracket above his head.

Sister Lewis of the Baptist persuasion arose at once, her hands akimbo, her eyes flashing.

"Brothah Stringah, you take yo' lousy coat down off dese sacred walls! Aint you Meth'dis' got no gumption in the house uh washup?"

Stringer did not answer her, but he cast over a glance that said as plain as day, "Just try and make me do it!"

Della Lewis snorted, but Stringer took his seat complacently. He took his seat, but rose up again as if he had sat on a hot needle point. The reason for this was that Brother Hambo on the Baptist side, a nasty scrapper, rose and rolled his eyes to the fighting angle, looking at Stringer. Stringer caught the look, and hurriedly pawed that coat down off that wall.

Sister Taylor (M.) took up the gauntlet dropped like a hot potato by Stringer. "Some folks," she said with a meaning look, "is a whole lot moh puhtic'lar bout a louse in they church than they is in they house." A very personal look at Sister Lewis.

"Well," said that lady, "mah house mought not be exactly clean. But nobody caint say *dat*"—indicating an infinitesimal amount on the end of her finger—"about my chaRACter! They didn't hafta git de sheriff to make Sam marry ME!"

Mrs. Taylor leaped to her feet and struggled to cross the aisle to her traducer but was restrained by three or four men. "Yas, they did git de sheriff tuh make Sam marry me!" She shouted as she panted and struggled, "And Gawd knows you sho oughter git him agin and make *some* of these men marry yo' Ada."

Mrs. Lewis now had to be restrained. She gave voice and hard, bone-breaking words flew back and forth across the aisle. Each was aided and abetted by her side of the house. His Honor was all the time beating the pulpit with his gavel and shouting for order. At last he threatened to descend in person upon the belligerents.

"Heah! You moufy wimmen! Shet up. Aint Ah done said cote was set? Lum Boger, do yo' duty. Make them wimmen dry up or put 'em outa heah."

Marshall Boger who wore his star for the occasion was full of the importance of his office for nineteen is a prideful age; he hurried over to Mrs. Taylor. She rose to meet him. "You better gwan 'way from me, Lum Boger. Ah jes' wish you would lay de weight of yo' han' on me! Ahd kick yo' cloes up round yo' neck lak a horse collar. You impident limb you."

Lum retreated before the awful prospect of wearing his suit about his neck like a horse collar. He crossed the aisle to the fiery Della and frowned upon her. She was already standing and ready to commence hostilities. One look was enough. He said nothing, but her threats followed him down the aisle as he retreated to the vestibule to shoo the noisy children away. The women subsided and the Mayor began.

"We come heah on very important business," he said. "Stan' up dere, Jim Weston. You is charged wid 'ssaultin' Dave Carter here wid a mule bone, and robbin' him uh his wild turkey. Is you guilty or not guilty?"

Jim arose, looked insolently around the room and answered the charge: "Yas, Ah hit him and took de turkey cause it wuz mine. Ah hit him and Ahll hit him agin, but it wasnt no crime this time."

His Honor's jaw dropped. There was surprise on the faces of all the Baptist section, surprise and perplexity. Gloating and laughter from the Methodists. Simms pulled Jim's coattail.

"Set down Jim," he cooed, "youse one of mah lambs. Set down. Yo' shepherd will show them that walks in de darkness wid sinners and republicans de light."

Jim sat down and the pastor got to his feet.

"Looka heah, Jim, this aint for no foolishness. Do you realize dat if youse found guilty, youse gonna be run outa town?"

"Yeah," Jim answered without rising. "But Ah aint gonna be found no guilty. You caint find me." There was a pleasurable stir on his side of the house. The Baptists were still in the coma which Jim's first statement had brought on.

"Ah say too, he aint guilty," began Rev. Simms with great unction in his tones. "Ah done been to de cot-house at Orlando an' set under de voice of dem lawyers an' heard 'em law from mornin' tell night. They says you got tuh have a weepon befo' you kin commit uh 'ssault. Ah done read dis heah Bible fum lid tuh lid" (he made a gesture to indicate the thoroughness of his search) "and it aint in no Bible dat no mule bone is a weepon, an' it aint in no white folks law neither. Therefo' Brother Mayor, Ah ast you tuh let Jim go. You gotta turn 'im loose, cause nobody kin run 'im outa town when he aint done no crime."

A deep purple gloom settled down upon the Mayor and his followers. Over against this the wild joy of the Methodists. Simms already felt the reins of power in his hands. Over the protest of the Mayor he raised a song and he and his followers sang it with great gusto.

Oh Mary dont you weep, dont you mourn
Oh Mary, dont you weep dont you mourn
Pharaoh's army got drownded,
O-O-oh Mary, dont you weep

The troubled expression on the face of the Baptist leader, Rev. Long, suddenly lifted. He arose while yet the triumphant defense is singing its hallelujah. Mayor Clarke quieted the tumult with difficulty. Simms saw him rise but far from being worried, he sank back upon the seat, his eyes half closed, hands folded fatly across his fat stomach. He smirked. Let them rave! He had built his arguments on solid rock, and the gates of Baptist logic could not prevail against it!

When at last he got the attention of the assembly, he commanded Dave to stand.

"Ah jus want you all tuh take a look at his head. Anybody kin see dat big knot dat Jim put on dere." Jim, the Rev. Simms and all his communicants laughed loudly at this, but Long went on calmly. "Ah been tuh de cote-house tuh Orlando an' heard de white folks law as much as any body heah. And dey dont ast whether de thing dat a person gits hurt wid is uh weepon or not. All dey wants tuh fin' out is, 'did it hurt?' Now you all kin see dat mule bone did hurt Dave's head. So it must be a weepon cause it hurt him.—"

Rev. Simms had his eyes wide open now. He jumped to his feet.

"Never mind bout dem white folks laws at O'landa, Brother Long. Dis is a colored town. Nohow we oughter run by de laws uh de Bible. Dem white folks laws dont go befo' whuts in dis sacred book."

"Jes' hold yo' hot potater, Brother Simms, Ahm comin' tuh dat part right now. Jes lemme take yo' Bible a minute."

"Naw indeed. You oughter brought one of yo' own if you got one. Furthemo' Brother Mayor, we got work tuh do—Wese workin' people. Dont keep us in heah too long. Dis case is through wid."

"Oh, naw it aint," the Mayor disagreed, "you done talked yo' side, now you got tuh let Brother Long talk his. So fur as de work is concerned, it kin wait. One thing at a time. Come on up heah in yo' pulpit an' read yo' own Bible, Brother Long. Dont mind me being up heah."

Long ascended the pulpit and began to turn the leaves of the large Bible. The entire assembly slid forward to the edges of the seat.

"Ah done proved by de white folks law dat Jim oughter be run outa town an' now Ahm gointer show by de Bible—"

Simms was on his feet again. "But Brother Mayor—"

"Set down Simms" was all the answer he got. "Youse *entirely* outa order."

"It says heah in Judges 15:16 dat Samson slewed a thousand Philistines wid de jaw-bone of a ass," Long drawled.

"Yas, but this wasnt no ass, this was a mule," Simms objected.

"And now dat bring us to de main claw uh dis subjick. It sho want no ass, but everybody knows dat a donkey is de father of every mule what ever wuz born. Even little chillen knows dat. Everybody knows dat little as a donkey is, dat if he is dangerous, his great big mule son is mo' so. Everybody knows dat de further back on a mule you goes, de mo' dangerous he gits. Now if de jawbone is as dangerous as it says heah, in de Bible, by de time you gits clear back tuh his hocks hes rank pizen."

"AMEN!! Specially Brazzle's ol' mule," put in Hambo.

"An' dat makes it double 'ssault an' batt'ry," Long continued. "Therefo' Brother Mayor, Ah ast dat Jim be run outa town fuh 'ssaultin Dave wid a deadly weepon an' stealin' his turkey while de boy wuz unconscious."

It was now the turn of the Baptists to go wild. The faint protests of Simms were drowned in the general uproar.

"I'll be henfired if he aint right!" the Mayor exclaimed when he could make himself heard. "This case is just as plain as day."

Simms tried once more. "But Brother Mayor—"

"Aw be quiet, Simms. You done talked yo'self all outa joint already." His Honor cut him short. "Jim Weston, you git right outa *mah* town befo sundown an' dont lemme ketch you back heah under two yeahs, neither. You folks dats so rearin' tuh fight, gwan outside an' fight all you wants tuh. But dont use no guns, no razors nor no mule-bones. Cote's dismissed."

A general murmur of approval swept over the house. Clarke went on; unofficially, as it were. 'By ziggity, dat ol' mule been dead three years an' still kickin'! An' he done kicked more'n one person outa whack today." And he gave Simms one of his most personal looks.

from black no more
1931

a huge silver monoplane glided gracefully to the surface of
Mines Field in Los Angeles and came to a pretty stop after a short
run. A liveried footman stepped out of the forward compartment armed
with a stool which he placed under the rear door. Simultaneously a high-
powered foreign car swept up close to the airplane and waited. The rear
door of the airplane opened, and to the apparent surprise of the nearby
mechanics a tall, black, distinguished-looking Negro stepped out and
down to the ground, assisted by the hand of the footman. Behind him
came a pale young man and woman, evidently secretaries. The three
entered the limousine which rapidly drove off.

"Who's that coon?" asked one of the mechanics, round-eyed and
respectful, like all Americans, in the presence of great wealth.

"Don't you know who that is?" inquired another, pityingly. "Why that's
that Dr. Crookman. You know, the fellow what's turnin' niggers white. See
that B N M on the side of his plane? That stands for Black-No-More. Gee,
but I wish I had just half the jack he's made in the last six months!"

"Why I thought from readin' th' papers," protested the first speaker,
"that th' law had closed up his places and put 'im outta business."

"Oh, that's a lotta hockey," said the other fellow. "Why just yesterday
th' newspapers said that Black-No-More was openin' a place on Central
Avenue. They already got one in Oakland, so a coon told me yesterday."

" 'Sfunny," ventured a third mechanic, as they wheeled the big plane
into a nearby hangar, "how he don't have nuthin' but white folks around
him. He must not like nigger help. His chauffeur's white, his footman's
white an' that young gal and feller what was with him are white."

"How do you know?" challenged the first speaker. "They may be
darkies that he's turned into white folks."

"That's right," the other replied. "It's gittin' so yuh can't tell who's who. I think that there Knights of Nordica ought to do something about it. I joined up with 'em two months ago but they ain't done nuthin' but sell me an ole uniform an' hold a coupla meetin's."

They lapsed into silence. Sandol, the erstwhile Senegalese, stepped from the cockpit grinning. "Ah, zese Americains," he muttered to himself as he went over the engine, examining everything minutely.

"Where'd yuh come from, buddy?" asked one of the mechanics.

"Den-vair," Sandol replied.

"Whatcha doin', makin' a trip around th' country?" queried another.

"Yes, we air, what you callem, on ze tour inspectione," the aviator continued. They could think of no more to say and soon strolled off.

Around an oval table on the seventh floor of a building on Central Avenue, sat Dr. Junius Crookman, Hank Johnson, Chuck Foster, Ranford the Doctor's secretary and four other men. At the lower end of the table Miss Bennett, Ranford's stenographer, was taking notes. A soft-treading waiter whose Negro nature was only revealed by his mocking obsequiousness, served each with champagne.

"To our continued success!" cried the physician, lifting his glass high.

"To our continued success!" echoed the others.

They drained their glasses, and returned them to the polished surface of the table.

"Dog bite it, Doc!" blurted Johnson. "Us sho is doin' fine. Ain't had a bad break since we stahted, an' heah 'tis th' fust o' September."

"Don't holler too soon," cautioned Foster. "The opposition is growing keener every day. I had to pay seventy-five thousand dollars more for this building than it's worth."

"Well, yuh got it, didn't yuh?" asked Johnson. "Just like Ah allus say: when yuh got money yuh kin git anything in this man's country. Whenever things look tight jes pull out th' ole check book an' eve'ything's all right."

"Optimist!" grunted Foster.

"I ain't no pess'mist," Johnson accused.

"Now gentlemen," Dr. Crookman interrupted, clearing his throat, "let's get down to business. We have met here, as you know, not only for the purpose of celebrating the opening of this, our fiftieth sanitarium, but also to take stock of our situation. I have before me here a detailed report of our business affairs for the entire period of seven months and a half that we've been in operation.

"During that time we have put into service fifty sanitariums from Coast to Coast, or an average of one every four and one-half days, the average capacity of each sanitarium being one hundred and five patients. Each place has a staff of six physicians and twenty-four nurses, a janitor, four orderlies, two electricians, bookkeeper, cashier, stenographer and record clerk, not counting four guards.

"For the past four months we have had an equipment factory in Pittsburgh in full operation and a chemical plant in Philadelphia. In addition to this we have purchased four airplanes and a radio broadcasting station. Our expenditures for real estate, salaries and chemicals have totaled six million, two hundred and fifty-five thousand, eighty-five dollars and ten cents." . . .

"He! He!" chuckled Johnson. "Dat ten cents mus' be fo' one o' them bad ceegars that Fostah smokes."

"Our total income," continued Dr. Crookman, frowning slightly at the interruption, "has been eighteen million, five hundred thousand, three hundred dollars, or three hundred and seventy thousand and six patients at fifty dollars apiece. I think that vindicates my contention at the beginning that the fee should be but fifty dollars—within the reach of the rank and file of Negroes." He laid aside his report and added:

"In the next four months we'll double our output and by the end of the year we should cut the fee to twenty-five dollars," he lightly twirled his waxed mustache between his long sensitive fingers and smiled with satisfaction.

"Yes," said Foster, "the sooner we get this business over with the better. We're going to run into a whole lot more opposition from now on than we have so far encountered."

"Why man!" growled Johnson, "we ain't even stahted on dese darkies yet. And when we git thu wi' dese heah, we kin work on them in th' West Indies. Believe me, Ah doan *nevah* want dis graft tuh end."

"Now," continued Dr. Crookman, "I want to say that Mr. Foster deserves great praise for the industry and ingenuity he has shown in purchasing our real estate and Mr. Johnson deserves equally great praise for the efficient manner in which he has kept down the opposition of the various city officials. As you know, he has spent nearly a million dollars in such endeavors and almost as much again in molding legislative sentiment in Washington and the various state capitals. That accounts for the fact that every bill introduced in a legislature or municipal council to put us out of business has died in committee. Moreover, through his corps of secret operatives, who are mostly young women, he has placed numbers of officials and legislators in a position where they cannot openly oppose our efforts."

A smile of appreciation went around the circle.

"We'll have a whole lot to do from now on," commented Foster.

"Yeh, Big Boy," replied the ex-gambler, "an' whut it takes tuh do it Ah ain't got nuthin' else but!"

"Certainly," said the physician, "our friend Hank has not been over-burdened with scruples."

"Ah doan know whut dat is, Chief," grinned Johnson, "but Ah knows whut a check book'll do. Even these crackers tone down when Ah talks bucks."

"This afternoon," continued Crookman, "we also have with us our three regional directors, Doctors Henry Dogan, Charles Hinckle and Fred Selden, as well as our chief chemist, Wallace Butts, I thought it would be a good idea to bring you all together for this occasion so we could get better acquainted. We'll just have a word from each of them. They're all good Race men, you know, even if they have, like the rest of our staff, taken the treatment."

For the next three-quarters of an hour the three directors and the chief chemist reported on the progress of their work. At intervals the waiter brought in cold drinks, cigars, and cigarettes. Overhead whirred the electric fans. Out of the wide open windows could be seen the panorama of bungalows, pavements, palm trees, trundling street cars and scooting automobiles.

"Lawd! Lawd! Lawd!" Johnson exclaimed at the conclusion of the meeting, going to the window and gazing out over the city. "Jes gimme a coupla yeahs o' dis graft an' Ah'll make Henry Foahd look like a tramp."

Meanwhile, Negro society was in turmoil and chaos. The colored folk, in straining every nerve to get the Black-No-More treatment, had forgotten all loyalties, affiliations and responsibilities. No longer did they flock to the churches on Sundays or pay dues in their numerous fraternal organizations. They had stopped giving anything to the Anti-Lynching campaign. Santop Licorice, head of the once-flourishing Back-To-Africa Society, was daily raising his stentorian voice in denunciation of the race for deserting his organization.

Negro business was being no less hard hit. Few people were bothering about getting their hair straightened or skin whitened temporarily when for a couple of weeks' pay they could get both jobs done permanently. The immediate result of this change of mind on the part of the Negro public was to almost bankrupt the firms that made the whitening and straightening chemicals. They were largely controlled by canny Hebrews, but at least a half-dozen were owned by Negroes. The rapid decline in this business greatly decreased the revenue of the Negro weekly newspapers who depended upon such advertising for their sustenance. The actual business of hair straightening that had furnished employment to thousands of colored women who would otherwise have had to go back to washing and ironing, declined to such an extent that "To Rent" signs hung in front of nine-tenths of the shops.

The Negro politicians in the various Black Belts, grown fat and sleek "protecting" vice with the aid of Negro votes which they were able to control by virtue of housing segregation, lectured in vain about black solidarity, race pride and political emancipation; but nothing stopped the exodus to the white race. Gloomily the politicians sat in their offices, wondering whether to throw up the sponge and hunt the nearest Black-No-More sanitarium or hold on a little longer in the hope that the whites might put a stop to the activities of Dr. Crookman and his associates. The latter, indeed, was their only hope because the bulk of Negroes, saving their dimes and dollars for chromatic emancipation, had stopped gambling, patronizing houses of prostitution or staging Saturday-night brawls. Thus the usual sources of graft vanished. The black politicians appealed to their white masters for succor, of course, but they found to their dismay that most of the latter had been safely bribed by the astute Hank Johnson.

Gone was the almost European atmosphere of every Negro ghetto: the music, laughter, gaiety, jesting and abandon. Instead, one noted the same excited bustle, wild looks and strained faces to be seen in a war time soldier camp, around a new oil district or before a gold rush. The happy-go-lucky Negro of song and story was gone forever and in his stead was a nervous, money-grubbing black, stuffing away coin in socks, impatiently awaiting a sufficient sum to pay Dr. Crookman's fee.

Up from the South they came in increasing droves, besieging the Black-No-More sanitariums for treatment. There were none of these havens in the South because of the hostility of the bulk of white people but there were many all along the border between the two sections, at such places as Washington, D.C., Baltimore, Cincinnati, Louisville, Evansville, Cairo,

St. Louis and Denver. The various Southern communities attempted to stem this, the greatest migration of Negroes in the history of the country, but without avail. By train, boat, wagon, bicycle, automobile and foot they trekked to the promised land; a hopeful procession, filtering through the outposts of police and Knights of Nordica volunteer bands. Where there was great opposition to the Negroes' going, there would suddenly appear large quantities of free bootleg liquor and crisp new currency which would make the most vigilant white opponent of Black-No-More turn his head the other way. Hank Johnson seemed to be able to cope with almost every situation.

The national office of the militant Negro organization, the National Social Equality League, was agog. Telephone bells were ringing, mulatto clerks were hustling excitedly back and forth, messenger boys rushed in and out. Located in the Times Square district of Manhattan, it had for forty years carried on the fight for full social equality for the Negro citizens and the immediate abolition of lynching as a national sport. While this organization had to depend to a large extent upon the charity of white folk for its existence, since the blacks had always been more or less skeptical about the program for liberty and freedom, the efforts of the society were not entirely unprofitable. Vistas of immaculate offices spread in every direction from the elevator and footfalls were muffled in thick imitation-Persian rugs. While the large staff of officials was eager to end all oppression and persecution of the Negro, they were never so happy and excited as when a Negro was barred from a theater or fried to a crisp. Then they would leap for telephones, grab telegraph pads and yell for stenographers; smiling through their simulated indignation at the spectacle of another reason for their continued existence and appeals for funds.

Ever since the first sanitarium of Black-No-More, Incorporated, started turning Negroes into Caucasians, the National Social Equality League's income had been decreasing. No dues had been collected in months and subscriptions to the national mouthpiece, *The Dilemma*, had dwindled to almost nothing. Officials, long since ensconced in palatial apartments, began to grow panic-stricken as pay days got farther apart. They began to envision the time when they would no longer be able for the sake of the Negro race to suffer the hardships of lunching on canvasback duck at the Urban Club surrounded by the white dilettante, endure the perils of first-class Transatlantic passage to stage Save-Dear-Africa Conferences or undergo the excruciating torture of rolling back and forth across the United States in drawing-rooms to hear each lecture on the Negro problem. On meager salaries of five thousand dollars a year they had fought strenuously and tirelessly to obtain for the Negroes the constitutional rights which only a few thousand rich white folk possessed. And now they saw the work of a lifetime being rapidly destroyed.

Single-handed they felt incapable of organizing an effective opposition to Black-No-More, Incorporated, so they had called a conference of all of the outstanding Negro leaders of the country to assemble at the League's headquarters on December 1, 1933. Getting the Negro leaders together for any purpose except boasting of each other's accomplishments had previously been impossible. As a usual thing they fought each other with a vigor only surpassed by that of their pleas for racial solidarity and unity of action. This situation, however, was unprecedented, so almost all of the representative gentlemen of color to whom invitations had been sent agreed with alacrity to come. To a man they felt that it was time to bury the hatchet before they became too hungry to do any digging.

In a very private inner office of the N. S. E. L. suite, Dr. Shakespeare Agamemon Beard, founder of the League and a graduate of Harvard, Yale and Copenhagen (whose haughty bearing never failed to impress both Caucasians and Negroes) sat before a glass-topped desk, rubbing now his curly gray head, and now his full spade beard. For a mere six thousand dollars a year, the learned doctor wrote scholarly and biting editorials in *The Dilemma* denouncing the Caucasians whom he secretly admired and lauding the greatness of the Negroes whom he alternately pitied and despised. In limpid prose he told of the sufferings and privations of the downtrodden black workers with whose lives he was totally and thankfully unfamiliar. Like most Negro leaders, he deified the black woman but abstained from employing aught save octoroons. He talked at white banquets about "we of the black race" and admitted in books that he was part-French, part-Russian, part-Indian and part-Negro. He bitterly denounced the Nordics for debauching Negro women while taking care to hire comely yellow stenographers with weak resistance. In a real way, he loved his people. In time of peace he was a Pink Socialist but when the clouds of war gathered he bivouacked at the feet of Mars.

Before the champion of the darker races lay a neatly typed resolution drawn up by him and his staff the day before and addressed to the Attorney General of the United States. The staff had taken this precaution because no member of it believed that the other Negro leaders possessed sufficient education to word the document effectively and grammatically. Dr. Beard re-read the resolution and then placing it in the drawer of the desk, pressed one of a row of buttons. "Tell them to come in," he directed. The mulattress turned and switched out of the room, followed by the appraising and approving eye of the aged scholar. He heaved a regretful sigh as the door closed and his thoughts dwelt on the vigor of his youth.

In three or four minutes the door opened again and several well-dressed blacks, mulattoes and white men entered the large office and took seats around the wall. They greeted each other and the President of the League with usual cordiality but for the first time in their lives they were sincere about it. If anyone could save the day it was Beard. They all admitted that, as did the Doctor himself. They pulled out fat cigars, long slender cigarettes and London briar pipes, lit them and awaited the opening of the conference.

The venerable lover of his race tapped with his knuckle for order, laid aside his six-inch cigarette and rising, said:

"It were quite unseemly for me who lives such a cloistered life and am spared the bane or benefit of many intimate contacts with those of our struggling race who by sheer courage, tenacity and merit have lifted their heads above the mired mass, to deign to take from a more capable individual the unpleasant task of reviewing the combination of unfortunate circumstances that has brought us together, man to man, within the four walls of the office." He shot a foxy glance around the assembly and then went on suavely. "And so, my friends, I beg your august permission to confer upon my able and cultured secretary and confidant, Dr. Napoleon Wellington Jackson, the office of chairman of this temporary body. I need not introduce Dr. Jackson to you. You know of his scholarship, his high sense of duty and his deep love of the suffering black race. You have doubtless had the pleasure of singing some of the many sorrow songs he has written and popularized in the past twenty years, and you must know of his fame as a translator of Latin poets and his authoritative work on the Greek language.

"Before I gratefully yield the floor to Dr. Jackson, however, I want to tell you that our destiny lies in the stars. Ethiopia's fate is in the balance. The Goddess of the Nile weeps bitter tears at the feet of the Great Sphinx. The lowering clouds gather over the Congo and the lightning flashes o'er Togoland. To your tents, O Israel! The hour is at hand."

The president of the N. S. E. L. sat down and the erudite Dr. Jackson, his tall, lanky secretary got up. There was no fear of Dr. Jackson ever winning a beauty contest. He was a sooty black, very broad shouldered, with long, ape-like arms, a diminutive egg-shaped head that sat on his collar like a hen's egg on a demitasse cup and eyes that protruded so far from his head that they seemed about to fall out. He wore pince-nez that were continually slipping from his very flat and oily nose. His chief business in the organization was to write long and indignant letters to public officials and legislators whenever a Negro was mistreated, demanding justice, fair play and other legal guarantees vouchsafed no whites except bloated plutocrats fallen miraculously afoul of the law, and to speak to audiences of sex-starved matrons who yearned to help the Negro stand erect. During his leisure time, which was naturally considerable, he wrote long and learned articles, bristling with references, for the more intellectual magazines, in which he sought to prove conclusively that the plantation shouts of Southern Negro peons were superior to any of Beethoven's symphonies and that the city of Benin was the original site of the Garden of Eden.

"Hhmm! Hu-umn! Now er—ah, gentlemen," began Dr. Jackson, rocking back on his heels, taking off his eye glasses and beginning to polish them with a silk kerchief, "as you know, the Negro race is face to face with a grave crisis. I-ah-presume it is er-ah unnecessary for me to go into any details concerning the-ah activities of Black-No-More, Incorporated. Suffice er-ah umph! ummmmh! to say-ah that it has thrown our society into rather a-ah bally turmoil. Our people are forgetting shamelessly their-ah duty to the-ah organizations that have fought valiantly for them these-ah many years and are now busily engaged chasing a bally-ah will-o-the wisp. Ahem!

"You-ah probably all fully realize that-ah a continuation of the aforementioned activities will prove disastrous to our-ah organizations. You-ah, like us, must feel-uh that something drastic must be done to preserve the integrity of Negro society. Think, gentlemen, what the future will mean to-uh all those who-uh have toiled so hard for Negro society. What-ah, may I ask, will we do when there are no longer any-ah groups to support us? Of course, Dr. Crookman and-ah his associates have a-uh perfect right to-ah engage in any legitimate business, but-ah their present activities can-not-ah be classed under that head, considering the effect on our endeavors. Before we go any further, however, I-ah would like to introduce our research expert Mr. Walter Williams, who will-ah describe the situation in the South."

Mr. Walter Williams, a tall, heavy-set white man with pale blue eyes, wavy auburn hair and a militant, lantern jaw, rose and bowed to the assemblage and proceeded to paint a heartrending picture of the loss of pride and race solidarity among Negroes North and South. There was, he said, not a single local of the N. S. E. L. functioning, dues had dwindled to nothing, he had not been able to hold a meeting anywhere, while many of the stanchest supporters had gone over into the white race.

"Personally," he concluded, "I am very proud to be a Negro and always have been (his great-grand-father, it seemed, had been a mulatto), and I'm willing to sacrifice for the uplift of my race. I cannot understand what has come over our people that they have so quickly forgotten the ancient glories of Ethiopia, Songhay and Dahomey, and their marvelous record of achievement since emancipation." Mr. Williams was known to be a Negro among his friends and acquaintances, but no one else would have suspected it.

Another white man of remote Negro ancestry, Rev. Herbert Gronne of Dunbar University, followed the research expert with a long discourse in which he expressed fear for the future of his institution whose student body had been reduced to sixty-five persons and deplored the catastrophe "that has befallen us black people."

They all listened with respect to Dr. Gronne. He had been in turn a college professor, a social worker and a minister, had received the approval of the white folks and was thus doubly acceptable to the Negroes. Much of his popularity was due to the fact that he very cleverly knew how to make statements that sounded radical to Negroes but sufficiently conservative to satisfy the white trustees of his school. In addition he possessed the asset of looking perpetually earnest and sincere.

Following him came Colonel Mortimer Roberts, principal of the Dusky River Agricultural Institute, Supreme General of the Knights and Daughters of Kingdom Come and president of the Uncle Tom Memorial Association. Colonel Roberts was the acknowledged leader of the conservative Negroes (most of whom had nothing to conserve) who felt at all times that the white folks were in the lead and that Negroes should be careful to guide themselves accordingly.

He was a great mountain of blackness with a head shaped like an upturned bucket, pierced by two pig-like eyes and a cavernous mouth equipped with large tombstone teeth which he almost continually displayed. His speech was a cross between the woofing of a bloodhound and the explosion of an inner tube. It conveyed to most white people an impression of rugged simplicity and sincerity, which was very fortunate since Colonel Roberts maintained his school through their contributions. He spoke as usual about the cordial relations existing between the two races in his native Georgia, the effrontery of Negroes who dared whiten themselves and thus disturb the minds of white people and insinuated alliance with certain militant organizations in the South to stop this whitening business before it went too far. Having spoken his mind and received scant applause, the Colonel (some white man had once called him Colonel and the title stuck), puffing and blowing, sat down.

Mr. Claude Spelling, a scared-looking little brown man with big ears, who held the exalted office of president of the Society of Negro Merchants, added his volume of blues to the discussion. The refrain was that Negro business—always anemic—was about to pass out entirely through lack of patronage. Mr. Spelling had for many years been the leading advocate of the strange doctrine that an underpaid Negro worker should go out of his way to patronize a little dingy Negro store instead of going to a cheaper and cleaner chain store, all for the dubious satisfaction of helping Negro merchants grow wealthy.

The next speaker, Dr. Joseph Bonds, a little rat-faced Negro with protruding teeth stained by countless plugs of chewing tobacco and wearing horn-rimmed spectacles, who headed the Negro Data League, almost cried (which would have been terrible to observe) when he told of the difficulty his workers had encountered in their efforts to persuade retired white capitalists, whose guilty consciences persuaded them to indulge in philan-thropy, to give their customary donations to the work. The philanthropists seemed to think, said Dr. Bonds, that since the Negroes were busily solving their difficulties, there was no need for social work among them or any collection of data. He almost sobbed aloud when he described how his collections had fallen from $50,000 a month to less than $1000.

His feeling in the matter could easily be appreciated. He was engaged in a most vital and necessary work: i.e., collecting bales of data to prove satisfactorily to all that more money was needed to collect more data. Most of the data were highly informative, revealing the amazing fact that poor people went to jail oftener than rich ones; that most of the people were not getting enough money for their work; that strangely enough there was some connection between poverty, disease and crime. By establishing these facts with mathematical certitude and illustrating them with elabo-rate graphs, Dr. Bonds garnered many fat checks. For his people, he said, he wanted work, not charity; but for himself he was always glad to get the charity with as little work as possible. For many years he had succeeded in doing so without any ascertainable benefit accruing to the Negro group.

Dr. Bonds' show of emotion almost brought the others to tears and many of them muttered "Yes, Brother" while he was talking. The conferees were getting stirred up but it took the next speaker to really get them excited.

When he rose an expectant hush fell over the assemblage. They all knew and respected the Right Reverend Bishop Ezekiel Whooper of the Ethiopian True Faith Wash Foot Methodist Church for three reasons: viz., his church was rich (though the parishioners were poor), he had a very loud voice and the white people praised him. He was sixty, corpulent and an expert at the art of making cuckolds.

"Our loyal and devoted clergy," he boomed, "are being forced into manual labor and the Negro church is rapidly dying" and then he launched into a violent tirade against Black-No-More and favored any means to put the corporation out of business. In his excitement he blew saliva, waved his long arms, stamped his feet, pummeled the desk, rolled his eyes, knocked down his chair, almost sat on the rug and generally reverted to the antics of Negro bush preachers.

This exhibition proved contagious. Rev. Herbert Gronne, face flushed and shouting amens, marched from one end of the room to the other; Colonel Roberts, looking like an inebriated black-faced comedian, rocked back and forth clapping his hands; the others began to groan and moan. Dr. Napoleon Wellington Jackson, sensing his opportunity, began to sing a spiritual in his rich soprano voice. The others immediately joined him. The very air seemed charged with emotion.

Bishop Whooper was about to start up again, when Dr. Beard, who had sat cold and disdainful through this outbreak of revivalism, toying with his gold-rimmed fountain pen and gazing at the exhibition through half-closed eyelids, interrupted in sharp metallic tones.

"Let's get down to earth now," he commanded. "We've had enough of this nonsense. We have a resolution here addressed to the Attorney General of the United States demanding that Dr. Crookman and his associates be arrested and their activities stopped at once for the good of both races. All those in favor of this resolution say aye. Contrary? . . . Very well, the ayes have it . . . Miss Hilton please send off this telegram at once!"

They looked at Dr. Beard and each other in amazement. Several started to meekly protest.

"You gentlemen are all twenty-one, aren't you?" sneered Beard. "Well, then be men enough to stand by your decision."

"But Doctor Beard," objected Rev. Gronne, "isn't this a rather unusual procedure?"

"Rev. Gronne," the great man replied, "it's not near as unusual as Black-No-More. I have probably ruffled your dignity but that's nothing to what Dr. Crookman will do."

"I guess you're right, Beard," the college president agreed.

"I know it," snapped the other.

The Honorable Walter Brybe, who had won his exalted position as Attorney General of the United States because of his long and faithful service helping large corporations to circumvent the federal laws, sat at his desk in Washington, D.C. Before him lay the weird resolution from the conference of Negro leaders. He pursed his lips and reached for his private telephone.

"Gorman?" he inquired softly into the receiver. "Is that you?"

"Nossuh," came the reply, "this heah is Mistah Gay's valet."

"Well, call Mister Gay to the telephone at once."

"Yassuh."

"That you, Gorman," asked the chief legal officer of the nation addressing the National Chairman of his party.

"Yeh, what's up?"

"You heard 'bout this resolution from them niggers in New York, aint you? It's been in all of the papers."

"Yes I read it."

"Well, whaddya think we oughtta do about it?"

"Take it easy, Walter. Give 'em the old run around. You know. They ain't got a thin dime; it's this other crowd that's holding the heavy jack. And 'course you know we gotta clean up our deficit. Just lemme work with that Black-No-More crowd. I can talk business with that Johnson fellow."

"All right, Gorman, I think you're right, but you don't want to forget that there's a whole lot of white sentiment against them coons."

"Needn't worry 'bout that," scoffed Gorman. "There's no money behind it much and besides it's in states we can't carry anyhow. Go ahead; stall them New York niggers off. You're a lawyer, you can always find a reason."

"Thanks for the compliment, Gorman," said the Attorney General, hanging up the receiver.

He pressed a button on his desk and a young girl, armed with pencil and pad, came in.

"Take this letter," he ordered: "To Doctor Shakespeare Agamemnon Beard (what a hell of a name!), Chairman of the Committee for the Preservation of Negro Racial Integrity, 1400 Broadway, New York City.

"My dear Dr. Beard:

The Attorney General has received the solution signed by yourself and others and given it careful consideration.

Regardless of personal views in the matter (I don't give a damn whether they turn white or not, myself) it is not possible for the Department of Justice to interfere with a legitimate business enterprise so long as its methods are within the law. The corporation in question has violated no federal statute and hence there is not the slightest ground for interfering with its activities.

Very truly yours,

WALTER BRYBE.

"Get that off at once. Give out copies to the press. That's all."

Santop Licorice, founder and leader of the Back-to-Africa Society, read the reply of the Attorney General to the Negro leaders with much malicious satisfaction. He laid aside his morning paper, pulled a fat cigar from a box near by, lit it and blew clouds of smoke above his woolly head. He was always delighted when Dr. Beard met with any sort of rebuff or embarrassment. He was doubly pleased in this instance because he had been overlooked in the sending out of invitations to Negro leaders to join the Committee for the Preservation of Negro Racial Integrity. It was outrageous, after all the talking he had done in favor of Negro racial integrity.

Mr. Licorice for some fifteen years had been very profitably advocating the emigration of all the American Negroes to Africa. He had not, of course, gone there himself and had not the slightest intention of going so far from the fleshpots, but he told the other Negroes to go. Naturally the first step in their going was to join his society by paying five dollars a year for membership, ten dollars for a gold, green and purple robe and silver-colored helmet that together cost two dollars and a half, contributing five dollars to the Santop Licorice Defense Fund (there was a perpetual defense fund because Licorice was perpetually in the courts for fraud of some kind), and buying shares at five dollars each in the Royal Black Steamship

Company, for obviously one could not get to Africa without a ship and Negroes ought to travel on Negro-owned and operated ships. The ships were Santop's especial pride. True, they had never been to Africa, had never had but one cargo and that, being gin, was half consumed by the unpaid and thirsty crew before the vessel was saved by the Coast Guard, but they had cost more than anything else the Back-To-Africa Society had purchased even though they were worthless except as scrap iron. Mr. Licorice, who was known by his followers as Provisional President of Africa, Admiral of the African Navy, Field Marshal of the African Army and Knight Commander of the Nile, had a genius for being stuck with junk by crafty salesmen. White men only needed to tell him that he was shrewder than white men and he would immediately reach for a check book.

But there was little reaching for check books in his office nowadays. He had been as hard hit as the other Negroes. Why should anybody in the Negro race want to go back to Africa at a cost of five hundred dollars for passage when they could stay in America and get white for fifty dollars? Mr. Licorice saw the point but instead of scuttling back to Demerara from whence he had come to save his race from oppression, he had hung on in the hope that the activities of Black-No-More, Incorporated, would be stopped. In the meantime, he had continued to attempt to save the Negroes by vigorously attacking all of the other Negro organizations and at the same time preaching racial solidarity and coöperation in his weekly newspaper, "*The African Abroad*," which was printed by white folks and had until a year ago been full of skin-whitening and hair-straightening advertisements.

"How is our treasury?" he yelled back through the dingy suite of offices to his bookkeeper, a pretty mulatto.

"What treasury?" she asked in mock surprise.

"Why, I thought we had seventy-five dollars," he blurted.

"We did, but the Sheriff got most of it yesterday or we wouldn't be in here today."

"Huumn! Well, that's bad. And tomorrow's pay day, isn't it?"

"Why bring that up?" she sneered. "I'd forgotten all about it."

"Haven't we got enough for me to get to Atlanta?" Licorice inquired, anxiously.

"There is if you're gonna hitch-hike."

"Well, of course, I couldn't do that," he smiled deprecatingly.

"I should say not," she retorted surveying his 250-pound, five-feet-six-inches of black blubber.

"Call Western Union," he commanded.

"What with?"

"Over the telephone, of course, Miss Hall," he explained.

"If you can get anything over that telephone you're a better man than I am, Gunga Din."

"Has the service been discontinued, young lady?"

"Try and get a number," she chirped. He gazed ruefully at the telephone.

"Is there anything we can sell?" asked the bewildered Licorice.

"Yeah, if you can get the Sheriff to take off his attachments."

"That's right, I had forgotten."

"You would."

"Please be more respectful, Miss Hall," he snapped. "Somebody might overhear you and tell my wife."

"Which one?" she mocked.

"Shut up," he blurted, touched in a tender spot, "and try to figure out some way for us to get hold of some money."

"You must think I'm Einstein," she said, coming up and perching herself on the edge of his desk.

"Well, if we don't get some operating expenses I won't be able to obtain money to pay your salary," he warned.

"The old songs are the best songs," she wise-cracked.

"Oh, come now, Violet," he remonstrated, pawing her buttock, "let's be serious."

"After all these years!" she declared, switching away.

In desperation, he eased his bulk out of the creaking swivel chair, reached for his hat and overcoat and shuffled out of the office. He walked to the curb to hail a taxicab but reconsidered when he recalled that a worn half-dollar was the extent of his funds. Sighing heavily, he trudged the two blocks to the telegraph office and sent a long day letter to Henry Givens, Imperial Grand Wizard of the Knights of Nordica—collect.

"Well, have you figured it out?" asked Violet when he barged into his office again.

"Yes, I just sent a wire to Givens," he replied.

"But he's a nigger-hater, isn't he?" was her surprised comment.

"You want your salary, don't you?" he inquired archly.

"I have for the past month."

"Well, then, don't ask foolish questions," he snapped.

JAMES WELDON JOHNSON

brer rabbit, you's de cutes' of 'em all
1935

Once der was a meetin' in de wilderness,
All de critters of creation dey was dar;
Brer Rabbit, Brer Possum, Brer Wolf, Brer Fox,
King Lion, Mister Terrapin, Mister B'ar.
De question fu' discussion was, "Who is de bigges' man?"
Dey 'pinted ole Jedge Owl to decide;
He polished up his spectacles an' put 'em on his nose,
An' to the question slowly he replied:

"Brer Wolf am mighty cunnin',
Brer Fox am mighty sly,
Brer Terrapin and Possum—kinder small;
Brer Lion's mighty vicious,
Brer B'ar he's sorter 'spicious,
Brer Rabbit, you's de cutes' of 'em all."

Dis caused a great confusion 'mongst de animals,
Ev'y critter claimed dat he had won de prize;
Dey 'sputed an' dey arg'ed, dey growled an' dey roared,
Den putty soon de dus' begin to rise.
Brer Rabbit he jes' stood aside an' watched 'em w'ile dey fight,
Brer Lion he mos' tore Brer B'ar in two;
W'en dey was all so tiah'd dat dey couldn't catch der bref
Brer Rabbit he jes' grabbed de prize an' flew.

Brer Wolf am mighty cunnin',
Brer Fox am mighty sly,
Brer Terrapin an' Possum—kinder small;
Brer Lion's mighty vicious,
Brer B'ar he's sorter 'spicious,
Brer Rabbit, you's de cutes' of 'em all.

STERLING BROWN

slim in atlanta
1932

Down in Atlanta,
  De whitefolks got laws
For to keep all de niggers
  From laughin' outdoors.

    Hope to Gawd I may die
      If I ain't speakin' truth
    Make de niggers do deir laughin
      In a telefoam booth.

Slim Greer hit de town
  An' de rebs got him told,—
"Dontcha laugh on de street,
  If you want to die old."

    Den dey showed him de booth,
      An' a hundred shines
    In front of it, waitin'
      In double lines.

Slim thought his sides
  Would bust in two,
Yelled, "Lookout, everybody,
  I'm coming through!"

    Pulled de other man out,
      An' bust in de box,
    An' laughed four hours
      By de Georgia clocks.

Den he peeked through de door,
An' what did he see?
Three hundred niggers there
In misery.—

Some holdin' deir sides,
Some holdin' deir jaws,
To keep from breakin'
De Georgia laws.

An' Slim gave a holler,
An' started again;
An' from three hundred throats
Come a moan of pain.

An' everytime Slim
Saw what was outside,
Got to whoopin' again
Till he nearly died.

An' while de poor critters
Was waitin' deir chance,
Slim laughed till dey sent
Fo' de ambulance.

De state paid de railroad
To take him away;
Den, things was as usural
In Atlanta, Gee A.

slim lands a job?
1932

Poppa Greer happened
  Down Arkansaw way,
An' ast for a job
  At Big Pete's Cafe.

    Big Pete was a six foot
      Hard-boiled man
    Wid a forty-four dungeon
      In his han'.

"Nigger, kin you wait?"
  Is what Pete ast;
Slim says, "Cap'n
  I'm jes' too fast."

    Pete says, "Dat's what
    I wants to hire;
    I got a slow nigger
    I'm gonna fire—

Don't 'low no slow nigger
  Stay roun' hyeah,
I plugs 'em wid my dungeon!"
  An' Slim says "Yeah?"

    A noise rung out
    In rush a man
    Wid a tray on his head
    An' one on each han'

Wid de silver in his mouf
  An' de soup plates in his vest
Pullin' a red wagon
  Wid all de rest. . . .

De man's said, "Dere's
  Dat slow coon now
Dat wuthless lazy waiter!"
  An' Slim says, "How?"

    An' Slim threw his gears in
      Put it in high,
    An' kissed his hand to Arkansaw,
      Sweetheart . . . good-bye!

crispus attucks mckoy
1965

I sing of a hero,
Unsung, unrecorded,
Known by the name
Of Crispus Attucks McKoy,
Born, bred in Boston,
Stepson of Garvey,
Cousin of Trotter,
Godson of Du Bois.

No monastic hairshirt
Stung flesh more bitterly
Than the white coat
In which he was arrayed;
But what was his agony
On entering the drawing-room
To hear a white woman
Say slowly, "One spade."

He threw up his job,
His scorn was sublime,
And he left the bridge party
Simply aghast;
Lo, see him striding
Out of the front door
A free man again
His infamy past.

Down at the Common,
The cradle of freedom,
Another shock nearly
Carried him away
Someone called out "Shine"
And he let loose a blue streak,
And the poor little bootblack
Slunk frightened away.

In a bakery window
He read with a glance
"Brown Betties for sale"
And his molars gnashed;
Up came the kerbstone,
Back went his trusty arm,
Swift was his gesture,
The plate glass was smashed.

On the sub, Crispus
Could have committed murder,
Mayhem and cannibalism,
When he heard a maid
Say to the cherub
Opposite to her,
"Come over here, darling,
Here's a little shade."

But down at the Gardens,
He knew was his refuge,
Recompense for insults,
Solace for grief,
A Negro battler,
Slugging Joe Johnson
Was fighting an Irishman
Battling Dan O'Keefe.

The garden was crammed,
Mickeys, Kikes, Bohunks,
Polacks and Dagoes,
All over the place,
Crispus strode in,
Regally, boldly,
The sole representative
Of his race.

The fight was even,
When Joey hit Dan,
The heart of Crispus
Shone with a steady glow,
When Dan hit Joey,
Crispus groaned "foul,"
"Oh the dirty low-down
So-and-so."

In the tenth round,
Dan got to swinging,
Joey was dazed,
And clinched and held,
When suddenly,
Right behind Crispus,
"Kill the Nigger!"
Somebody yelled.

Crispus got up
In all of his fury;
Lightning bolts zigzagged
Out of his eyes,
With a voice like thunder
He blurted his challenge,
"Will the bastard who said that
Please arise."

Thirty-five thousand
Nordics and Alpines,
Hebrews and Gentiles,
As one man arose,
See how our hero,
Armed with his noble cause,
Armored with righteousness
To battle goes.

They found an ankle in Dedham,
A thighbone in Maldon,
An elbow in Somerville,
Both nostrils in Lynn,
And on Boston Common
Lay one of his eyebrows,
The cap of his knee,
And a piece of his shin.

Peabody Museum
Has one of his eardrums;
His sound heart was found
In Lexington;
But over the reaches
From Cape Cod to Frisco
The soul of our hero
Goes marching on . . .

GWENDOLYN BROOKS

at the hairdresser's
1945

Gimme an upsweep, Minnie,
With humpteen baby curls.
'Bout time I got some glamour.
I'll show them girls.

Think they so fly a-struttin'
With they wool a-blowin' 'round.

Wait'll they see my upsweep.
That'll jop 'em back on the ground.

Got Madam C. J. Walker's first.
Got Poro Grower next.
Ain't none of 'em worked with me, Min.
But I ain't vexed.

Long hair's out of style anyhow, ain't it?
Now it's tie it up high with curls.
So gimme an upsweep, Minnie.
I'll show them girls.

one reason cats . . .
1968

One reason cats are happier than people
is that they have no newspapers . . .

a song in the front yard
1945

I've stayed in the front yard all my life.
I want a peek at the back
Where it's rough and untended and hungry weed grows.
A girl gets sick of a rose.

I want to go in the back yard now.
And maybe down the alley,
To where the charity children play.
I want a good time today.

They do some wonderful things.
They have some wonderful fun.
My mother sneers, but I say it's fine
How they don't have to go in at a quarter to nine.
My mother she tells me that Johnnie Mae
Will grow up to be a bad woman.
That George will be taken to jail soon or late.
(On account of last winter he sold our back gate.)

But I say it's fine. Honest I do.
And I'd like to be a bad woman too,
And wear the brave stockings of night-black lace,
And strut down the streets with paint on my face.

adventure
c. 1962

"**a**dventure is a great thing," said Simple, "which should be in everybody's life. According to the Late Late Show on TV, in the old days when Americans headed West in covered wagons, they was almost sure to run into adventure—at the very least a battle with the Red Skins. Nowadays, if you want to run into adventure, go to Alabama or Mississippi where you can battle with the White Skins."

"'Go West, young man, go West,' is what they used to say," I said. "'*Pioneers! O pioneers!*' cried Whitman."

"'Go South, young man, go South,' is what I would say today," declared Simple. "If I had a son I wanted to make a man out of, I would send him to Jackson, Mississippi, or Selma, Alabama—and not in a covered wagon, but on a bus. Especially if he was a white boy, I would say, 'Go, son, go, and return to your father's house when you have conquered. The White Skins is on the rampage below the Mason-Dixon line, defying the government, denying free Americans their rights. Go see what you can do about it. Go face the enemy.'"

"You would send your son into the maelstrom of Dixie to get his head beaten by a white cracker or his legs bitten by police dogs?"

"For freedom's sake—and adventure—I might even go South myself," said Simple, "if I was white. I think it is more important for white folks to have them kind of adventures than it is for colored. Negroes have been fighting one way or another all our lives—but it is somewhat new to whites. Until lately, they did not even know what a COLORED ONLY sign meant. White folks have always thought they could go anywhere in the world they wanted to go. They are just now finding out that they cannot go into a COLORED WAITING ROOM in the Jim Crow South. They cannot even go into a WHITE WAITING ROOM if they are with colored folks. They never knew before that if you want adventure, all you have to do is cross the color line in the South."

"Then, according to you," I said, "the Wild West can't hold a candle to the Savage South any more."

"Not even on TV," said Simple. "The Savage South has got the Wild West beat a mile. In the old days adventures was beyond the Great Divide. Today they is below the Color Line. Such adventures is much better than the Late Late Show with Hollywood Indians. But in the South, nobody gets scalped. They just get cold cocked. Of course, them robes the Klan sports around in is not as pretty as the feathers Indians used to wear, but they is more scary. And though a Klan holler is not as loud as a Indian war whoop, the Klan is just as sneaky. In cars, not on horseback, they come under cover of night. If the young people of the North really want excitement, let them go face the Klan and stand up to it.

"That is why the South will make a man of you, my son,' I would say. 'Go South, baby, go South. Let a fiery cross singe the beard off your beatnik chin. Let Mississippi make a man out of you.'"

"Don't you think white adults as well as white youth should be exposed to this thing?" I asked.

"Of course," said Simple. "If the white young folks go as Freedom Riders, let the white old folks go as sight-seers—because no sooner than they got down there, they would be Freedom Riders anyhow. If I owned one of these white travel bureaus arranging sight-seeing tours next summer to Niagara Falls, Yellowstone Park, the Grand Canyon, and Pike's Peak, I would also start advertising sight-seeing tours to Montgomery with the National Guard as guides, to Jackson with leather leggings as protection against police dogs, to the Mississippi Prison Farms with picnic lunches supplied by Howard Johnson's, and to the Governor's Mansion with a magnolia for all the ladies taking the tour—and a night in jail without extra charge.

"Negroes would be guaranteed as passengers on all tours, so that there would be sure adventures for everybody. My ads would read:

SPECIAL RATES FOR A WEEK-END
IN A TYPICAL MISSISSIPPI JAIL.

Get arrested now, pay later. Bail money not included. Have the time of your lives living the life of your times among the Dixie White Skins. Excitement guaranteed. For full details contact the Savage South Tours, Inc., Jesse B. Semple, your host, wishing you hell."

GARY BELKIN (WRITING AS MUHAMMAD ALI)

clay comes out to meet liston
1963

In august 1963, Cassius Clay recited this blow-by-blow description of the final round of his February 1964 championship fight against Sonny Liston.

Clay comes out to meet Liston
And Liston starts to retreat,
But if Liston goes back an inch further
He'll end up in a ringside seat.

Clay swings with his left,
Clay swings with his right;
Look at young Cassius
Carry the fight.

Liston keeps backing
But there's not enough room.
It's a matter of time
Ere Clay lowers the boom.

Now Clay lands a right—
What a beautiful swing!
The punch raises Liston
Up out of the ring.

Liston's still rising
And the ref wears a frown
For he can't stop counting
Till Sonny comes down.

Now Liston disappears from view:
The crowd is getting frantic.
But our radar stations have picked him up—
He's somewhere over the Atlantic.

Who would have thought
When they came to the fight
That they'd see the launching
Of a human satellite?

Yes, the crowd did not dream
When they put down their money
That they would see
A total eclipse of the Sonny!

I AM THE GREATEST!

double nigger
1965

"Yeaah!" said grease. ". . . and evah time I grunt, that damn peckerwood, he say to hisself, 'Damn if you ain't the workinest nigger I ever seed.'"

We laughed at Grease, but we won't payin him no mind. He was the onliest one who done taken his shoes off tryin to keep off that hot pike.

We was makin it back to New Hope, Grease, Blue, Fish and me. We had just got done with bustin up some road for a white man, helpin out his constructin gang.

We was feelin good, headin back home with four dollars apiece. We'd all take out them bills evah mile or so, count 'em and match 'em up to see whose was the newest. They was the prettiest damn dollar bills we evah made. Totin rocks and stumps for that white man almost busted out natural backs.

"Shet up, nigger," Blue said to Grease. "Your mouth runnin like a stream." Blue was walkin along on the other side of the road even with me. We were fanned out a bit. Fish was ahead. Grease, he was behind him, jumpin off and on to the hot pike to cool his feet.

"Yeaah!" I said. "Put your shoes on. Ain't you got no civilization?"

"Yeaah!" said Grease, wavin his greens back at me and Blue. "He say, 'Niggah,' and yall know what it mean when a white man call a nigger a niggahhh, don't you?"

"Naw," said Blue. "What it mean?"

Old Grease, he half fell over laughin, but then he straightened up and posed hisself like he was a preacher givin us a lesson.

"Nigggahhh. That mean whatever you can do, it take *two* niggers to keep up with you. Then you a Double Nigger," and he fell to laughin again.

We moved on, payin Grease little mind, but glad he wasn't gettin tired. He funny sometime, but he nevah know when to stop clownin.

We come to a hill. The road turned around the hill. It was really hot. Your spit almost boil. We stopped under a shade tree. "I'm so damn thirsty," said Fish, "I could drink my own spit."

We all agreed.

"If yall come on," said Blue, "we be in Rock Hill less'n hour."

Grease said, "I bet that peckerwood there'll let us buy soda water with money look this pretty."

"Naw," said Fish, lookin over the hill. "I think we oughta cut yonder ways, hit the Creek and be home fore dark."

"Boy, you crazy!" shouted Grease. "Tired as my feet is, and full of snakes as that creek is . . ."

"What you say, Tate?" Fish asked me.

"All I want is one bucket of water now," I said.

"What bout you, Blue?"

"It don't matter one way t'other," he said. "We done come this far, we might as well walk the rest."

"Well, yall go ahead," said Grease, pretendin he wasn't payin us no mind. "I'll be drinkin soda water and snatchin on that black gal Lucille as soon as I gets to Rock Hill, and then I catch a bus or a ride with some niggers comin through."

"Yeah," said Blue, "you little squiggy nigger, and you get home tomorrow mornin too. Ain't no more bus comin through Rock Hill."

"Yes it is."

"Naw," said Fish.

"Yeah," I added. "If you do get home messin round down there, you have a rope around your neck. Ain't no colored people livin out here."

"The hell there ain't."

"Come on," said Fish. Blue and me broke off with Fish cross the field.

We knew that Greasemouth was only playin, but he had worked over this way once with some white man sawin lumber. It was just before school started. I member, cause Grease ain't come to school hardly that whole year.

We climbed through the barbed wire fence settin way off the road. There was a creek over that way somewheres. If we went this way, it would cut off five miles, goin over the hills stead round them.

"Creek is yonder way," Blue said. We stood lookin over the area. We hadn't looked back to see if Grease was followin. We didn't much care.

He had stopped laughin at us, and when we turned around, we didn't see him.

"Let that greasemouth nigger go," said Blue. "One of them razorback peckerwoods'll catch him sniffin round down over yonder and they'll saw that nigger's lips off."

"If the grease don't stop 'em," said Fish.

We laughed. We always had fun with Grease when he was with us or not. We called him Grease cause whenevah he ate anythang, he let the grease pile up in the corners of his mouth and all over, like he nevah chewed his food but just slide it down with grease and lard.

We all come together now, walkin down the slope, watchin for bulls, dogs, wild hogs, crazy peckerwoods, devils and anything that moved. We might be trespassin. After a while we got deep into the trees. All we saw was a few birds and a rabbit.

"As ugly as Grease is," said Fish, "them peckerwoods'll wind up sending for us and then they pay us to take that nigger outa their sight."

We doubled over laughin. I tripped on a rock and sat there, catchin up on my wind. Blue was just ahead of me. He walked under a shade tree. He was so black that everybody called him Blue. Fish, he wasn't too much lighter. He was about my complexion and they called him Fish cause he could stroke good. Natural fish, he was. They called me Tate cause my head shaped like a potato. I nevah could find no damn potato on my head, but they just keep callin me that anyway, and so I do like everybody else and tease ole crazy Greasemouth. Then I can stand them better teasin me. I stopped laughin and got up. I picked up a stick and thought about throwin it at Blue, but kept it and went runnin on down to catch up.

I don't recollect what I thought it was at first. But all of a goddamn sudden! there comes this wild-buck thang chargin at us from behind a bunch of trees, yellin.

Blue broke in front of me, screamin somethin I ain't nevah heard, and before all three of us knew anythang, ole Greasemouth was doubled over laughin at us.

Fish was the first to holler at him, cause Fish probably saw him fore any of us, and he wasn't taken aback by him jumpin out like that.

"Get up, boy. You ain't scared nobody but yourself," Fish said to Grease.

But he kept wallerin there on the ground, laughin.

"Scared all of you!" he hollered. He began rollin down the hill, still laughin.

"You shoulda seen that . . ." And he pointed at Blue, who was standin just shakin his head as if to signify on Grease for makin a fool out of hisself. But Blue was really scared a little bit. Me too, a little.

". . . that nigger get ready to run. Did yall see that?"

Blue swung his arm on a limb and chunked some leaves at Grease.

"Ah, get up, boy. As ugly as you is, the trees leanin over away from you."

Grease got up and kept on teasin us. We moved on now through the patches of trees and washed out ditches and holes. Grease had put on his shoes now and was way up front, call hisself singin.

Then he hauled off and stopped singin.

"Hey, yonder's a well!" We all ran over and looked where he was pointin.

"Ah, now damn!" said Blue. We stood there lookin.

"Told yall niggers live up here," Grease said.

It was a house sittin beside a busted-in barn and a old wellshed. About half an acre of shale dirt full of weeds was behind that house. Nothin grow on dirt like that but scorpions and mean peckerwoods.

"Dammit, Grease," hollered Fish, "you know it ain't no niggers livin there . . ."

"That's right, and I can't drink that damn house," said Blue.

"Hell," I said, "don't think a peckerwood mind givin four niggers some water."

"Who's gonna ask?" said Grease.

"You, nigger," said Fish. "Didn't you find the place?"

"Yall said I was ugly," he said, "and I don't want to scare nobody, as thirsty as I is."

"Just whoever do the askin, leave the gate open and watch for nigger-eatin dogs," I said.

As we moved toward the house, Blue said, "Ain't nobody livin there. Look, ain't no smoke in the chimney."

Nobody said nothin to that, but we didn't trust it for gettin us water. We moved in slow, waitin for a dog to smell us and start to barkin.

When we had come off the hill into a ditch that run up longside a little dirt road that run in front of the house, sure nough a damn dog caught scent of us, and come runnin. But it wasn't nothin to get scared of. That dog was a sissy-puppy, a fool dog, we called them. It was still a pup, but it was jumpin and switch-tailin round, lickin at strangers so fast it look like it was chasing its tail.

"Toe fleas got that damn dog," said Blue.

"Hey, get away, dog!" Grease stomped his feet. "Toe-fleas got 'im itchin to beg." We headed for the well. "Up his ass and down his legs."

The place did look like nobody was home. We ran to the well. Fish hollered for somebody and then went round back. Me and Blue snatched that rope and let the well bucket down. Grease was throwin sticks for the fool dog to run after. "Sic 'em," he was shoutin, "sic 'em!" But the dog liked us too much. She just wiggled her tail, lickin Greasemouth's feet.

"Look here!" said Grease. "I found somethin worse'n a nigger."

"What's that?" Fish said, comin back.

"A nigger's dog."

"Shet up, boy," Blue grunted. We were pullin up the bucket. The well was old, and the rope was so rotten it shot dust tween our fingers. One of the boards under us squeaked and then that sissy-puppy come up waggin its tail under our feet too.

"Peckerwoods live here," said Blue.

"Ain't nobody home, though," said Fish.

"Les drink and git," I said.

"I want to drink but that dog got to git," said Grease, and he kept tryin to sic that pup off.

Then we heard a loud crashin sound come from inside the well. Blue stopped pullin on the bucket. He leaned over. "I got it," I said.

"What's goin on?" asked Grease. "Hurry and get me some water."

I began pullin again. I could feel the ground shakin under me. The well was fallin, crashin in and givin away. But the bucket was almost up.

"Wait!" shouted Grease. "This is it. Blue, you right!"

I kept on pullin. "Right about what?" Blue asked.

Grease waved us all quiet and he began runnin around the well, lookin at it real close and pointin. Then he ran over near the house and began to study it. He looked dead serious. He almost tripped over a fruit jar, but he kicked it as if he knew it was there and didn't have to look.

He came back to us. I had the bucket up to the top. Grease began pointin at the well. "Don't drink this here maggot water, boys. I know I'm tellin you the truth."

"What's in here, Grease?" Blue asked.

"Look round here. Can't yall smell this place stinkin like a beaneater?"

"Hurry, yall," said Fish. "That nigger's lyin." But nobody was gettin ready to take the first drink.

"Naw, naw, Fish," Grease said. "It's somethin that woulda clear skipped my mind, cept for this here fool-dog. He was a pup then . . . Yall member back last year when I was workin for Tulsom Lumber?"

We ain't say nothin. I pulled the big dirty bucket up and sat it there. Cool water was shootin out the holes. I was gettin ready to plunge my mouth in when Grease said, "Go head, Tatehead. Your head swell up bigger'n a punkin, and when it bust you member my words. Go head."

We ain't say nothin. Then Blue asked him what he knew. He started tellin a long tale about how he was passin by with a white man who knew the peckerwoods that lived there. That's what he meant by Fish bein right, right that white people lived there, not colored. Fish walked off and spit. He nevah believed nothin Grease said.

When we looked in that bucket, we saw pieces of wood in there, dirt and a couple of dead bugs floatin around. Blue smelled it and frowned. I smelled it and Fish came over. The fool-dog was jumpin all over Fish now, and he was wavin it off.

"And here's the thang I couldn't help . . ." Grease lowered his voice. "That white man woulda killed me sure as hell is below high water if he find out what I done to his well. But it won't my fault."

"What happen?" asked Blue.

"It was night, see. That damn fool-dog's mama was a mean bitchhound, then. I was waitin in the truck for this here white man to come out. But he wouldn't come. It started gettin dark. I had to go bad. So I ain't want to bother nobody cause I knowed what he was up to in that house. There was a little ole skinny peckerwood gal in there. I was headin out past the well, see, and no sooner I got jumpin distance from the well, here come that fool-dog's mama towards me, growlin like she wanted some nigger leg. Hell, I ain't have no place to run. I jumped up on the well cover and must've busted it then, cause it's gone now as yall can see, and jist bout time I got up, the bitchhound was snappin at me, mean as a peckerwood's dog wants to be.

"I had to go bad, and that damn dog wouldn't let me down. And that sucker inside wouldn't get off that gal and come out, to help this nigger.

"So, brothers," he said, as if we woulda all done the same thing, "I had to crap in that man's well."

"Get this lyin nigger!" Fish shouted, and we all grabbed Grease. He started shakin his head, but I come right up to him with my fist drawed back, while Fish locked that devil's arms. Grease, he started tryin to shake us off. Blue got a hold on his legs and we started swingin that nigger all round.

"Hold him, yall!" I said, and we all was laughin, but we wanted to teach him a lesson.

"Go head, Tate," Fish said to me, "git your drink."

I cleared the dirt off the top of the water and got me some. That water was good.

Then I got a new hold on Grease who was still hollerin. "Come on now, can't yall take a tale?"

"Yeah, yours," Blue said.

After Blue and Fish got their drink, we drug Grease long towards the road. He was yellin. That damn sissy-dog got scared of us and started to bark, tuckin her tail under and peepin from under that raggedy house.

Before I left, I got that jar on the ground and filled it full of the dirtiest water on top, rot-wood and all. Then I stuck the jar in my back pocket and caught up with them niggers pushin ole Grease long. He kept up a natural plea with us, but we ain't listen to him. We act like we ain't even know him anymore.

"What we gonna do with this nigger, Tate?" Fish asked me.

"Make him eat a half sack of salt."

"What you say, Blue?"

"I tell you guys. That was the stinkiest water I evah tasted. I think we oughta let this nigger go back and drink a whole bucket full. If he let one drop fall, we tie his ass to the well and let that peckerwood find 'im there."

"That's too good," said Fish. "Les tie his mouth up. This nigger talks too much. Then les pour creek water over his head."

"Naw," I said. "Les lift him up by his big foot to the first low tree we come to and let that sissy-dog lick 'im till he slimes up from dog spit, and his mouth and eyelids stick shut."

All the time Grease was whinin. But we pulled and pushed him along. We got over a mile down the road. We was all sweatin with that squiggy nigger by now, and gettin tired of the game. We figured we was too far now for him to turn around and go back. So we turned him loose and soon as we did, that nigger broke out laughin at us again. He said that while we was tusslin with him he had picked our pockets, and had all that good money. He waved some bills in his hand. Damn, if that didn't get to us.

"Grease, you the lyinest nigger I evah met up with," said Fish, after drawin out his money and lookin at it. We did too, and was about to grab him again when we heard the sound of a truck comin up that dirt road.

We all got serious and pulled together. Round the corner came this beat-up truck with a skinny ole red-necked hillbilly bent over the wheel and a wide-eyed freckled faced gal sittin side him. The truck was goin so goddamn slow that I coulda read a whole chapter of God's Holy Bible by the time it passed us. But it didn't pass.

That peckerwood stopped it and called us over.

Fish stood where he was, but me, Blue and Grease come off the side of the ditch.

"You boys lookin for somethin?"

"Naw, sir," said Grease real fast. "We goin home."

"What you lookin fer around here?"

"We done two days work other side of Rock Hill," said Grease. "We work for a white man named Mr. Nesbit. He paid us and said, 'That's it, boys,' so we goin back to Bainesville . . ."

"You niggers lyin?"

"Naw, sir," said Blue. He looked back at Fish who was gettin mad, if he wasn't already. We coulda all beat that old man's ass, but if we did we'd have to leave the state. Even a poor white man like him could mess over niggers and niggers couldn't do a damn thing about it. Right then I wished Grease's tale hada been true.

"They puttin a cutoff out on the Memphis Highway," I said. "They know bout it in Rock Hill."

"How come you niggers ain't go round through Rock Hill like you ought to? I got a good mind to make yall go back the way you come. We don't allow no niggers over here."

We all just stood there. That young gal was steady twitchin and twitchin. We ain't look at her, but I could see her out of the corner of my eye, twitchin round in that seat like she sittin on a pile of rocks.

All of a sudden that old man hauled off and slapped her.

"Now keep still," he said.

Then he got up a shotgun.

"You niggers come long this road a far piece?"

Fish stood straight now and came towards us. I thought he was gonna say somethin, but Grease beat him to it.

"Naw, sir, we just come off that hill." He pointed. "We tryin to get to the creek, but I tole 'em we passed the creek and best keep on, since . . ."

"How come yall comin this away?"

"We thought we knowed the way cross these hills, but I reckon we got lost."

"How long yall come along this road?"

"We just got on it bout the time we hear a truck comin round the bend, and then it was you," said Grease.

"If I find you niggers lyin, and been in my house, I'm gonna come back here and make buzzard meat outa your asses."

"Naw, sir, we ain't seen no house since we left the highway."

He raced the engine coupla times, then he turned and looked at me. "Nigger, what's that you got in your back pocket? Let me see."

I jerked my hand back there. I done forgot. Fish come over, but Grease beat him to the words. "That's mine," said Grease. I took out the jar of water.

"That's niggerwater for my feet," said Grease. "I got bad feet, and suffer with short wind."

"What you talkin about?" The old man looked like he mighta laughed then, but he didn't. He cocked his head.

"I fell out. Tate, he carryin the water for me." Grease rolled his eyes.

"I ain't never heard of a nigger fallin out," the old man said.

"Naw, sir, it ain't like you think. I was totin a rock weigh three times my size. I come near bustin myself."

The old man looked at each of us. We was all dressed dirty and sweat was pourin off us. He looked at the jar of water, then at Greasemouth, who was showin off how sick he was.

". . . wide open." Grease kinda motioned with his whole self to where he mighta busted hisself, but because that gal was sittin there, Greasemouth didn't point or say no more.

"All right, boy," said the old man. "Thas nough now." He turned to each of us.

"This nigger tellin the truth?"

We all said a loud "Yes Sir." Even Fish said it.

"All right. Yall niggers done missed the creek. You way off, and you better get hell outa my hills. Don't stop till yall hit thet highway. Now git!"

We moved off quickly. That old man still held that shotgun up in the air. He had braked the truck on the hill, but we never heard it no more, cause when we got round that bend we broke into the woods off the road, runnin fan-wise, cussin, movin down that road like we were four boats in a downriver. We didn't stop till Fish slowed and leaned up ginst a tree, puffin. . . .

"What the hell we runnin for?"

"Gimme my water," puffed Grease.

"What you talkin bout, your water?"

"All right, I'm goin back and tell that peckerwood yall busted into his house, stole his water and pissed and shit in his well."

"Yeah? And that white man shoot the first nigger he see, you first," I said.

Greasemouth must've been really thirsty then, because he was chokin. He was gaspin for breath.

I took out that jar of water and almost put my own mouth to it, but Grease was on it like a rat on cheese.

We all watched. We wanted some of that water so damn bad.

Then old Grease do somethin we ain't expect him to do. He saved back nough for each of us to have one swallow, and then he twisted up his mouth. "I ought not to give you lyin niggers nothin."

"Go head, boy, and drink your water," said Fish, but he didn't mean it. Me and Blue took one swallow each.

Grease took that jar and gave it to Fish. "I knowed a Christian was livin in that devil heart of yours," he said, and he finished it.

We went on, pullin together, and not laughin anymore.

"You just watch," said Blue. "You just watch that nigger Greasy when he gits back. He gonna tell everybody how he did this here and did dat dere. You watch. He be done run a white man down, took his gun off him, whopped the white man's ass and then climbed upon the white man's well and shit in it just for devilment."

We were puffin a bit still, and everytime Blue took a step he puffed and dragged his words.

That fool old man wasn't comin after us. We knew that. We slowed down and Blue kept on teasin Greasy.

Fish was movin longside me now.

We laughed and kidded about what Blue was sayin.

Grease wasn't payin no mind to none of us. He kept movin long, puffin as much as any of us. Then he hauled off and stopped, scratched his head like a mosquito had struck him one.

"Listen up, you niggers," Grease said. "I know the truth now. Goddammit, I know it."

We ain't paid too much attention to him, but we did slow down.

"I got it all right here." He touched his heart. "You see how that peckerwood jump at me when I tell him the truth. That was God Almighty truth what I told him. But that sucker, he ain't hear me, uh?" He grunted like Rev. Weams do when he windin himself up.

"The truth is the thing. May a dead dog draw red maggots as sure as you niggers hear me. I swear fore livin God, may cowshit stand up and walk, I swear. You niggers listenin? I swear, I ain't foolin round no more. No more lies for me. The truth for me!"

"Aw, you a damn lie," said Fish. "You a lie and don't know why. Shet up and come on."

"Yeaah," said Blue. "Double Niggaahh!!"

from yellow back radio broke-down
1969

t he saddle stiffs from the Purple Bar-B were congregated in Big
Lizzy's Rabid Black Cougar drinking Rot-Gut and Two-Bits-Per-
Throw. Some of the cowpokes were seated at tables playing poker or
being entertained by the hurdy gurdy girls.

Skinny McCullough the foreman was at the bar conversing with Sam
the bartender.

Man, that boss is really getting timid in the noggin, Skinny said.

Can you blame him? Monstrous births, weird parties, his nag stolen,
herd wiped out by mysterious animals, toes, fingers and hindlegs rotting
away, I mean how can you blame the guy? But I don't care if he turns into
black straw so long as he coughs up the deeds he promised us.

He brings us up there every Sun, and he reads those awful words from
the good book. Sometimes I feel so skerry I go back to my bunk and have
dreams in which blank-eyed and stupid demons do handsprings on my
chest. I think as soon as this season comes to an end I'm going to take my
roll and go over to join the Lincoln County forces against that anarchist
bandit Billy the Kid. It's nice and peaceful on the front.

Did you see his latest symptoms? the bartender said. Sits up there on the
hill. Got all the servants building a monument he designed for himself.
Said he might kick off any day now. Case he feels it coming and wants to
get it over with quick. And to add to that each night the coyote howls
outside his house and he raises himself and sez: Who's that! Who's that
howling about my door?

Good evening Marshal.

Good evening Sam, Skinny. Damn, what time of day is it? Looks half
and half, like a land assessor's coffee break. Let's have something special
today. Hows about some of that imported Lacrymose Christi?

Marshal, Skinny said, I was just telling the bartender that Drag is getting spookier than a son of a bitch. He's a mere whisper of his former self. Each morning we find those effigies on the doorstep. Before you know it he'll be making an appearance before the Riders of Judgement. He thinks the Loop Garoo Kid has put some kind of so-called magical spell on him or something. While he's out there building his tomb that new mail order bride of his plays with them funny cards.

Poker?

No, some kind of weird cards, one of em had death on it, with a scythe cutting across the grim reaper's foot.

You don't believe in that malarkey do you boys? the Marshal asked.

No I'm a Fanny Wrightite, Skinny said.

And I'm a Baptist, the bartender offered, that pagan nonsense cuts nothing with me.

Just then Royal Flush Gooseman, Furtrapper and sometimes bald-headed Cowthief, and Mighty Dike entered the room:

O.K. all you brush poppers, ranahans, limb skinners, and saddle warmers, this is Royal Flush Gooseman all the way from St. Louis!!!!!!!!

All the cowpokes rose from their tables with gosh, golly stares on their faces. The Marshal and bartender and the foreman were a little more nonchalant, each having been as far as the Mississippi River a few times apiece.

What you need, cowpokes? Rectifyers to heal them bruises, blankets, boots, firearms, bottle of rum all the way from Boston? Come outside and inspect my mule train. You got the money I got the time.

Little hand of poker while you're at it. I even got posters of that greenhorn President of the East case you want to mount them on your bunk walls and spit tobaccy at em.

All the buckaroos laughed and followed Royal Flush outside to examine his mule train of goods. Some of them were already reaching into their jeans for silver with which to make purchases.

The Marshal, foreman and bartender continued their conversation.

Man, pass me another whiskey. This place is really getting eerie, never seed no town like this; all the planks holding up the buildings seem to lean, like tilt over, and there's a disproportionate amount of shadows in reference to the sun we get—it's like a pen and ink drawing by Edward Munch or one of them Expressionist fellows.

Huh?

See, got me talking out of my noodle. What's your theory Marshal?
Skinny McCullough asked.

Well you know me, boys, why if I hadda been at that party the other
night instead of at the Law Enforcement Convention up the creek there, it
would have been me and the Kid. Hell, me and the Earp brothers use to
ambush people and shoot em in the back like they wuz dogs. He'd better
not show his snake in Yellow Back Radio. Big Lizzy the owner of the
Rabid Black Cougar entered. A giant square-jawed woman with a
tomboy haircut, her flabby breasts hung around her roped in waist.
She wore an apron over a drab calico dress, with leggings and boots,
and her hands were covered with hair. Below the nose bridge could be
seen the faint print of a mustache.

She spoke in a low husky voice that sounded like sand paper rubbing
together. She carried a moose over her shoulder and under her arm a
Winchester Rifle.

Evening Big Lizzy, what's that you got with you? Well I'll be, the
Marshal said scratching his head, it's a moose!

Yeah, Lizzy answered, bagged him up in the hills while I wuz hunting.
She swung the moose over her shoulder and onto the floor. Chinaboy go
get me some beer mugs out of the latrine so's I can give the boys a drink
and clean up that ear that wuz shot off a couple of weeks back, it's
beginning to smell. I need a drink of Red-Eye after what I saw up there in
the hills.

Whaddya see Big Lizzy? Skinny asked.

There was this woman cooking some smelly stuff in a cauldron. I came
upon her about the third evening out. She was stirring with some long
pole, when all of a sudden this black cowboy come riding out of the
shadow and hitched up her skirts and whipped his pecker on her right on
the spot. I had to put my hand on the dying moose's mouth so he
wouldn't make no noise, cause then things really started to freak out.

What happened then Big Lizzy? one of the steerbusters gambling at the
table asked as the others put down their cards and gathered around the bar
to listen closely to Big Lizzy's strange narrative.

Well they were on the ground making out and she started to writhe and
hiss like a serpent and say skerry things like: mash potatoes all over my
motherfucking soul. Then after it was over he gathered her up and they
rode off to the cemetery where tombs shone against the moon like white
plates.

How did the woman look? Skinny asked.

She was wearing shades even in the night, a black velvet dress and a jade locket. Had long black hair and olive skin. A real beauty. Bilt like a brick shit house.

Hey that sounds like the boss's old lady, one of the hands said. Let me go up to the ranch and tell him he'd better see about his old lady.

The foreman grabbed the man by the collar:

Hold on you idiot, wait until the season's over. The way he's wasting away like he might be in a vile mood. You see how he flogged us the other night, next thing you know he'll be asking us to milk the cows or something harebrained like that. Be cool till the eagle flies, that way we won't get in Dutch.

The cowpokes who had gone outside with Royal Flush returned loaded down with goods. One went to the group at the bar.

Geez you know he cleaned us out. Had a little stand set up in the street and had Royal Flushes in poker four times straight, never seed nothing like it!

The Marshal, foreman, Big Lizzy and the bartender chuckled.

What happened to the last wife? Big Lizzy inquired.

She's up in the hills Big Lizzy, tomato, in the plural these days.

O I see.

Big Lizzy ever since we burnt down the circus strange things have been happening. There was this nigger bull-dogger guy who performed. He could bring down steer with his teeth and he used a whip like most men fire a pistol. Anyway he rode off and the townspeople haven't come down from those devil's pills them wicked kids gave them, them horrible urchins we knocked off.

Town 50 miles from here the kids were found in caves smoking injun tobaccy and the herd Drag sent up the Chizzum was stampeded by Giant Sloths which is crazy as hell Big Lizzy, cause Giant Sloths haven't lazed around the Plains of North America for thousands of years. Sometimes I think the whole continent is accursed.

The Preacher Rev. Boyd is going around like the town kook. Nobody goes to his Church any more and he's weaving some kind of allegorical prophecies.

The Preacher Rev. Boyd entered the bar and through his three week old beard began to recite from a yellow pad attached to a cupboard. He reeled about the room.

stomp me o lord!!
i am the theoretical mother of all insects!!
mash my 21 or so body segments!!
tear the sutures which join my many abdomens!!
make me a mass of stains of thy choice
an ugly blotch under thy big funny clodhoppers!!

The door swung open on the last line.

The men seated dropped their poker cards and slowly moved away from their chairs. The moose got to its feet and clomped through the side of the building, sending splinters of wood flying.

Hear you're looking for me, Marshal.

Big Lizzy, Skinny McCullough and the bartender eased away from the bar. The other cowpokes froze.

Now Kid, the Marshal said, what's a Western without tall tales and gaudy romance? Have a drink.

Pretending to reach for his change the Marshal drew his shooting iron. Too bad. Too slow. Not fast enough.

The lash whistled across the room and popped off the Marshal's holster, a second lash flicked the gun from his hand, a third lash cracked off the Marshal's hat, a fourth lash unbuckled his belt with its persuader, which caused the Marshal's pants to fall, and came within a thousandth of an inch of his shirt, unpinning the star, which dropped to the floor.

The moose peeked in through the big hole he had made in the wall, but seeing no improvement in the situation, galloped towards a lake in the distance.

Loop Garoo the lord of the lash walked over to the end of the bar to where the Preacher was crouched on the floor.

He was scribbling furiously on his yellow pad.

When he saw the Loop standing over him, Rev. Boyd brought forth his crucifix. Nothing happened. He took out a pocket mirror and aimed it into Loop's face. Loop used the opportunity to straighten his fedora which had slid to the side of his head when he gave the Marshal such a good behind whipping.

Finished? Loop asked.

The Preacher backed away a few paces with a dipshit grin on his face.

Loop lashed the crucifix from his breast without tearing into the man's flesh. The crucifix dropped to the floor and the little figure attached to it scrambled into the nearest moose hole.

Didn't you say something about spade poets having gone up in tinder when I walked into the party the other night? Come on Preacher don't start your thing, I don't want to hear anything about Matthew Chapter and Verse in ditty bop talk. I get sick of "Soul" sometimes. All right then, Loop said.

(CRACK!) Whenever you say something like that. (CRACK!! CRACK!!) In the future. Check out some sources. (CRACK!! CRACK!!) Motherfucker!! (CRACK! CRACK!) Ask you mama. (CRACK!) Yo wife. (CRACK! CRACK!) Guillaume Apollinaire. (CRACK! POP! CRINKLE! SNAP!) Anybody you want to ask. (CRACK!) But get your information right next time. (NICK!) O.K.?

The Preacher lay on the floor a quivering mumbling heap.

Loop folded his whip and looked about the room. He winked at Big Lizzy. Anybody else want some of this ringing stinging?

The cowpokes shook their heads.

Loop put a rolled cigarette into the Marshal's mouth and walked outside the bar. The townspeople who had been peeking through the door ran in different directions.

Loop mounted his green horse which kind of did a slow high-stepping trot out of town.

The Marshal just stood there for a moment taking a long swig of whiskey. Big Lizzy's eyes were two lights she was so much in glee. Her jaws swelled with laughter. The cowpokes all stood, pushing their feet around the floor and eyes downcast in embarrassment.

The Marshal picked at the edges of his mustache. His eyes became moist. He knelt and picked up his badge. He pulled up his pants, covering his red and black colored BVD's.

Well folks, I'm not going to make excuses. The Kid made a fool of me. Got nothing on but my shorts. I'm a scoundrel, a rogue and a bully. Later for Yellow Back Radio. I've met my match here so now it's time to move on down the line.

He shook hands with everybody in the bar then walked outside and stood in front of the saloon.

The street was a dumpheap of Brueghel faces, of Hogarth faces, of Coney Island hot-dog kissers, ugly pusses and sinking mugs, whole precincts of flat peepers and silly lookers. The sun's wise broad lips smiled making the goats horny with cosmic seed as monstrous shapes who could never unbend their hands all looked as the Marshal ripped off his badge, boarded his horse and rode out of town. Each side was lined with spectators. He rode past his beloved Hat and Boot store, the Feed store and on into the Black Forest.

TONI CADE BAMBARA

the lesson
1972

back in the days when everyone was old and stupid or young and foolish and me and Sugar were the only ones just right, this lady moved on our block with nappy hair and proper speech and no makeup. And quite naturally we laughed at her, laughed the way we did at the junk man who went about his business like he was some big-time president and his sorry-ass horse his secretary. And we kinda hated her too, hated the way we did the winos who cluttered up our parks and pissed on our handball walls and stank up our hallways and stairs so you couldn't halfway play hide-and-seek without a goddamn gas mask. Miss Moore was her name. The only woman on the block with no first name. And she was black as hell, cept for her feet, which were fish-white and spooky. And she was always planning these boring-ass things for us to do, us being my cousin, mostly, who lived on the block cause we all moved North the same time and to the same apartment then spread out gradual to breathe. And our parents would yank our heads into some kinda shape and crisp up our clothes so we'd be presentable for travel with Miss Moore, who always looked like she was going to church, though she never did. Which is just one of things the grownups talked about when they talked behind her back like a dog. But when she came calling with some sachet she'd sewed up or some gingerbread she'd made or some book, why then they'd all be too embarrassed to turn her down and we'd get handed over all spruced up. She'd been to college and said it was only right that she should take responsibility for the young ones' education, and she not even related by marriage or blood. So they'd go for it. Specially Aunt Gretchen. She was the main gofer in the family. You got some ole dumb shit foolishness you want somebody to go for, you send for Aunt Gretchen. She been screwed into the go-along for so long, it's a blood-deep natural thing with her. Which is how she got saddled with me and Sugar and Junior in the first place while our mothers were in a la-de-da apartment up the block having a good ole time.

So this one day Miss Moore rounds us all up at the mailbox and it's puredee hot and she's knockin herself out about arithmetic. And school suppose to let up in summer I heard, but she don't never let up. And the starch in my pinafore scratching the shit outta me and I'm really hating this nappy-head bitch and her goddamn college degree. I'd much rather go to the pool or to the show where it's cool. So me and Sugar leaning on the mailbox being surly, which is a Miss Moore word. And Flyboy checking out what everybody brought for lunch. And Fat Butt already wasting his peanut-butter-and-jelly sandwich like the pig he is. And Junebug punchin on Q.T.'s arm for potato chips. And Rosie Giraffe shifting from one hip to the other waiting for somebody to step on her foot or ask her if she from Georgia so she can kick ass, preferably Mercedes'. And Miss Moore asking us do we know what money is, like we a bunch of retards. I mean real money, she say, like it's only poker chips or monopoly papers we lay on the grocer. So right away I'm tired of this and say so. And would much rather snatch Sugar and go to the Sunset and terrorize the West Indian kids and take their hair ribbons and their money too. And Miss Moore files that remark away for next week's lesson on brotherhood, I can tell. And finally I say we oughta get to the subway cause it's cooler and besides we might meet some cute boys. Sugar done swiped her mama's lipstick, so we ready.

So we heading down the street and she's boring us silly about what things cost and what our parents make and how much goes for rent and how money ain't divided up right in this country. And then she gets to the part about we all poor and live in the slums, which I don't feature. And I'm ready to speak on that, but she steps out in the street and hails two cabs just like that. Then she hustles half the crew in with her and hands me a five-dollar bill and tells me to calculate 10 percent tip for the driver. And we're off. Me and Sugar and Junebug and Flyboy hangin out the window and hollering to everybody, putting lipstick on each other cause Flyboy a faggot anyway, and making farts with our sweaty armpits. But I'm mostly trying to figure how to spend this money. But they all fascinated with the meter ticking and Junebug starts laying bets as to how much it'll read when Flyboy can't hold his breath no more. Then Sugar lays bets as to how much it'll be when we get there. So I'm stuck. Don't nobody want to go for my plan, which is to jump out at the next light and run off to the first bar-b-que we can find. Then the driver tells us to get the hell out cause we there already. And the meter reads eighty-five cents. And I'm stalling to figure out the tip and Sugar say give him a dime. And I decide he don't need it bad as I do, so later for him. But then he tries to take off with Junebug foot still in the door so we talk about his mama something ferocious. Then we check out that we on Fifth Avenue and everybody dressed up in stockings. One lady in a fur coat, hot as it is. White folks crazy.

"This is the place," Miss Moore say, presenting it to us in the voice she uses at the museum. "Let's look in the windows before we go in."

"Can we steal?" Sugar asks very serious like she's getting the ground rules squared away before she plays. "I beg your pardon," say Miss Moore, and we fall out. So she leads us around the windows of the toy store and me and Sugar screamin, "This is mine, that's mine, I gotta have that, that was made for me, I was born for that," till Big Butt drowns us out.

"Hey, I'm goin to buy that there."

"That there? You don't even know what it is, stupid."

"I do so," he say punchin on Rosie Giraffe. "It's a microscope."

"Whatcha gonna do with a microscope, fool?"

"Look at things."

"Like what, Ronald?" ask Miss Moore. And Big Butt ain't got the first notion. So here go Miss Moore gabbing about the thousands of bacteria in a drop of water and the somethinorother in a speck of blood and the million and one living things in the air around us is invisible to the naked eye. And what she say that for? Junebug go to town on that "naked" and we rolling. Then Miss Moore ask what it cost. So we all jam into the window smudgin it up and the price tag say $300. So then she ask how long'd take for Big Butt and Junebug to save up their allowances. "Too long," I say. "Yeh," adds Sugar, "outgrown it by that time." And Miss Moore say no, you never outgrow learning instruments. "Why, even medical students and interns and," blah, blah, blah. And we ready to choke Big Butt for bringing it up in the first damn place.

"This here costs four hundred eighty dollars," say Rosie Giraffe. So we pile up all over her to see what she pointin out. My eyes tell me it's a chunk of glass cracked with something heavy, and different-color inks dripped into the splits, then the whole thing put into a oven or something. But for $480 it don't make sense.

"That's a paperweight made of semi-precious stones fused together under tremendous pressure," she explains slowly, with her hands doing the mining and all the factory work.

"So what's a paperweight?" asks Rosie Giraffe.

"To weigh paper with, dumbbell," say Flyboy, the wise man from the East.

"Not exactly," say Miss Moore, which is what she say when you warm or way off too. "It's to weigh paper down so it won't scatter and make your desk untidy." So right away me and Sugar curtsy to each other and then to Mercedes who is more the tidy type.

"We don't keep paper on top of the desk in my class," say Junebug, figuring Miss Moore crazy or lyin one.

"At home, then," she say. "Don't you have a calendar and a pencil case and a blotter and a letter-opener on your desk at home where you do your homework?" And she know damn well what our homes look like cause she nosys around in them every chance she gets.

"I don't even have a desk," say Junebug. "Do we?"

"No. And I don't get no homework neither," say Big Butt.

"And I don't even have a home," say Flyboy like he do at school to keep the white folks off his back and sorry for him. Send this poor kid to camp posters, is his specialty.

"I do," says Mercedes. "I have a box of stationery on my desk and a picture of my cat. My godmother bought the stationery and the desk. There's a big rose on each sheet and the envelopes smell like roses."

"Who wants to know about your smelly-ass stationery," say Rosie Giraffe fore I can get my two cents in.

"It's important to have a work area all your own so that . . ."

"Will you look at this sailboat, please," say Flyboy, cuttin her off and pointin to the thing like it was his. So once again we tumble all over each other to gaze at this magnificent thing in the toy store which is just big enough to maybe sail two kittens across the pond if you strap them to the posts tight. We all start reciting the price tag like we in assembly. "Handcrafted sailboat of fiberglass at one thousand one hundred ninety-five dollars."

"Unbelievable," I hear myself say and am really stunned. I read it again for myself just in case the group recitation put me in a trance. Same thing. For some reason this pisses me off. We look at Miss Moore and she lookin at us, waiting for I dunno what.

"Who'd pay all that when you can buy a sailboat set for a quarter at

Pop's, a tube of glue for a dime, and a ball of string for eight cents? "It must have a motor and a whole lot else besides," I say. "My sailboat cost me about fifty cents."

"But will it take water?" say Mercedes with her smart ass.

"Took mine to Alley Pond Park once," say Flyboy. "String broke, Lost it. Pity."

"Sailed mine in Central Park and it keeled over and sank. Had to ask my father for another dollar."

"And you got the strap," laugh Big Butt. "The jerk didn't even have a string on it. My old man wailed on his behind."

Little Q.T. was staring hard at the sailboat and you could see he wanted it bad. But he too little and somebody'd just take it from him. So what the hell. "This boat for kids, Miss Moore?"

"Parents silly to buy something like that just to get all broke up," say Rosie Giraffe.

"That much money it should last forever," I figure.

"My father'd buy it for me if I wanted it."

"Your father, my ass," say Rosie Giraffe getting a chance to finally push Mercedes.

"Must be rich people shop here," say Q.T.

"You are a very bright boy," say Flyboy. "What was your first clue?" And he rap him on the head with the back of his knuckles, since Q.T. the only one he could get away with. Though Q.T. liable to come up behind you years later and get his licks in when you half expect it.

"What I want to know is," I says to Miss Moore though I never talk to her, I wouldn't give the bitch that satisfaction, "is how much a real boat costs? I figure a thousand'd get you a yacht any day."

"Why don't you check that out," she says, "and report back to the group?" Which really pains my ass. If you gonna mess up a perfectly good swim day least you could do is have some answers. "Let's go in," she say like she got something up her sleeve. Only she don't lead the way. So me and Sugar turn the corner to where the entrance is, but when we get there I kinda hang back. Not that I'm scared, what's there to be afraid of, just a toy store. But I feel funny, shame. But what I got to be shamed about? Got as much right to go in as anybody. But somehow I can't seem to get hold of the door, so I step away for Sugar to lead. But she hangs back too. And I look at her and she looks at me and this is ridiculous. I mean, damn, I have never ever been shy about doing nothing or going nowhere. But then

Mercedes steps up and then Rosie Giraffe and Big Butt crowd in behind and shove, and next thing we all stuffed into the doorway with only Mercedes squeezing past us, smoothing out her jumper and walking right down the aisle. Then the rest of us tumble in like a glued-together jigsaw done all wrong. And people lookin at us. And it's like the time me and Sugar crashed into the Catholic church on a dare. But once we got in there and everything so hushed and holy and the candles and the bowin and the handkerchiefs on all the drooping heads, I just couldn't go through with the plan. Which was for me to run up to the altar and do a tap dance while Sugar played the nose flute and messed around in the holy water. And Sugar kept givin me the elbow. Then later teased me so bad I tied her up in the shower and turned it on and locked her in. And she'd be there till this day if Aunt Gretchen hadn't finally figured I was lyin about the boarder takin a shower.

Same thing in the store. We all walkin on tiptoe and hardly touchin the games and puzzles and things. And I watched Miss Moore who is steady watchin us like she waitin for a sign. Like Mama Drewery watches the sky and sniffs the air and takes note of just how much slant is in the bird formation. Then me and Sugar bump smack into each other, so busy gazing at the toys, 'specially the sailboat. But we don't laugh and go into our fat-lady bump-stomach routine. We just stare at that price tag. Then Sugar run a finger over the whole boat. And I'm jealous and want to hit her. Maybe not her, but I sure want to punch somebody in the mouth.

"Watcha bring us here for, Miss Moore?"

"You sound angry, Sylvia. Are you mad about something?" Givin me one of them grins like she tellin a grown-up joke that never turns out to be funny. And she's lookin very closely at me like maybe she plannin to do my portrait from memory. I'm mad, but I won't give her that satisfaction. So I slouch around the store bein very bored and say, "Let's go."

Me and Sugar at the back of the train watchin the tracks whizzin by large then small then gettin gobbled up in the dark. I'm thinkin about this tricky toy I saw in the store. A clown that somersaults on a bar then does chin-ups just cause you yank lightly at his leg. Cost $35. I could see me askin my mother for a $35 birthday clown. "You wanna who that costs what?" she'd say, cocking her head to the side to get a better view of the hole in my head. Thirty-five dollars could buy new bunk beds for Junior and Gretchen's boy. Thirty-five dollars and the whole household could go visit Granddaddy Nelson in the country. Thirty-five dollars would pay for the rent and the piano bill too. Who are these people that spend that much for performing clowns and $1,000 for toy sailboats? What kinda work they do and how they live and how come we ain't in on it? Where we are is who we are, Miss Moore always pointin out. But it don't necessarily have to be that way, she always adds then waits for somebody to say that poor people have to wake up and demand their share of the pie and don't none of us know what kind of pie she talkin about in the first damn place. But she ain't so smart cause I still got her four dollars from the taxi and she sure ain't gettin it. Messin up my day with this shit. Sugar nudges me in my pocket and winks.

Miss Moore lines us up in front of the mailbox where we started from, seem like years ago, and I got a headache for thinkin so hard. And we lean all over each other so we can hold up under the draggy-ass lecture she always finishes us off with at the end before we thank her for borin us to tears. But she just looks at us like she readin tea leaves. Finally she say, "Well, what did you think of F.A.O. Schwarz?"

Rosie Giraffe mumbles, "White folks crazy."

"I'd like to go there again when I get my birthday money," says Mercedes, and we shove her out the pack so she has to lean on the mailbox by herself.

"I'd like a shower. Tiring day," say Flyboy.

Then Sugar surprises me by sayin, "You know, Miss Moore, I don't think all of us here put together eat in a year what that sailboat costs." And Miss Moore lights up like somebody goosed her. "And?" she say, urging Sugar on. Only I'm standin on her foot so she don't continue.

"Imagine for a minute what kind of society it is in which some people can spend on a toy what it would cost to feed a family of six or seven. What do you think?"

"I think," say Sugar pushing me off her feet like she never done before, cause I whip her ass in a minute, "that this is not much of a democracy if you ask me. Equal chance to pursue happiness means an equal crack at the dough, don't it?" Miss Moore is besides herself and I am disgusted with Sugar's treachery. So I stand on her foot one more time to see if she'll shove me. She shuts up, and Miss Moore looks at me, sorrowfully I'm thinkin. And somethin weird is goin on, I can feel it in my chest.

"Anybody else learn anything today?" lookin dead at me. I walk away and Sugar has to run to catch up and don't even seem to notice when I shrug her arm off my shoulder.

"Well, we got four dollars anyway," she says.

"Uh hunh."

"We could go to Hascombs and get half a chocolate layer and then go to the Sunset and still have plenty money for potato chips and ice-cream sodas."

"Uh hunh."

"Race you to Hascombs," she say.

We start down the block and she gets ahead which is O.K. by me cause I'm goin to the West End and then over to the Drive to think this day through. She can run if she want to and even run faster. But ain't nobody gonna beat me at nuthin.

ETHERIDGE KNIGHT

dark prophecy: i sing of shine
1973

And, yeah, brothers
while white / america sings about the unsink-
able molly brown
(who was hustling the titanic
when it went down)
I sing to thee of Shine
the stoker who was hip enough to flee the fucking ship
and let the white folks drown
with screams on their lips
(jumped his black ass into the dark sea, Shine did,
broke free from the straining steel).
Yeah, I sing to thee of Shine
and how the millionaire banker stood on the deck
and pulled from his pockets a million dollar check
saying Shine Shine save poor me
and I'll give you all the money a black boy needs—
how Shine looked at the money and then at the sea
and said jump in mothafucka and swim like me—
And Shine swam on—Shine swam on—
and how the banker's daughter ran naked on the deck
with her pink tits trembling and her pants roun her neck
screaming Shine Shine save poor me
and I'll give you all the pussy a black boy needs—
how Shine said now pussy is good and that's no jive
but you got to swim not fuck to stay alive—
And Shine swam on Shine swam on—

How Shine swam past a preacher afloating on a board
crying save *me* nigger Shine in the name of the Lord—
and how the preacher grabbed Shine's arm and broke his stroke—
how Shine pulled his shank and cut the preacher's throat—
And Shine swam on—Shine swam on—
And when the news hit shore that the titanic had sunk
Shine was up in Harlem damn near drunk

memo #9
1973

doze o blk / capitalists
ain't shit,
the blk / poet sung,
as he hustled his books
for 10.95.

rehabilitation & treatment in
the prisons of america
1973

the convict strolled into the prison administration building to get assistance and counseling for his personal problems. Inside the main door were several other doors proclaiming; Doctor, Lawyer, Teacher, Counselor, Therapist, etc. He chose the proper door, and was confronted with two more doors: Custody and Treatment. He chose Treatment, went in, and was confronted with two more doors: First Offender and Previous Offender. Again he chose the proper door and was confronted with two *more* doors: Adult and Juvenile. He was an adult, so he walked through that door and ran smack into two *more* doors: Democrat and Republican. He was democrat, so he rushed through that door and ran smack into two *more* doors: Black and White. He was Black, so he rushed—*ran*—through that door—and fell nine stories to the street.

KYLE BAKER

from the cowboy wally show
1988

Chapter Two : Sands of Blood

The Cowboy Wally Show. © 1988, 1996 Kyle Baker. All Rights Reserved.
Used with permission of DC Comics.

Chapter Two: SANDS OF BLOOD
(Drama, 1986)

Cowboy Wally's first starring role in
a motion picture and his second
directorial effort (See "Ed Smith, Lizard
of Doom"), **Sands of Blood** was a milestone
in his career. For him, it meant a return
to acting, a return to the limelight,
and a return to sleeping with the kind
of fabulous babes who normally
wouldn't give him the time of day.

   Sands of Blood was also the film that
introduced the writing and acting
talents of Lenny Walsh. As Stanley, the
young recruit who is forced to kill
twelve men, Lenny Walsh exudes a
quiet intensity and the refreshing
vulnerability of youth. And a
vivacious alienation, too.

   A hauntingly tragic, but vastly
entertaining film.

Hi.

Hi, yourself.   Where you going?

I'm going to France.

Right. Dumb question. Of course you're going to France. I mean, this is a boat to France. Where else could you be going? I mean, you're not going to jump off the boat in the middle of the Pacific Ocean! It's Atlantic. I knew that. Pacific is...

I thought you meant where am I going in France. I was just teasing you when I said, "France." It was a joke.

I'm sorry. It's a pretty good joke now that I think about it.

Thanks. You should calm down. You seem kind of tense.

No, not really. Well, maybe. It's funny. I have a lot of trouble speaking to beautiful women. I don't know why I just said that. This isn't a pickup, you know.

Oh. Okay.

"Oh. Okay"?

What?   You said "Oh. Okay". What do you mean by that? Would you like this to be a pickup? I mean if you want, it could be. I just said it's not a pickup because I thought you didn't want me to pick you up. But I could make it a pickup. If you want.

No.

Oh, then I was just kidding.

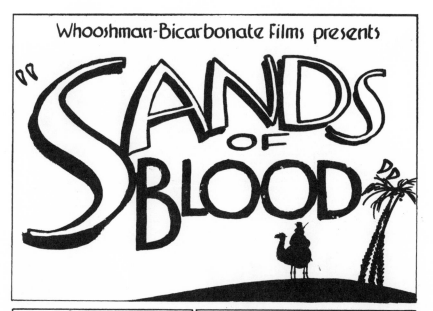

Whooshman-Bicarbonate Films presents

"SANDS OF BLOOD"

Hello I'd like to join the French Foreign Legion.

Fine. We'll need your name, Social Security number, and the name of the girl you're trying to forget. That is, if you're up to it. If you're not going to start crying or anything. I know it's painful.

I'm fine. Don't worry about me.

Really? To be honest, you look like a crier to me. Don't get me wrong, now. I understand completely. I just don't want to have to look at it. Maybe we'll just do the paperwork later. Just give me your first name for now.

Stanley.

Well, hello, Stanley, and welcome to the French Foreign Legion. We congratulate you for taking this giant step toward chasing away nasty old Mr. Blues. In the years that follow, we hope you'll come to think of us here in the Legion as your friends. Have a balloon.

Thank you.

You gonna be okay? You look like you're getting kind of misty. I really don't want to have to watch that. I'll show you to your quarters now. Try not to bust out crying until we get there.

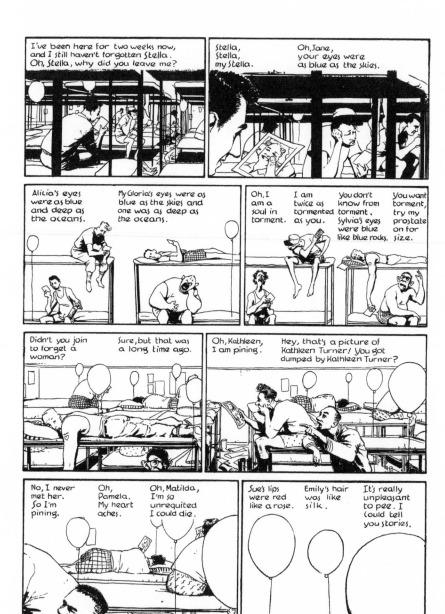

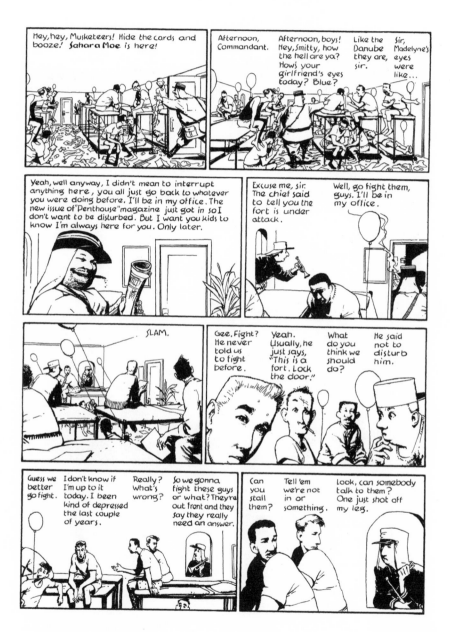

BANG BANG BANG BANG BANG BANG BANG BANG BANG BANG BANG BANG
Die, Alice! Eat hot lead, Nina! You're brain soup now, Pamela!

BANG BANG BANG BANGBANG BANG BANG BANG BAN
...And this is for "I'll love you forever, Harry." BANG! ...And this is for "I wish you'd trust me and open up, Harry." BANG! ... And this is for "I think we should see other people, Harry." BANG! ... And this is for "We'll still be friends, Harry." BANG!

BANG BANG BANG BANG BANG BANG BANG BANG B
Hey, you, hey! Look up here! Up here! Shoot me! Shoot me! I'm worthless! Please kill me! Hey! You! Hey! 'Tis a far, far better thing I do! Hey!

NG BANG BANG BANG BANG BANG BANG BANG BANG BAN
Hey, Guys. Cut that out. Come on. Why should we, Stanley? We're morons. We deserve to die. What do we have to live for anyway, huh, Stan?

They're showing "Porky's II" on cable tonight. Oh, okay.

BANG BANG BANG BANG BANG BANG BANG BAN
And stay down, for cryin' out loud! "Kill me, kill me, boo hoo hoo." Why, I oughta ... Gee, Stan, we'd be dead for sure if you hadn't come along. Wow, you're a hero!

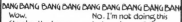

BANG BANG BANG BANG BANG BANG BANG BANG BANG

Wow. Stanley the hero. That must feel great. Being a hero and all that.

No. I'm not doing this to be a hero. I just don't want to see you get kilt.

BANG BANG BANG BANG BANG BANG BANG BANG BANG

Yeah, but I'll bet you still get kind of a rush standing there with that gun. But you feel like Clint Eastwood or something. I know I would.

Come on, cut it out. I hate guns.

BANG BANG BANG BANG BANG BANG BANG BANG BANG BA

Yeah, right.

No, really. I just didn't want you guys to get hurt. I'd rather not be here, if you want to know the truth. I don't like fighting. I don't like guns, I don't like killing. I don't want to be a hero.

BANG BANG BANG BANG BANG BANG BANG BANG BANG

Wow.

Oops. Almost missed one.

BANG BANG BANG BANG BANG BANG BANG BANG B

Hey, Stanley, do you think I could hold the gun for a minute, huh?

No, you can't hold the gun for a minute. Get down.

BANG BANG BANG BANG BANG BANG BANG BANG BANG BAN

Come on, just for a minute. Let me just shoot one guy, and then I'll give it right back.

No, sit down. You'll get shot.

BANG BANG BANG BANG BANG BANG BANG BANG BANG B

Oh, okay. I see how it is, Mr. Rambo.

No, that's not it at all. It's just that you'll get killed, you want to die.

BANG BANG BANG BANG BANG BANG BANG BANG BAN

No I don't. Really. That was before. I've changed. I'm a completely different guy now. Rugged and manly and stuff.

So grow a beard. Sit down.

BANG BANG BANG BANG BANG BANG BANG BANG BANGB

So what do you say? Lemme get the gun for a minute, huh?

I don't know. How can I be sure? I mean, suppose you're just lying to me so I'll let you up here to kill yourself? I'd better just hold onto the gun.

NG BANG BANG BANG BANG BANG BANG BANG BANG BANG

You think I'd do that? You really think I'd lie to get myself killed? If I got killed right after lying, I'd go straight to Hell for sure!

What?

BANG BANG BANGBANG BANG BANG BANG BANG BANG BAN

No, really! It happened to a guy in my neighborhood!

Guy in your neighborhood went to Hell.

BANG BANG BANG BANG BANG BANG BANG BANG BANG BA

Yeah, he lied to his wife about working late, and then got hit by a car and went to Hell.

How did you find out he went to Hell?

BANG BANG BANG BANG BANG BANG BANG BANG BANG B

He appeared to his son in a dream and said,"I lied to your mother, and now I'm in Hell, and boy, am I sorry."

Right.

NG BANG BANG BANG BANG BANG BANG BANG BANG BANG BAN

Really. The kid was on TV and everything! That "60 Minutes" show. Mike Wallace interviewed him.

I'll bet Wallace was impressed.

BANG BANG BANG BANG BANG BANG BANG BANG BANG B

Actually, Wallace tore him apart. Asked the kid all sorts of dumb questions to make him look bad. Stuff like "What did your father say Hell looked like?

So what did the kid say?

NG BANG BANG BANG BANG BANG BANG BANG BANG BANG

He said it looked like Jackson Heights, Queens. In New York. It's all these fourteen-year old kids wearing plaid flannel shirts over Def Leppard T-shirts. And no black people, hardly.

Probably couldn't afford the rent.

You know what we should do? We should celebrate. We should do guy stuff. Manly stuff. On account of our newfound manliness and masculinity.

So we should do guy stuff. What's guy stuff, for instance?

Like beer. We could drink beer. That's a manly thing. We could drink a lot of beer and yell "Go go go go" and "Ay ay ay ay." And belch. Belching is manly.

We could watch a sporting event while drinking beer.

I want to spit and swear and adjust my shorts on a street corner. That would be guy stuff. Can we do that?

Hey, let's drive around and yell out of car windows at women.

And drink beer.

And drink beer.

Hey, Stanley! Want to do guy stuff?

Sure! We'll go!

Jeez, you mean you're gonna bring your wimp friends with you? Holy crap. They'll ruin everything.

We're not wimps, we're just sensitive.

Yeah, sensitive.

Whatever. I don't think you should be allowed to do guy stuff.

How come?

Yeah, how come?

Because you shouldn't, that's why. Because... because you didn't kill anybody. You didn't kill anybody, so now you shouldn't be allowed to do guy stuff. Sure, that makes sense, doesn't it? Stanley can come, because he's a hero. He killed a bunch of guys.

I was gonna kill some people. I was working up to it.

Well, here we are. A hardy band of Legionnaires out for a night on the town.

We're glad you could come along, Commandant.

You kidding? To watch you do guy stuff, I'd miss my own funeral.

Thanks for letting us come along, too.

What letting? You followed us.

Of course we followed you. We thought we were invited.

That's why you followed us with the lights off. That's why you waited around the corner while we got gas. That's why you spent most of the trip disguised as old ladies.

So, what're you saying?

Hey, come on. I want to do guy stuff! What are we gonna do first?

How 'bout we go into this bar and knock back a few Brewskis.

And arm wrestle.

Yahoo! Let's go!

I'll be along in a minute. I want to swear and spit awhile out here first.

Something wrong, Ike?

No, it's just that, well, what if somebody asks me, "See the game last night?" If I tell them I didn't, they'll think I'm a fag or something.

So say you saw it.

What if they quiz me?

So, what do you do?

We're coat-check girls.

Oh, really?

No, we just said that to impress you.

Blanche, that wasn't nice.

That's okay, it was a pretty good joke.

I'm sorry. I don't know what's the matter with me. I shouldn't pick on you. You seem like a nice guy. I mean, you've got it bad enough as it is, without me picking on you.

What do you mean?

It's just an awkward situation. You're trying to pick Fifi up, but you don't want to offend her friend, namely me. So you're being a good sport and talking to both of us, even though you really just want to talk to Fifi.

You probably also hate yourself for the fact that you're more attracted to Fifi than to me. You think it's wrong to prefer Fifi just on the basis of her looks, but at the same time you can't help yourself. You suspect that I may secretly be jealous of Fifi because men usually ask her out and not me.

You're probably thinking about asking me out because you feel sorry for me. Or because you feel guilty. But you really want Fifi. She's so beautiful. The kind of girl every guy wants. Every guy. She probably has zillions of guys. Big guys. Rich guys. Most likely, she wouldn't go out with you. You think maybe you'd have better luck with me because I'm less attractive. Yep, it's an awkward situation all right.

I hear you're coat-check girls. That sounds like interesting work.

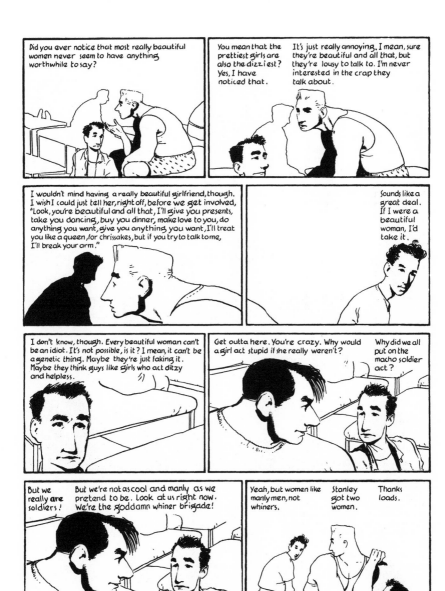

Sure he got two women. Stanley's a nice guy. We're all nice guys. We just don't have faith in our own appeal and so we put on acts.

Damn straight, I put on an act. If I don't put on an act, I'll just be a normal guy. There's nothing special about me.

So be a normal guy, for chrissakes! It'll make you stand out from the crowd. There aren't too many normal guys around anymore. Everybody's got an act. Some are better than others, but they're still acts. Deep down, everybody's the same, anyway. All anyone wants is to be loved. That goes for women as well as men.

Wow, that's beautiful. I'm touched. I really am. I'd cry, but it makes me look like Oprah Winfrey. Look, I hate to break up this rap session, but we've got a fight scheduled in fifteen minutes and I want you all to get showered.

Fight?

Yeah, remember? I told you guys yesterday.

Commandant, enemy sighted on the horizon. They should be here in a minute.

But sir, we can't fight.

Damn. They're ten minutes early.

Sir, Murphy's on cannons. He said to ask you if we have any of the good cannonballs left.

What do you mean, you can't fight?

Sir? We've kind of got a situation out here. We really need to know about those cannonballs.

We can't fight them, they're soldiers like us. Maybe they have the same problems we have.

Yeah.

I doubt it. I can hardly believe that **you** have the problems you have.

Sir, Murphy says— Oh, never mind. They got Murphy, sir.

We're sorry, sir, but it's how we feel.

Oh, this is great, just great. We're dead men. I wish you guys had told me about this earlier. I would have had time to sneak out the back.

Can I come in, sir? I have to go to the bathroom.

This sucks. This really sucks. I hope you know that.

I'm sorry, sir, we can't fight them. It would be wrong.

We're dead men. This really, really sucks, guys.

Come on, let me in, sir, please.

Maybe if we surrender, they won't kill us.

I'd rather die.

You're in luck, sir. They'd rather kill us.

We could kill ourselves.

That's brilliant.

I wonder what it'll be like, being dead.

Do you believe in God, sir?

I did until about 30 seconds ago. Now if you'll excuse me, I figure I've got about two minutes left to get stinking drunk.
It's sad, really. We could have done so much together. Don't you see? We weren't just fighting men, we were defending a way of life!

Making the world a safer place for our children and ensuring the rights of every freedom-loving man and woman! And now we're throwing it all away. Can you do that? Can you sit back and watch our precious way of life be destroyed by these monsters? Can you? No! You'll fight! Fight like lions! Fight because you must! Fight for what's just!

Wait a minute. Sometimes I'm so dumb I could puke. This is a fort! Lock the door.

the
end

a cowboy wally production

from do the right thing
1989

EXT: *STREET—DAY*

Officers Ponte and Long drive down the block and at the corner they stop, glare at the Corner Men.

CLOSE—OFFICER POINTE

CLOSE—SWEET DICK WILLIE

CLOSE—OFFICER LONG

CLOSE—COCONUT SID

ANGLE—POLICE CAR

OFFICER PONTE

What a waste.

ANGLE—CORNER

Sweet Dick, ML, and Coconut Sid stare right back at the cops.

ANGLE—POLICE CAR

It drives off.

ANGLE—CORNER

COCONUT SID

As I was saying before we were
so rudely interrupted by the
finest.

ML

What was you saying?

Coconut Sid blanks.

SWEET DICK WILLIE

Motherfucker wasn't saying shit.

ML

Look at that.

COCONUT SID

Look at what?

ML points across the street to the Korean fruit and vegetable stand.

ML

It's a fucking shame.

SWEET DICK WILLIE

What is?

ML

Sweet Dick Willie.

SWEET DICK WILLIE

That's my name.

ML

Do I have to spell it out?

COCONUT SID

Make it plain.

ML

OK, but listen up. I'm gonna
break it down.

SWEET DICK WILLIE

Let it be broke.

ML

Can ya dig it?

SWEET DICK WILLIE

It's dug.

CLOSE—ML

ML

Look at those Korean motherfuckers
across the street. I
betcha they haven't been a year
off da motherfucking boat before
they opened up their own place.

CLOSE—COCONUT SID

COCONUT SID

It's been about a year.

CLOSE—ML

ML

A motherfucking year off the
motherfucking boat and got a
good business in our neighborhood
occupying a building that
had been boarded up for longer
than I care to remember and
I've been here a long time.

CLOSE—SWEET DICK WILLIE

SWEET DICK WILLIE

It has been a long time.

CLOSE—COCONUT SID

COCONUT SID

How long?

CLOSE—ML

ML

Too long! Too long. Now for
the life of me, I haven't been
able to figger this out. Either
dem Koreans are geniuses or
we Blacks are dumb.

This is truly a stupefying question and all three are silent. What is the answer?

COCONUT SID

It's gotta be cuz we're Black.
No other explanation, nobody
don't want the Black man to
be about shit.

SWEET DICK WILLIE

Old excuse.

ML

I'll be one happy fool to see
us have our own business right
here. Yes, sir. I'd be the
first in line to spend the
little money I got.

Sweet Dick Willie gets up from his folding chair.

SWEET DICK WILLIE

It's Miller time. Let me go
give these Koreans s'more
business.

ML

It's a motherfucking shame.

COCONUT SID

Ain't that a bitch.

EXT: *STOOP—DAY*

Da Mayor sits on his stoop and a kid, EDDIE, runs by.

DA MAYOR

Sonny! Sonny!

Eddie stops.

DA MAYOR

Doctor, what's your name?

EDDIE

Eddie Lovell.

DA MAYOR

How old are you?

EDDIE

Ten.

DA MAYOR

What makes Sammy run?

EDDIE

My name is Eddie.

DA MAYOR

What makes Sammy run?

EDDIE

I said my name is Eddie Lovell.

DA MAYOR

Relax, Eddie, I want you to go
to the corner store. How
much will it cost me?

EDDIE

How would I know how much it's
gonna cost if I don't know
what I'm buying?

DA MAYOR

Eddie, you're too smart for
your own britches. Listen
to me. How much do you want
to run to the store for Da
Mayor?

EDDIE

Fifty cents.

DA MAYOR

You got a deal.

He gives Eddie some money.

DA MAYOR

Git me a quart of beer, Budweiser,
say it's for your father, if
they bother you.

Eddie runs down the block just as Ahmad, Cee, Punchy, and Ella pass him.

AHMAD

Who told him he was Da Mayor
of this block?

CEE

He's self-appointed.

ELLA

Leave him alone.

PUNCHY

Shut up.

DA MAYOR

Go on now. Leave me be.

AHMAD

You walk up and down this block
like you own it.

CEE

Da Mayor.

PUNCHY

You're old.

AHMAD

A old drunk bum.

Da Mayor stands up from his seat cushion on the stoop.

AHMAD

What do you have to say?

DA MAYOR

What do you know 'bout me?
Y'all can't even pee straight.
What do you know? Until you
have stood in the doorway and
heard the hunger of your five
children, unable to do a damn
thing about it, you don't
know shit. You don't know
my pain, you don't know me.
Don't call me a bum, don't
call me a drunk, you don't
know me, and it's disrespectful.
I know your parents raised you
better.

The teenagers look at Da Mayor.

ELLA

He told you off.

Da Mayor sits back down on his seat cushion on his stoop.

INT: *SAL'S FAMOUS PIZZERIA—DAY*

ANGLE—PAY PHONE ON WALL

Mookie is on the phone.

MOOKIE

I know I haven't seen you in
four days. I'm a working man.

TINA (VO)

I work too, but I still make time.

MOOKIE

Tina, what do you want me to
do?

TINA (VO)

I want you to spend some time
with me. I want you to try and
make this relationship work.
If not, I'd rather not be
bothered.

MOOKIE

Alright. Alright. I'll be
over there sometime today.

TINA (VO)

When?

MOOKIE

Before I get off work.

TINA (VO)

Bring some ice cream, I'm
burning up. Do you love me?

MOOKIE

Do I love you?

CLOSE—SAL

SAL

Mookie, get offa da phone.

CLOSE—MOOKIE

MOOKIE

Be off in a second. Tina, I
dedicated a record on Mister
Señor Love Daddy's show to you.

TINA (VO)

Big deal.

CLOSE—SAL

SAL

Mookie! How is anybody gonna
call in?

CLOSE—MOOKIE

MOOKIE

Big deal? If that's not LOVE,
I don't know what is.

CLOSE—PINO

PINO

You deaf or what?

CLOSE—MOOKIE

MOOKIE

Gotta go. See ya soon.
(he hangs up)
Everybody happy now?

The phone rings right away and Pino picks it up.

ANGLE—PINO

> **PINO**
>
> Sal's Famous Pizzeria, yeah,
> two large pizzas, pepperoni and
> anchovies, hold on. . . . See,
> Pop, Mookie fucking talking on
> the phone and people are trying
> to call in orders. He's making
> us lose business.

CLOSE—SAL

> **SAL**
>
> Mookie, you're fucking up.

> **PINO**
>
> Twenty minutes.
> (he hangs up the phone)
> How come you niggers are so
> stupid?

CLOSE—MOOKIE

> **MOOKIE**
>
> If ya see a nigger here, kick
> his ass.

CLOSE—PINO

> **PINO**
>
> Fuck you and stay off the phone.

CLOSE—VITO

> **VITO**
>
> Forget it, Mookie.

ANGLE—PIZZERIA

MOOKIE

Who's your favorite basketball
player?

PINO

Magic Johnson.

MOOKIE

And not Larry Bird? Who's your
favorite movie star?

PINO

Eddie Murphy.

Mookie is smiling now.

MOOKIE

Last question: Who's your
favorite rock star?

Pino doesn't answer, because he sees the trap he's already fallen into.

MOOKIE

Barry Manilow?

Mookie and Vito laugh.

MOOKIE

Pino, no joke. C'mon, answer.

VITO

It's Prince. He's a Prince freak.

PINO

Shut up. The Boss! Bruuucce!!!!

MOOKIE

Sounds funny to me. As much as
you say nigger this and nigger
that, all your favorite people
are "niggers."

PINO

It's different. Magic, Eddie,
Prince are not niggers, I mean,
are not Black. I mean, they're
Black but not really Black.
They're more than Black. It's
different.

With each word Pino is hanging himself even further.

MOOKIE

Pino, I think secretly that
you wish you were Black. That's
what I think. Vito, what do
you say?

PINO

Y'know, I've been listening and
reading 'bout Farrakhan, ya didn't
know that, did you?

MOOKIE

I didn't know you could read.

PINO

Fuck you. Anyway, Minister
Farrakhan always talks about

the so-called "day" when the
Black man will rise. "We will
one day rule the earth as we
did in our glorious past."
You really believe that shit?

MOOKIE

It's e-vit-able.

PINO

Keep dreaming.

MOOKIE

Fuck you, fuck pizza, and fuck
Frank Sinatra, too.

PINO

Well, fuck you, too, and fuck
Michael Jackson.

CUT TO:

RACIAL SLUR MONTAGE
The following will be a QUICK-CUTTING MONTAGE of racial slurs,
with different ethnic groups pointing the finger at one another. Each
person looks directly INTO THE CAMERA.

CLOSE—MOOKIE

MOOKIE

Dago, wop, garlic-breath, guinea,
pizza-slinging, spaghetti-
bending,
Vic Damone, Perry
Como, Luciano Pavarotti, Sole
Mio, nonsinging motherfucker.

CUT TO:

CLOSE—PINO

PINO

You gold-teeth, gold-chain-
wearing, fried-chicken-and-
biscuit-eatin', monkey, ape,
baboon, big thigh, fast-running,
three-hundred-sixty-degree-
basketball-dunking spade
Moulan Yan.

CUT TO:

CLOSE—STEVIE

STEVIE

You slant-eyed, me-no-speak-
American, own every fruit and
vegetable stand in New York,
Reverend Moon, Summer
Olympics '88, Korean kick-
boxing bastard.

CUT TO:

CLOSE—OFFICER LONG

OFFICER LONG

Goya bean–eating, fifteen in a
car, thirty in an apartment,
pointed shoes, red-wearing,
Menudo, meda-meda Puerto Rican
cocksucker.

CUT TO:

CLOSE—KOREAN CLERK

KOREAN CLERK

It's cheap, I got a good price
for you, Mayor Koch, "How I'm
doing," chocolate-egg-cream-

drinking, bagel and lox, B'nai
B'rith asshole.

CUT TO:

INT: *WE LOVE RADIO STATION CONTROL ROOM—DAY*

CLOSE—MISTER SEÑOR LOVE DADDY

MISTER SEÑOR LOVE DADDY

Yo! Hold up! Time out! Time
out! Y'all take a chill. Ya
need to cool that shit out . . .
and that's the truth, Ruth.

CUT TO:

CLOSE—WHITE-HOT SUN

INT: *SAL'S FAMOUS PIZZERIA—DAY*

Mookie picks up his two pizza pies for delivery.

MOOKIE

Sal, can you do me a favor?

SAL

Depends.

MOOKIE

Can you pay me now?

SAL

Can't do.

MOOKIE

Sal, just this once, do me
that solid.

PATRICIA SMITH

boy sneezes, head explodes
1991

Inspired by a headline in a supermarket tabloid

There are no pictures with this story,
strange when one considers the possibilities.

There could be a pre-sneeze montage,
dim photos of a boy being bounced
on his father's knee,
a terse 8th grade graduation shot,
or something taken at Boy Scout camp
four years ago.
Any shot with his head still
attached to his shoulders
would pretty much get the point across.

Or afterward, man-on-the-street candids
of surprised passersby
showered with bits of gray matter,
shards of nostril,
clumps of hair,
ragged shreds of facial tissue.

The tabloids could run
full color action shots
of the poor guy's torso
teetering back and forth
doing that crazy circumstance dance
and finally falling,

flopping on the sidewalk
like an orgasmic guppy.

The electronic media would be sure
to pick up the audio
as some witness jerk
mumbles "gesundheit"
or even worse,
"God bless you."

But I guess
anything in the way of illustration
would either be too early
or too late.
Who could see the pinpoint of irritation
growing insistent like a hot white light in his head?
Who could follow that errant bit of dust
driven deep by the wind?
How could he know, when he opened his mouth,
that once he closed it
it wouldn't be there?

lil' black zambo, *from* negrophobia
1992

lil' Black Zambo was a little nigger boy. Or pickaninny. Or jigaboo. Or any number of names we have for little colored children—shine, smoke, snowball, dinge, dust, inky, eggplant, and chocolate moonpie. And since Lil' Black Zambo lived with his mammy in a one-room hut made of mud and leaves near a croc-infested swamp in the Jungle, we can call him 'gator bait, too.

There was not much in the hut where Zambo and his mammy lived: a dirt floor, several pairs of dice (Zambo and his mammy liked to roll the bones), and hundreds of big, brown cockroaches with wings snapping *clickity-click splat* as they buzzed through the hut and slapped against the walls.

Zambo's pappy, Tambo, who liked to drink cheap coconut wine, ran off long before Zambo was born, so Zambo and his mammy were very, very poor. They didn't give out welfare checks in the Jungle. The Jungle was uncivilized. Or at least that's what Zambo's mammy, Mambo, said. "When we gwine git civilized so I can git on d'welfare?"

Zambo's mammy was as big as a gorilla and looked like one, too. She had big, red lips stretched out of shape by two clay plates stuck in her face and a big, white bone pushed through her nose. Her knuckles even dragged on the ground.

Zambo was no looker himself. "Lawd! What I do to deserve such an ugly chil'?" his mammy moaned. "An' why you give him such *nappy* hair? It look like d'wool knotted up on a sheep's ass!"

Zambo was real, real, black. *Spear-chucker chocolate*, his mammy said. She clacked her lips and told Zambo he d'darkest chil' she ever seen. Darker than her frying pan even.

"Dat pretty damn *dark*!" Zambo said.

"*Damn right!*" Mammy exclaimed. "When you born, you so dark, d'docta slapped me!"

Zambo's eyes grew big and sad when his mammy said that, thinking, "What I do to be so black an' blue?"

(Sometimes Louie Armstrong flew out to the Jungle with his band and jammed for the Jungle Bunnies. That's where Lil' Black Zambo picked up all his blues references. All the Jungle Bunnies in the Jungle would show up, dressed in their finest feathers, and smoked the Mezz. As Pops blew, the Jungle Bunnies, high as a kite, cheered, "Oooga-booga!"*)

Now Lil' Black Zambo loved to eat watermelons. He didn't eat the red juicy part because he didn't like the seeds.

"What I look like sittin' in d'Jungle spittin' a bunch o' seeds?" he said. "Can't kill no lions wif a moufful o' seeds!"

So he ate the rind and threw the rest away.

But more than watermelon, Zambo loved pancakes. He loved pancakes more than he loved his saucer-lipped mammy. Mile-high stacks of pancakes dripping with sweet sugary syrup and lots of hot yellow butter. Zambo's lips got greasy just thinking about it. *Ummumm!*

Zambo's mammy made him pancakes three times a day, every day. She made her pancakes from scratch. They didn't have Aunt Jemima in the Jungle.

Zambo liked missionary sausage with his pancakes real special. "Mammy, when we gwine eat mo' Bibletotin' whyte folks?"

So Zambo's mammy would file her teeth, streak her face with fresh daubs of paint, and go into the bush, trapping herself a nice, plump white missionary. She'd grind him into wormy bits of red meat, stuff him into a tube of monkey's intestines, and fry him up grease-poppin' brown.

"Uuuumm-yum, Mammy! I *love* whyte people!"

One day, as Zambo's mammy stirred pancake batter made from scratch, and battled an airborne squadron of flying cockroaches, she complained:

"We so uncivilized! We don't have welfare checks or Aunt Jemima mix or nuffin in d'Jungle! When we gwine git civilized an' go pick cotton fo' d'rich whyte folks in America?"

Zambo tugged at the fringes of his mammy's straw skirt. (Zambo's mammy wore a straw skirt and nothing more. When her picture was published in *National Geographic*, baring her black bushbabe bod and flat

* Editor's Note: "That nigga can play his ass off!"

Jungle Woman tits, she knew she'd finally been civilized. She could just
see the welfare checks flying in.) "An' not only dat, Mammy!" he said.
"We ain't got no hot yellow butter, neither!"

"Oh no!" his mammy wailed. "We ain't got no hot yellow butter!
What me an' my poor chil' gwine do now? He gone haf t'eat his pancakes
wif sweet sugary syrup! Damn dis uncivilized Jungle life!"

With her face buried in her hands, she dropped to her knees on the hut's
dirt floor and began to cry.

"Don't cry, Mammy!" Zambo said, forking a pancake into his mouth.
"Look! I eatin' it! It good wif jus' d'sweet sugary syrup! I don't need no
old hot yellow butter! Hot yellow butter ain't good fo' you no way! It
high in cholesterol, it harden on yo' arteries, an' give you hypertension,
d'number-one killer o'black folks today! Dat one thing I'll say fo' dese
damn flyin' cockroaches. Dey strict vegetarians!"

As was the habit of his kind, Zambo was lying.

While his mammy howled like a horse-whipped hound, Zambo took
his plate of pancakes and marched from the hut with a pout. He was in a
huff.

"Shoot! I'm gone git me some hot yellow butter! Sittin' 'round whinin'
fo' d'rich whyte folks t'come civilize us pickin' cotton wif Aunt Jemima
an' welfare checks ain't gone git me no hot yellow butter! What cotton
anyway? Shoot!"

Zambo walked through deep, dark jungle with the pancakes stacked
high on his plate. Suddenly, a Tiger sprang out from behind a coconut
tree. "Hey boy! Can't you read the sign? It says, *no darkies allowed!*"

"No," said Zambo. "I can't read. I ain't been civilized. What's a
'darkie'?"

"Don't talk smart at me, boy!" said the Tiger. "We eat little darkies like
you where I come from!"

"*You does?*" Zambo trembled, his eyes wide with fear.

"Yes. I 'does,'" said the Tiger with considerable condescension. "Like
hell you does!" Zambo zipped to the top of the coconut tree, trailing a
plume of dust.

The Tiger was confounded by the little nigger boy's speed.

"You sneaky little burrhead! Come down here this instant!"

Zambo stared down at the Tiger from the top of the coconut tree with
the plate of pancakes balanced on his lap. He looked like a lump of coal.

"Is you out yo' rat mind? Does you think I'm gonna climb down there jus' 'cause you say so? An' let you eat me, too? Dis might be d'Jungle, Mr. Tiger, but my mammy didn't raise no fool!"

Zambo's grin displayed a set of perfectly white teeth.

The Tiger's face turned red with frustration. He stomped his paws and thrashed his tail.

"You insolent little ragoon!" the Tiger fumed. "We give you people all the mud and leaves you need for your roach-infested huts, plenty of open space to chuck your spears, all the monkeys and coconuts you can eat, and all I ask for in return is one lousy meal! Is this how you people show your gratitude?"

"What 'graptitude,' Mr. Tiger?" Zambo asked innocently.

The Tiger grew blind with rage at Zambo's niggerheadedness. He rolled his paw into a ball and shook it at the sky.

"Just one woolhead little Jungle Bunny! That's all I asked for! One kinky-haired little ink spot! Who's going to miss him? His big, ugly, bone-through-the-nose, gorilla-lookin' mammy? Not that fat, funky, water-melon and pancake eatin' bitch! She done lost her mind and don't know *that's* gone yet!"

That made Zambo mad. The tiger was talking about his mammy! She might be big, black, and ugly with a bone through her nose but she was *his* mammy. What was wrong with that Tiger? Didn't he have enough sense to know you didn't go around talking about other people's mammies like they were pellets of monkey doo-doo?

"You talkin' junk now, sucka!" said Zambo. "Don't lemme haf t'come down there an' beat th'stripes off yo' butt!"

The Tiger laughed. "I'll slap the black out of you and that fat flapjack freak you live with! Now what you got to say to that, *punk*?"

Zambo hit the Tiger in the head with a coconut.

The coconut raised a big, throbbing lump between the Tiger's ears. He staggered around the coconut tree with a circle of stars revolving around his head. Birds chirped *tweet-tweet*. An asteroid flashed past his eyes.

Upon recovery, the Tiger angrily shook his balled paw at Lil' Black Zambo.

"I'm gonna put a hurtin' on you now, you Uzi-armed little crackhead! When I get through with you, you'll never listen to rap music again!"

The Tiger began running in circles around the coconut tree.

"I hope you enjoy the view up there, boy, 'cause when I get my claws in you, you gonna be a *dead* nigger with an attitude!"

The Tiger ran faster and faster and faster. He ran so fast he looked like a yellow ring of swiftly spinning light.

"*Burrhead!*" the Tiger roared. "*Jungle bunny! Ink spot!*"

The Tiger ran faster still. "*Spear-chucker! Mau-mau lips!*"

Suddenly, there was the gleam of flame and the acrid smell of smoke. The glare hurt Zambo's eyes. In an instant the Tiger was gone. Lil' Black Zambo blinked in amazement.

He couldn't believe what his eyes had just seen. He rubbed them with his tiny fists and blinked again. It was true. The Tiger had vanished.

And directly below him, in a bright puddle circling the foot of the coconut tree, was seven-hundred pounds of hot yellow butter.

Lil' Black Zambo smacked his lips.

His last thought, just before he shimmied down the trunk of the coconut tree, was how he'd like, with his pancakes, to sink his freshly filed teeth into a string of sizzling missionary sausage.

return of the funky man
1992

Chorus:
Mad brothers know his name. Yeah, it's him again.
Mad brothers know his name. Yeah, it's him again.
Mad brothers know his name. Yeah, it's him again.
Mad brothers know his name. Yeah, it's him again.

Lord Finesse got something for your eardrums
Back on the scene, long time, no hear from
It's the funky man, the brother with the same sound
I've been coolin' about a year and some change now
So hand over the microphone cause it's my turn
The brother with a fade, half-moon, and long sideburns
Nice, dope, and keep the girls scopin'
Say the funky shit and get all the niggas open
So heed that, don't try to yap and give me feedback
I'll get in that ass, believe that
Can it, I'll steal your show like a bandit
I get papes while you're broke like mass transit
You're not as smooth as this, so what can you do with this
Brothers need to stop and step with that foolishness
I'm the type to interrupt a party
I don't need a phone to reach out and touch somebody
Gimme a mic, it's just as good as one
Leave the party is what you wack MC's should of done
Cause y'all starvin', I'm living extra large 'n'
I'm swingin' shit as if my name was Tarzan
Yeah, cause I'm on some old new shit
Got more styles than you see in a Kung Fu flick

Mic to cease, wax opponents off with ease
I'm more deadly than a venereal disease
So think twice, those who think Imma fall
I'm shining more than a tire full of Armor All
It's Lord Finesse and I got shit planned
Hot damn, it's the Return of the Funky Man

(Chorus)
Mad brothers know his name. Yeah, it's him again.
Mad brothers know his name. Yeah, it's him again.
Mad brothers know his name. Yeah, it's him again.
Mad brothers know his name. Yeah, it's him again.

Brothers get cash, but I get way more
In the '90s, I'm getting paid for
Rhyme and envy, 21st century
When asked, Who's the funkiest? You better mention me
I go all out while a lot of crews be fronting
I know and they know that they can't do me nothin'
Cause I'm smooth and wise, the skills I utilize
Lyrics all advanced you'd think my brain was computerized
So who needs a partner or a sidekick?
When it comes to being funky, I got all that old fly shit
The rough and rugged, plus the pimp smooth rhyme
I polish opponents off like a shoe shine
They be frontin' like they on the crazy tip
Tryin' to hang but they softer than baby shit
Frontin' like they wild with they bullshit style
I'll put they ass on trial, pull they card and they file
I'm hardcore, but I still keep the scene pumpin'
So all that singing and dancing, that shit don't mean nothin'
MCs suffer Lord Finesse lately
Some of them hate me, think that they can take me
I'll take on some of them, bring a whole ton of them
I'll take them all on and stomp each and every one of them
I just chill, relax and flaunt my cash
You wanna riff, I'll be quit to stomp that ass
And let you know that you can't get with this

Come one come all and get burnt by the quickness
Greater, creator, drop stupid data
If I ever got served it had to be by a waiter
I lounge and I rest until my song is done
I plan to be straight with papes in the long run
Cause when it comes to rhymes I give you more than you ask for
Bring a whole task force, I rhyme my fuckin' ass off
I stand in command with the mic in my hand
Aw shit, it's the Return of the Funky Man

(Chorus)
Mad brothers know his name. Yeah, it's him again.
Mad brothers know his name. Yeah, it's him again.
Mad brothers know his name. Yeah, it's him again.
Mad brothers know his name. Yeah, it's him again.

Stand back, I'm about to flip here
Got dissed last year so I'm kickin' ass this year
Brothers were stressing me, strictly overworking me
(They jerked you last year) Yeah, that fits perfectly
Cool, cause I'm still kinda fed with them
Who gives a fuck, I'm about 20 steps ahead of them
Now I'm established, they feel all embarrassed
'Cause I'm with Warner Brothers and my man Gary Harris
Spread the news or should I say buzz?
(Finesse is paid!) Thought I wasn't when I was
The last label was confusing me, jerking me, fooling me
Now that I'm paid, you know what y'all can do for me
Since I sound funky a lot of labels want me
But I'll be damned to be another man's flunky
I can never be a stool pigeon, I'd rather be a full pigeon
Fuck the bullshittin'
'Cause in the '90s I got more than a little game
It's Lord Finesse and funky is my middle name
Plus my title and everybody wants mine
It's the brother with compounds and punchlines
I can still put my foot all in your ass
I'm crazy funky plus smoother than Teddy Pendergrass

I'm the man to put words in a simile
(He's a funky technician) Yeah, y'all remember me
I'm real and actual, the man out taxing you
I got rhymes and Mike got a scratch or two
So ain't no use trying to eat us for din-din
Brothers better off trying their luck with Win-10
To my opposition: I'm the man out burning ya'
I'll dust a rapper off like furniture
So take our stand, I'll foil your plan
Goddamn, it's the Return of the Funky Man.

(Chorus)
Mad brothers know his name. Yeah, it's him again.
Mad brothers know his name. Yeah, it's him again.
Mad brothers know his name. Yeah, it's him again.
Mad brothers know his name. Yeah, it's him again

the only one
1994

One night last spring, the fashion editor André Leon Talley attended an all-male nude revue at the Gaiety Theatre, on West Forty-sixth Street. He was dressed in a red waist-length military jacket with gold epaulets and black cuffs, black military trousers with a gold stripe down each leg, black patent-leather pumps with grosgrain bows, gray silk socks with black ribbing, white gloves, and a faux-fur muff. Accompanying him, rather like another accessory, was the young English designer John Galliano.

As the driver opened the car door in front of the theatre, Talley, characteristically, issued a directive followed by a question: "I shall expect you here upon my return at once! Lord, child, how am I gonna get out of this car in all this drag?" He did not pause for an answer. He stretched out his long left leg, placed his foot on the sidewalk, and, grabbing the back of the driver's seat, hoisted himself up and out—a maneuver whose inelegance he countered by adjusting his muff with a flourish.

Appearances are significant to André Leon Talley, who seeks always to live up to the grand amalgamation of his three names. He has sienna-brown skin and slightly graying close-cropped hair. He is six feet seven and has large hands and large feet and a barrel chest. He has been described as "a big girl." He is gap-toothed and full-mouthed. His speech combines an old-school Negro syntax, French words (for sardonic emphasis), and a posh British accent. Though a wide audience may know him from his periodic television appearances on CNN and VH1, it is in the world of magazines that he has made his name. Currently the creative director of *Vogue*, formerly the creative director of *HG* and a writer, stylist, and photographer for *Women's Wear Daily, Interview*, and the *Times Magazine*, André Leon Talley is, at forty-six, fashion's most voluble arbiter, custodian, and promoter of glamour.

Inside the Gaiety—a small, dark space with a stage, a movie screen, and two tiers of seats—some men sat in various states of undress and arousal while others dozed quietly. Talley and Galliano stood in the middle of the aisle to the left of the stage and waited for the dancers to appear. Talley was hoping for a "moment." He finds moments in other people's impulses ("I can tell you were about to have a moment"), work ("What Mr. Lagerfeld and I were after in those photographs was a moment"), architecture ("This room could use a certain . . . moment"), social gatherings ("These people are having a moment"). When the dancers entered, one by one, Talley said, "This is a major moment, child." Swaying to loud disco music and against a backdrop of gold lamé, the young men, who were either nude or partly so, offered the men in the front row a thigh to be touched, a biceps to be rubbed.

"Ooh!" Talley exclaimed. "It's *nostalgie de la boue!* It's 'Déjeuner sur l'Herbe,' no? Manet. The flesh. The young men. The languorous fall and gall of the flesh to dare itself to fall *on the herbe.*" André Leon Talley came down hard on the word *herbe* as he caught sight of a lavishly tanned young man onstage who was naked except for cowboy boots and, as his smile revealed, a retainer. "What can one do?" Talley moaned. "What can one do with such piquant insouciance? How can one live without the *vitality* of the cowboy boots and teeth and retainers and so forth?"

Before the end of the performance, Talley led Galliano into a room on one side of the theatre, where several other men were waiting for the dancers. Upon identifying André Leon Talley as "that fashion man off the TV," a black drag queen, who wore jeans, a cream-colored halter top, and an upswept hairdo, and sat on the lap of a bespectacled older white man, said, "That's what I want you to make me feel like, baby, a white woman. A white woman who's getting out of your Mercedes-Benz and going into Gucci to buy me some new drawers because you wrecked them. Just fabulous."

"This is charming," Talley said, calling attention to a makeshift bar with bowls of pretzels and potato chips and fruit punch. "For the guests who have come to pay homage to the breathtaking ability of the personnel." His muff grazed the top of the potato chips.

The room contained framed photographs from Madonna's book "Sex," which depicted scenes of louche S & M violence (Madonna, in an evening dress, being abused; nude dancers, with collars, being ridden by Daniel de La Falaise in a dinner jacket). The scenes had been enacted and photographed at the Gaiety. "*Miss* Ciccone," Talley said, with disdain, barely looking at the photographs. "My dear, we do *not* discuss the vulgar."

In inspecting and appraising his surroundings, André Leon Talley was working—the creative director in pursuit of inspiration. It is the same sort of work he does in the more conventional environs of his working day. At *Vogue*, Talley is many things—art director, stylist, fashion writer, and producer. As a producer, Talley suggests unlikely combinations, hoping for interesting results. Recently, he arranged to have Camilla Nickerson, a young fashion editor at *Vogue* and a proponent of the glamour-misshapen-by-irony look, design a photo spread on Geoffrey Beene, a designer committed to glamour not misshapen by anything. As an art director, Talley from time to time oversees cover shoots, especially those involving celebrities. He tries to insure that the photographer will produce an image that makes both the clothes and the celebrity look appealing and provides enough clear space in the frame for the magazine's art director to strip in cover lines. At the same time, Talley encourages the celebrity to project the kind of attitude that *Vogue* seeks to promote on its covers: relaxed and elegant but accessible. He does so by acting as both therapist and stylist. He soothes his subjects' anxieties about the cover shoot by exclaiming, as he dresses them, that this or that garment has never looked better.

It is in the production of stories he conceives on his own that Talley employs all his talents simultaneously. Before a season's new designer collections are shown to the press, Talley visits various houses to look for recurring motifs, in order to build a story around them. During a recent season, he discerned that two or three collections featured lace. *Vogue* then devised a story based on the mystery of lace, and had Helmut Newton photograph lace gloves, lace boots, and lace bodices in a way that enhanced the mystery. Talley chose which details of the clothes should be photographed. In conjunction with Newton, he also chose the models, the hair-and-makeup people, and the locations.

Talley will sometimes write the text to accompany the fashion spread he has conceived. At other times, he will act simply as a cultural reporter, writing pieces on new designers and choosing the best examples of their work to be photographed. Talley has written on interiors, too, directing the photographer to capture images that complement his text. "My dear, an editor must, *must* be there to fluff the pillows!" he says, explaining his presence at these photo shoots.

ANDRÉ LEON TALLEY's office at *Vogue* in Paris, where he is based, is a high-ceilinged space, painted white, with large windows facing the Boulevard Saint-Germain; it is surprisingly bare, except for two desks and many photographs on the walls, including a large one in color by Karl Lagerfeld of Talley carrying a big fur muff. There Talley will sometimes perform a kind of boss-man theatre—throw papers about, slam telephones down, noisily expel the incompetent. "This is too much. What story do we need to be working on, children? What *story*? Let's get cracking, darlings, on fur. *Fuh, fuh, fuh.* One must set the mood around the *fuh* and the heels, the hair, the skin, the nipples under the *fuh*, the hair around the nipples, the *fuh* clinging to the nipples, sweat, oysters, champagne, *régence!*" He conveys not only dissatisfaction but also the promise that, once he is satisfied, his reflexive endearments ("darling," "child," and so forth) will be heartfelt.

André Leon Talley, in a blue pin-striped suit, walked into his office one day making several demands that could not be met, since his assistant was not there to meet them. That Talley had, hours before, dismissed his assistant for the day was a fact he chose to ignore. He sat at his desk and began upsetting papers on it—papers that had clearly been left in some order. He then complained about the lack of order. He complained about the lack of a witness to the lack of order. He summoned by intercom a young woman named Georgie Newbery, an assistant in the fashion department, to be such a witness.

"Georgie!" Talley exclaimed as she quietly entered the room. Her eyes were focussed on Talley, who, as a result of the attention, seemed to grow larger. "I told Sam never, *nevah* to leave my desk in this state of . . . disorder! I can't find my papers."

"What papers, André?" Newbery asked.

"The papers, darling! The papers! I need a telephone number on the . . . papers! Can you believe this, child?" Talley asked of no one in particular. "I need the number of the soirée, darling," he said, slumping in a caricature of weariness. He covered his face with his hands and moaned. Newbery picked a piece of paper off his assistant's desk and handed it to him. Talley looked at the paper: on it was the telephone number. There was a silence; Talley seemed dissatisfied at having the phone number, the problem solved, the event over. He paused, as if to consider the next event he would create. Looking up at Newbery, Talley said, "Georgie, I need three thousand francs! At *once!*"

ANDRÉ LEON TALLEY has been the creative director of *Vogue* for six years. During that time, he has seen many looks come and go—the grunge look, the schoolgirl look, the sex-kitten look, the New Romantic look, the reconstituted-hippie look, the athletic-wear-meets-the-street look. In the years I have known him, though, Talley's own look has consistently been one of rigorous excess. In his way, he has become the last editorial custodian of unfettered glamour, and the only fashion editor who figures at all in the popular imagination. He is the fashion editor who, seemingly sparing no expense for models, clothes, props, photographers, and airplane tickets to far-flung locations—a farm in Wales, a burlesque house on West Forty-sixth Street—pursues that which the public will perceive, without naming it, as allure.

This pursuit begins in Talley's Paris apartment, which is situated near the Invalides, where Napoleon is entombed. The apartment is small but rich in talismans of allure: scented candles, flower-patterned draperies that puddle on the floor, a large flower-patterned screen, a Regency bed, books artfully arranged on a table in the vestibule. The walls are covered in beige rice paper. There is a small dark room off the vestibule with a VCR attached to an oversized television; on the walls are a number of drawings by Karl Lagerfeld and a poster-size, black-and-white photograph of a black man's torso by Annie Leibovitz.

Talley begins telephoning in the morning, often as early as six o'clock, to suss out what might be "the next thing." When Talley telephones a designer, he may ask, "Darling, have you had a moment?" In an industry notoriously suspicious of language, Talley's grandiloquence transports the designer into the role of artist. It does so by placing the designer's work in the realm of the historic: "This collection is more divine than the last, Monsieur Ferrè, in that it is a high moment of Grecian simplicity, of fluted skirts in the material of a high rustling mega-moment, from room to room, à la the essence of King Louis XV, à la the true spirit of couture!"

On the other hand, Talley does not see the work without the frame of commerce around it; in this sense, he is like an art dealer, whose survival is based on an evaluation of the market and of how the work at hand will shape the market, or be shaped by it, in future months. When Chanel, Dior, de la Renta, and other couture and ready-to-wear houses advertise in *Vogue*, they signal the affinity between their aesthetic and the world that André Leon Talley has created. Designers trust him, the moneyed women he brings to the designers trust him, and the women's husbands trust him with their wives. Drawing on this fund of trust, Talley presents, in the pages of *Vogue*, the work of European designers in an atmosphere of guilt-free exuberance that an American audience, standing in line at the supermarket reading *Vogue*, can trust.

"Magazines are not a Diderot moment of œuvreness," Talley says. "They are monthly ventures that should amuse and earn money by showing how *kind* money can be." In the stories that Talley has produced for *Vogue* in recent years—"The Armani Edge," "Feets of Brilliance," "Which Way Couture?," and "The Couture Journals," among others—everything is seduction. Talley's delicate orchestration and manipulation of the designers and buyers and photographers and editorial staff contributing to his vision are never seen, of course. What matters most to André Leon Talley is the image in his head of a woman looking at the page and imagining herself on it, unaware of all that André Leon Talley has contributed to her imagination.

ANDRÉ LEON TALLEY says he owes his desire to uphold what he calls "the world of opulence! opulence! opulence! maintenance! maintenance! maintenance!" to the late Diana Vreeland, who was the fashion editor for twenty-five years at *Harper's Bazaar*, the editor-in-chief of *Vogue* for eight years, and thereafter a special consultant to the Metropolitan Museum's Costume Institute, where she mounted audacious shows on Balenciaga, the eighteenth-century woman, equestrian fashion, and Yves Saint Laurent. It was during Vreeland's planning and installation of one such show—"Romantic and Glamorous Hollywood Design," in 1974—that Talley and Vreeland first met, through the parents of one of his college classmates. He later came to work for her as an unpaid assistant.

Vreeland was the most recognizable person in the fashion industry—indeed, the very image of the fashion editor—with her heavily rouged cheeks and lips, red fingernails, and sleek black hair; her red environments; her pronouncements (bluejeans "are the most beautiful things since the gondola"; Brigitte Bardot's "lips made Mick Jagger's lips *possible*"); her credos ("Of course, you understand I'm looking for the most *far-fetched* perfection"; "There's nothing more boring than narcissism—the tragedy of being totally . . . me"); her standards (having her paper money ironed, the soles of her shoes buffed with rhinoceros horn); and her extravagance of vision (photographic emphasis on nudity, drugs, and jewels).

By the time they met, Talley had gradually constructed a self that was recognizably a precursor of the André Leon Talley of today. And its most influential component was the formidable chic of his maternal grandmother. Talley was born in Washington, D.C., and when he was two months old he was sent by his parents to live with his grandmother Bennie Frances Davis, in Durham, North Carolina. "An extraordinary woman with blue hair, like Elsie de Wolfe" is how he describes her. "You know what one fundamental difference between whites and blacks is? If there's trouble at home for white people, they send the child to a psychiatrist. Black folks just send you to live with Grandma."

As a teenager, Talley made regular trips to the white section of Durham to buy *Vogue*, and these forays were another significant influence on his development. "My uncles cried 'Scandal! Scandal!' when I said I wanted to grow up to be a fashion editor," he says. "I discovered so early that the world was *cruel*. My mother didn't like my clothes. Those white people in Durham were so awful. And there I was, just this lone jigaboo . . . creature. And fashion in *Vogue* seemed so kind. So *opulently* kind. A perfect image of things. I began to think like an editor when I began to imagine presenting the women I knew in the pages of *Vogue*: my grandmother's style of perfection in the clothes she made; her version of couture."

In a snapshot of Talley from his college days, he is sitting with two female friends. What makes him recognizable is not just his physical appearance—the long, thin body; the large, vulnerable mouth jutting out from the long, thin face—but also his clothes. Unlike the other students, who are dressed in T-shirts and jeans, Talley wears a blue sweater with short sleeves over a white shirt with long sleeves, a brooch in the shape of a crescent moon, large aviator glasses with yellow lenses, and a blue knit hat. He looks delighted to be wearing these clothes. He looks delighted to be with these women.

Talley earned a B.A. in French literature at North Carolina Central University in 1970. His interest in the world of allure outside his grandmother's closet, away from Durham, coincided with his interest in French. He says of his discovery that couture was a part of French culture, and that his grandmother practiced her version of it, "You could have knocked me over with a feather! And it was stretching all the way back to the ancien régime, darling! Introduced to me by my first French instructor, Miss Cynthia P. Smith, in the fields of Durham, North Carolina! The entire French œuvre of oldness and awfulness flipping one out into the Belle Époque bodice of the music hall, Toulouse-Lautrec, an atmosphere of decadence, leading us to Josephine Baker and . . . me!"

Talley's immersion in French gave him a model to identify with: Baudelaire, on whose work he wrote his master's thesis, at Brown University in the early seventies. And it was while he was at Brown, liberated by the Baudelairean image of the flaneur, that Talley began to exercise fully his penchant for extravagant personal dress. He was known for draping himself in a number of cashmere sweaters. He was known for buying, on his teaching-assistant stipend, Louis Vuitton luggage.

"Obviously, he was not going to teach French," Dr. Yvonne Cormier, a schoolmate of Talley's at Brown, says. "André thought it was just good manners to look wonderful. It was a *moral* issue. And his language reflected that. André could never just go to his room and study. He had to *exclaim*, 'They've sent me to this prison! Now I have to go to my chambers and have a moment.'"

After Talley left Brown and completed his stint as a volunteer with Diana Vreeland at the Met, he became known in New York fashion circles for these things: insisting, at his local post office, on the most *beautiful* current stamps and holding up the line until they materialized; serving as a personal shopper for Miles Davis at the request of Davis's companion, Cicely Tyson; answering the telephone at Andy Warhol's *Interview*, in his capacity as a receptionist, with a jaunty *"Bonjour!"* and taking down messages in purple ink (for bad news) and gold (good news); wearing a pith helmet and kneesocks in the summer; being referred to by the envious as Queen Kong; becoming friends with the heiress Doris Duke and attending, at her invitation, many of her appearances as a singer with a black gospel choir; overspending on clothes and furnishings and running up personal debts in his habitual effort to live up to the grand amalgamation of his three names.

The late seventies, when André Leon Talley came into his own, is the period when designers like Yves Saint Laurent and Halston produced the clothes that Talley covered at the beginning of his career as a fashion editor at *WWD*, clothes often described as glamorous. It is the period referred to in the clothes being produced now by designers like Marc Jacobs and Anna Sui. "It was a time when I could take Mrs. Vreeland and Lee Radziwill to a

LaBelle concert at the Beacon and it wouldn't look like I was about to mug them," Talley says.

Daniela Morera, a correspondent for Italian *Vogue*, has a different recollection. "André was privileged because he was a close friend of Mrs. Vreeland's," she says. "Black people were as segregated in the industry then as they are now. They've always been the don't-get-too-close-darling exotic. André enjoyed a lot of attention from whites because he was ambitious and amusing. He says it wasn't bad, because he didn't know how bad it was for other blacks in the business. He was successful because he wasn't a threat. He'll never be an editor-in-chief. How could America have *that* dictating what the women of America will wear? Or representing them? No matter that André's been the greatest crossover act in the industry for quite some time. Like forever."

TALLEY's fascination stems, in part, from his being the *only one*. In the media or the arts, the only one is usually male, always somewhat "colored," and almost always gay. His career is based, in varying degrees, on talent, race, nonsexual charisma, and an association with people in power. To all appearances, the only one is a person with power, but is not *the* power. He is not just defined but controlled by a professional title, because he believes in the importance of his title and of the power with which it associates him. If he is black, he is a symbol of white anxiety about his presence in the larger world and the guilt such anxiety provokes. Other anxieties preoccupy him: anxieties about salary and prestige and someone else's opinion ultimately being more highly valued than his. He elicits many emotions from his colleagues, friendship and loyalty rarely being among them, since he does not believe in friendship that is innocent of an interest in what his title can do.

Talley is positioned, uniquely, at the intersection of fashion, magazine publishing, television, and high society. He regards his position as a privilege, and he flaunts it. "A large part of his life is *Vogue*," Candy Pratts Price, the magazine's fashion director, says about him. "Which explains the vulnerable, intense moods he goes through when he thinks someone here is against him. We've all been there with those moods of his, and *there* is pretty intense."

Talley's emotional involvement with women rises in part from nostalgia. He seems to project his grandmother's intentions and concerns for him, and Cynthia P. Smith's and Diana Vreeland's as well, onto his female colleagues at *Vogue*, and he seems to feel spurned when they exercise the independence inherent in a modern-day professional relationship. Often, the results are disastrous. When Talley is in favor, his colleagues adopt him as a totem of editorial success; when he is not, they regard him as a glittering but superfluous accessory.

His interest in romance is nostalgic, too. For him, romance is not about ending his loneliness; rather, it flows from the idea, expounded by Baudelaire, that love is never truly attained, only yearned for. (Talley's contemporary version of this: "No man, child," he might say, telephoning from his apartment in Paris. "No man. Just another video evening alone for the child of culture.") Talley's romantic yearnings are melancholic: he is susceptible to the prolonged, unrequited "crush" but is immune to involvement. He avoids engaging men he is attracted to. Generally, he is attracted to men who avoid him. He avoids the potential rejection and hurt that are invariable aspects of romantic love. Going to a gay bar with Talley, then, is an odd experience. In gay bars, as a rule, all bets are off: everyone is the same as everyone else because everyone is after the same thing. In a sense, the common pursuit divests everyone present of his title. Talley rarely speaks to anyone in this sort of environment. Mostly, he glowers at men he finds appealing and lays the blame for their lack of immediate interest in him on racism, or on the sexually paranoid environment that AIDS has fostered everywhere. Perhaps he just prefers the imagery of love made familiar by fashion magazines: images of the subject exhausted by "feeling," undone by a crush, recuperating in an atmosphere of glamour and allure.

Once, in New York, I had dinner with Talley and his friend the comedian Sandra Bernhard. She asked me how long I had known André. I said, "I fell in love with him in Paris." There was a silence—a silence that André did not fill with being pleased at or made shy by my comment. He grew large in his seat. He grew very dark and angry. And then he exclaimed, with great force, "You did not fall in love with me! You were in love with Paris! It was all the fabulous things I showed you in Paris! Lagerfeld's house! Dior! It wasn't me! It wasn't! It was Paris!"

When I first met Talley, I did not tell him that my interest in him was based in part on what other blacks in the fashion industry had said about him, on the way they had pointed him out as the only one. Blacks in the fashion industry have spoken of Talley with varying degrees of reverence, envy, and mistrust (which is how non-blacks in the fashion industry have spoken of him as well). One black American designer has called André Leon Talley "a fool. He'll only help those kids—designers like Galliano—if they've got social juice, if they're liked by socialites, the women who tell André what to do." Talley complains about people who underestimate the difficulty of his position. "It's exhausting to be the only one with the access, the influence, to prevent the children from looking like jigaboos in the magazine—when they do appear in the magazine. It's lonely."

TALLEY gave a luncheon in Paris a few years ago to celebrate the couture season's start. The people he welcomed to the luncheon—held in the Café Flore's private dining room, on the second floor—included Kenneth Jay Lane, a jewelry designer; Inès de la Fressange, a former Chanel model and spokesperson; Joe Eula, a fashion illustrator; Roxanne Lowitt, a photographer; and Maxime de La Falaise, a fashion doyenne, and her daughter, LouLou, the Yves Saint Laurent muse.

Following shirred eggs and many bottles of wine, Roxanne Lowitt, her black hair and black Chinese jacket a blur of organization, invited the guests to assemble in order to be photographed. LouLou de La Falaise removed an ancient huge round compact from her purse and began to powder her nose as her mother sat in readiness. Joe Eula ignored Lowitt and continued drinking. Talley got up from his seat to sit near Maxime de La Falaise, who had admired a large turquoise ring he wore.

"Look, LouLou!" Talley shouted. "The color of this ring is divine, no? Just like the stone you gave me!"

"What?" LouLou de La Falaise asked, barely disguising her boredom.

"This ring, child. Just like the stone you gave me, no?"

LouLou de La Falaise did not respond. She nodded toward Roxanne Lowitt, and Lowitt instructed her to stand behind Maxime de La Falaise and Talley. LouLou de La Falaise said, "I will stand there only if André tries not to look like such a nigger dandy."

Several people laughed, loudly. None laughed louder than André Leon Talley. But it seemed to me that a couple of things happened before he started laughing: he shuttered his eyes, his grin grew larger, and his back went rigid, as he saw his belief in the durability of glamour and allure shatter before him in a million glistening bits. Talley attempted to pick those pieces up. He sighed, then stood and said, "Come on, children. Let's *see* something. Let's visit the House of Galliano."

JOHN FARRIS

in the park after school with the girl & the boy
1994

Characters

GIRL
BOY
GOOD HUMOR MAN
STRANGER
JOGGERS
POLICEMEN
FRIENDS
VARIOUS OTHER ENTITIES

A PARK
THUMB PIANO ALTERNATES WITH M-80'S THROUGHOUT

GIRL: No. No.

BOY: Why?

GIRL: [GIGGLING] I don't know.

BOY: What's wrong, then?

GIRL: Stop.

BOY: Stop what?

GIRL: Look at her. If I dressed the way that girl does over there, I'd be a bourgeois too. See? Everybody's flirting. Even the birds. Funny how those pines make a Japanese landscape out of this place. I went to Japan once . . .

BOY: With who?

GIRL: With my parents! Who'd you think I went with?

BOY: Your boyfriend. That guy I saw you with the other day.

GIRL: What guy?

BOY: C'mon . . . You know what guy.

GIRL: C'mon . . . What do you mean, "C'mon!" What am I, a mind reader? And I don't remember seeing you the other day . . .

BOY: You didn't. But I saw you . . . Who was he?

GIRL: I'm with a lot of guys. I'm with you, right? It could have been anybody.

BOY: I'm anybody?

GIRL: You know what I mean.

BOY: No. Tell me . . .

GIRL: I mean I like being with guys more than with girls. You know what I mean.

BOY: No.

GIRL: Then—well—you're stupid.

BOY: Don't try to change the subject. Tell me! Why not?

GIRL: Why should I? You'll only use it against me.

BOY: I won't.

GIRL: You're already doing it!

BOY: You're crazy! How can I be using, "it" against you, when I don't even know what "it" is?

GIRL: You won't respect me . . . You'll tell everybody . . .

BOY: I will not!

GIRL: I'll bet it's a Smith and Wesson . . .

BOY: No, it's a Glock! Plastic!

GIRL: Ooh . . . Show it to me! I love plastic! Let me feel it! Show it
to me!

STRANGER RUNS BY. BOY SHOOTS STRANGER. STRANGER
FALLS.

STRANGER: [SCREAMING] HELP! Help!

BOY: See?

GIRL: Oh. Oh. Oh. It's so beautiful! Can I touch it!

STRANGER: HELP! Help!

BOY: Are you sure?

GIRL: Oh, please—I told you—I just love it.

BOY: Well, okay. Just me, right?

GIRL: I swear. I swear to god. Only with you.

BOY SHOWS PISTOL TO GIRL

STRANGER: Help!

GIRL: [FONDLING PISTOL] Ooh. I love it. What's your name?

BOY: Soldier.

GIRL: That's a nice name—Soldier. Say, where'd you get a name like
that?

BOY: In the war. It just came to me.

GIRL: Gee, it does have sort of—you know—a nice ring to it. You
know what? I think I want a name like that. I think I would die
for a name like that. That's a name to die for. Soldier. Oh, soldier.

STRANGER: Help, please!

GIRL: Soldier. Soldier. Will you give me a name like that—will you?

BOY: I don't know—I'm young, yet. But—but what's your name
now?

GIRL: Is that important? Why?

BOY: Tell me.

GIRL: Oh, alright. It's Piece. No Piece. My Father wanted to name me Any, but my mother said, No. Mother got her way. She usually does.

BOY: Mine, too . . . My father used to beat her but now that she has one of these . . . [HOLDING UP PISTOL]

GIRL: It's sooo beautiful . . . Do you have a silencer? Let me see it again.

BOY: Of course I do . . . I was born in N.Y.

GIRL: We were born in Kansas. My brother doesn't have one.

BOY SHOWS HER SILENCER, FITS IT TO PISTOL.

STRANGER: Help! Somebody please help me! Police!

BOY AIMS PISTOL AT STRANGER.

GIRL: Oh, please, why don't you let me do it?

BOY: Are you sure you're ready? Do you want to?

GIRL: Oh, yes, Soldier—more than anything else in the world!

STRANGER: HELP! Help!

BOY: Don't you think you should wait?

GIRL: Why?

BOY: Why—I don't know—well, because you're a woman. Shouldn't you—

GIRL: Hey—talk about your double standards! I should wait just because I'm a woman? No, I am a woman—that's why I want it now.

BOY: [TEASING] Really—do you want it, really? [WAVING PISTOL. IT IS JUST OUT OF REACH.]

GIRL: Oh, you—why are you so macho? I thought you might be different. Just a bit. [MEASURING WITH THUMB AND FOREFINGER] But you're just like everybody else.

BOY: That's me.

STRANGER: Help me! Help me!

GIRL: You sure are. Give it to me!

SHE LUNGES FOR PISTOL. THEY STRUGGLE. PISTOL GOES OFF. BOY GOES LIMP.

GIRL: [AFTER A MOMENT] Soldier! Soldier? [SHAKING HIM] Oh! He's dead . . . It's got to be up to me now.

GIRL WALKS OVER TO STRANGER

STRANGER: No! No!

GIRL SHOOTS STRANGER

GIRL: Somebody's got to do it . . .

GOOD HUMOR MAN ENTERS RINGING BELL AND PUSHING CART

GIRL: Good Humor Man! Say—Good Humor Man! Give me an ice cream bar!

GHM: Don't have any ice cream.

GIRL: No ice cream! What is this? What do you have in there?

GHM: Fish. I have fish.

GIRL: Fish?

GHM: Fish.

GIRL: Fish? You know, it occurs to me I haven't seen one of those in a long time!

GHM: That's because I have them all in here. [PATTING CART]

GIRL: Chocolate?

GHM: Everything. I have everything. One chocolate coming up. [OFFERS GIRL CHOCOLATE FISH] That will be three clams.

GIRL: Clams? I don't have any clams. How about three dollars?

GHM: Dollars? Dollars are not good. They look sick. Weak. Their eyes are not good. If you look carefully, their eyes are all weak.

GIRL: Weak, weak, weak. I suppose that might be true. I just don't have any clams on me right now.

GHM: That's too bad. The fish is good. Clams are good.

GIRL: I'm sorry. I don't have any clams.

GHM: That's because I have them all. Right here. [PATS FREEZER]

GIRL: Well, what do you need with mine?

GHM: You don't have any.

GIRL: [WAVING PISTOL AT GHM] What do you need with them?

GHM: Time. I'm trying to buy time! Obviously.

GIRL: What's it worth to you?

GHM: One clam.

GIRL: One? It might as well be ten thousand.

GHM: One. I already have a Jaguar. It's a wreck.

GIRL: [LEVELING THE PISTOL] Give me the clam.

GHM: Wait. Do you—

GIRL: [IMPATIENTLY] Give me the clam!

GHM: You can wait—it's I that haven't the time. Do you swear to take this clam—

GIRL: Give it to me! [HOLDING OUT A HAND]

GHM: One clam coming up! [SLAPS CLAM INTO HER HAND]

GIRL: Okay, now give me another!

GHM: What?

GIRL: I said, give me another . . . NOW!

GHM: Do you mean another? I can't. That one was the very last clam in the clam bed. You have all the clams now.

GIRL: Every one?

GHM: Every one. You know, suddenly, clams don't matter so much anymore . . .

GIRL: And I've got it. I've got it! Wait. Clams are bivalves. Where there is one, there will soon be two!

GHM: Screw it!

GIRL: Why are you in such a bad humor? You're the Good Humor Man! You should make me laugh.

GHM: I got to make a living!

GIRL: I want ice cream!

GHM: Go fish! Chocolate! Look, it's melted. Too late! I'm all in.

GIRL: Strawberry?

GHM: I'm all out.

GIRL GOES OVER TO BOY. KICKS BOY.

GIRL: [TO BOY] Can't you get up? [TO GHM] He's dead. It was an accident.

SHOTS RING OUT OFFSTAGE. COUPLE STAGGERS ONSTAGE, DIE.

GIRL: [TO GHM] How about vanilla?

GHM: That will cost you one bean.

THREE SISTERS ENTER, DRESSED IN PINAFORES, GIGGLING.

GIRL: [TO SISTERS] You're so silly—will you ever stop being so silly?

SISTERS: [TOGETHER] We're girls. We have to be silly. [THEY GIGGLE]

GIRL SHOOTS THREE SISTERS. THEY FALL, SHRIEKING.

GIRL: [TO NO ONE IN PARTICULAR] They were just silly! It was an accident . . .

GHM PATS FREEZER. GIRL HOPS ON. THEY GO AROUND AND AROUND IN A CIRCLE.

GIRL: [AFTER A COUPLE OF TIMES AROUND] There are so many fences . . .

GHM: There have always been fences—real or imagined . . .

GIRL: [DECLAIMING] Give me liberty or give us death! I'm hungry . . . Give me a fish.

GHM: Nothing is free. Not even where the buffalo roam. There is at least the cost of labor, and I am always a specialist.

GIRL: Now!

GHM: [GOES INTO THE FREEZER. FEELS AROUND. LOOKS] Oops! Would you believe—no vanilla? Well . . . I could have sworn—[ACCUSATORY] What do you know about this?

SIREN SOUNDS, AMBULANCE, FIRE ENGINE, MORE GUN-SHOTS. RAP SONGS FROM DIFFERENT SOURCES PLAYED AT DIFFERENT INTERVALS. A JAGGED RONDO.

GIRL: What are you going to do?

GHM: I have an idea . . . [REMOVES FISHING TACKLE FROM A JACKET POCKET] You'll have to move over.

GIRL SHIFTS. GOOD HUMOR MAN SITS BESIDE HER, FEELING IN HIS POCKETS.

GHM: No. There are no worms . . . [SHRUGS] Eh? [DROPS A LINE INTO FREEZER] Maybe. [EXAMINES LINE] Nope!

GIRL: I love that song, don't you?

GHM: I can't hear you. Wait. [GRABS AT AIR] There. Flies are good. [ATTACHES FLY TO HOOK. LOWERS LINE INTO FREEZER]

GIRL: Oh, isn't it romantic?

GHM: Shhh!

GIRL: Hey! Don't shush me!

GHM: You're going to scare the fish. Shut up and steer north.

GIRL: North?

GHM: North. By Northwest.

GIRL: East.

GHM: To where?

GIRL: South.

GHM: By what?

GIRL: God!

GHM: By god!

GIRL: That's a good line.

GHM: What are you doing?

GIRL: Bending.

GHM: What now?

GIRL: Your ear.

GHM: You're giving me the bends.

GIRL: Help! He's around the bend! Steady matey. Steady. All roads lead to the cooler.

GHM: Do you see anything?

GIRL: It's dark.

GHM: There must be stars!

GIRL: I can't see them.

GHM: I'm exhausted. Wait.

GIRL: Wait for what?

GHM: Wait for the wagons.

GIRL: Oh, you're good. Wait for the wagons?

GHM: [PULLING AT LINE, TESTS IT] Here come the wagons.

GIRL: Tongue. Some tongue.

GHM: Wagging.

GIRL: Waggin'.

GHM: Somebody's talking about us.

GIRL: Talking about us? Who?

GHM: Let that be a lesson to you.

GIRL: Wait.

GHM: Wait for what? Wait broke the wagon.

GIRL: I'm broke.

GHM: I don't know matey. Looks to me like it might be your tail. Where's the tail? Where is it!

GIRL: It was an accident.

GHM: Indeed.

GIRL: The deed.

GHM: Indeed.

GIRL: It was a whale of a tale.

GHM: A wail?

GIRL: A low wail . . .

GIRL SOBS.

GHM: I'm going to whale the tar out of you . . . Shut up.

GIRL: [LAUGHS. WAVES PISTOL DRUNKENLY] Oh, yeah?

GHM: Wait! It's just a line. [EXAMINES LINE] Do you like me? Do
   you like me, you li'l booger? Do you like my line?

GIRL: What line?

GHM: What ho'?

GIRL: What ho'? Give me some slack.

GHM: I'm giving you a line . . .

GIRL: What's my line?

GHM: A-hunting we will go, a-hunting we will go, hi-ho, the dairy-
   o, a-hunting we will go!!

GIRL: I'm hungry. I'm wailing.

GHM: Wait. Don't wail so loudly. You'll scare something.

GIRL: Hopefully. I'll scare something up . . .

GHM: Go fish.

GIRL: Fish are so dear . . .

GHM: Dear fish.

GIRL: Dear deer . . .

GHM: Allez, move!

GIRL: I'm whipped.

GHM: Do you see anything?

GIRL: [PEERING INTO FREEZER] Nothing. [CROSSING HER
   ARMS] I'm cold.

GHM: Sometimes. Sometimes you are!

GIRL: [GLARES MENACINGLY] Sometimes you need to eat!

GHM: Wait! Don't do anything rash. [STANDING UP ON FREEZER. GOOD HUMOR MAN DROPS HIS PANTS, SQUATS OVER OPENING, GRUNTING] Nope! Nothing . . .

GIRL: Something stinks . . .

GHM: Your stinking ass. You speak rashly, you scurvy rat.

GIRL: My teeth are falling out.

GHM: We're being knocked out. [STRAINS] Wait. Let's see. [PEERS INTO OPENING] Nope. Nothing.

GIRL KICKS HIM IN THE ASS. GOOD HUMOR MAN FALLS, GETS UP, PULLS HIS PANTS UP, GRABS CART, PUSHES IT IN CIRCLES. THEY GO AROUND A COUPLE OF TIMES. GIRL BUMPS INTO HIM, DROPS PISTOL.

GHM: Wait! Stop!

GIRL FREEZES.

GHM: Do you know what this is? This is a disaster! [LUNGES FOR PISTOL. GRABS IT. GROWLS LIKE LONG JOHN SILVER] Now, me matey! We'll see what this here is all about. Won't we . . .?

JOGGER RUNS BY. GOOD HUMOR MAN SHOOTS JOGGER. JOGGER FALLS.

GHM: You see when I make a play for you, you make the wrong move, you could die. Just like that. [WAVES PISTOL]

GIRL: Nothing's changed.

GHM: Nothing ever changes. Names, dates, places, modes of technology. The wind.

GIRL: You're farting.

GHM: That's something. Let's see. [TESTING LINE] Ahh! [PULLS IT UP, REMOVES FLY, PRESENTS IT TO GIRL, TRIUMPHANT]

GIRL: It's the fly!

JOGGER: Help! Help me!

GIRL: [EATING FLY] Good Humor Man, let me do it, please. Let me help that person.

GOOD HUMOR MAN SHOOTS JOGGER. JOGGER DIES.

GHM: Beggar! Plagiarist!

GIRL: It's the code of the West!

GHM: East!

GIRL: North!

GHM: South!

GIRL: Mideast!

GHM: Midwest!

GIRL: Blow wind!

GHM: Softly.

GIRL: Quietly . . .

GHM: As a morning sunrise.

GIRL: Good Humor Man, where are we going?

GHM: That's "captain" to you. Captain Good Humor Man.

GIRL: "Captain" to me, where are we going?

GHM: [GROWLING] In strictly nautical terms, nowhere. We're going nowhere . . .

GIRL: Going with the flow. Drifting . . .

GHM: On a reed . . .

CHARLIE PARKER'S "DRIFTING ON A REED" IS HEARD FROM OFFSTAGE.

GHM: Wait! Shut up!

MUSIC STOPS.

GIRL: What's that?

GHM: I don't hear anything . . . What ship is this?

GIRL: Captain—it's the Bull Rush . . .

GHM: How many men are we?

GIRL: Well, sir, captain, sir . . . there is just you and me . . . unless you count those poor souls over there . . .

GHM: They're dead. They are our ancestors now.

GIRL: Lovers. Brothers. Sisters. Fathers. Mothers.

GHM: Our cousins . . . Our aunts and uncles . . .

GIRL: Great people. Saints . . .

GHM: Ground down. Crushed.

GIRL: At sea . . . maybe there's something to eat . . .

GHM: I wouldn't count on it. Those people are rotten. Rotten, I tell you. Pushovers. Push 'em over.

GIRL: They'll pop up, maybe.

GHM: We'll see. I wouldn't count on it . . .

GIRL: Let's save our strength . . .

GHM: I see. S.O.S.

GIRL: Is that Trinidad?

GHM: [PEERING INTO OPENING] Where? What? I don't see anything. Do you?

GIRL: That light over there with those clouds hovering over it.

GHM: That mountain over there that appears to be a mountain to my sore eyes? No—that's China. Where the magnificent khans play . . .

GIRL: We're on the road to Mandalay!

GHM: Flying fishes! Have you ever seen such a thing? I think we're onto something. What do you think?

GIRL: I think we're Yankees!

GHM: We're Dodgers!

GIRL: [TO THE HEAP OF BODIES] You're Indians. Do you want to play a game? We'll get our hits in and you run around. Okay?

GHM: The object of the game is to steal home.

GIRL: He says his name is Guacanagari, Captain!

GHM: That's funny . . . That's not a name. He doesn't know his own name . . . We'll have to give him one . . . It should be Con. Surname—Vict. Hmm . . . [PEERS INTO OPENING] Con Vict. I think we're getting somewhere.

GIRL: At last! Do you have any corn? I'm a commodities man.

GHM: Look here, my fine feather of a friend. I'm the Good Humor Man. I'm a Christian. Do you have any gold, Gua-Gua . . . I can't even pronounce it . . . It makes me choke. I'll make a report . . . Killed while trying to escape.

GIRL: Good Humor Man—! Let me do it!

GHM: [TURNS, LEVELING PISTOL AT HER] Avast, there, woman!

GIRL: [TO BODIES] Got any berries? [GOES TO BOY] Soldier? Nope. Nothing. He's dead . . . It was an accident. It was not a freak of nature. It was our destiny. We were going to get married. Four score and twenty years ago, I think that was it.

GHM: He was a disaster! [SHOOTS BOY AGAIN] Oh, god. What a waste of ammunition! We'll have to save our shots . . .

GIRL: S. O. S.

GHM: Steady, woman! Don't show any fear—Steady!

GIRL: I need some coffee.

GHM: Role call. How would you like your orange juice?

GIRL: In the can.

GHM: White bread?

GIRL: Jeffrey Dahmer . . .

GHM: David Rabinowitz.

GIRL: Oliver North.

GHM: I have to tell you something . . . a confession. This is not china.

GIRL: What is it?

GHM: It's porcelain laced with lead. Sugar?

GIRL: Please.

GHM: That will be one clam.

GIRL: I don't have any clams . . . I ate it.

JOGGERS RUN BY. GOOD HUMOR MAN SHOOTS THEM. THEY FALL.

GHM: [PEERING INTO THE OPENING] Nothing's real. It's all symbolic . . . Red, white, and blue.

COPS ENTER, RUNNING.

COP: What's fishy now?

GHM, GIRL: [TOGETHER] Nothing, officer!

COP: I need a report!

GHM: The days are getting shorter . . .

GIRL: Don't say that!

GHM: That's right! I'm not dead yet. Am I . . .? [SHOOTS COPS]
There. How's that for a report. That should get you a raise.

GIRL: Wait, what's that?

GHM: Sounds like shooting.

GIRL: What for?

GHM: Sounds like it's coming from that house over there.

GIRL: That's a nice one.

GHM: Somebody's already took a shot at it. It's not on the map. It's
out of the park. You'll have to aim for something else.

GIRL: Can you push for a while?

GHM: Look, it's gotten to where you'll have to push your own load.
At your age, you should be comfortable with mine too. You should
also know that there is no such thing as a free ride.

GIRL: Don't try to give me that. You can't give me that anymore.

GHM: That's what I'm saying. Keep pushing.

GIRL: You have pushed me to my limits.

GHM: No limits I can see. None. We must push for the frontiers of
space.

GIRL: Out of uniform, you look like a pirate.

GHM: It ain't softball.

GIRL: I want to play. Give me a shot.

GHM: I've been having a ball by myself.

GIRL: You've got all the balls. I can see that.

GHM: You've got some smart ass.

GIRL: Are we getting anywhere?

GHM: I'm getting off.

GIRL: We can get on together.

GHM: Get on with you. You're pulling my leg.

GHM: Whatever you put out is what you get in.

GIRL: We're going in circles.

GHM: I think we're getting somewhere. Circle the wagons.

GIRL: It's your shot. Aim anywhere. Try where that house was.

GHM: That's nothing.

GIRL: I've been there. I think when I was very young.

TWO WELL-DRESSED MEN, LATE THIRTIES, SITTING ON A BENCH. THEY ARE "FRIENDS."

1ST FR: I would like to have you over for tripes.

2ND FR: Tripe?

1ST FR: Tripes. We call it—them—"tripes"! At least, my wife does. She's not of our persuasion.

2ND FR: With an "s"?

1ST FR: What an "s." The most elegant I've ever seen. That's why she's the wife. And guess where I ran into her.

2ND FR: Where?

1ST FR: At an intersection. I almost tore her fender off. The door. She survived. It wasn't anybody's fault. We both had insurance—I figured, hey—what the hell! I tell you I caught myself a beauty. A real shiner. It was all the way out to here! That was when I found out about that "s." It was the coolest, most level-headed thing I have ever done. Dead on. Pretty much the way I ran into you. Only with a car.

2ND FR: More liability.

1ST FR: You got that right. The deductible was not negligible. But you know what—nothing is an accident. With one fell stroke of the pen I acquired myself quite some "s."

2ND FR: Capital! Capital!

1ST FR: Not in this case. Small. A career.

2ND FR: I see. As you must know, I love tripe. Even with an "s" as
    you so elegantly put it.

1ST FR: Jowls too! And trotters!

2ND FR: Stop it. You make me want to roll my eyes.

1ST FR: You just go right ahead. You remember that old saying,
    don't you?

2ND FR,
1ST FR: [TOGETHER, LIKE A RAP SONG] Yo' eyes may shine.
    Yo' teeth may grit, but none o' dese trotters shall you get!

LOOKING AROUND GUILTILY AND SEEING NO ONE
THEY LAUGH UPROARIOUSLY, SLAPPING PALMS AND
THIGHS.

2ND FR: We'll I'll be a monkey's uncle. You. You haven't forgotten
    . . . You haven't forgotten! After all these years.

1ST FR: You tell me. How could I? How could I? Particularly in this
    business, and that's conventional wisdom.

2ND FR: Why yes, but should I take that literally?

1ST FR: Not at all.

2ND FR: Strictly business.

1ST FR: You are a friend. You are a dear friend and that is a grand
    idea, isn't it? It's so comforting we bumped into each other. You
    are the very first person I thought of. [STARTLED] Did you hear
    that?

2ND FR: What?

1ST FR: That noise. It sounded like a shot.

2ND FR: A shot? No, no. I can't say that I did.

1ST FR: [LISTENING] Hey, that was another!

2ND FR: Really? Shots? Are you sure? [LOOKING AROUND, HALF CROUCHING]

1ST FR: My god—it sounds like a war!

2ND FR: [STILL CROUCHING] That's funny. I can't hear a thing.

1ST FR: It's funny how we perceive things as existing or not existing according to our sensibilities.

2ND FR: Some things have to be seen to be believed.

GIRL ENTERS FOLLOWED BY GOOD HUMOR MAN.

2ND FR: Oh good. There's the Good Humor man. I'd like some. Wouldn't you?

GOOD HUMOR MAN SHOOTS 2ND FRIEND. 2ND FRIEND SLUMPS, DEAD. FIRST FRIEND STARES IN HORROR.

1ST FR: My god, you shot my friend! I think you killed him! Who are you? What did you do that for? Look, don't you hurt me. I can give you money. Listen, don't shoot—see—my wallet—if that's not enough, we can go to the cash machine. This just might be your lucky day. I'm a wealthy man. I can give you as much as you like, but you'll have to take me—see—it's a special machine with video imaging. I swear!

GIRL: [TO GOOD HUMOR MAN] My! He sure can talk, can't he? Knows all the right sounds to make. I don't understand. I want ice cream, that's all. Do you have any of that?

1ST FR: But your friend there—he is your friend—isn't he—doesn't he—if he doesn't, I can get you some—how about a sundae— sundae hell—a frappé, just don't shoot!

GHM: You see you are addressing the wrong person. As you can see, I am the one with the gun . . . and I don't want ice cream.

1ST FR: What—do you want? I can get—you anything you want!

GHM: It's not enough. [RAISES PISTOL]

1ST FR: Stop—Stop—Why are you doing this?

GHM: [SHOOTS] I do it because I can.

FIRST FRIEND DIES.

GIRL: Why'd you do that? He was going to get ice cream.

GHM: [HOPPING ONTO CART] Shut up. Just shut up. Stop whining and push.

BLACK

ELIZABETH ALEXANDER

talk radio, d.c.
1996

Leave fatback and a copper penny
on a wound 'til it draw out the poison,
'til the penny turn green.

Tobacco's what works on a bee-sting,
but for poison ivy—I'm serious, now—
catch your first morning urine in your hands
and splash it on that rash.

When they had the diptheria epidemic
I was burning up with fever, burning and burning.
When the doctor left the house, my grandmother
snuck in the back door with a croaker sack of mackerel.
She wrapped me all up in that salt mackerel.
The next morning, my fever had broke
and the fish was all cooked.

ERIKA ELLIS

from good fences
1999

1988: Blackflight

". . ."

". . ."

". . . man oh man oh man . . ."

". . ."

"Damn. That geechee bitch you was bonin' befo' musta put a curse on your ass, Spade my man."

"Sheeet."

"I feel for you, my brother, but thank GAWD I'm not in your shoes. Your shit is in the pan, about to get deep-fried."

"Give me some dap on that one, my brother." Lloyd, from Idaho, got up off the bed and did a slow pimp across the area rug and banged fists with George, from Silver Springs. The air was thick with soul. Tommytwo ground his teeth. He was like, not in the mood.

"He be fucked."

"His ass be grass."

Tommytwo sure wished they'd all shut the hell up. He'd come to these guys for maybe some practical advice, maybe a little bit of sympathy, not for Shaft and Blackula to remind him that he'd flushed his life down the toilet.

"Daaaamn!" Clyde from down the hall erupted, fingers snapping so hard as he slid into the room that he could have been flicking off red ants. Tommytwo could not believe his luck. First he gets somebody pregnant—pregnant! pregnant!—and then he ends up in here with this bunch of lunchboxes when what he needed was some privacy and a Ginzu knife.

Oh God—was Dad right? Always remove yourself from a bad situation, his dad had been urging him each and every time they spoke for the past three years. Transfer. Anyplace but Morehouse, anywhere but Atlanta. He wondered what Dad would say when he found out Tommytwo was an unwed father. Dad had sworn this place would bring out the nigger in him.

"Yo, nigga, you sure she said anti-abortion?"

"Twice."

As far as Tommytwo was concerned, pregnancy was the creature from the black lagoon. When she said the word . . . oy-yoy-yoy. It came at him like a meat cleaver. PRREEGGNNNAAANNNTT, there it still was, echoing in his hollow head. Pregnant, she'd snapped at him again when he just stood there trying to figure out what in the heck a guy was supposed to say.

Woman, don't start trippin' out on me, he'd snapped at her, out of the blue. About the last muhfucka I need is a baby. He'd said that, in the same Superfly voice he used with the guys. To LaKisha, who knew him, the real him. She'd smacked him with her book bag, out in the middle of the quad, then run away.

If there was any slight silver lining to this fiasco, it was that now everyone on campus would know for sure that Tommytwo was nobody's piece of Spam. Oh yeah, he knew other guys had their doubts about him. He hadn't known how to play bidwist freshman year, he'd thought Don Cornelius was a Spanish explorer. But he had his own doubts about some of them. He'd seen George at Lenox Mall playing video games with white dudes in Emory sweatshirts. And he'd heard plenty of guys in bio asking for recommendations, diction white as milk. He'd heard Pinky in lab one afternoon answering to the name Burgess like a fucking puppy. Burgess. If there ever was a guy with a name whiter than Burgess would he speak now or forever hold his peace. Oh boy. Oh boy boy boy. Tommytwo was screwed.

"Yo ass be grass, my brother."

"Yo, like, could you guys please chill."

"All I was saying was you Fucked, my brother. With a capital *F*."

Tommytwo stuffed his fists into his ears and hummed "The Star-Spangled Banner." Oh yeah, and his mom, oh man. His mom was going to keel. As for his dad, being at Morehouse was bad enough, let alone getting some girl pregnant. Let alone getting some girl named LaKisha pregnant. LaKisha was different, the real deal. She was from Detroit, down and dirty, knew guys who'd taken heroin, had gone out with a guy who'd stabbed his cousin.

"She probably planned it, yo ass ax me. Probably took her a needle and poked a hole in the rubber, you ax me. Ax her before you go marryin' her, man, just ax her." Clyde, from Alaska, was the Christopher Columbus of discovering words in black English, but had never heard of overkill.

"Marry?! Nigger, you need to trip your black ass out the window. What law says brotherman got to go that far?"

"Word! Babycake come from the screets. Her mama be pleased as punch she found a college nigga to knock her ass up."

"I said chill," said Tommytwo. There was no rubber. Under all the gold jewelry, LaKisha was an old-fashioned girl. She didn't believe in modern technology separating her Esmerelda from his Big Daddy. That was what she called it. Big Daddy. Even in front of her girlfriends.

She was one of a kind, as far as Spelman went. Your typical Spelman girl would let a guy spend his last ten bucks on a plate of spaghetti marinara, then go bounding back inside her dorm like a kangaroo, forget the kiss. Not LaKisha. She'd cook a guy a meal on a hotplate. She carried herself like Miss Universe, and he'd figured she was safe.

"How she be lookin', ya'll?"

"She fine. Spader like 'em black but fine."

"Long hair?"

"Hell naw. To the neck. Baby got a body though."

"Today she got a body. Six months from now she'll be one big fat stank ho talkin' bout where the pickles—"

"I said chill!" These assnoses could talk trash all they wanted, but they better keep LaKisha out of it, period. If they'd seen her expression, talking about going to Detroit all by herself to raise the ba . . . the ba . . . the baby. He'd taken in about half the words she'd said out there in the quad, something about having the kid underwater in a birthing pool, teaching it how to swim from day one like a tadpole. LaKisha loved the ocean. Forced him to watch *Miami Vice* on Friday nights. Popped popcorn on the hotplate. Giggled every time the tinfoil blew up like a balloon. Son, remove yourself from bad situations. Screw you, Dad. I love her.

"Yo, hand me the phone."

The guys shouted Tommytwo down. Don't call her, was he out of his mind, leave the bitch be, wait her ass out. It was beginning to get on his nerves. It was his life, his choice.

"Hands me the phone, Pinky bro. I needs to calls my girl, make sure is she be doing okay." His soul train had jumped track, the words were falling off his tongue mangled, but it was okay for once. He loved LaKisha! They were going to have a baby! Cigars, what he needed was cigars.

PERCIVAL EVERETT

from erasure
2001

Story idea—a man marries a woman whose name is the same as that of his first wife. One night while making love he says her name and the woman accuses him of calling out the name of his first wife. Of course he in fact has called out the name of his first wife, but also he has called out his present wife's name. He tells her that he was not thinking of his first wife, but she says she knows what she heard.

I was driving up Highway 395 on my way to fish the South Fork of the Kern. At the junction of 178 and 395 I stopped for a bite. It was summer and dusk was coming on and so it was late enough and still eerie enough for the weirdos to be out. I sat in a booth and was called "sugar" by the middle-aged waitress while a couple of guys spoke French to each other in the booth behind me. When traveling, it is best to eat without regard to health or one might not eat at all. I was carving into what was called a chicken fried steak and was unable to detect chicken or steak, but it was clear that it was indeed fried, when a couple of stringy, gimme-capped, inbred bohunks came noisily into the restaurant. Their keen hearing, though it did not allow them to know it was French, picked up the annoying cadence of a "fern" language. They sat at the counter and cast more than a few glances toward the French-speaking men, until they could take it no longer and walked over to them.

"You boys funny?" The skinnier and taller of the two asked.

"Funny?" one of the Frenchmen asked.

"You know, queers," from the second long-fingernailed, backwoods, walking petri dish.

"Ah, queers," the Frenchman said. "Oui."

"Oui," from bumpkin number one, who looked at his buddy and shared a laugh. "Come on outside so we can kick your ass."

"I don't understand," the second Frenchman said.

Bumpkin two must have stepped or leaned closer. I registered the alarmed expression on the face of the waitress, who then called out that she didn't want any trouble.

"Outside, faggots. You ain't chickens, are you? It's two against two. That's fair."

"Actually, it's two against three," I said. I put the bite that was on my fork into my mouth.

Bumpkin one stepped over to look at me, then laughed to his pal, "I think we got the nigger riled."

I chewed my food, trying to remember all the posturing I had learned as an undersized teenager.

"You a faggot, too?" he asked.

I pointed to the fact that I was chewing. This confused him slightly and I could see for a split second his fear. "I might be," I said.

"So, you want to fight, too."

I didn't want to fight, but the fact of the matter was that I was already fighting. I said, and still I am proud of it, "Okay, if we're going to do this, let's do it. Just remember that this is one of the more important decisions you will ever make."

I'd overshot my mark. His fear grew and turned into rage and he hopped back and yelled for me to get up. I was afraid now that I might really have to do something I didn't do very well, throw punches. I stood and though I wasn't a skinny wire, I was not much larger than either of them. The second bumpkin yelled for the gay men to get up, too.

They did and I wished I'd had a camera to capture the expressions of those two provincial slugs. The Frenchmen were huge, six-eight and better, and healthy looking. The rubes stumbled over themselves backing away, then scrambled out of the diner.

I was laughing when the men asked me to join them, not at the spectacle of the rednecks running out, but at my own nerve and audacity, to presume that they needed my help.

C'est plus qu'un crime, c'est une faute.

from john henry days
2001

alphonse miggs lies on his bed half-naked, contemplating the fissures of a mothball. His striped boxer shorts almost reach his knees, the tops of his socks almost reach his knees, out of his T-shirt extrude soft fishbelly arms. He hasn't removed his shoes yet. Lying on the bed with his shoes on is something he would never do at home, not even on the pullout sofa in the basement where he sleeps these days, and is a luxury. He is in room 12 of the Talcott Motor Lodge, in a museum of previous guests' scratches and gouges, grateful to have a place to call his own.

The mothball's surface is too pocked and imperfect to roll away.

Rarely in his recent memory has he been as happy as when he unpacked his clothes. In any drawer he pleased. He had saved this task (extra-special treat) for after the banquet. In the top drawer Alphonse delicately placed his underwear and socks, in the second his shirts, and in the last his pants. One, two, three. Every item of clothing level in his palm as if he were handling packages of moody nitroglycerine. In the ledge above the sink he placed his travel kit just so. Eleanor was not there to stop or move his placements and each time his hand departed one of his possessions he felt a blush of freedom. A bona fide sensation.

Putting clothes in any old drawer feels like a political act because recently in the Miggses' household, 1244 Violet Lane, there has unfolded a cold war over spaces. It happens in every household of course, someone picks out a favorite chair or side of the couch; over time someone comes to a choice, or all at once—on the first day the new chair arrives in the house and is claimed. In Alphonse's home the usual pattern of domestic boundary erection has attained the aspect of warfare, with the attendant gamesmanship of posturing, deployment, arcane strategy. Not to mention hurt feelings on both sides.

Alphonse and Eleanor married for all the usual reasons: fear of death, fear of being alone, the compulsion to repeat the mistakes and debacles of their parents' marriage. It was a small ceremony; Eleanor's six-year-old niece caught the bouquet, leading to jokes at the expense of Eleanor's unmarried older sister, whom everybody pretended was not a lesbian. On the honeymoon cruise they made brief love several times, with the lights on for the first time ever, as there was no one who could see them except whatever beings lived in the darkness outside the porthole. Eventually they bought a home.

The prefabricated house at 1244 Violet Lane came equipped in its natural state with nooks and cubbies. These were areas in rooms that would offend the eye if not occupied by a thing or object. That corner in the living room. That somehow frightening blank spot in the foyer. The mantel, with its unbroken plane that spoke of manifest destiny. These were areas that needed to be filled or else something else might roost there that was unwanted, a negative feeling or perception. A great flood of refugees from knickknackland set up lean-tos where appropriate, dispossessed tchotchkes earned citizenship. Artificial flowers insinuated into the small nook between the bay windows in the dining room and doilies accepted their missions with a grim certitude that belied their frilly edges. Alphonse's second-place trophy from his senior year achievement in the hundred-yard dash posed in the foyer on a three-legged table whose radius forbid objects larger than single-flower vases or small pictures, perfect for the submajestic dimensions of the die-cast second-place trophy. Whether the architects of the house placed these nooks out of a farsighted sense of need or mere perversity is beyond telling, but Alphonse and Eleanor passed the test with flying colors and swiftly the house looked lived in. Together they chose where things went.

A routine of married life settled in. For the first couple of years Alphonse spent an inordinate amount of time looking at his hands. Lifelines and their mysteries crisscrossed and terminated in his palms. His cuticles obtained nicks and imperfections that healed over time and he observed the process. Alphonse tried to read something there, a clue or two. He took this preoccupation as a symptom of incompleteness, despite what surface appearances told him. He had a good job, for example; middle management was only a better tie away. Around him the house was in great shape, as they outgrew the wisdom of the home decorating magazines. Sometimes they entertained other married couples of their acquaintance for dinner to discuss the issues of the day. But still. Then one afternoon, in his doctor's office as he waited for his annual physical, Alphonse discovered an article about hobbies. It caught his eye. The article elaborated about a psychological need common to most folks, a hole that needs filling. Stamp collecting, the article suggested, was a wholesome interest amenable to the beginner but equally rewarding for the seasoned collector. He showed the article to Eleanor, who nodded, and he sent away for a starter kit from one of the philately companies recommended in the article.

The basement proved perfect for this new interest. The basement was great for storage and one day would make a fine barracks for the washer and dryer, but in the early period of their marriage served only as the home of the fuse box, oft-worshiped during hurricane season. Then the stamps arrived. He scraped a table down the stairs, untangled an extension cord to power the lamp and created a space for himself not far from the water heater. Above him spiders wove secretions into traps amid a maze of bent copper tubing. The basement became a place that was completely his, different from the communal nooks and cabinets and drawers upstairs, the spaces that testified to their shared effort to make a home together. They agreed where to put the vase, the porcelain unicorn, together they ratified the placement of the wedding picture, but the basement was his. An inequity blossomed. It was a full third of the house's cubic space and he had claimed it. It was a place to masturbate and think about the world and mount his stamps, glory over his collection of railroad stamps.

Stamps like to be touched in a certain way. Soak them until they are wet to separate them from envelopes, and when they are wet enough they have to be handled just so. With tongs. It is his hobby. And so it went on for years. She never went down there. And then Eleanor retaliated. It took years but it happened.

With Eleanor lately there has been this flurry of clubs. It is almost as if he looked up one day and she'd gone through the Yellow Pages or ripped off every contact number from every flyer in every laundromat in town. Or maybe one club leads to another club, a pyramid scheme of interest and hobby. She makes one friend and the friend is a clue to another friend in another club. "It's just something to pass the time," she says when he asks her to explain the newest prop in her repertoire, the next alien thing she has brought into the house, bylaws or instructional literature. When she says this she is returning his stamp excuse to him and it is not lost on either party.

She is on the steering committee of two maybe three charities now. The book club. Every month there's another discounted hardcover from the local big chain. He's never heard of the books before he takes them into his hands and reads the dust covers. They seem to be about women overcoming, or women suffering, and then there is a little note of triumph at the end. Eleanor affects a note of irritation whenever he asks a simple question about the books. Sometimes he'll be reading a philately magazine and will look up to see Eleanor squinting at him over the hardcover edge as if he lives in its pages. It seems the only time she cooks nowadays is to test out the storage capabilities of her latest acquisition from her plastics club. In this club the membership requirements are that you like to get together to trade plastic food storage devices. He opens the door after a long, a too long, day at work, to a smell fit for the kitchen of a really fancy restaurant, one they might visit on a special occasion, if they still celebrated their anniversary for example. But there will be nothing on the dining room table except the honed gleam of the wood polish. In the kitchen the grand repast is already interred in her plastic containers, in flat lozenges, in sleek cylinders, in deep rectangles with rounded corners. Half a liter, liter and two liter and in between. The tops are available in many different colors, everything stacks inside everything else conveniently. The plastic is opaque and he can barely make out the contents. He'll tilt one and watch a brown liquid collect in the bottom corner. Eleanor will be in the living room with a book while he inspects container after container. The things in the plastic containers are not leftovers in the strict sense for they have been prepared specifically for storage. She throws them out the next day in preparation for the next configuration of containers. Sometimes he'll happen into the kitchen during the cleaning ritual. Certain orange globules of grease resist the capabilities of the soft side of the sponge and force her to turn it over to the abrasive side. Then the plastic becomes clean.

The storage devices necessitated her membership in a recipe club so she could have novel foodstuffs with which to fill her containers, which in turn required the purchase of cookbooks. Exotic recipes from foreign lands necessitated the purchase of rare herbs, ingredients that would never be used again yet required still more storage. His cereal was exiled to a not as convenient cabinet, displaced by carmine dust (for color) and lime green relishes (for tangy aftertaste). He went downstairs one day and noticed his World War II spy novels, all twenty years' worth, in boxes on the floor of the basement; their homelands upstairs had been invaded by cookbooks.

His racing trophy was on the floor next to them; it had been displaced by a group photograph of the steering committee of the Clothes for Orphans fund-raising dinner. He has no idea where things he might need are stored these days. Scissors, duct tape, the menus of establishments that deliver food, they have been replaced by Eleanor's diverse materials and cannot be found. How could he not see it as revenge for the basement?

Perhaps they had had a decent conversation lately but about what he doesn't know.

Perhaps he'd feel better if she had bruises on the inside of her thighs or worked late at the office or constantly returned to him thin excuses, but instead it's these clubs. As a gesture—no, it was more than that it was an attempt at de-escalation—he said she could use his computer down in the basement, but Eleanor was adamant about getting her own. Instead she took him up on his other offer, made a decade and a half before, to use the guest room as her office, and in there she made a clubhouse for her clubs. Her new computer makes invitations and bulletins and flyers a snap. The new word processing programs make everyone into a desktop publisher. Slowly she mastered fonts. They had not used the pullout sofa in the guest room for years; she moved a desk in its place, and one of her club friends helped her move the sofa downstairs one afternoon. Now Alphonse sleeps there nights. They had long before grown bored with each other's bodies and laid off the sex thing. Some nights he comes out only for food.

The drawers in room 12 are uncontested and his.

He can hear periodic laughter from one of the rooms down the row. Probably those journalists. They have their fun and he has his. For about an hour now he has been staring at the mothball. The small moon on the bedside table. From a few feet away it looks smooth but the more he looks at it the more the imperfections become apparent. His eyes dip between granules and go as far into the thing as they can, then clamber on to the next ridge. He has decided to make the thing into his lucky charm. Certainly there is a reason he chose that suit as his last suit, and a reason the mothball decided to come along.

This night he saved a man's life. He was the first to recognize the symptoms of choking, drilled into him by years of staring at the walls of restaurants as he ate by himself, with his paper already read and still half a plate of his greasy meal left on the plate. At such moments there is little to read except choking prevention signs and the wretched faces of his fellow diners. Alphonse was the first to notice that the black man was choking.

Two years earlier he saved the life of a woman at The Chew Shack when she indulged too enthusiastically in a plate of all-you-can-eat shrimp. He knew what to do. But he found himself staring at the black man. It seemed as if every feature of the man's face, as it was manipulated and contorted by suffocation, became discrete and separate from the rest. His bowed left eyebrow one object, his twitching right nostril part of something else. Each of these things could be collected and put in a separate mount on its own page in one of his stamp volumes. A special edition series. In its special place on a basement shelf. It was only when he realized his indifference to whether the man lived or died that Alphonse jumped up to help. The man didn't say thanks, but given the excitement, Alphonse didn't blame him.

He props himself on his elbows, peering down the soft, foreign slope of his body, fixating on his knees and the slack skin congealed into those ugly lumps. Then he finally removes his shoes. The heels of his blue-toed socks are stiff with blood. He bought new shoes for the occasion and they break him in as much as he breaks them in. His heels are raw and torn and tarred with dried blood. He hasn't felt the pain because all he's felt since he arrived in Talcott is this feeling of inevitability.

WILLIE PERDOMO

should old shit be forgot
2003

Papo the Poet started kicking a
Poem while Dick Clark put the
City on the count

Once again we pledge down for
Whatever until the day we die
Love forever in one minute it takes
Sixty seconds to forget the one who
Left you waiting at the bus stop

And I was like:
All that shit you sayin'
Sounds good but let's
Talk about the thirty
Dollars you owe me

I hear you I hear you I hear
What you sayin'
We boys and we should
Be happy when big ass
Disco balls drop on
151 proof resolutions

Father Time says
He's only gonna smoke
On the weekends

New Year cornets
Are swept off the street
Like old friends

Champagne corks ricochet
Off ballroom walls

Roast pork burns while we
Puff and pass in project halls

Bullets kill El Barrio sky to
Celebrate holding it down
The same ole same ole shit we
Say every year
Fuck it
Pass that rum
It's cold out here
Who wants some?
You could say pleeze
You could freeze
Whatever
Happy New Years
Feliz Año Nuevo
I'm out here for a reason
Not the season
Should old shit be forgot
And all that good stuff
But I want my money
Before next year

black absurdity

t he funniest, and oftentimes the saddest, folks realize that if it weren't for absurdity, life wouldn't make any sense. Chester Himes was a man whose life was so full of rejection and sundry inexplicables that it took two four-hundred-page autobiographies to sort it all out. The first volume is called *The Quality of Hurt*, the second *My Life of Absurdity*, which begins: "Albert Camus once said that racism is absurd. Racism introduces absurdity into the human condition. Not only does racism express the absurdity of the racists, but it generates absurdity in the victims. And the absurdity of the victims intensifies the absurdity of the racists, ad infinitum. If one lives in a country where racism is held valid and practiced in all ways of life, eventually, no matter whether one is a racist or a victim, one comes to feel the absurdity of life."

If, like Himes, an American does come to feel the absurdity of life, it's a subject we dare not address. There are no statutes. No government proclamations have been issued demanding our silence. None need be when we censor ourselves. To identify anything in this country as absurd is to stand up at the wedding ceremony when the official asks for dissenters to speak now or forever hold their peace and say, "Yeah, I have some reasons. First off, the bride is still sleeping with her brother. Second off, the groom and his grandmother are secretly videotaping their trysts and selling them on the Internet at IncestIsBest.com. And last off, the institution of marriage is indentured servitude to the patriarchal heterosexist power structure."

"Yes, but is that any reason why this couple shouldn't be united in holy matrimony?"

"No, on second thought, I guess it isn't. Sorry for the interruption. Proceed."

"What was the name of that Web site?"

"IncestIsBest.com."

Maybe the reason so few people are funny these days is that nothing is identified as being absurd anymore. The only folks who use the word are elected officials who bandy it about during congressional hearings. Steroids in baseball? Absurd! The Bush administration used September 11th as pretext for invading Iraq? Absurd! Excuse me, Senator, what's absurd, that 9/11 was a pretext for the invasion or that it wasn't? Absurd! High-strung and invariably monocled bank managers who are being tormented on afternoon television by the Marx Brothers or the Three Stooges like to point their fat fingers at the ceiling and shout, "Why, that's absurd!" Other than that, the word is rarely even used, because for the dutiful American to acknowledge the absurdity of life implies responsibility. We don't stand for inequity and incongruence. All contradictions must be rectified. All wrongs must be righted. The problem with making things rational is that it's a lot of work. It's much easier to ignore absurdity than to deal with it. So when someone is confronted with irrationality, they'll say, "Wow, man, that's so *surreal*." If some happening is surreal, you're absolved. Can't make the surreal real, dude. Can't do anything about it except hang it on the wall of a modern art museum.

There's a wonderful Dave Chappelle bit about being in the back of a limousine driving through the 'hood at three o'clock in the morning. The car stops, Chappelle rolls down the window and sees a baby standing nonchalantly on the street corner. Saddened at the sight of a lone baby on a dimly lit ghetto corner, he wants to help, but he doesn't trust the baby. He's not frightened for the baby; he's frightened of the baby. "The old 'baby on the corner' trick, eh? Not going to fall for that shit." Turns out the baby's selling weed. Chappelle knows this is absurd, but he doesn't try to locate the baby's parents or alert the authorities. Instead he buys a dime bag.

It takes a bold person to buy a dime bag of absurdity. The speakers and writers in this section may not be smokers, but they're brave souls indeed, unafraid to confront life's black imponderables. This is black humor, and I don't mean African-American black.

ZORA NEALE HURSTON

book of harlem
c. 1921

1. A pestilence visiteth the land of Hokum, and the people cry out. 4. Toothsome, a son of Georgia returns from Babylon, and stirreth up the Hamites. 10. Mandolin heareth him and resolveth to see Babylon. 11. He convinceth his father and departs for Babylon. 21. A red-cap toteth his bag, and uttereth blasphemy against Mandolin. 26. He lodgeth with Toothsome, and trieth to make the females of Harlem, but is scorned by them. 28. One frail biddeth him sit upon a tack. 29. He taketh council with Toothsome and is comforted. 33. He goeth to an hall of dancing, and meeting a damsel there, shaketh vehemently with her. 42. He discloseth himself to her and she telleth him what to read. 49. He becometh Panic. 50. The Book of Harlem.

1. And in those days when King Volstead sat upon the throne in Hokum, then came a mighty drought upon the land, many cried out in agony thereof.

2. Then did the throat parch and the tongue was thrust into the cheek of many voters.

3. And men grew restless and went up and down in the land saying, "We are verily the dry-bones of which the prophet Ezekiel prophesied."

4. Then returned one called Toothsome unto his town of Standard Bottom, which is in the province of Georgia. And he was of the tribe of Ham.

5. And his raiment was very glad, for he had sojourned in the city of Babylon, which is ruled by the tribe of Tammany. And his garments putteth out the street lamps, and the vaseline upon his head, yea verily the slickness thereof did outshine the sun at noonday.

6. And the maidens looked upon him and were glad, but the men gnasheth together their bridgework at sight of him. But they drew near

unto him and listened to his accounts of the doings of Babylon, for they all yearned unto that city.

7. And the mouth of Toothsome flapped loudly and fluently in the marketplace, and the envy of his hearers increased an hundredfold.

8. Then stood one youth before him, and his name was called Mandolin. And he questioned Toothsome eagerly, asking "how come" and "wherefore" many times.

9. And Toothsome answered him according to his wit. Moreover he said unto the youth, "Come thou also to the city as unto the ant, and consider her ways and be wise."

10. And the heart of Mandolin was inflamed, and he stood before his father and said, "I beseech thee now, papa, to give unto me now my portion that I may go hence to great Babylon and see life."

11. But his father's heart yearned towards him, and he said, "Nay, my son, for Babylon is full of wickedness, and thou art but a youth."

12. But Mandolin answered him saying, "I crave to gaze upon its sins. What do you think I go to see, a prayer-meeting?"

13. But his father strove with him and said, "Why dost thou crave Babylon when Gussie Smith, the daughter of our neighbor, will make thee a good wife? Tarry now and take her to wife, for verily she is a mighty biscuit cooker before the Lord."

14. Then snorted Mandolin with scorn and he said, "What care I for biscuit-cookers when there be Shebas of high voltage on every street in Harlem? For verily man liveth not by bread alone, but by every drop of banana oil that drippeth from the tongue of the lovely."

15. Then strove they together all night. But at daybreak did Mandolin touch the old man upon the hip, yea verily upon the pocket-bearing joint, and triumphed.

16. So the father gave him his blessing, and he departed out of Standard Bottom on his journey to Babylon.

17. And he carried with him of dreams forty-and-four thousands, and of wishes ten thousands, and of hopes ten thousands.

18. But of tears or sorrows carried he none out of all that land. Neither bore he any fears away with him.

19. And journeyed he many days upon the caravan of steel, and came at last unto the city of Babylon, and got him down within the place.

20. Then rushed there many upon him who wore scarlet caps upon the head, saying "Porter? Shall I tote thy bags for thee?"

21. And he marvelled greatly within himself, saying, "How charitable are the Babylons, seeing they permit no stranger to tote his own bag! With what great kindness am I met!"

22. And he suffered one to prevail and tote his bag for him. Moreover he questioned him concerning the way to Harlem which is a city of Ham in Babylonia.

23. And when he of the scarlet cap had conducted Mandolin unto a bus, then did Mandolin shake hands with him and thank him greatly for his kindness, and stepped upon the chariot as it rolled away, and took his way unto Harlem.

24. Then did the bag-toter blaspheme greatly, saying, "Oh, the cock-eyed son of a wood louse! Oh, the hawg! Oh, the sea-buzzard! Oh, the splay-footed son of a doodle bug and cockroach! What does he take me for? The mule's daddy! The clod-hopper! If only I might lay my hands upon him, verily would I smite him. yea, until he smelt like onions!"

25. But Mandolin journeyed on to Harlem, knowing none of these things.

26. And when he had come unto the place, he lodged himself with Toothsome, and was glad.

27. And each evening stood he before the Lafayette theatre and a-hemmed at the knees that passed, but none took notice of him.

28. Moreover one frail of exceeding sassiness bade him go to and cook a radish, and seat himself upon a tack, which being interpreted is slander.

29. Then went he unto his roommate and saith, "How now doth the damsel think me? Have I not a smiling countenance, and coin in my jeans? My heart is heavy for I have sojourned in Harlem for many weeks, but as yet I have spoken to no female."

30. Then spoke Toothsome, and answered him saying, "Seek not swell Shebas in mail-order britches. Go thou into the marketplace and get thee Oxford bags and jacket thyself likewise. Procure thee shoes and socks. Yea, anoint thy head with oil until it runneth over so that thou dare not hurl thyself into bed unless thou wear weed chains upon the head, lest thou skid out again."

31. "Moreover lubricate thy tongue with banana oil, for from the oily lips proceedeth the breath of love."

32. And Mandolin hastened to do all that his counsellor bade him.

33. Then hied him to the hall of dancing where many leaped with the cymbal, and shook with the drums.

34. And his belly was moved, for he saw young men seize upon damsels and they stood upon the floor and "messed around" meanly. Moreover many "bumped" them vehemently. Yea, there were those among them who shook with many shakings.

35. And when he saw all these things, Mandolin yearned within his heart to do likewise, but as yet he had spoken to no maiden.

36. But one damsel of scarlet lips smiled broadly upon him, and encouraged him with her eyes, and the water of his knees turned to bone, and he drew nigh unto her.

37. And his mouth flew open and he said, "See now how the others do dance with the cymbal and harp, yea, even the saxophone? Come thou and let us do likewise."

38. And he drew her and they stood upon the floor. Now this maiden was a mighty dancer before the Lord; yea, of the mightiest of all the tribe of Ham. And the shakings of the others were as one stricken with paralysis beside a bowl of gelatine. And the heart of the youth leaped for joy.

39. And he was emboldened, and his mouth flew open and the banana oil did drip from his lips, yea even down to the floor, and the maiden was moved.

40. And he said, "Thou sure art propaganda! Yea, verily thou shakest a wicked ankle."

41. And she being pleased, answered him, "Thou art some sheik thyself. I do shoot a little pizen to de ankle if I do say so myself. Where has thou been all my life that I have not seen thee?"

42. Then did his mouth fly open, and he told her everything of Standard Bottom, Georgia, and of Babylon, and of all those things which touched him.

43. And her heart yearned towards him, and she resolved to take him unto herself and to make him wise.

44. And she said unto him, "Go thou and buy the books and writings of certain scribes and Pharisees which I shall name unto you, and thou shalt learn everything of good and of evil. Yea, thou shalt know as much as the Chief of the Niggerati, who is called Carl Van Vechten."

45. And Mandolin diligently sought all these books and writings that he was bidden, and read them.

46. Then was he sought for all feasts, and stomps, and shakings, and none was complete without him. Both on 139th Street and on Lenox Avenue was he sought, and his fame was great.

47. And his name became Panic, for they asked one of the other, "Is he not a riot in all that he doeth?"

48. Then did he devise poetry, and played it upon the piano, saying:

> *Skirt by skirt on every flirt*
> *They're getting higher and higher*
> *Day by day in every way*
> *There's more to admire*
> *Sock by sock and knee by knee*
> *The more they show, the more we see*
> *The skirts run up, the socks run down*
> *Jingling bells run round and round*

CHESTER HIMES

dirty deceivers
1948

a ll of his family were very fair. The most through examination of any sort could not have disclosed their Negro Blood. Yet in the small town in Tennessee where he was born his family were known as Negroes. This is not uncommon in the South. His family accepted their position as Negroes without obvious rancor and worked diligently to secure a comfortable living.

Following high school he attended Fisk University, and was graduated in 1931. He came to New York City seeking employment and worked for a year as a Red Cap. But he did not like the job; it was too demanding. The hours were long and the pay was short.

In the Spring of 1933 he was offered a job as deck hand on a freighter bound for Italy. He took it. When the freighter docked in Lisbon, Portugal, for supplies, he jumped ship. He avoided discovery by going inland immediately.

For the following seven years he lived in Portugal, engaging in a number of casual occupations. He assumed the name of Ferdinand Cortes, and in time learned the language quite proficiently. In 1940 he forged papers, proving himself a native of Portugal, and applied for a passport and U.S. visa. He returned to this country as a Portuguese and when war broke out he enlisted and was stationed in Lisbon as an interpreter, where he remained for the duration.

After the war he got a job as an interpreter on Ellis Island and immediately applied for naturalization papers.

There was a beautiful young Spanish girl, named Lupe Rentera, who worked in his department. He was attracted to her on sight, but the knowledge that he was part Negro restrained him from making the first advance. She was also attracted to him. Finally, one day, she gave him an encouraging smile. He responded by asking her to lunch.

He learned that she roomed with a family of Mexicans on the fringe of the Spanish community in Brooklyn: delightedly he announced that he roomed nearby. They discovered that they rode the same line to work and wondered how they had missed seeing each other. After that he waited for her in the morning and rode home with her at night. He began dating her regularly and in a month they were engaged.

Two months later they applied for their marriage license. He recorded his race as white, his nationality as Portuguese; she recorded her race as white, her nationality as American. Their fellow workers gave them an office party when they were married. They spent their honeymoon in Brooklyn looking for an apartment.

Two places were offered them, but both were in communities mixed with Negroes, and they declined. Finally they found a place in South Brooklyn that suited them and they spent all of their savings furnishing it.

They should have been blissfully happy, but there was a strain in their relationship. He was continuously fearful that his Negro blood would be discovered. Since his discharge he had been communicating with his relatives in Tennessee, but to avoid discovery he had rented a post office box where he received his mail. They did not know his assumed name, his address, nor his occupation. As soon as he read their letters he destroyed them.

But he was afraid that Lupe might discover signs of his Negro blood in his appearance. He kept himself scrupulously clean and used an after shave lotion which contained a slight bleach. Each week he got a hair cut and a massage. But fearing that the neighborhood barbers might guess his Negro origin from the texture of his hair, he patronized a Negro barbershop uptown in Harlem. Each Saturday afternoon when they returned from their half day at work, he departed for his jaunt uptown and did not return until dark. After getting his haircut and massage, he spent the rest of the time wandering about the streets of Harlem. It was the only time during the week that he felt comfortably relaxed.

Unknown to him, Lupe also had a problem. She, too, felt strained in their relationship for she was also part Negro. And as with him, she was fearful of his discovering it. She took the same precautions against its discovery as did he. She bathed frequently, used quantities of bleach creams, and patronized a Negro hairdresser uptown in Harlem. Each Saturday she left the house exactly a half-hour after his departure, used the same transportation, and arrived at her beauty parlor at the time he was in his barbershop not more than four blocks away. She also spent part of the afternoon visiting friends in Harlem before returning, although she managed always to get home a few minutes before his arrival. But for those Saturday afternoon sessions with her Negro friends, she could not have endured the strain.

He told her he spent the time in school, taking a course in electronic engineering. He never knew that she went out at all. In fact he did not know that her hair was the type that required straightening. He was too preoccupied with his own fear of being discovered to notice.

To make matters worse, both exhibited extreme prejudice against Negroes. Of course, they did so in an effort to hide their identity. But the effect it had was only to increase their trepidation. As they labored more and more desperately to avoid detection, the strain between them increased. In time they became the most prejudiced people in all of New York City.

Due to his excellent war record, some of the red tape concerning his application for citizenship was avoided, and he became a naturalized citizen of the United States sooner than he had expected. It had an immediate effect of security on him. But her fears increased proportionately. She had visions of being discovered and put in jail for falsifying her race on the application for a marriage license. He would have the marriage annulled. He was so prejudiced against Negroes he might even kill her for deceiving him. Her days became filled with constant dread.

Shortly after this when he stopped at his box for mail he found a letter saying his mother had died. His father had died years before. It was from his elder sister. She wanted him to come home for the funeral.

He was so upset he forgot to destroy the letter. He slipped it into his side pocket. Then he began to scheme how he could make the trip without Lupe discovering his destination. At dinner he told her he'd have to spend a week in Cincinnati to complete his engineering course. She thought it strange but said nothing.

Then she noticed the tip of the letter extending from his pocket. This surprised her more than the other. She had never known him to receive a letter before.

That night, after he was asleep, she got out of bed and read the letter. To her complete astonishment she learned that he had Negro blood. In fact, he was from the same little town in Tennessee where she'd been born. As she continued to read she recognized his family. She had known them well. They were distantly related to her family. She even recalled having

Both from the same town

seen him when she was a child, but he was ten years older and wouldn't remember her.

She was so happy and jubilant over the discovery she awakened him. Waving the letter, laughing and crying at the same time, she cried, "I'm one, too, Ferdy! I'm one, too, darling." She fell on the bed and began kissing him passionately.

But he pushed her roughly aside and jumped to his feet. His face was white and stricken: he was shaken to the core. "One what?" he yelled. "What are you talking about?"

"I'm like you," she said, laughing at him. "See, I read the letter. I'm from Pinegap, Tennessee; I'm a Williams, too. My Mamma was Dora Williams. I'm Sadie. I even remember you—you're Clefus."

The color came back into his face. He sat down on the side of the bed. "Well, what do you know!" he exclaimed.

For the first few days they were jubilant over the discovery that they both had Negro blood. Now they would not have to live in a constant state of dread and apprehension. They would not have to take so many baths or spend so much on bleach preparations. They could go together uptown on Saturday afternoons, he to the barbershop, she to the hairdresser. Afterwards they could stop at the Savoy and dance to the good hot rhythm of the Negro bands.

They felt they had discovered the happy combination of being white and colored too.

Of course, he took her with him on the trip to Tennessee. They visited their families and told them the whole story. Everything worked out perfectly.

On their return they looked forward to a life of bliss. It was such great fun fooling all the white people with whom they worked. They laughed about it at night and felt like great conspirators.

But after the jubilance wore off, and they had settled down to the daily routine of living, a strange disillusionment came. They began feeling betrayed by each other. Each experienced bitter disappointment in the knowledge that the other was not "pure white." They realized that had they known of the other's Negro blood they would not have become married.

Each became furious at the other's deceit. In fact, they got so mad at each other they quit speaking and are now suing for divorce on the grounds of false pretenses.

RALPH ELLISON

from invisible man
1952

a t first i had turned away from the window and tried to read but
my mind kept wandering back to my old problems and, unable to
endure it any longer, I rushed from the house, extremely agitated but
determined to get away from my hot thoughts into the chill air.

At the entrance I bumped against a woman who called me a filthy
name, only causing me to increase my speed. In a few minutes I was several
blocks away, having moved to the next avenue and downtown. The
streets were covered with ice and soot-flecked snow and from above a
feeble sun filtered through the haze. I walked with my head down, feeling
the biting air. And yet I was hot, burning with an inner fever. I barely
raised my eyes until a car, passing with a thudding of skid chains whirled
completely around on the ice, then turned cautiously and thudded off
again.

I walked slowly on, blinking my eyes in the chill air, my mind a blur
with the hot inner argument continuing. The whole of Harlem seemed to
fall apart in the swirl of snow. I imagined I was lost and for a moment there
was an eerie quiet. I imagined I heard the fall of snow upon snow. What
did it mean? I walked, my eyes focused into the endless succession of
barber shops, beauty parlors, confectioneries, luncheonettes, fish houses,
and hog maw joints, walking close to the windows, the snowflakes lacing
swift between, simultaneously forming a curtain, a veil, and stripping it
aside. A flash of red and gold from a window filled with religious articles
caught my eye. And behind the film of frost etching the glass I saw two
brashly painted plaster images of Mary and Jesus surrounded by dream
books, love powders, God-Is-Love signs, money-drawing oil and plastic
dice. A black statue of a nude Nubian slave grinned out at me from
beneath a turban of gold. I passed on to a window decorated with switches
of wiry false hair, ointments guaranteed to produce the miracle of

whitening black skin. "You too can be truly beautiful," a sign proclaimed. "Win greater happiness with whiter complexion. Be outstanding in your social set."

I hurried on, suppressing a savage urge to push my fist through the pane. A wind was rising, the snow thinning. Where would I go? To a movie? Could I sleep there? I ignored the windows now and walked along, becoming aware that I was muttering to myself again. Then far down at the corner I saw an old man warming his hands against the sides of an odd-looking wagon, from which a stove pipe reeled off a thin spiral of smoke that drifted the odor of baking yams slowly to me, bringing a stab of swift nostalgia. I stopped as though struck by a shot, deeply inhaling, remembering, my mind surging back, back. At home we'd bake them in the hot coals of the fireplace, had carried them cold to school for lunch; munched them secretly, squeezing the sweet pulp from the soft peel as we hid from the teacher behind the largest book, the *World's Geography*. Yes, and we'd loved them candied, or baked in a cobbler, deep-fat fried in a pocket of dough, or roasted with pork and glazed with the well-browned fat; had chewed them raw—yams and years ago. More yams than years ago, though the time seemed endlessly expanded, stretched thin as the spiraling smoke beyond all recall.

I moved again. "Get yo' hot, baked Car'lina yam," he called. At the corner the old man, wrapped in an army overcoat, his feet covered with gunny sacks, his head in a knitted cap, was puttering with a stack of paper bags. I saw a crude sign on the side of the wagon proclaiming YAMS, as I walked flush into the warmth thrown by the coals that glowed in a grate underneath.

"How much are your yams?" I said, suddenly hungry.

"They ten cents and they sweet," he said, his voice quavering with age. "These ain't none of them binding ones neither. These here is real, sweet, yaller yams. How many?"

"One," I said. "If they're that good, one should be enough."

He gave me a searching glance. There was a tear in the corner of his eye. He chuckled and opened the door of the improvised oven, reaching gingerly with his gloved hand. The yams, some bubbling with syrup, lay on a wire rack above glowing coals that leaped to low blue flame when struck by the draft of air. The flash of warmth set my face aglow as he removed one of the yams and shut the door.

"Here you are, suh," he said, starting to put the yam into a bag.

"Never mind the bag, I'm going to eat it. Here . . ."

"Thanks." He took the dime. "If that ain't a sweet one, I'll give you another one free of charge."

I knew that it was sweet before I broke it; bubbles of brown syrup had burst the skin.

"Go ahead and break it," the old man said. "Break it and I'll give you some butter since you gon' eat it right here. Lots of folks takes 'em home. They got their own butter at home."

I broke it, seeing the sugary pulp steaming in the cold.

"Hold it over here," he said. He took a crock from a rack on the side of the wagon. "Right here."

I held it, watching him pour a spoonful of melted butter over the yam and the butter seeping in.

"Thanks."

"You welcome. And I'll tell you something."

"What's that?" I said.

"If that ain't the best eating you had in a long time, I give you your money back."

"You don't have to convince me," I said. "I can look at it and see it's good."

"You right, but everything what looks good ain't necessarily good," he said. "But these is."

I took a bite, finding it as sweet and hot as any I'd ever had, and was overcome with such a surge of homesickness that I turned away to keep my control. I walked along, munching the yam, just as suddenly overcome by an intense feeling of freedom—simply because I was eating while walking along the street. It was exhilarating. I no longer had to worry about who saw me or about what was proper. To hell with all that, and as sweet as the yam actually was, it became like nectar with the thought. If only someone who had known me at school or at home would come along and see me now. How shocked they'd be! I'd push them into a side street and smear their faces with the peel. What a group of people we were, I thought. Why, you could cause us the greatest humiliation simply by confronting us with something we liked. Not *all* of us, but so many. Simply by walking up and shaking a set of chitterlings or a well-boiled hog maw at them during the clear light of day! What consternation it would cause! And I saw myself advancing upon Bledsoe, standing bare of his false humility in the crowded lobby of Men's House, and seeing him there and him seeing me and ignoring me and me enraged and suddenly whipping out a foot or two of chitterlings, raw, uncleaned and dripping sticky circles on the floor as I shake them in his face, shouting:

"Bledsoe, you're a shameless chitterling eater! I accuse you of relishing hog bowels! Ha! And not only do you eat them, you sneak and eat them in *private* when you think you're unobserved! You're a sneaking chitterling lover! I accuse you of indulging in a filthy habit, Bledsoe! Lug them out of there, Bledsoe! Lug them out so we can see! I accuse you before the eyes of the world!" And he lugs them out, yards of them, with mustard greens, and racks of pigs' ears, and pork chops and black-eyed peas with dull accusing eyes.

I let out a wild laugh, almost choking over the yam as the scene spun before me. Why, with others present, it would be worse than if I had accused him of raping an old woman of ninety-nine years, weighing ninety pounds . . . blind in one eye and lame in the hip! Bledsoe would disintegrate, disinflate! With a profound sigh he'd drop his head in shame. He'd lose caste. The weekly newspapers would attack him. The captions over his picture: *Prominent Educator Reverts to Field-Niggerism!* His rivals would denounce him as a bad example for the youth. Editorials would demand that he either recant or retire from public life. In the South his white folks would desert him; he would be discussed far and wide, and all of the trustees' money couldn't prop up his sagging prestige. He'd end up an exile washing dishes at the Automat. For down South he'd be unable to get a job on the honey wagon.

This is all very wild and childish, I thought, but to hell with being ashamed of what you liked. No more of that for me. I am what I am! I wolfed down the yam and ran back to the old man and handed him twenty cents. "Give me two more," I said.

"Sho, all you want, long as I got 'em. I can see you a serious yam eater, young fellow. You eating them right away?"

"As soon as you give them to me," I said.

"You want 'em buttered?"

"Please."

"Sho, that way you can get the most out of 'em. Yessuh," he said, handing over the yams, "I can see you one of these old-fashioned yam eaters."

"They're my birthmark," I said. "I yam what I am!"

"Then you must be from South Car'lina," he said with a grin.

"South Carolina nothing, where I come from we really go for yams."

"Come back tonight or tomorrow if you can eat some more," he called after me. "My old lady'll be out here with some hot sweet potato fried pies."

Hot fried pies, I thought sadly, moving away. I would probably have indigestion if I ate one—now that I no longer felt ashamed of the things I had always loved, I probably could no longer digest very many of them. What and how much had I lost by trying to do only what was expected of me instead of what I myself had wished to do? What a waste, what a senseless waste! But what of those things which you actually didn't like, not because you were not supposed to like them, not because to dislike them was considered a mark of refinement and education—but because you actually found them distasteful? The very idea annoyed me. How could you know? It involved a problem of choice. I would have to weigh many things carefully before deciding and there would be some things that would cause quite a bit of trouble, simply because I had never formed a personal attitude toward so much. I had accepted the accepted attitudes and it had made life seem simple . . .

But not yams, I had no problem concerning them and I would eat them whenever and wherever I took the notion. Continue on the yam level and life would be sweet—though somewhat yellowish. Yet the freedom to eat yams on the street was far less than I had expected upon coming to the city. An unpleasant taste bloomed in my mouth now as I bit the end of the yam and threw it into the street; it had been frost-bitten.

from the wig
1966

TRYING to get RID OF the big Rat !!

One magnificent rat, premium blue-gray, and at least twenty-five inches long, walked boldly into the center of Nonnie Swift's cluttered living room, its near-metallic claws making a kind of snaredrum beat on the parquet floor.

"I started to call the ASPCA," Nonnie whispered.

"I'll handle this mother," I said.

"Please be careful."

"Sure thing." An old proverb crossed my mind: Bravery is a luxury; avoid it at all cost. "Take the gun," I said to Nonnie.

"Oh! Les . . ."

"Take it."

A terrified Nonnie reached for the spear gun. "I'm praying as fast as I can, Lester Jefferson."

"This is gonna be child's play," I said. "Hell. I thought he'd come on like a tiger," and just then, before I could get into a quarterback position, the rat bit my left big toe.

"The sneaky son of a bitch," I yelled, hopping on one foot.

"Are you wounded?" Nonnie cried.

"No. I got tough feet."

The rat moved back. He had a meek Quaker expression and the largest yellow-green eyes I've ever seen on a rat.

"He's the lily of the valley," Nonnie said, foolishly, I thought.

"Shut up," I warned and knelt down and held out my hand. "Here, rattie, rattie," I crooned. "Come here, you sweet little bastard. Let's be pals."

"Call him Rasputin. They love that," Nonnie advised.

"Rasputin, baby. Don't be shy. Let's be pals, Rasputin."

Rasputin lowered his head and inched forward slowly.

"That's a good boy, Rasputin," I said.

And the little bugger grazed my hand lovingly. Rasputin's fake chinchilla fur was warm, soft.

"That's a good little fellow," I smiled sweetly and clamped my hands so hard around Rasputin's throat that his yellow-green eyes popped out and rolled across the parquet like dice.

"Oh, my gracious," Nonnie exclaimed. "You killed him with your bare hands. Oh, my gracious!"

"It was a fair fight."

"Yes, it was, Lester Jefferson. You killed the white bastard with your hands."

"Yeah. He's a dead *gray* son of a bitch," I said happily.

"He's a dead *white* son of a bitch," Nonnie insisted. "White folks call you people coons, but never rat, 'cause that's *them*."

"I didn't know that."

"It's a fact. I should know. They got plenty of rats in New Orleans. But none in the Garden District, where I was born."

"Well, well," I said. "You never get too old to learn." Seizing my rusty Boy Scout knife from my patched hip pocket, I began skinning Rasputin I. "Do you think the others will be afraid to come out because they smell the odor of death?" I said.

A delighted cackle from Miss Swift. She lifted her skirt and displayed rose, well-turned knees. "Let'm come. You can handle'm."

"You're right for once."

Nonnie walked over to me, like a fifty-year-old cheer-leader. She touched my shoulder lightly. "Your true glory has flowered," she said. "Samson had his hair and, by god! you got your Wig."

Modesty forbade me to answer Miss Swift, but her voice rang sweetly in my ears. I would have kissed her, except my hands were soaked with blood.

"Are you ready, warrior?"

"At your service, Ma'am."

"That's the spirit," Nonnie said. "I'll get the coal shovel and bang against the wall. Then I'll close my eyes. I don't want my baby to be born with the sign of a rat on him."

Waiting for Nonnie's overture, I stood up and stretched. The blood had caked on my hands, making them itchy.

"This is gonna be more fun than a parade," Nonnie said. She spat on the coal shovel for luck.

"I'm ready when you are," I said, bracing my shoulders and sucking in my belly.

"Here we go," Nonnie cried, and banged the shovel against the wall three sharp whacks.

Lord! Eight rats bred from the best American bloodlines (and one queer little mouse) jumped from holes in the *chinoiserie* panels. Nonnie had her eyes tight shut and was humming "Reach Out for Me." Or were the rats humming? I couldn't quite tell.

Fearless, I didn't move an inch. Images of heroes marched through my Wigged head. I would hold the line. I would prove that America was still a land of heroes.

Widespread strong hands on taut hips, fuming, ready for action—I stomped my feet angrily. If I'd had a cape, I'd have waved it.

The rats advanced with ferocious cunning.

Perhaps for half a second, I trembled—slightly.

With heavy heart and nothing else, Nonnie Swift prayed. Through the thin wall, I heard Mrs. Tucker wheeze a doubtful, "Amen."

Then, suddenly feeling a more than human strength (every muscle in my body rippled), I shouted, "All right, ya dirty rats!"

My voice shook the room. Nonnie moaned, "Mercy on us." I could hear Mrs. Tucker's harvest hands applauding on the other side of the wall. The rats had stopped humming but continued to advance.

And I went to meet them, quiet as Seconal (this was not the moment for histrionics)—it would have been fool-hardy of me to croon, "Rasputin, old buddy."

Arms outstretched, the latest thing in human crosses, I tilted my chin, lifted my left leg, and paused.

They came on at a slow pace, counting time. The mouse shrewdly remained near the wastebasket, just under the lavabo.

"Yes!" Nonnie cried out.

I didn't answer. The rats had halted, a squad in V-formation. Connoisseurs of choice morsels—of babies' satin cheeks, sucking thumbs, and tender colored buttocks—they neared the front for action.

"Come a little closer," I sneered.

"Oh, oh," Nonnie cried. "I can't wait to tell *him* about this moment! I am a *witness* of the principality!"

She was obviously nearly out of her mind, so I said only, "Patience, woman."

"Yes, my dear. But do hurry. He's beginning to kick. We're both excited."

I stood my ground. The rats seemed to be frozen in position, except for one glassy-eyed bastard, third from the end.

He broke ranks and came to meet me.

I flung my Dizzy Dean arms, made an effortless Jesse Owens leap, lunged like Johnny Unitas, and with my cleat-hard big toe kicked the rat clear across the room. He landed on Nonnie's caved-in sofa.

But I'll hand it to the others: they were brave little buggers, brilliantly poised for attack.

Strategy was extremely difficult. I had to map out a fast plan.

"Les, Les . . . are you all right?"

"Yeah," I breathed and started to close up ground.

One rat, a second-stringer, made a leap but I crotched him with my right knee. He nose-dived, his skull going crack on the floor. Another zeroed in on that famed big toe, but I was ready for him too. Kicking wildly—because four were sneaking from the left flank—I could only knock him unconscious.

Now the four and I waltzed. One-two-left. One-two-right. One-two-left, one-two-right. One-two-left, one-two-rightonetwoleftonetwo—and then the biggest son of a bitch of all leaped as if he'd had airborne training.

I hunched down fast and he sailed right over my head. I spun around just in time to land a solid right in his submachinegun mouth.

Panting hard, I watched him go down slow, his head bobbing in a kind of ratty frug.

I felt good.

"They at war!" I heard Mrs. Tucker yell. I looked over at Nonnie. She was backed against the door, mesmerized with admiration.

When I turned to face the enemy again, two rats were retreating.

Pursuing as fast as I could, I slipped on the waxed floor and fell smack on the remaining three. But I fell easily and was careful not to damage the fur.

I lay there briefly, rolled over, and scouted for the deserters. Two were making a beeline for the wastebasket, which was brass and steel and filled with empty Fundador bottles.

I was decent. I waited until they thought they were safe, only to discover that they were actually ice-skating on the brandy bottles.

I knelt down and called, "Rasputin, Rasputin." They raised their exquisite heads and I put my hands in the wastebasket, grabbed both by the neck—I squeezed, squeezed until the fur around their neck flattened. It was easy.

"You can open your eyes, Nonnie," I said in a tired voice.

"A Good Man Is Hard to Find," the gal from Storyville sang.

I was tired. I made a V-for-victory sign, winked, and started skinning rats.

Someone knocked at the door.

Nonnie was excited. "Oh, Les. The welcoming committee has formed already!"

"Wanna sub for me, cupcake."

"Delighted."

Another knock. "It's Mrs. Tucker, your next-door neighbor, and I couldn't help but hear what was going on . . ."

"There ain't no action in this joint, bitch," said Nonnie.

"I just wanted to offer my heartfelt congratulations to young Master Jefferson."

"Is that all you wanna offer him?" said Nonnie bitchily.

"Now that's no way to talk, Miss Swift, and you a Southern-bred lady."

"You're licking your old salty gums," Nonnie taunted. "You smell fresh blood. If you're hungry, go back to yo' plantation in Carolina."

"I will in due time, thank you." Mrs. Tucker withdrew in a huff.

"Go! Go!" Nonnie said, and turned abruptly and walked over to where I sat on the floor. "I guess you know those skins ain't tax-free," she said.

Engrossed in my job and thinking of The Deb, I did not answer.

"I could report you," Nonnie went on. "You don't have a license for rat killing."

"But *you* invited me over. You were afraid they'd kill you!"

"That's besides the point," Nonnie said sharply. "There are laws in this land that have to be obeyed."

"You didn't mention the law when you were trying to break down my door."

"Smart aleck! Ambitious little Romeo. I want a percentage on every perfect skin!"

"But I'm not gonna sell them," I said clearly.

"Listen, conkhead! You'll put nothing over on me."

"Never fear, cupcake."

"You try to outsmart me and I'll see your ass in jail if it's the last thing I do."

I looked up at Nonnie and laughed. Rat killing was a manly sport and there was always the warmth of good sportsmanship after the game. I split open the belly of Rasputin number nine. The rich blood gushed on the parquet and I thought of the long red streamers on a young girl's broad-brimmed summer hat.

"At least you could give me some for broth," Nonnie cried. "Don't be so mean and selfish. I'm only a poor widow and soon there'll be another mouth to feed."

I wasn't really listening to Nonnie; in my mind I saw the tawny face of The Deb, saw her rapture upon receiving the magnificent pelts. We would talk and laugh and later make love. My penis, which I have never measured, flipped snakewise to an honest Negro's estimate of seven-and-a-half inches.

MRS. Tucker threatens Jafferson to lock him up for killing rats.

black stereotype (big penis)

BOB KAUFMAN

abomunist manifesto
1965

Do's -N- DONTS
↓

ABOMUNISTS JOIN NOTHING BUT THEIR HANDS OR LEGS, OR OTHER SAME.

ABOMUNISTS SPIT ANTI-POETRY FOR POETIC REASONS AND FRINK.

ABOMUNISTS DO NOT LOOK AT PICTURES PAINTED BY PRESIDENTS AND
UNEMPLOYED PRIME MINISTERS.

IN TIMES OF NATIONAL PERIL, ABOMUNISTS, AS REALITY AMERICANS,
STAND READY TO DRINK THEMSELVES TO DEATH FOR THEIR
COUNTRY.

ABOMUNISTS DO NOT FEEL PAIN, NO MATTER HOW MUCH IT HURTS.

ABOMUNISTS DO NOT USE THE WORD SQUARE EXCEPT WHEN TALKING TO
SQUARES.

ABOMUNISTS READ NEWSPAPERS ONLY TO ASCERTAIN THEIR
ABOMINUBILITY.

ABOMUNISTS NEVER CARRY MORE THAN FIFTY DOLLARS IN DEBTS ON
THEM.

ABOMUNISTS BELIEVE THAT THE SOLUTION OF PROBLEMS OF RELIGIOUS
BIGOTRY IS, TO HAVE A CATHOLIC CANDIDATE FOR PRESIDENT AND
PROTESTANT CANDIDATE FOR POPE.

ABOMUNISTS DO NOT WRITE FOR MONEY; THEY WRITE THE MONEY
ITSELF.

ABOMUNISTS BELIEVE ONLY WHAT THEY DREAM ONLY AFTER IT COMES
TRUE.

ABOMUNIST CHILDREN MUST BE REARED ABOMUNIBLY.

ABOMUNIST POETS, CONFIDENT THAT THE NEW LITERARY FORM FOOT-
PRINTISM HAS FREED THE ARTIST OF OUTMODED RESTRICTIONS,
SUCH AS: THE ABILITY TO READ AND WRITE, OR THE DESIRE TO
COMMUNICATE, MUST BE PREPARED TO READ THEIR WORK AT
DENTAL COLLEGES, EMBALMING SCHOOLS, HOMES FOR UNWED
MOTHERS, HOMES FOR WED MOTHERS, INSANE ASYLUMS, USO
CANTEENS, KINDERGARTENS, AND COUNTY JAILS. ABOMUNISTS
NEVER COMPROMISE THEIR REJECTIONARY PHILOSOPHY.

ABOMUNISTS REJECT EVERYTHING EXCEPT SNOWMEN.

*don't reject
whiteman*

heavy water blues
1967

The radio is teaching my goldfish Jujutsu
I am in love with a skindiver who sleeps underwater,
My neighbors are drunken linguists, & I speak butterfly,
Consolidated Edison is threatening to cut off my brain,
The postman keeps putting sex in my mailbox,
My mirror died, & can't tell if i still reflect,
I put my eyes on a diet, my tears are gaining too much weight.

I crossed the desert in a taxicab
only to be locked in a pyramid
With the face of a dog
on my breath

I went to a masquerade
Disguised as myself
Not one of my friends
Recognized

I dreamed I went to John Mitchell's poetry party
in my maidenform brain

Put the silver in the barbeque pit
The Chinese are attacking with nuclear
Restaurants

The radio is teaching my goldfish Ju Jutsu
My old lady has taken up skin diving & sleeps underwater

I am hanging out with a drunken linguist, who can speak butterfly
And represents the caterpillar industry down in Washington D.C.

★

I never understand other peoples' desires or hopes,
until they coincide with my own, then we clash.

I have definite proof that the culture of the caveman,
disappeared due to his inability to produce one magazine,
that could be delivered by a kid on a bicycle.

When reading all those thick books on the life of god,
it should be noted that they were all written by men.

It is perfectly all right to cast the first stone,
if you have some more in your pocket.

Television, america's ultimate relief, from the indian disturbance.

I hope that when machines finally take over,
they won't build men that break down,
as soon as they're paid for.

i shall refuse to go to the moon,
unless i'm inoculated, against
the dangers of indiscriminate love.

After riding across the desert in a taxicab,
he discovered himself locked in a pyramid
with the face of a dog on his breath.

The search for the end of the circle,
constant occupation of squares.

Why don't they stop throwing symbols,
the air is cluttered enough with echoes.

Just when i cleaned the manger for the wisemen,
the shrews from across the street showed up.
The voice of the radio shouted, get up
do something to someone, but me & my son
laughed in our furnished room.

CECIL BROWN

from the life and loves
of mr. jiveass nigger
1969

[handwritten annotation: George & Reb buy liquor from head & tail.]

One spring day him and Reb let the school bus leave them. They walked along the road kicking an old tin can. Then they went over to Heads and Tails to buy some liquor. They walked into the living room and George told Head he wanted a pint. Don't you boys 'spoze to be in school, Tail said. Tail was Head's twin brother. They were around forty and had drunk so much rot-gut liquor which they made themselves that both of them had the reddest eyes you ever saw. The house was filthy and stinking with dog shit. They had an old rabbit dog they called Lightnin'. But he was the laziest ass dog in the county. He had red eyes, too, and was probably the same age as Head and Tail. Man, what you talking about school fer, Reb said. Shit, you never went to school. Hell, I quit school in the first grade, Tail said, laughing. What the fuck you talking about then, Reb said. Head came back with the pint. George gave him a dollar. That pint is a dollar and a quarter, Head said. Man, I'll give it to you sometime. Now come on and gimme my quarter, boy. I ain't got no mo' money, Head, I swear 'fore God, you kin search me, George said and held up his arms. Go to hell, Head said. Reb put the jar to his lips. Gimme a swig of that, Tail said. Give this fat motherfucker a drink, George said. I didn't say anything about your mother, did I now, Tail said. He took the jar from Reb. You better not, I beat the lard outa your fat ass, George said. You better go beat your old man, Head said. Ah shet up, nigger, George said. What happened, his old man kicked his ass, Reb said. Stomp a mud-hole in his ass, Head said. Tail said, shor did. I thought he was gonna kill that po' boy. Oh, man, he just hit at me and I ducked, George said. You ducked all right, you ducked the wrong way, and man, he was on your little narrow ass like a streak of lightnin' and a bowl of heat. Sheet, George said. Reb was laughing. No, he didn't, did he, Reb said, bent over. These niggers lying, George said. Now why would I lie, huh? Both of us saw it. Ole George was coming around the end of the field with that fast-back mule, which one is that, Georgie boy, you know, and old Willie said now I told that boy to be careful with that drag and old George was whipping the mule with the lines but he didn't know Willie was watching him, and he came flying around that curve and the drag went one way and 'bacco went another and Willie went to Georgie boy's ass. Man, he turned that nigger's ass every way but loose. Reb was down on his knees, laughing. The jar was in Head's hand. George reached over and got it. Sheet, he said. Now, didn't he kick yo' ass, Georgie boy? Now, didn't he? Come on, tell the truth, ain't no sense in lying, now wasn't yo' old man kicking yo' ass down that 'bacco patch like he was driving a tractor, Head was saying. Sheet, George said. He took a swig, a great big one, and began to chuckle to himself. Reb was slapping his hand on his knees, breaking up. Oh man, git the shit up off that flo' 'fore I kick *your* ass. He kicked that po' boy's ass so bad that he ruined a whole half acre of 'bacco, Tail said. A whole half acre of 'bacco, Reb howled from the floor, not a whole half acre, not *that* much! It was almost a acre, Head said, and they all burst out laughing. George had to laugh a little bit himself. Head took the jar and took a swig. Man, get up from that flo', 'fore I start talking 'bout yo' old chicken-eating pappy, George said. Reb got up from the floor, brushing off his pants. Lookit there, got dog shit all over 'im, George said. Where, man, where, Reb said. Oh, that nigger just lying, he mad 'cause his old man kicked his ass in front of everybody, Head said, laughing. Reb started to fold up on the floor again. Sheet, George said, you niggers done drink up all my liquor. Gimme a drink, Reb said. Give you shit, nigger, George said, and took a swig big enough to finish it, but there was still a corner left, so he hand it over to Reb. Niggers drink up all the liquor, Reb said, licking his lips. Hey, Head, I want you to give me back a quarter, George said. Fer what? Fer what? Fer drinking up my liquor. That's what! Your liquor, Head said, hell I just drink the part you didn't pay for. Shit, I paid for all of it, George said. Hey, look you niggers ain't gonna start that shit in my house, Tail said. Man, you call this shit-hole a house, Reb said, with dog shit all over the place and chinches walking around in broad daylight. Git the shit out of 'er, Head said. C'm on let's go. George said, you some crazy motherfuckers, selling people liquor and then heping them drink it up. C'm on let's go, Reb.

They walked out the alley, and Reb asked George what he wanted to do and George said he wanted to go somewhere and read and Reb said shit man that's all you ever think about is reading. Then George said, shit he didn't care what they did. You wanna hitch down to Armour, Reb said. George said O.K. They went out to the highway and caught a ride with a young cracker in a '55 Ford.

Where you boys going, the cracker said.

Just down the road a piece. We'll tell you where, Reb said.

My name is Richard, the cracker said, what's yours.

My name is Byron, George said, and this here is Shelley.

Reb looked over at George, surprised.

Them's some mighty strange names, the cracker said.

We come from up North, George said, we just come down here to visit wit our relatives.

You did, that's very inneresting. I use to live in New York City, the cracker said.

That's where we from, George said, from Harlem.

Well, I'll be, I been to Harlem, once.

It's a very inneresting city, George said, looking out the window. He felt Reb's leg putting pressure on his.

Is that so, the cracker said, glancing over at the boys.

It's a inneresting city, but we rather live in the South, 'cause in the South you kin always get something to eat, see. But sometimes in Harlem you kin go for weeks without a mouthful to eat. I had a brother who went up North, I mean to say, we wuz already living up there and my brother starved to death because he couldn't get no food.

Is that so, the cracker said, you sho' can always get enough to eat down in the South, can't you. There is some colored folks we use to have to feed. We use to live in Bladen County then. Then we move to Wilmington in the city and there ain't no colored around, so my grandmother she goes all the way over across town sometimes to give food to some colored people who used to work for us on the farm back in Bladen County. At first they say they don't want our food, but then they start to coming to they senses and now we git along right nicely.

I know they really appreciate that food, George said, there's a lot of people in the North, like the white people, who have a heart.

Is that so, the cracker said, let me ask you boys something. Y'all had any breakfast?

Breakfast? George said. We ain't have no breakfast in a long time.

Y'all wanna stop and git some?

We as hungry as we can be, but . . .

But what, the cracker said, looking over at George.

We just don't think it right to be eating with white people, George said, we don't wanna eat with white people and we don't want nobody forcing us to. Not even white people.

The cracker didn't say anything. Just stared at the road.

Y'all don't wanna eat with white people, huh, he said.

No, we don't think it's right, George said.

Y'all don't think it's right, huh, the cracker said.

No, we don't think it's any more right for colored to be eating with white people, George said, any more than it's right for white people to be eating with colored people.

I swear, you boys the funniest Northern colored boys I ever met, the cracker said, tell you what I'm gonna do—

At that point George looked out the window, out past the railroad track, and saw his father and mother and the hired hands hoeing in the field. He could tell by the color of the clothes which speck was his mother and which was his father. Dumb motherfuckers always digging in the dirt. Like animals. Niggers always working in the soil like woodchucks.

—tell you what I'm gonna do. 'Fore I let you boys off, I'm gonna give you some money so you kin get a decent meal. And when you go back up North, up there in—

Harlem, George said.

—When you get up there in Harlem, you kin tell them colored people they better come back down here and get something to eat.

I shor will tell 'em, George said, I think I'm gonna be a writer one day and if'n I do, well, I'll just write a book about it; the name of the book'll be called, All the Starving Colored People of the North, Come Home to the South, Supper's on the Table.

Ha, ha, ha, the young cracker laughed, you shor is a smart rastle, ain't you.

What's yo' name, George said, I'll put it on the first page of the book.

My name is Jim Morgan, I got a middle name too. You better use that, 'cause they maybe some other Jim Morgans around, though maybe not in these parts, and it's Melvin. Kin you remember all that?

Let me write it down, George said. He got out a pencil and scribbled in his notebook: Jim Dumbass Cracker Morgan.

You kidding about that book?

No, I ain't kidding, you'll see.

The cracker chuckled.

We gonna get off at the next road, Reb said weakly.

We really appreciate the money, George said.

I ain't give it you, yet, the cracker said, obviously pleased with himself. The car pulled to the side of the road, and the cracker took out two dollars from his pocket.

You boys buy some food with this money, and don't fergit me.

We won't ever fergit you, and when we get back to Harlem, I'll tell everybody about you.

Ha, ha, ha, the cracker said. He had yellow hair and a large, knife-like Adam's apple. They slammed the door and the car drove off.

Goddamnit, Reb said, why'd you tell all them lies.

Shit, how'didya think we got this money? He wouldn't give us shit if'n he knowed we're from here.

But you just start lying *before* that, you were just lying for the fun of it.

Oh, I don't know, George said, it just comes natural with me. I jive people if I don't trust them, see. I jive that mother-fucker because I don't feel right with him, you dig my meaning. That white cracker ain't no friend of mine, so I jive him.

And where you get them names, what was it you call me?

I call you Shelley and me Byron. They're poets, man. They were friends, though, because they were into two different things, see. They were rivals.

What's that.

Rivals, you know. They were always doing battle on each other if they met in the street. They're dead now, though.

They white?

Yeah, George said. They crossed the highway and were now walking into the woods.

Why you wanna call me white, man?

I just said that, man, I mean Byron was just like me, man, he was a jive too. And you serious just like Shelley, see.

What you mean by jive, man, you mean he told lies like you?

Reb, everything is a lie. Life is a lie. But people don't know that, see. Only smart people like me know that.

You jiveass nigger, Reb said, laughing.

No, I'm telling the truth.

You jiveass nigger, get away from here.

Well, shit I guess you right, Reb. I am jiving because jiving is the truth, and I'm the living truth.

You the living shit if you don't give me my dollar.

Let's get some wine with it.

No, man, I wanna grease with mine.

What you mean "mine," shit, you ain't got none unless I decide to give you some out of the benevolence of my heart.

What does that mean, Reb asked.

It means the same thing as goodness.

Bee-nevo-LENSE, like that, Reb said.

No, it's Be-NEV-olence, the accent is on the second syllable.

Be-NEV-olence, Reb repeated over and over quietly to himself.

George knew Reb was going to use the word as soon as he got an audience, just to show off. George didn't care. Reb was his main man. They followed the woods around until they could see the high school from between the trees. They sneaked across the road over to the candy store and got some potato chips, two poor boys, and two Pepsis. They had fifty cents left and they went behind the shop and bought a gallon of wine from Jabbo's Uncle Mose. By the time it was three o'clock, they were high off the wine. They went out to catch the school bus back home. They got to the bus, but Buddy Boy who was driving wouldn't open the door. Don't let 'em in, Flossie Belle was shouting from the back window, they didn't go to school t'day, and they half drunk too.

Shit, Reb said, you motherfuckers better open up this here door before I kick your ass out of the be*nev*olence of my heart.   ⟨⟩⟩

being smartass

STEVE CANNON

from groove, bang and jive around
1969

Annette Duffs: But, Oh, What a Nutty Trip

Seventy-two hours after having dropped the coins in the juke
at the Gumbo House, excusing herself from Dip and heading for the
john, Annette was further away from home than she'd ever been before.
Fine, dandy, together and down, so ran her feelings; she was ready to take
on the world, the whole universe, give love a chance and do her own
thing.

Bookbag in hand, purse thrown over her shoulder and clutching the red
handkerchief tight in her fist, she tipped up the ramp on her way away
from home.

Images of Marie lying in the coffin filtered through her mind as she felt
something hard inside the handkerchief. But she never gave it a second
thought.

She hurried through the cardboard and plastic passengers with frowns
on their faces, their children, little monsters, and headed for the gate.

A sign overhead screamed out to be read:

GATE TWELVE . . . 12 . . . STRAIGHT AHEAD

She hurried underneath the sign. A pink face, grey hair, eyes and dull grey
teeth in a reversed collar, black shirt and suit waved at her. Max. He was
back into his priest's bag.

"I was so worried," he started, grabbing her bookbag and kissing her
embarrassingly on the cheek. "I thought you weren't going to make it."

"What's this?" She pulled back away from him, wiping the saliva off her
cheek. He smelled like garlic bread blended with King Bee tobacco.
"Some kind of super-sad joke?" His rags turned her around.

"Sssssh!" He put his index finger to his lips, blew air through his teeth and glanced around to see who was listening.

Two brats in harnesses slapped palms, got their jollies; one cupped a hand over its mouth, the other to the ear, and pointed to Max.

He felt like two cents. "No, this is what I do for a living," he whispered. He was really scared she was going to put him down. Real hard. Call him a no-count, faggoty, pussy-sucking toothless Jesuit with a bad case for black eyes and vampire plans—a schemeless sissy who didn't know where dick was at.

Annette dug it. The words flowed through her mind, but she kept her thoughts under wraps. Her head was into duffing, getting away from New Orleans, she had had it. All of it!

Max hurriedly led her through the swinging doors into the cool air-filled night. A burning star turned red, then black—vanishing into the darkness as they mounted the portable steps, leading to the plane.

Annette saw a dead bird on the plane's wing—a hawk.

Max was so busy talking he saw nothing but her. "I was lucky. The Governor's plane was just stopping down here to refuel; you know he just returned from a tour of *our* South American colonies and I hitched this ride. That's why I wasn't able to meet you, but sent the car instead."

Annette said nothing. Her eyes were on the woman holding a clipboard in her hand, next to the door of the plane. Virginia Dare. A tall metallic blonde with lips painted orange, skin the color of sandalwood, showing pearl molars. As they entered the ship she checked off their names.

The interior of the plane was designed like a conversation pit in a slick townhouse. The color scheme was white on blue in red. It contained a bar, kitchenette, lounge chairs, phones, a three-inch-TV screen, ear-phones and a bubble gum machine.

The Governor, his two aides—a Mexican and a Cuban—Reverend Afterfacts and his wife, a big Swedish broad with volley-balls for breasts and big fine thighs, sat around in white lounge chairs, all looking very important. Dignified!

Annette cupped a hand over her mouth. The thought occurred to her—from the Gumbo House shithouse to *this*? She cracked up. So this was how the other half, the sedate types, acted. Too much!

Max introduced her around, saying she was an orphan who had not only lost her parents, but also her home. He was taking her to Heaven (that was his metaphor for West Hell) and put her in his Church.

Annette looked at him kind of curiously but said nothing. Her thoughts were into thinking . . . once in the city, the Big City, she was going to cut him loose.

They settled in two lounge chairs opposite Reverend Afterfacts (a tall lean spade preacher with a Castro beard and mod sunglasses) and his wife. Annette squatted near a window. She had a thing about planes. (But this was her first trip, you say? I know, but she still had a thing about 'em.) She didn't trust 'em. Max got her bag and threw it atop the luggage rack.

"As I was saying," Max settled in his seat and glanced around at the others, "did you see Marie or her mother before you left?"

"No, just Charles," Annette cut him short. Images of Marie in the coffin with black candles flickering rushed through her mind. Outside a priest, inside a thief, attending Voo Doo ceremonies just so he could get a nut. Annette sized him up.

"You know, they're some marvelous people. Simply marvelous."

"Yeah, I know, they turned me on to a whole woop of shit, especially about the way you *mothers* are playing it."

Max let that one slide. Afterfacts grinned but didn't say anything. His wife frowned.

Green neon lights in the front of the plane blinked on:

NO SMOKING   FASTEN SEAT BELTS

The big plane taxied up to the runway sounding like a Cecil B. DeMille epic of the Second World War, got take-off instructions from the tower and, like some technological thingamajig about to give birth, it moaned, groaned, revved its four engines—the wings tremblin', rattlin' and shakin' like they were about to break, straining under its own weight like trying to take a constipated shit—and with enough noise to make you think the whole globe had exploded, it started slowly down the runway, gathered momentum and was in the air, circling the city after at least ten minutes of all that bullshit.

Annette unlocked the safety belt. The pilot's voice filled the belly of the jet, sounding as though he were speaking from the plane's substructure or was down in hell, his voice cracking through the metallic walls.

They were flying on Statecraft One and were due to land in Heaven at 0500 hours in the morning. The captain's name was Buck Rogers, his co-pilot's name was Miles Standish. And the stewardesses were Susan B.

Anthony and Virginia Dare. Flight engineer aboard was Estavanico. Little Stephen to some. The Dap Daddy.

Annette and Reverend Afterfacts exchanged broad grins at the word that a brother from way back was plotting the course. Can you dig it?

His wife pouted. She didn't know what dick was all about. Just that the whole mess was tricky.

Virginia Dare, blonde with blue eyes, and Susan B. Anthony, red hair and green eyes (could have been a stand-in for Rita Hayworth any time) passed out pillows and blankets, leaning over everyone asking if they cared for anything more.

"Max? Do they have any grease on this heap?" Annette snapped. "I'm so hungry I could eat a nation of pigs."

"Sssssh." Max turned red as this page, lips turned blue; he glanced around at everyone present, then looked again at Annette. "Call me father, honey," he pleaded. "Don't let on we're equals."

Annette's eyes popped. She honestly thought he'd lost his marbles. She pointed to herself. "What? Me? Fool! You? Father? Must be nutty as a fruitcake." Then she loud-talked him. "Back at Marie's when you were giving me all that head, you damn near called me mother, you jive-time cracker. I met you as Max, think of you as Max, and I ain't gon' change now, no matter what you ax."

Max's face went through the whole spectrum of colors; from black to blue, green yellow purple white—and tightened up on red.

Everyone in the plane snickered except for Afterfacts. He clapped his hands, pounded his feet, slapped his knees and haw-haw-hawed. Lawd, he couldn't hold it back. "She got you that time, Max. Put all your business in the street."

Max sat there with his eyes downcast. He was feeling so bad, he couldn't help but blush. Then he went into fits of coughing like he was having spasms or something.

Susan B. was standing directly behind his chair. She'd heard the entire conversation. Nervously, with Scotch on her breath, she asked, patting his back, "Do you need a tranquilizer, Father? What is it?"

He felt like he'd been turned inside out. Asshole in his mouth, mouth in his balls, purple blue and red outside.

Rev Afterfacts busted out laughing a second time.

Annette was sitting there clenching her little fists, madder than ten Nixons caught in a nigger trick. Call him *father*, ain't that a blip? And he sucks hind tit.

Max was still coughing, his hand up to his mouth, bent over at the waist, clutching his stomach, his face beet-red. A spider slowly crawled down from the side of the plane and dropped down his back. He jumped up and did a fan dance, trying to get it out of his shirt.

Rev Afterfacts cracked, clapping his hands and pounding his feet; he hadn't seen anything so funny since the Irish brothers got fixed and Dago red was caught with the bitch.

Susan B. helped him as best she could. The booze was messing with her head. She stuck her hand down around his behind and pulled his shirt up from the rear while he attacked it from the front. He did a funny kind of jig, real funky, like he had a lot of soul, and dropped his pants to the floor.

"Max. You dun had it." Afterfacts again.

Annette didn't even laugh. Spiders were her thing. And Max? Crazy motherfucker—really, really out of it. She got up and brushed past the two of them strugglin' in the aisle, bumped into Virginia and asked: "Where's the ladies' room, please?"

"Straight ahead, to your right, in the rear. You can't miss it." She half riffed it, half biffed it, and half rocked and bopped it, all together in a Laura Nyro voice, her eyes following Annette's behind and thighs, down to her sandalled feet, trying to get a peek through the bells. Ding! Bong! Bong! She really went for the way Annette moved, reminded her of herself when she first got to Heaven and got tied up with the red men, going from one to the other, till she vanished on the train.

Rev Afterfacts, who was all eyes anyway, was watching Virginia watching. He thought he detected a strange look in her eyes. But wasn't sure. He relaxed, rubbed his ol' lady's big fat, fine thigh underneath the table, and looked over at Max. He was still coughing and dancing in the aisles, trying to get his britches back up.

Susan B. finally got him to down two Alka-Seltzers and a glass of water. His face had turned grey.

The Governor called him over to have a seat opposite him. He spoke in a nasal voice. "Here, fella, come over here." He was a tall angular man, WASP written all over him, a pirate from the get-go, with manicured nails and sandy hair.

"There's nothing to worry about, Max. I mean, your screwing around with that young doll. At least you're not like Ted. He can't even take a joke—thinks of it as an insult."

"Oh, you talkin' 'bout the way he had that Polish chick to go down on him and give him all that head." Afterfacts jes' had to git into white folks' bizness. I'm telling you, he couldn't let up for a second. He started laughing, "It got so good to him, next thing he was off the bridge and into the water. Then came back and lied to the press about the whole thing. Denied it. That's what he did."

"Right." The Governor really didn't feel up to going into it, not with Afterfacts anyway. "But he's attempting to keep his image clean, no blemishes. That's how it is in this racket. Once they find out you're just as filthy, nasty and dirty as the next one, you wind up off the polls, or the low man thereon. Totem."

Max was feelin' gloomy; hence, he said nothing.

"Reach over in my bag and pull out that pound I brought back with me from Panama, willya, Pancho?" the Governor directed one of his aides. Then to Max, "This will get your head straight."

The Mexican with a fuzzy black mustache, wearing two bandoliers of ammo crisscrossed across his chest, got up and followed the instructions: "Si, Senor. *Excelente.*" He and Afterfacts winked at each other.

"Ya." Afterfacts just couldn't let it go. "All that little jive-assed stud had to do was to get on TV and say: 'Yeah, motherfuckers, I got the pussy and you can believe it was good. She was the best gold digger around. Fact is, I got films of the shit, in case anyone is interested.' That's all he had to say. I mean everybody can get to *that*, can't they?"

No one said a word. After all, it was the Governor's plane.

"Look, I mean with all the noise being made about faggots wanting the world to know they're faggots, lesbians in the same act, why can't those who fuck, suck and ball, admit it to each other? Talking 'bout open societies, ever heard of Alex Bennett? My main man and Girodias was on that show in New York, show run by R. Peter, talkin' 'bout good loving and erotic art; next thing you knowed, the dude was offed. I mean, offed. But now he's back. But dun toned his thing down." Afterfacts laughed, but he was the only one who did.

A red bantam rooster escaped out of the Governor's bag—a gift from Poppa Doc. Pancho chased it around the plane.

It headed straight for the ladies' room.

"Get that bird," the Governor shouted, his eyelids fluttering up and down. "Get him." He didn't know himself what he was so nervous about, 'less it was something that Duvalier had dropped on him about white zombies and Voo Doo dolls.

Pancho hustled back towards the ladies' room, caught the bantam rooster by the neck and brought it back to the lounge. It pecked at the table, its eyes darting, staring him dead in the face.

He tried to shoo it away. Nothing was happening. It stood there all proud and arrogant, like it knew the whole score, and stared. Pancho picked it up again and put it on the floor. It tipped around the lounge looking from one to the other.

"That's quite a bird you got there, Max. Where did you pick her up? The girl I mean . . . where did you find her?"

"She found *me*, Rocky. You might say . . ."

"On the floor at Marie's Secret Ceremony. He was down on the ground with his tongue sticking out. Getting wid it." Afterfacts socked it to the Governor, watching the Cardinal blush, slapping his knees and haw-haw-hawing all over the place.

By this time, Max was fuming. But just turned red, like folks do when they ain't got the *power*.

Even the Governor had to grin. "Well, I guess that's better than robbing the cradle in an orphanage."

"I had to tell you something," Max blurted.

The whole plane cracked up behind that one. Even Pancho, who had gotten the bag of reefer and placed it near the Governor's right hand. "*Ici, Senor.*" He spoke French-Spanish.

Virginia and Susan B. served drinks all around. Afterfacts had a glass of port with lemon. His wife—gin, on the rocks. Max stuck to coffee and brandy, and the Mexican and Cuban had their own brown bags. Tequila and rum. The Governor had sarsaparilla. He was on the wagon.

Susan B. poured herself four fingers of Scotch with crushed ice and sat on the arm of the Governor's chair. She started rolling joints, licking the papers and passing them around. Bombers.

The Governor dealt the cards, palming aces and spades, sipped his drink and looked at Max.

The Cardinal felt tired, dejected and drugged with the whole set. He wished the Pope would let him have his own plane so he could really go into his act, instead of having to beg, borrow or steal a ride with these clowns, Rocky and Afterfacts.

"I still say that's a nice young piece of ass you got there. What happened, the nuns cut you off?" Rocky grinned, showing rotten black teeth in the back of his mouth. Route canals. "Fella?"

Max gave him the evil eye. (He was part Jewish, you see.) "At least I'm not getting my jollies from checking out *Screw, Evergreen* and *Playboy* magazine, or getting the hot towel treatment, like some people I know."

Afterfacts had to let Max have that one. "Lawd! Lawd! Lawd! Go 'head, Max."

"You don't have to get personal, Bishop. After all, I was only joking with you on a friendly basis. Bitch."

(How low can you go?)

This changed the mood of the entire plane. Someone turned on the sound system, images of Sly and the Family Stone appeared on the miniature TV screens, the sound blasted out the walls.

The Governor cut the cards himself. And while Susan B. passed out the smoke, giving one to each of the aides, two to Max, and three to Afterfacts (he let his wife have one), and lighting one for herself, the Governor dealt.

Max inhaled on the reefer, his mind still on the conversation which had just gone down. His stomach muscles tightened and his throat contracted as images of eating pussy flashed through his mind. He thought about Annette.

RIFFS: To Be Blown on Meat Flutes or Piped-In Organs

Chorus: Take Four

The big plane soared higher into the black night, climbing past the tropopause into the stratosphere, the whole Earth catalogued in blackness with networks of lights far down below. The plane hummed along at cruising speed as if made of fluid—gone with the wind.

Estavanico sat at the controls in the Flight Engineer's cabin. He picked up a moving vision on the radar screen. It seemed to be rising from the Equator, south of New Orleans. He took off his sunglasses, dropped the pipe of hashish out of his mouth and put on his earphones. Space-science music on cosmic frequencies echoed through his skull. He took a fresh plug of American-grown marijuana and chewed on it for a while. The spot drifted like some glob, there and not there, all at the same time. Like some giant shadow. He swiveled in his chair, chewing the smoke, pressed a button and picked up Virginia with her tall self, entering the ladies' room where Annette stood before the mirror. First words to run through his mind were: "Who's the fine sister? WOW." He pressed another button and the picture on the screen changed to a view of the lounge.

He laughed to himself when he dug the rooster pecking corn on the floor, jump back on the table and stare Rocky down.

Max. The Governor. Afterfacts and his fat wife. Susan B. soused. And the two aides. He shook his head and grinned again. Actually he was mad about some shit that had gone down centuries before, when the Spaniards had him working as an Indian scout; he'd escaped, caught up with Virginia Dare who was running from the Indians, then when the technology got right, pulled this gig and brought her along. She and Buck, his main man. Zonked. He chewed.

His sonic-visual radar showed a visionary blip about the size of Africa rising with the speed of light somewhere on the left of the screen. He locked his sights. The image danced, sang, rocked back and forth, then became a huge drum. It vibrated like the Earth around the Sun, the Sun around this Galaxy, the whole Universe one pulsating rhythm inside Space. He flashed a message: EVERYTHING IS EVERY*THING*.

Annette listened to the brash metallic sound of the technological monster, the primordial machine as it slid through the darkness which encompassed that part of planet Earth.

Signs: Cornbread 2002, Kilroy killed 1947, moved to the sub-Urbs, War Babies. Liberation! Black. Loves. And So Forth were smudged with red lipstick around the sides of the john. No dirty pictures. Just dirty thoughts. Words!

She slowly undid the handkerchief, wondering about Marie, the changes at her parents' house, the Jive Five—it all seemed like it had happened in some unknown world—and then Max. "What a dip," slipped from her lips. Wondering what they, those she had left behind, would think of her now. She was glad she was gone. In more ways than one.

Inside the red handkerchief was a black cat bone and some goofer dust, taken from a recently made grave. A note was attached on catgut. It read:

> *BeWare of Snakes no matter what Color.*
> Signed,
> M.L.

Annette was more than a little puzzled. She quickly retied the hand-kerchief, leaving everything as it was, and was about to drop it down in her purse when she heard a noise at the door.

She quickly wiped her behind; the shit was black. (I don't know what the broad had been eating.) Stood before the mirror pulling up her drawers when in walked Virginia. She strolled in swaying her hips to the movement of the craft, her eyes slits, like she was high behind some good smoke. She eyed Annette's fine round young thighs.

Annette was wise to her eyes. She pulled up the bell-bottoms and tipped as the plane bounced, rocked and shook, moved towards the bowl and began combing her wig.

Virginia gave her a sidelong glance, dropped her drawers, lifted her skirt and sat down on the john. A quick glance told Annette that the bitch had black hair on her pussy and blonde hair on her head, "I've been holding this in since we left the airport. Feel like I'm about to burst." She splattered what sounded like a gallon of water into the commode.

Annette was always shy around people she didn't know. And . . . er . . . white folks, well, to her, let's face it, they smelled. (Of what? She never explained to me.) She gave Virginia a thin-lipped smile and concentrated on the tune going through her mind:

Runnin' thru the city goin' nowhere fast
You're on your own at last

"Man, you sure did tell that Max off, honey." Virginia finished peeing, didn't even wipe herself and pulled up her pink panties. She rubbed her tanned thighs—so unblemished, they looked like mannequin legs sitting in a Surrealist Pop-Art Trash Can. "Served him right, he ain't had no bizness telling that lie on you, honey. Served him right."

Annette glanced at her. Blonde hair on her head? Black hair around a pink-lipped pussy? Annette was having her troubles putting it all together. Virginia looked up and caught her looking at her thighs, then shot a message through her eyes. It hit Annette in the pit of her stomach, dropped to her womb and made her ass feel good. She quickly turned her head and continued to comb her blonde wig. "Damn, I'm hungry. Is there any food on this thing?" She talked to herself in the mirror.

Virginia acted as though she hadn't heard. She continued with her own line of questioning, dropping her skirt down over her twat. "You from Hoo Doo, right?"

A pain penetrated right above Annette's heart, right between her two lovely breasts. "Huh?"

Annette checked out Virginia's pinkish-brown, red face; the blue eyes and false eyelashes, and the arched eyebrows which had been plucked into crescent moons; the straight nose which might have been hooked in the first generation, and the thin, thin, red, painted orange lips. Virginia let her tongue roll slowly across her lips as she eyed Annette's hips.

"I was asking if you come from down there? You know, Gumbo?" Virginia moved closer to Annette, Annette could smell the best and worst of American beauty perfumes, colognes and bath oils emanating from her body.

Annette had to get the associations straight in her head before she answered. "Gurt Town. The projects."

The plane humped about ten thousand feet altitude, like flying over a big-titty woman. Annette held onto the wash basin. "Why?"

"Then that means you must know something about the Dark. Er . . . I mean mysteries—Voo Doo, the Occult. But that's what that word means, isn't it? Occult? Dark?"

"Beats me, Bones." Annette couldn't help but laugh, as the image of Marie in the coffin slipped back into her mind, candles burning upside-down, black snakes, the eternal, Sun, Moon and children of the night. Infidels. All this ran through her mind along with spirits, natural and supernatural, two heads ha'nts and curses. "Just that they kin put the bad-mouth on you, that's all."

Virginia was originally from the South. But in those days there wasn't such a thing. When she was a little baby, her father had abandoned her little ass and sailed back to England, left her to be attended by the Indians, then the Blacks took her and made her sell pussy; afterwards she went back to her own people and got a permanent position on the Governor's line. This way she didn't have to wash drawers, be humiliated and stuff, just push products instead. Autos, washers, vaginal sprays, cigarettes and Dope.

But she was a firm believer in the dark forces of the Universe, the Indians and Negroes had taught her all that, but when it came to Hoo Doo and root American lore, she was just as dumb as the rest of 'em, believing that everything good came from Europe, and everything that was home-grown was rotten to the core. She'd accept seaweed from China, pearls from Africa and everything from Latin America, before she'd buy dis folklore.

So when she heard Annette put those two words together, use that syntax, *bad-mouth*, her body started aching, her loins trembled, her box got hot, and her tongue was heavy, dripping saliva.

She grabbed Annette from the rear, cupped her breasts and kissed her on the neck.

"Hey, wait a minute, bitch." Annette turned and pushed her off to the side. "I don't play that shit."

Virginia hit the floor and her skirt came up. Red splotches showed on the crotch of her panties. Black hairs sticking out the sides.

Virginia got herself together off the floor and eased up a second time, talking in a low sensuous voice, almost blurring her words. "I think that you are the most beautiful colored girl . . . black . . . I mean *dinge* that I've ever seen. And really . . ."

At this point she placed her arms around Annette's waist; Annette struggled to get free. But Virginia had her in a clinch, breathing hard: "All I want is to suck and tongue-kiss your bad mouth. Is that how you say it? The one between your thighs? Nothing would turn me on more than that, huh?"

Strange creatures. STRANGE. The bitch wanted to play with her poodle but had to call it something else.

Mixed emotions swelled in her chest while Virginia, as best she could, felt her breasts. She smelled like she had been dumped in a vat of perfume with stagnating shit at the bottom. Bull's shit. Suddenly the thought occurred to her, since this was a one-way trip, no coming back this way, not really, suddenly she asked herself, *why not?* And turned, shoving piles of tongue down Virginia's hot mouth.

Virginia held her tightly, rubbing her stomach against Annette's, feeling her breasts with hers, hips crushing against one another. Annette closed her eyes and was still able to see Marie in the coffin. She opened them, looked at the black roots of Virginia's blonde hair, the freckles on her neck, and felt Virginia's wet tongue on her cheeks and in her ears—sending chills down her spine, her core touching her, boxes boxing and rubbing against one another.

Still they clung to one another, Virginia running the palms of her hands over Annette's well-curved hips and fat ass, feeling up her thighs; they swayed in the middle of the floor, listening to their own breathing and the plane's drone.

Annette dropped her hands around Virginia's hips, clutched the flesh of her behind, reached down, pulled up her skirt and felt the soft flesh between her thighs. Virginia opened her eyes, closed them real fast, saw images of nightingales dancing on stairs, then felt Annette's fingers inside the lips of her cunt, working slowly, faster, then slowly, and Annette was staring her in the eyes. They were in utter communication, two bodies moving as one; Virginia continued to rub her legs, thighs and wiggle her hips. The hot gushy liquids flowed slowly down her thighs. She grabbed Annette tightly around the waist, ran her hand up and down her spine, rubbed her shoulders and pulled her even closer to her. Being the taller of the two, Virginia leaned her head down and kissed Annette on the cheeks, the eyelids, all over her face. She whimpered softly in the shorter girl's ear: "Oh, baby, baby, darling, you're so beautiful. I could just love you each and every day. Up here in the airways, down there on the ground, you're the best finger-fucker around."

Quickly Virginia was down on her knees unzipping Annette's bell-bottoms, pulling down her drawers and kissing the pubic hairs of her cunt and the lower half of her stomach, pushing her backwards towards the commode. Annette sat down, and Virginia stuck her head between Annette's thighs.

Annette lifted her thighs slowly and leaned back on the toilet, looking up at the white indirect lighting and listening to the plane, thinking about Marie in the john, Willie at the Gumbo House, watching the golden-headed bitch goddess suck between her legs.

She brushed her hair with the tips of her fingers, held her tightly around the head, and wrapped her tanned brown thighs close around Virginia's head.

It was a nutty sight to witness, Annette sitting back on the john like that and Virginia down on her knees, head down, licking the top, sides, bottom of Annette's cunt, feeling her fat round thighs, and trying to get a finger up Annette's ass. It didn't work. She got so carried away, she bent down even further and stuck her tongue up there instead.

Annette let out a sigh that the ground crew could have heard.

(MEANWHILE)

Max and the Governor were deep into their game: five-card stud. The Governor was ahead. Ace-deuce-trey spread.

Susan B. was into her own thing: sipping Scotch, downing them quick, and blowing boo like nobody's biz.

Afterfacts sat in the corner reading the Scriptures: trying to get Jezebel's tricks straight with Salome's head. His wife, who was the quiet type, sat playing footsie with Pancho under the table.

While the Cuban aide copped nods: Dreams of future glories, *El Topo*'s gories, raced through his head—a thousand revolutionaries, all white in red.

Estavanico strolled past the card players, the Governor and Max and said, "All systems Go," half winked at Susan B., ignored the others and, like a quarterback returning to the huddle, eased back to the ladies' room.

Either it was the hashish, the American-grown marijuana, or the stogie which he had just dispensed with; whatever it was, it made him think twice. He could have swore that the white-haired mongrel was down between Annette's big thighs instead of Virginia Dare. He felt the black cat bone in his pocket, rubbed his John de Conqueror root around his neck, and clutched a hound dog's tooth in his left palm.

Annette looked up at him and smiled. Her eyes motioned. From just looking in her eyes, he could tell she was fly. Virginia kept reminding him of the bitch of Bucharest for some strange reason, maybe it was because she was down there on her knees, her tongue up Annette's asshole, her two forefingers squishing around in Annette's cunt, her head resting on the fine brown thighs.

Estavanico felt his nuts get tighter; his blood was at the boiling point, his insteps ached, he was so carried away his head began to spin. He walked over to the commode and opened his fly. His joint popped up, bounced, stiffened, aimed at Annette's rosy sexy lips.

Like a pro from the backwoods, Eve in cahoots with the snake, Annette took in five of his ten inches and juiced it around. She moved her head back and forth, kept her eyes closed for a moment dreaming of dill pickles with gristles and cucumbers made of flesh, feeling the head of his member on her tonsils, the foreskin on her tongue and the roof of her mouth, and bit down softly as a hot liquid slowly oozed out.

Estavanico looked down at her little girl's face, a smile on his lips, checked out Virginia who had caused Annette to get one discharge, and rubbed both their heads. He dropped his pants to the ground, leaned in closer to Annette, she still continued to work his johnson and saliva his joint. Virginia dug the action and knelt down behind him. She started licking his asshole, squeezing his balls and fingering her pussy all at the same time.

Estavanico felt like Damballah in the body of the Pope being worked over by nuns who were love machines.

He continued to rub both the broads' heads, pulled Annette's wig off, exposing her naps, and pulling Virginia's stringy hair. *She* looked like a witch. But he was feeling good inside; all down around his knees, he could feel his blood rushing to his temples, drop down around his shoulders and swell in his stomach. A fart escaped from his asshole. Virginia inhaled deeply and swallowed hard, her tongue still up his ass, her hands on his balls. Looking down at Annette's rosy lips, his joint jerked, got hard as a railroad torch, and he came in her mouth.

Annette felt the hot fluids sputtering down her throat, the foreskin on his member become more sensitive as it wiggled like a ramjet—really to her delight. Even Virginia could feel the pressure being released because his asshole tightened, the cheeks of his ass grew taut as the pressure behind the hot blast—which exploded in Annette's little girl's mouth—caused him to drop a one-inch turd, which Virginia swallowed like it was a Hershey.

Max had already lost five games to the Governor and had tired of hearing him telling fuck stories, about this time and that time and how he had turned queer. His thoughts were in the john, as visions of ninety thousand thirteen-year-old pussies floated outside in the sky. The reefer had done its job.

Reverend Afterfacts had drunk so much port and smoked so many reefers he'd fallen asleep with his hands inside his wife's drawers, dreaming of fair-haired, big-titty women and himself with a dick so long and nuts so big that they had to be transported by a dozen freight cars or four Jumbo Jets. Bitches coming to him from all over the world just to have a connaissance and kiss the head of his johnson. Faggots and sissies, lesbians and dykes, sending him poison-pen letters because people now wanted to get straight—forget about makes.

His wife looked over at him; he sat smiling in his sleep. Slowly she removed his hand from her crotch, it smelt of jism and dried-up come. She excused herself from the table and went to see what was happening in the rear of the plane.

Suddenly Afterfacts' dream changed drastically. He was back in Kenya. His Swedish wife lay on the bed, taking on natives one after another. He moaned in his sleep and laid his head down on the table.

The bantam rooster came over and pecked in his ear.

Without really realizing it, he got out his blade and cut the rooster's throat.

Wings fluttered, chicken legs spread, the rooster ran all over the lounge, blood gushing from its neck—crazy, wild, frenzied: a chicken without a head.

Susan B. wasn't really superstitious, but this little act gave her the shits. Her period came on the spot; she rushed to the ladies' room, trying to cover it up.

The Governor had dropped the cards. His dick had gotten hard. He ran around the table, dodged the headless rooster, tackled Susan near the ladies' room and stuck his head between her thighs.

She wasn't wearing any drawers, had gotten that bad habit since living on New York's Lower East Side (where brothers and P.R.s were grabbing broads in the Park), so he had the upper hand.

Her snatch tasted of blood, urine and salt and water. His tongue worked around her thighs, licked her stomach and tickled the edge of her asshole, before he smacked her snatch and caressed her thighs.

The Mexican and the Cuban dug the action, slapped palms, and signaled each other. They took off for the cockpit.

Susan B., so drunk, and now fucked around, laid there and moaned.

Afterfacts woke up with a fright, then dug the sight: Susan B. on the floor, the Governor's head between her big fat thighs, her legs around his back, and she whimpering. The sight of the rooster almost gave him a fit; its head on the table, eyes condemning him, the rest of the body over near the cockpit door. He dropped his pants, looked around for his wife, charged past Susan B. and her cunt-chaser, running for his life.

Max was too excited to do anything for a minute. He sat, frozen to his seat, smoking a reefer so fast, looked like he was doing a cancer ad. His mind returned to Annette getting up, Estavanico passing through the aisles, Virginia disappearing, then to the preacher's wife's last appearance. Put it all together, something definitely smelled *fishy*.

Action and reaction all around him, but still he hadn't budged. The reefer had him floating. His mind was into digging a trillion young cunts, not a single one a nun—in spite of what the Governor had tried to signify.

Finally he went over to the bubble gum machine, dropped in a couple of slugs, got two jawbreakers and sat chewing the cud.

Back to the john: Virginia lay stretched out on her back, romping and stomping, her shapely tan thighs around Estavanico's behind, his hands caressing her flat ass, squeezing, pushing and pulling like a gorilla gone wild. Annette sat on Virginia's face, moving her bottom slowly back and forth while swapping kisses with Little Stephen, the navigator—Estavanico's monicker.

Virginia felt hot all over: goose pimples broke out on her flesh, chills went up her spine, warm blood surged down around her loins and swelled her head (she had the big head) as she worked her hips slowly up and down. She felt Stevie's ten inches up to the hilt, sloshing around in her hole, working the corners and walls overtime, the head of his member banging against her womb.

She slipped her tongue in and out of Annette's cunt and licked her behind, cleaning out her ass—the chocolate butter—slipped it back inside her cunt and played around her clit, the juices spasmodically discharging all over her mouth. Her arms were wrapped around Annette's big spade ass. It felt so good to Virginia she refused to come up for air.

Annette's eyes were closed. She was still busy swapping spit with Estavanico, feeling the top of his joint rubbing V's clit, while she kissed him in the ears.

The preacher's wife got so excited she almost fell out on the floor. She dropped her skirt and her drawers, took off her blouse and literally crawled on the floor to where the three were working out.

Actually she was strung out on oral sex, being from a cold climate— sweetened in Sweden, if you will—but she didn't know where these people's heads were at, save for what she dug.

She laid her big Nordic body down next to Virginia—her head near V's ass, her ass near V's head. She jackknifed her legs, exposing muscular legs and firm round thighs, then eased them open, and at the same time shoved a hand underneath V's legs. She clutched Stevie's balls and squeezed gently.

He stopped kissing Annette—still working out atop V—long enough to see who it was. He couldn't go for some faggot playing with his balls. He nodded that was all right.

The preacher's wife smiled up at him, showing ruby red lips. She moved her head further under V's thighs while Steve, as best he could, maneuvered V's ass atop the bitch's breasts. V felt thighs next to her shoulders, a leg rubbing against her ears. She continued to work her tongue up in Annette's young but well-greased cunt, and dropped her right hand over to her side. She felt the preacher's wife's big round luscious thighs and got hotter than exploding dynamite. She came in jerks and spasms, while Steve was really working out. He hadn't had a hot pussy like this since Tricia sneaked him up to her quarters. He busted his nuts, feeling the tongue working around the bottom of his member taking care of his johnson while he worked it in and out of V's sloshing cunt.

V was working with her fingers, starting with two, built up to three, inside of the preacher's wife's hole, feeling her big thighs on her arms opening and closing, and still working her tongue inside Annette's box. She felt the fluids.

Virginia's body, without her control, went into tremors. She swished her ass up and down atop the preacher's wife's huge breast, feeling the tongue up her ass and working around her cunt as Steve's dick moved rapidly in, up to the hilt, back out to the lips, over and over and over again constantly, making her discharge in rapid succession. She shoved her thumb up the preacher's wife's cunt, her index finger up her asshole. Her whole body felt like it was turning to liquid, melting or something, and she wanted the world to realize and experience her thing too.

The preacher's wife worked, twisted and moved her ass from side to side, shook her hips up and down, down and up, meeting the jabs of V's thumb and finger working in counterpoint in her core and up her ass. Blindly, Virginia's tongue searched and explored every crevice and hidden place inside Annette's cunt, feeling the liquids oozing in her mouth, her nose up Annette's behind, still working out.

Annette wasn't feeling no pain either. You can bet your sweet ass on that, honeychile, sugarpie, whoever you are; she was working with Steve, swapping spit so thick it felt like peach syrup, running her hands up and down the length of his body while he played with her breasts, rubbed her brown thighs, and tickled her clit.

By the time the preacher got to the door (the headless rooster following him into the room), they were into a polyrhythmic motion that would cause the most advanced musician to go into retirement.

His wife's head was hidden by Virginia's fine thighs, but he felt like he was bobbing up and down. As her ass moved up, her head moved down; and as Steve Estavanico, who was mounted atop, made his deliveries and came back for strength, Virginia's hips came up to meet his stabs. Annette was moving her ass from side to side, slowly at first, then going round and round.

When the Reverend walked in the door all four of them had spent, but Annette and Steve and his wife were still hot. And Virginia—now that I think of it—felt like a bitch just out of heat. Slowly her legs stretched out on the floor; she maneuvered Annette's ass away from her face and took her thumb and forefinger out of the preacher's wife's crotch. Steve worked her slowly up and down until he was sure her load was spent. She lay sighing, moaning low on the floor.

Rev Afterfacts didn't know whether to get mad, glad, punch someone or laugh the whole thing off. He felt in his pocket, found a snort rag, stuck it to his nose and got a sniff of some coke. He checked out the rag, slowly unbuttoned his grey-striped pants, dropped his frock coat on the floor, and crawled on all fours directly to his wife's hole.

He realized that once she had eaten some pussy and sucked a little dick, she was ready to fuck straight up for at least an hour or more. He couldn't understand that part of it, but it was no big thing. He was crazy 'bout her big legs, her big wide hips, the fat firm breasts, in spite of the fact that her face was so ugly. She was worse than just ugly, her face was ruint, and looked like she had been beaten by a ton of bricks. But he loved her just then—some.

Steve got up, his member sticking straight up in the air dripping a little bit, while Annette joined him and rubbed it in her hand. They stood over near the commode. Steve started laughing at the preacher; he looked so funny, crawling across the floor in a white-on-white shirt with frills, and a red bowtie. His black ass exposed his johnson, almost touching the floor, stiff as a stick.

Annette got excited. Slowly she was falling in love with Steve. He was such a hoochie-coochie she didn't know what to do. She pulled on his joint and it stiffened and bounced a couple of times; she lifted her legs and tried to climb up on his hips.

Steve helped her. He held her under the knees, put his hands under her buttocks, leaned back against the wall and slipped his dick in her hole. Annette screamed, let out a sigh, moaned a little bit, then worked slowly up and down, feeling it seemingly all the way up in her chest around her throat, and defiantly inside her stomach.

Rev Afterfacts dropped the coke on his ol' lady's pink-lipped, thick pussy, rubbing it slowly around the lips like a mother cleaning off her baby's ass. When he was finished, he bent all the way down and gave it his official salute. This consisted of running his tongue around the lips five times slowly, between the crack of her ass twice, and slipping his tongue inside her cunt, working up near the upper part of her cunt four times, the bottom part four times, dead center eight times, making all the changes and slowly taking his tongue out, massaging the cunt with his goatee, slowly, then faster, then kissing it fully on the lips. This accomplished— which took up at least twenty minutes—his wife swooning, sighing softly, crying joyfully to herself, clutching his head and helping him in his ritual, he straddled her body, pulled on his eight inches and dropped two balls of sperm on her stomach. She immediately rubbed it all over the lower half of her body, twisting and shaking her hips, close to a state of delirium as he waited, sticking his big left toe up her cunt and working it around, her thighs closing in around it. He knelt and shoved his joint in her mouth. She sucked it for three minutes, working her head back and forth slowly, then rapidly, while he played with her right breast, leaning forward as best he could and shoving his finger up her ass.

This accomplished, they fucked for the next twenty minutes—the usual way.

She lifted her hole up to the ceiling, come dripping out of it—looking like silver nitrate oozing from a rubber baby doll—her pink lips all red, the flesh all chapped, as he crawled slowly towards it between her big round thighs and slipped it in. It went in so easily Rev Afterfacts knew all body fluids must control the universe, turn the forces around and make changes on the ground. He slipped it slowly in and out, his wife coming forward to meet his thrust, working in counter-motions now, both sighing and hollering, yelling words of good loving in each other's ears. They worked out so good together, not losing their strides, silently and noisily and even and smooth, Virginia got jealous and stomped out of the room. She carried her clothes in her hand.

The headless bantam rooster, not dead yet, followed after her. She almost tripped over Susan B. who was sitting Indian-fashion on the floor, with the Governor's head between her thighs, drinking a glass of Scotch. V wasn't shocked. She knew they constantly got together—anytime either of them were scared, and most of the time they were. Both of 'em were so superstitious, for crying out loud, they got shook if they couldn't find their shadows on an overcast day.

Susan B. rubbed the Governor's head with one hand, sighed a couple of times, grinned and waved at V when she passed, but was quiet mostly. She called the Governor her little ninnie and treated him as such.

The rooster's head still lay on the table, eyes open. A mouse crawled out of a hole in the side of the plane and headed toward the table. Virginia's eyes caught it in her peripheral vision and she thought she was seeing things. She kept going toward the kitchenette; she wanted something to drink. Anything. The mouse, its long tail sticking straight up in the air, jumped out on the table, stood on its hind legs and bared its teeth.

V almost had conniptions. She shrieked. At that instant the plane hit an air pocket and dropped two thousand feet, banked twenty degrees to the left, straightened out, rocked and rose four thousand feet, only to drop down two thousand a second time, straighten out and get back on course. V fell back on her ass, rolled over on her side, grabbed at the table and almost touched the mouse. Her face was an inch from the little creature's paws. Her skin crawled, goose pimples the size of forty-five slugs popped out on her flesh and she almost collapsed from fright.

The mouse did four steps of the new dance in town—called *popcorn*— stepped back and shimmied for a minute, then went over and picked up the bleeding rooster head.

Virginia collapsed and fainted on the floor from sheer exhaustion mixed with fright.

Susan B. had lost her drink during all the commotion. The Governor's head had banged her in the stomach, spilling her drink and knocking her against the wall; she lay spread like a cooked goose on a dining room table—legs jackknifed, head staring at the ceiling and arms outstretched, as the Governor continued to work out between her thighs, beating his own meat.

Reverend Afterfacts and wife, Annette and Steve, had rolled with the rocking and the falling of the plane, didn't miss a beat and had busted their nuts.

Annette clung tightly in Estavanico's arms, kissed him on the neck and chin and slobbered on his lips. He worked his joint up and down in her crotch, lowered her to the floor and continued to jab. She rocked up and down, twisted and turned, shouted bloody Marys when her nut came. She started climbing the walls of the ladies' room, her body shaking with convulsions—images of Dip, Willie, the Jive Five. Now this heavy stud, big dick and all, exploded her vagina and gave her womanhood. She lay after a while, panting on the floor, tears of joy running down her face.

Max, who had been left out of the whole episode, was thrown on the floor when the plane lost its balance. His head lay in V's smelly cunt. He grabbed her fine suntanned thigh, stuck his head between her legs, and went down after it, his tongue directly aimed. Virginia was exhausted; she had had her share of screwing. She kicked him in the head and on the shoulders and started yelling, "No, Bishop, no! Go on in the ladies' room and get your young friend."

Max was too far gone on the reefer and the liquor. He lay dead on the floor for a few seconds, feeling up her soft thighs anyhow, rubbing her knees and kissing her feet.

Virginia was so tired, she let him have at least that satisfaction.

SUCH A FLIGHT IT WAS!

When Pancho and the *gusano*—who really was a Chicano in disguise— entered the cockpit, Buck was reading a copy of eight-pages about TV's Hugh Downs and Barbara Walters and, instead of pictures about discussions, poverty, pollution and resolutions, they were heavy into orgies. Barbara was down on her knees blowing a male guest, while another was giving it to her up the ass. Hugh was stroking her back and feeling hanky-panky, winking through the cartoon picture at the audience and pulling on his dong. Buck was so excited by what he saw—really, his mind was into nothing since the machine flew itself—his dick in hand, he milked the same.

Miles was looking over the pages while playing with the controls, his head almost all the way down as if to suck Buck's johnson.

The warning light blinked *emergency* when Pancho and the Chicano entered, guns drawn, and demanded a change in flight directions.

Miles saw the nozzle of the thirty-eight shoved towards his face, then the mustache and fat face of the Mexican, and almost had a nervous break—he mistook him for Marlon Brando in some strange movie south of the border. It just *had* to be a joke, but he wasn't *that* certain.

Chavez, the Chicano, looked so much like Sirhan Sirhan, Miles could hardly believe his eyes. With a forty-five in one hand and a shiv in the other, someone was gonna have to apologize. And it wasn't gonna be the third world, you kin bet your sweets on that, tootsie.

Miles sounded the buzzer. It went off in Estavanico's quarters. But he wasn't there to get it.

He tried the intercom. Nothing.

The stewardesses: Virginia and Susan B. Where were they?

He didn't know.

Panic-stricken, he pressed the button on the closed-circuit TV. He was shocked out of his wits. Bits and Tits!

Was it real? The reel? Virginia on the floor, the Bishop's head up her cunt. The Governor giving Susan B. some head while in the aisle. And the guests on the plane: the colored girl and the preacher's wife, being screwed something god-awful by two burly black men!

Miles got so mad all he could see for the next five minutes was red. Even the cockpit, the instrument panel, the people in the cockpit, Buck's pink dick—everything was red. Even the black sky outside was a deep, deep maroon. From where Pancho was standing, *he* even looked red, but his lips were white.

Miles' hands began to tremble. His body shook. He was sore down around his asshole and his balls blued. He wanted to get his hands on those two colored fellas in the back fucking those dames. Miles wasn't originally from the South, but had been to the Delta so many times and had heard fantastic tales concerning the size and complications of Smokey's joint; he knew once they (Western man's sex symbol, white proud plastic cellophane!) had had it, it was over for the "white" man. Images of lynching niggers and cutting out their nuts danced inside his head. Which way World? He pondered. Hard!

Suddenly remembering the Mexican and Cuban standing behind him with guns drawn, he quickly unfastened his safety belt and with that constant pain in the ass, he got out of the chair and swung wildly with both fists, knocking them both out his way, and started towards the conversation pit. Mad. With the ass.

Pancho let go a rocket from the thirty-eight; it flew past Miles' head and lodged itself in the doorframe. That stopped him. Miles dropped his hands to his sides, then got up, trying to grab stars.

Buck, who had come out his act when the commotion started, glanced at the closed-circuit TV, got it confused with the eight-pages in his hands, lost his hard-on when he heard the gun report, looked around, and saw Miles standing there, red all over.

Chavez hopped into the driver's seat, his gun aimed at Buck Rogers, whose limp joint hung between his thighs, and popped: "You want to blow?"

Buck's eyes bucked and his teeth began to chatter, not because he was afraid of Chicanos but he had a thing about guns. He deuced in a sad, super-sad, high tenor voice: "Please, sir . . . er . . . put that away. I'll suck your dick, kiss your ass, let you fuck me in the ass. Anything."

Chavez checked out Pancho, Pancho checked out Chavez, they slapped palms with their free hands. POW! and cracked.

"Kneel, *yanqui!* Kneel, you artifact, fractured bastard. Come blow my Nixon." Chavez unzipped his fly and a big fat, roly-poly, like-every-girl-who's-ever-been-to-Mexico knows, reddish-pink carrot popped out.

Sweat popped out on Buck's brow. "You mean your johnson?"

Slap! Pow! Chavez hit him side the head with the back of his hand. "He evicted. Johnson. Evicted. Understand. Nixon I say. Suck."

Ding-dong went the marbles inside Buck's skull. He closed his eyes and the saliva—because of the fear he was enduring and the sight of Chavez's big red dick—thickened in his mouth, his tongue got heavy and his stomach growled. Obediently he got down on his knees, stuck his head between Chavez's legs, grabbed the member in his hand and stroked it a little, then licked all around its head, stuck it in his mouth, felt it buck, jerk and get good to him—a baby bottle's nipple.

Miles Standish was up against the wall, looking into the barrel of Pancho's thirty-eight. "Senor, I would advise you not to try any more funny shit. You might end up pushing daisies sooner than you think."

Smooth as a feather, the big plane flew through the darkness averaging four hundred and eighty knots, with networks of white light far down below, and oceans gleaming gems on their surface as the plane banked, swerved, and floated past what seemed to be stars.

Estavanico sensed that the plane had changed directions. But he still had his dick inside Annette. She smiled with delight, hoping there was no end.

Afterfacts and his wife had given the whole thing up. He stepped over to the face bowl to clean himself off.

His wife got up off the floor, grabbed a towel off the rack, wiped between her thighs, then did his face—using the same towel. Afterfacts fell backwards; then suddenly it dawned on him as he grabbed at her body, grinning.

She held him off at arm's length, spreading juicy come all over his face.

He got the word, the reason for her actions. But she didn't have to worry about him trying to get some other broad; *he* was all *hers*. Not other women. Her cunt was big, fat, pink and juicy enough to last him three eternities. He just loved every moment, lying between those big fat thighs.

Afterfacts haw-hawed, washed his face a second time, licking his lips, and said: "Baby, you know I'm *yours*." Put on his grey-striped pants and frock coat.

"I was making sure," his wife answered, twisting into her drawers, the skirt, blouse and coat (gaucho suit), and they pranced—hand in hand—back to the conversation pit.

The Governor was asleep on the floor with his head up Susan B.'s crotch. She lay reading a copy of N.Y. *Screw* about hostesses on American planes who loved to finger-fuck. Balls.

Afterfacts and his wife walked on by. . . . The bantam rooster, headless but still alive, stood by the door of the cockpit flapping its wings, trying to shake off sudden death.

Max was still down on the floor with his nose up V's smelly box. He came up for air as Afterfacts and his wife passed, smiled, then went back to work, gnawing and biting like some huge rat. Virginia was totally relaxed—as if he wasn't really there. She looked up at the ceiling and wondered about the Spanish music coming out the speakers. She sensed something had to be *wrong*. Different.

She pressed down on Max's skull, moved her fine luscious thigh to her right, got up, straightening out her mini (she didn't have on any drawers, they were back in the john—lost), and strolled past Afterfacts and his ol' lady, towards the cockpit door.

The Reverend and his wife took seats in the white lounge chairs, their elbows on the table. "Hey, V, as long as you're up, bring us some more port. Two glasses. Haw! Haw! Ha!"

Virginia looked back at him like she was some strange bitch witch, eyes all wide and scary-looking, hair all entangled and stringy, lipstick smeared and clothes on all crooked. A sight! Her eyes caught a glimpse of the mouse doing the *funky chicken* with the rooster's head. She lifted her skirts. Her bare ass showed.

Afterfacts cracked.

Immediately, Virginia changed her mind about going into the cockpit (the bantam was still dancing before the doors), and went instead to the bar and got Afterfacts' order.

"Thank you, honey. Haw! Haw!" She placed the tall glasses before them. "Now how about a couple bombers so's I kin relax and con-template the Scriptures?"

She sat opposite them and silently rolled the joints. But her mind was still in the cockpit. And she remembered that she hadn't seen Pancho and Chavez.

Afterfacts watched her: "Baby, that sure was some other shit yaw'll had going on in the ladies' room." He paused. "Yaw'll do that often? Haw, haw, haw."

Virginia slipped him the joints without saying a word. She sat with her hands on the table, fingers intertwined.

"Wasn't that something, honey?" Afterfacts nudged his wife in the ribs. She smiled but continued to give V the eye.

V's paranoia was slowly getting the best, or what was left, of her. She wanted to go into the cockpit, find out what was happening, but her fears about the headless rooster were keeping her out. "Would you do me a favor?"

"What's that?" Afterfacts eyes got *biggggg*, he rolled them like Sambo and inhaled deeply on the joint. Signifying.

"Move that fucking rooster out of the way. I think something's wrong in the cockpit."

Afterfacts gave V one of his Dracula smiles. The pot had gone to his head. "For a price."

His black face shined in the neon light. It looked sinister to Virginia, as if he were Satan's double. Price? She'd never heard of such a mess. But decided to play it for what it was worth. "What's the price? Listen, something is definitely wrong inside the cabin. Where are those two *wetbacks?*"

"Your head in my lap." Afterfacts grinned. His wife panned, but still eyed Virginia, her long tan thighs, slender hips, flat ass and all.

Virginia gave him a sneer, as if to say, up yours, and watched Estavanico and Annette dance out of the ladies' room and up the aisle. Annette wore her yellow bell-bottom trousers, the black cat bone on a string around her neck; the goofer dust and note from Marie were still in the red handkerchief which she carried in her left hand, her purse in the right.

Little Stephen was stepping as if there were no tomorrow, dancing through the conversation pit on his way back to the navigator's place. They had their arms around one another and fell out laughing when they spied the Governor on the floor, fast asleep, his head still in the pussy—and Susan B., drunk but trying to read an Olympia book.

Virginia smiled up at Estavanico and winked at Annette, hoping that he would do the trick. As the rule goes, if one blood refuses to work for a

white woman, get yourself another. Afterfacts had a price. She popped the
question as they passed.

But Estavanico was too busy cracking up over the mouse with the
rooster's head, doing the *funky butt*. Suddenly a spider tripped hurriedly
across the table and stood on its hind legs, its tongue sticking out at
Virginia's face.

She shrieked. Afterfacts cracked. So did Annette. The Governor
yawned and shifted his position. Drunk in the hole. Max, his collar
off, his black shirt all soiled and pants open, tried to get up off the floor
when he heard all the commotion. But he was too stoned to move very
far. He grabbed his cock and snored some more—still on the floor looking
like Christ's father, the old man in the game.

Virginia stood before them. Latin soul music blared from the speakers.
"Stevie, I think something's wrong in there." She pointed towards the
cockpit.

Estavanico saw the dead rooster, gave Annette a sly grin and answered:
"Naw, baby, in there, everything is everything—under control. Dig?"

Virginia stepped aside, watched them as they disappeared down a flight
of stairs, still grinning, and thought about what he had said. Da-Da-Da.
Da-Da-Da. Everything is everything. What did it *really* mean?

Annette followed Little Stephen into the navigator's control center. He
turned on the audio-visual radar, the closed-circuit TV and dug the action
in the cockpit: Miles' hands were tied behind his back and a gag was stuck
in his mouth. Buck leaned back in his seat, panting, reading the instrument
panel, checking the amount of fuel on board.

Estavanico looked over at Annette. They both smiled, *knowingly*.

In the conversation pit, Afterfacts sat reading the story of David and
Goliath to Virginia and his wife. V sat rubbing her hands, listening, but
thinking about Da-Da-Da, Da-Da-Da, and watching the black candle
flickering on the table.

As drunk as she was, Susan B. had thrown a blanket over the Governor,
and moved over to sit next to Max. He wanted to complain about
Annette. "Tricked," he said. "Bamboozled."

Susan B. read Max's palm. Telling him like it is: Beware of young foxes
from Gumbo, they will trip you up every *trip*.

Estavanico called Chavez on the intercom. "You got it now, baby."

"Got it," Chavez echoed. "A three-sixty turn, heading due north, then
south, east and landing in the west. O.K.?"

"That's it, my man." Estavanico checked out the dials on the computerized flight plan, the stars, then added. "We'll be there, in Oo-bla-dee, in less than an hour. Fifty-nine-fifty-nine minutes, seconds. Right off!"

"Whee, baby!" Chavez shouted into the mike, grinning at Pancho. "On time. And on schedule. Straight ahead."

Buck banked the big bird twenty degrees, did a three-sixty, called Oo-bla-dee's tower and got landing instructions: Wind. Temp. Cloud cover. And barometric pressure.

Estavanico pulled out some fried chicken, potato salad, Falstaff beer, sloe gin and vanilla ice cream, and he and Annette scarfed all the way to the set.

FRAN ROSS

from oreo
1974

[handwritten: black / 3 / white]

[handwritten: dropping school / ? / marriage to Black girl]

1. Mishpocheh

First, the bad news

When Frieda Schwartz heard from her Shmuel that he was *(a)* marrying a black girl, the blood soughed and staggered in all her conduits as she pictured the chiaroscuro of the white-satin *chuppa* and the *shvartze*'s skin; when he told her that he was *(b)* dropping out of school and would therefore never become a certified public accountant—*Riboyne Shel O'lem!*—she let out a great *geshrei* and dropped dead of a racist/my-son-the-bum coronary.

[handwritten: boy / mother dead]

The bad news *(cont'd)*

When James Clark heard from the sweet lips of Helen (Honeychile) Clark that she was going to wed a Jew-boy and would soon be Helen (Honeychile) Schwartz, he managed to croak one anti-Semitic "Goldberg!" before he turned to stone, as it were, in his straight-backed chair, his

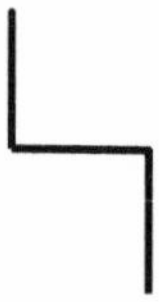

[handwritten: Boy / jew]

body a rigid half swastika, discounting, of course, head, hands, and feet.

Major and minor characters in part one of this book, in order of birth

Jacob Schwartz, the heroine's paternal grandfather
Frieda Schwartz, his wife (died in paragraph one but still, in her own quiet way, a power and a force)

James Clark, the heroine's maternal grandfather (immobilized in paragraph two)

Louise Butler Clark, the heroine's maternal grandmother (two weeks younger than her husband)

Samuel Schwartz, the heroine's father

Helen Clark Schwartz, the heroine's mother

Christine (Oreo), the heroine

Moishe (Jimmie C.), the heroine's brother

Concerning a few of the characters, an *aperçu* or two

Jacob: He makes boxes ("Jake the Box Man, A Boxeleh for Every *Tchotchkeleh*"). As he often says, "It's a living. I *mutche* along." Translation: "I am, *kayn aynhoreh*, a very rich man."

James and Louise: In the DNA crapshoot for skin color, when the die was cast, so was the dye. James came out nearest the color of the pips (on the scale below, he is a 10), his wife the cube. Louise is fair, very fair, an albino *manquée* (a just-off-the-scale −1). James is a shrewd business-man, Louise one of the great cooks of our time.

Samuel Schwartz: Just another pretty face.

Helen Clark: Singer, pianist, mimic, math freak (a 4 on the color scale).

Colors of black people

white	high yellow (pronounced YAL-la)		yellow	light-skinned
1	2		3	4

light brown-skinned	brown-skinned	dark brown-skinned
5	6	7

dark-skinned	very dark-skinned	black
8	9	10

NOTE: There is no "very black." Only white people use this term. To blacks, "black" is black enough (and in most cases too black, since the majority of black people are not nearly so black as your black pocketbook). If a black person says, "John is very black," he is referring to John's politics, not his skin color.

A word about weather

There is no weather per se in this book. Passing reference is made to weather in a few instances. Assume whatever season you like throughout. Summer makes the most sense in a book of this length. That way, pages do not have to be used up describing people taking off and putting on overcoats.

6. Ta-ta Troezen

Oreo's good-byes to her tutors

Milton the milkman came up on the porch and said to Oreo, "I hear you're leaving us to go find your father. Well, good luck to you. Funny thing about trips. You ever notice that if you meet somebody where they're not supposed to be, in a foreign country, say, or another city, you're happier to see them than if you bumped into them every now and then where they *were* supposed to be? I mean, take me, for instance. You see me almost every day and you're glad to see me, but we're just acquaintances, right? You couldn't call us friends. But if you saw me in Cincinnati, we'd act like we were long lost buddies. And if we met in France—why, there'd be no separating us. Then we'd meet again in Philly and we'd be back to being just acquaintances again, right? Now, before you go, I'd like to tell you my theory of divorce, based on the experience of a friend of mine. Now, this friend of mine—let's call him Stan—and his wife—let's call her Alice—had a big problem. She preferred a night bath *before* sex, he liked a morning shower *after* sex. What with one thing and another, one of them was always too clean or too dirty for the other one. So they rarely got together, so they got a divorce. Now, my theory is that the divorce rate could be reduced by ninety percent if, before marriage, couples would honestly discuss, one, the time of day they like to have sex and, two, the time of day they like to take baths and/or showers. A lot of heartache could be avoided later if they did this, because you can tell a lot about a person's character from these two things. Well, goodbye, kid. It's been a pleasure serving you all these years. Take care, and remember to drink at least a quart of milk a day."

"Good-bye, Milton."

Douglas Floors interrupted a crucial discussion of the Sino-Soviet War on Oreo's last day with him to inveigh against Central Park. "It is not quite so bad as Fairmount Park, of course, being smaller, but it is bad enough. The foul Sheep Meadow, the treacherous Great Lawn, and—I actually get a *frisson* every time I think of it—the Ramble, where benighted creatures actually go to watch *birds*." He shuddered behind his dark glasses and turned his chair more directly to the wall, the better to avoid seeing Louise's bare arm as she passed through the room. Her vaccination scar reminded him of a chrysanthemum. "I contribute to an enlightened East Coast group determined to pave all the parks. We'd like to start with Central. Our research indicates we have the best chance there. Of course, there are the lunatic conservation groups to contend with, but they will soon be neutralized by hay fever, poison ivy, ticks, and all the other little goodies their beloved Mother Nature inflicts on them whenever they go a-Maying." He snickered with nonnatural satisfaction.

"Remember," he said as he was leaving, "look out for rock out-croppings. Manhattan is full of schist."

And so are you, thought Oreo, misunderstanding him.

"Good-bye, Oreo."

"Good-bye, Doug."

Professor Lindau, after all his years of giving blood, was now taking. We went daily for a transfusion of the blood he had donated over the last decade, convinced by Milton the milkman that getting back his callow plasma, his jejune erythrocytes, his puerile leukocytes, his tender platelets would make him young again. Oreo believed that his conflations with his latest wedge were doing more for his rejuvenation than any old stale blood.

For her last assignment, the professor had given her a standard treatise in the field of economic agronomy upon which she was to model an essay on the same subject. She read the first and last words of the treatise, titled *Lying Fallow, or What You Should Know About Federal Subsidies*, and started and ended her essay with similar words. In *Lying Fallow*, the first word was *snow* and the last word was *potatoes*. In her book-length essay (*Secretaries of Agriculture I Have Known, or God: The First Economic Agronomist*), Oreo experimented with *monsoon* and *broccoli* as her first and last words, but decided they were too exotic, and, what is more, *monsoon* had too many syllables. Already she had strayed from the obvious pattern *Fallow*'s author had established with his forceful yet sensitive first and last words. After an evening with Roget, Oreo decided that her first word would be *rain* and her last word *rice*. She was more than willing to sacrifice syllables (her two to *Fallow*'s four) for alliteration. She quickly filled in the middle section of her essay, using the same technique. What she sacrificed in cogency, she gained in mechanicality (her serendipitous assembly-line gobbledygook against *Fallow*'s numbing agroeconomic clarity). Thus a typical sentence in *Fallow:* "Wheat farm B showed a declining profit-loss ratio during the harvest season," became in Oreo's manuscript: "Oat ranch wasp played the drooping excess-death proportion while a crop pepper." The professor was amused by Oreo's little farewell drollery, which ran to more than six hundred pages, single-spaced.

After the lesson, the professor excused himself and went to the bathroom. When he returned, he said, "Now that I have sifted out, I shall not go into a long wearing away. I shall merely give you a big comfort and take my leave." He hugged Oreo.

"Good-bye, professor."

"God be with ye, Oreo."

Oreo's good-byes to her family

The family farewells took three days because Louise needed the time to prepare a box lunch for her granddaughter to take on her journey perilous. The peroration of those good-byes went as follows.

Oreo said good-bye to her grandfather first, since that would take the shortest amount of time. "Good-bye, Grandfather," she said, kissing him on the cheek.

James, who had been grinning a second before, stopped grinning. There was a vacant stare on his face. This often happened and signaled the fact that he was giving his facial muscles a rest.

Oreo went next to Louise. "You look real nice, chile. Yo' white dress is spotless—you might eem say maculin." Louise dragged over Oreo's box lunch—more accurately, her duffelbag lunch, since that was what it was in. They could not find a box big enough for all the food Louise had prepared.

Oreo strapped the lunch to her backpack frame. Since the food took up so much space, Oreo had to repack the other equipment she was taking on her journey. She soon grew tired of shifting it around, said, "Oh, the hell with it," and shoved it into the duffel bag next to the lunch. It was a toothbrush, but difficult to pack because its interproximal stimulator, or rubber tip, and its bristles faced in opposite directions. Oreo kissed Louise. "Good-bye, Grandmother."

Louise kissed her. " 'Bye, Oreo."

Jimmie C. made a long speech in cha-key-key-wah, telling Oreo how much he loved her and promising not to be a *yold*. Then he said, "I know

grandparents first (bye)

you won't be gone for a spavol time, but"—and he sang this—"nevertheless and winnie-the-pooh, verily, I'm going to miss you." His voice had changed with age. His sweet countertenor was now a sweet boy soprano.

She kissed him on both cheeks. "Good-bye, Jimmie C."

"Vladi, Oreo."

When Helen embraced Oreo, she did not say anything, but her head equation, brought on by Jimmie C.'s keening in the background, was a simple

$$L = P + GD$$

where L = leavetaking, mph

P = pain, ppm

G = *gevalts*, cwt

D = *davening*, pf

"Good-bye, Oreo," Helen said when her equation was over. She was doubly sad, since she too would soon be leaving, to go on the road again.

"Good-bye, Mother."

Suddenly there was a sound like the primal rasp of a rusty hinge on a long unopened door—the pearly gates, perhaps. "Now, as I was saying . . . ," James croaked in his disused voice.

The whole family was stunned. They gaped at James in amazement. He was not aware of it now, but a few moments earlier all the good-byes had led him to believe that he was being abandoned. The shock of this fearful defection had quickened his broken blood vessel, which reached out across the vascular gap like a severed snake, probing the brain's topography for its other half. It made a slipknot around the break as a temporary measure until it could repair itself permanently. His anterograde amnesia disappeared. He stood up with a crisp popping and cracking of joints, the sound of Louise snapping gigantic green beans. His half swastika straightened into a ramrod.

His wife and daughter embraced him joyously, and he was reintroduced to his grandchildren for perhaps the umpty-third time.

"Well, I hate to greet and run . . . ," Oreo began. She had no shame.

When Oreo's impending journey was explained to him, a shudder ran through him at the mention of Samuel's name. But the slipknot in his brain held fast. James was somewhat consoled when he was told that

Samuel and Helen had been divorced for years. Helen promised to
postpone going on her road trip for a few days in order to help Louise
catch James up on all that he had missed during his years of amnesia. She
had come to love the road, but once James was fully recovered and
making money again, she could make shorter swings and come home
more often.

Louise timidly approached her husband. "Do de name Will Farmer ring
a gong?" she asked.

James thought a while, shook his head. "No, can't say that it does. Do I
know him?"

"No, and I don' neither," she said, a glaze coming over her eyes as she
lied in her teeth. "De name jus' come to me in a dream. I was dreaming
'bout one dem horny-back Baptist churches."

"You mean hard-shell," James said.

"Yeah, one dem. Anyway, a man was rollin' in de aisles, and de
preacher say, 'You bet' come on out cho ack, Will Farmer.' Jus' thought
you might recomember 'body by dat name."

James put a strain on his slipknot trying to figure out why he should
know someone in Louise's dream, but he shook it off and went on to other
things. "Helen, what do you think of this idea? I was thinking of making a
special mailing to all the homes for used Jews and—"

"You mean old folks' homes?" asked Helen.

"Naturally. Well, I was thinking—"

Oreo interrupted to initiate a final round of good-byes, then slipped out
the door as unobtrusively as she could, considering her backpack.

Betty the nymphomaniac tore herself away from her father long enough
to wave good-bye from her bedroom window and shout, "Don't forget
those dirty postcards you promised me!"

"Vladi, vladi," Jimmie C. called wistfully from the front porch until she
was out of sight.

And Oreo was on her way.

7. Periphetes

On the subway-elevated to Thirtieth Street Station

Oreo did what she always did on subways. She speculated or she
compared. She speculated on how many people in, say, Denver, Colo-

rado, were at that very moment making love. How many people in Cincinnati were having their teeth filled? As the El passed the Arena and the gilded dome of Provident Mutual's clock tower, in a mad rush to become a true subway with its plunge into the Fortieth Street stop, Oreo wondered how many people in Honolulu were scratching themselves. Was the number of people taking books out of the library in Duluth higher than one-tenth of one percent of the city's car owners? she mused. And what about the ratio of nose picking per thousand population in Portland, Oregon—or Portland, Maine, for that matter?

When she had tired of speculating, she went on to comparing. She looked up and down both sides of the car. On her first sweep, she concentrated on the size and shape of all the noses she could see. She awarded appropriate but valueless (imaginary) prizes to the possessors of the largest, smallest, and most unusual. A man wearing an astrakhan cap won the prize for the largest, with a nose big enough to accommodate nostrils that put Oreo in mind of adjacent plane hangars, fur-lined. His prize: free monthly vacuuming with a yet-to-be-invented nose Hoover. Modeling clay, the prize for the smallest nose, went to a red-headed woman with the nose of an ant. A hand passing from the redhead's formicine brow to her mouth would have to make no humanoid detours around cartilaginous prominences. Most unusual was the cross-eyed young man whose nose pointed to his left ear. Picasso *réchauffé*. His prize wasn't really his. It was a blindfold for others to wear in his presence.

Before she could go on to hands and shoes, Oreo got a seat. Sitting on the edge of the seat because of her backpack, she felt at the neck of her dress to make sure the mezuzah was still in place. She loosened the drawstring of her black handbag (the kind that looks like a horse's feed bag), pushed aside the bed socks her father had left her, and took out the coffee-stained list of clues.

1. Sword and sandals
2. Three legs
3. The great divide
4. Sow
5. Kicks
6. Pretzel
7. Fitting
8. Down by the river

9. Temple
10. Lucky number
11. Amazing
12. Sails

She crossed off the first item on the list. If number 2 was as
farfetched as number 1 had been, "Three legs" could mean anything
from a broken chair to Siamese twins. No matter. She was ready for
any kind of shit, prepared to go where she was not wanted, to butt
in where she had no business, to test her meddle all over the map.
Oreo was one pushy chick.

Her bravery was beyond question. She had chosen, against the
advice of older, more cautious adventurers, to eschew the easy canoe
trip up the Delaware, piece-of-cake portage across the swamplands of
New Jersey, and no-sweat glissade across the Hudson to Manhattan
and to travel instead the far more problematic overland route via the
Penn Central Railroad. What further ensign of Oreo's courage need
be cited?

The subway concourse at Thirtieth Street

Oreo knew that there were several stiff trials ahead before she
reached the official starting point of her overland journey, the
Waiting Room of Thirtieth Street Station. The first and second
trials came together: the Broken Escalator and the Leaky Pipes.
Countless previous travelers had suffered broken ankles and/or
Chinese water torture as they made their way between the subway
and Thirtieth Street Station. With the advent of wide-heeled ugly
shoes, which replaced hamstring-snapping spike heels, much of the
danger had been taken out of the Broken Escalator's gaping treads.
Much—in fact, all—of the movement had been taken out of the
B.E. almost immediately after it began its rounds. Thus it had had
a life of only two minutes and thirty seconds as a moving staircase before it expired to become the Broken Escalator of
Philadelphia legend. Oreo had prepared for this leg of the journey
by wearing sandals, which provided firm footing on the treads of
the B.E. and also served as a showcase for her short-toed perfect
feet.

The Leaky Pipes filled the traveler's need for irritation, humiliation, irrigation, and syncopation. According to the number of drops that fell on the traveler from the Leaky Pipes, he or she was irritated, humiliated, or irrigated. These degrees were largely a function of the Pipes' syncopation. With a simple one, *two*, three, *four*, a few even simpler souls would be caught by the drops of the offbeat. One who fell victim three or more times to this rhythm could safely be said to have passed beyond the bounds of irritation and into the slink of humiliation. The unlucky ones were those who got caught in a *one*, two, three, *four*, —, six, seven, eight. They would end up soaking wet by the time they got to the foot or the head (depending on their direction) of the Broken Escalator. Ninety percent of those caught by the *one*, two, three, *four*, —, six, seven, eight were white. They just couldn't get the hang of it. Black people were usually caught by the normal, unsyncopated, *one*, two, *one*, two—it was so simple, they couldn't believe it.

Oreo stood at the top of the B.E. and closed her eyes. She did not want to be distracted by looking at the drops. She just listened. She was in luck. The Pipes were in the one, *two*, three, *four* phase. She opened her eyes and observed that the drops *(two)* and *four)* hit the same side of the B.E. on every other tread. It was a simple matter then to make her way down along the dry side, leaping over the treads on which the drops fell to avoid lateral splash. She did so hastily—and just in time too, for the Pipes switched into a different cycle just as her sandal hit the last tread, and one drop narrowly missed her exposed heel.

The third trial was suffering through the graffiti of Cool Clam, Kool Rock, Pinto, Timetable, Zoom Lens, and Corn Bread (the self-styled "King of the Walls," who crowned his *B* with a three-pronged diadem). It was not considered fair to squint and stumble along the passageway to the station. No, the fully open eye had to be offered up to such xenophobic, no-news lines as

DRACULA AND MANUFACTURERS HANOVER TRUST SUCK

the polymorphous-perversity of

BABE LOVES

BILL & MARY & LASSIE & SPAM

the airy, wuthering affirmation of

CHARLOTTE & EMILY LIVE!

the Platonic pique of

SOCRATES THINKS HE KNOWS ALL THE QUESTIONS

Oreo stared at these writings, a test of her strength. So intense was her concentration that at first she paid little notice to a tickle at her right shoulder. She felt it again and whirled to look into the eyes of a lame man she had passed near the Babe-Bill-Mary-Lassie-Spam graffito. One of the foil-wrapped packages from her duffel-bag lunch was in his hand. He had been picking her packet! She reached out to grab it but ducked when she saw the man's arm go around in a baseball swing. There was a *whoosh!* as molecules of air bumped against one another, taking the cut her head should have taken. Strike one. With the count 0–1, she noticed that the bat was a cane. She ducked again for strike two. "Well, aint this a blip!" Oreo said aloud, finally getting annoyed. She grabbed the cane and gave the man a mild *hed-blō*. She did not want to strike a lame old man with a full-force *hed-krac*. When the old pickpacket saw the look in her eye, he turned and ran down the passageway at Olympic speed. He was really hot*footing* it, honey! He was really picking them up and putting them down! Because of her backpack, Oreo did not catch him until he neared the end of the passageway. Felling him with a flying *fut-kik*, she pressed on his Adam's apple with his cane until he promised he would not try to get up until she gave him leave.

She asked him his alias and his m.o. Perry recounted how he had gone into a hardware store and asked for a copper rod. The proprietor brought it to him, saying they were having a special on copper rods that day and that he was entitled to a fifteen percent discount. Perry, caviling emptor, who had read in the papers that the discount was supposed to be twenty percent, took the rod and racked up the storekeeper's head with it. He paid not a copper but, rather, copped the copper before the coppers came and he had to cop a plea. He had taken the rod home, sheathed it in wood, crooked one end, and brazenly decorated the other end with a brass ferrule. With this cupreous cudgel and a fake limp, he had been lurking in the subway concourse, preying on unwary commuters, rampaging up and down the passageway.

"So why haven't I read about this in the papers?" Oreo asked. "We're only a stone's throw from the *Bulletin* building."

"Oh, I just started fifteen minutes ago. You were my first victim, not counting the hardware guy."

Oreo helped Perry up off the ground, advising him that better he should be home waiting for his social security check. She confiscated his cane and admonished him that the way of the cutpurse was hard and drear. He wasn't convinced. Then she said, "I can sum up your ability as a *gonif* in one word."

"What's that?"

"Feh!"

He was convinced.

Oreo in the waiting room of Thirtieth Street Station

The trials of Getting a Ticket, Checking Departure Time, Finding the Track, and Waiting for the Late Train are too typical to chronicle here. While Oreo was in the state of Waiting for the Late Train, she decided to cross "Three legs" off her list. If Perry's cane, now her walking stick, was not the third leg of the Sphinx's hoary riddle about old age, she did not care what it was. She also decided that since this was, after all, her quest (so far a matter of low emprise), she would cross all the other clues off her list whenever she felt justified in doing so. This was not logical, but tough syll. For instance, number 4 on the list was "Sow." Did this pig in a poke indeed refer to something piglike or to something seedlike? To a pork chop or to a Burpee catalog? If her father was going to give such dumb clues, she was going to prove she was her father's daughter. When necessary, she could outdumb any scrock this side of Jimmie C. The arrival of the Silver Gimp—two hours and twelve minutes late—interrupted her smug assessment of how dumb she could be if given half a chance.

Oreo on the train

She had passed through the Finding a Seat phase and was now in the state of Hoping to Have the Seat All to Myself. She took off her backpack and put it on the overhead rack. As each potential seatmate came down the aisle, Oreo gave a hacking cough or made her cheek go into a rapid tic or

talked animatedly to herself or tried to look fat, then she laid her handbag
and walking stick on the adjoining seat and put a this-isn't-mine expression on her face. But these were seasoned travelers. They knew what she
was up to. Since most of them were in the pre-Hoping to Have the Seat
All to Myself phase, they passed on down the aisle, avoiding the eyes of the
shlemiels who were Hoping to Have Someone Nice to Talk to All the Way
to New York. As the train filled, the hardened travelers knew that it was
pie-in-the-sky to hold out for a double seat, and each of them settled
down to the bread-and-butter business of Hoping My Seatmate Will Keep
His/Her Trap Shut and Let Me Read the Paper and the even more fervent
Hoping No Mewling Brats Are Aboard.

One young blond had been traipsing up and down the aisles for five
minutes. Oreo's first thought when she saw him was that he was almost
as good-looking as she was, and she enjoyed watching the other
passengers watch him. On this trip, the young man stopped in front
of her with arms akimbo, resigned, and said, "All right, honey, I've
checked, and next to me you're the prettiest thing on this train, so we
might as well sit together. Give these Poor Pitiful Pearls something to
look at."

Oreo smiled appreciatively at his *chutzpah* and moved her handbag and
cane off the seat.

Before he sat down, he put a black case, about the size of a typewriter,
on the overhead rack. He tried to move Oreo's backpack over, but it
wouldn't budge. "Is this yours?" he asked.

Oreo nodded.

"What's in it—a piece of Jupiter?"

Oreo laughed. "No, my lunch. On Jupiter it would weigh more than
twice as much—between skatey-eight and fifty-'leven pounds."

"Good, good. I see I can talk to you."

By the time the train pulled into North Philadelphia, Waverley
Honor—"Can you *believe* that name?" he said. "In this case Honor is
a place, not a code, thank God!"—knew eight things about Oreo. "Okay,
that's enough about you. Now, go ahead, ask me what I do."

"What do you do, Waverley?" Oreo said dutifully.

"Are you ready for this?" He paused. "I'm a traveling executioner."

Oreo did the obligatory take.

"See that black case?" Waverley pointed to the overhead rack.

Oreo nodded. "It looks like a typewriter case."

"Guess what's in it."

"A small electric chair," Oreo said, playing straight.

"Good guess. No, a typewriter."

"Oh, shit," said Oreo.

Waverley placated her. "But it *was* a good guess. It's my Remington electric. Carry it with me on special jobs. It's a Quiet-Riter."

"So tell me, already, and cut the crap," said Oreo.

Waverley explained that he was a Kelly Girl, the fastest shift key in the East among office temporaries. Whenever a big corporation was having a major shake-up anywhere on the eastern seaboard, Waverley got the call to pack his Remington.

"Yes, but what exactly do you do?" asked Oreo.

"I thought you'd never ask." He moved closer to Oreo so that their conversation could not be overhead. "My last job was typical. I get the call from Kelly, right? They say, 'So-and-so Corporation needs you.' So-and-so Corporation shall be nameless, because, after all, a boy can't tell *everything* he knows." He paused for the laugh. "But believe me, honey, this is a biggie. I mean, you can't fart without their having something to do with it. Anyway, I show up at the building—one of those all-glass mothers. I flash my special pass at the guard. I wish I could use that identification card on all my jobs—absolutely *adorable* picture of me. Anyway, I take the back elevator to the fifty-second floor. The receptionist shows me to my cubicle. A man comes in a minute later with a locked brief-case. He opens it and explains the job. It's straight copy work. What I am doing is typing the termination notices of four hundred top executives. Off with their heads! That's why I call myself the traveling executioner. I mean, honey, most of those guys had been with that company since 1910, and they don't know *what* the fuck is going to hit them in their next pay check." He raised his eyebrows, an intricate maneuver involving a series of infinitesimal ascensions until the brows reached a plateau that, above all, tokened a pause for a rhetorical question. "Can you believe that? Well, my *dear*, the work was *so* mechanical and *so* boring that I *insisted* on having a radio the second day. So while I was decapitating these mothers from Scarsdale and Stamford and Darien, I was digging Aretha and Tina Turner and James Brown. Talk about ironic! While Tina is doing her thing on 'I Want to Take You Higher,' I'm lowering the boom on these forty-five-thousand-dollar-a-year men. Made me feel just *terrible!* I really sympathize with upper-income people, honey. They're *my* kind of minority."

While Waverley went to get a drink of water, Oreo stared at the dirty cardboard on the back of the seat in front of her:

Thanks for riding Penn Central   Have a pleasant trip

She looked out the window as the train passed a small station and saw another sign that, for an instant, made her think she was in a foreign country, until she realized that some letters were missing:

TRA

OCATION 5

As the train pulled into Trenton, Oreo got hungry. She hauled her backpack from the overhead rack and was about to start in, when she realized she was being selfish—besides, it wouldn't hurt to have a carload of travelers in her debt. Reserving only a few choice bundles, she enlisted Waverley's aid and distributed the rest to the other passengers. In a few minutes, groans and moans were heard amidst all the *fressing*.

Between bites, Waverley kept saying, "Oh my God, it's so good I'm coming in my pants."

The whole car broke into applause when Oreo went to get a cup of water. She bowed this way and that as she came back to her seat. She sat there for a while digesting Louise's Apollonian stuffed grape leaves, her revolutionary piroshki. She was trying to decide what shade of blue the sky was. It was the recycled blue of a pair of fifty-dollar French jeans (or jeannettes) that had been deliberately faded. She decided that from now on, she would call that shade jive blue. Douglas Floors would approve.

Waverley was looking over her shoulder. Suddenly he sat back and sighed. "You're the first nice person I've talked to in a long time. Can I drop my beads?"

"Sure, go ahead."

He confided that he was not only a traveling executioner, but also a *gay* traveling executioner.

"*Nu*, so vot else is new?" she said, doing one of her mother's voices.

He made a stage swishy gesture. "I'm beginning to think the whole world is." He then gave a list of movie stars, past and present, who were "that way"; it included everyone except Rin-Tin-Tin and John Wayne. "Even though the Duke's real name is Marion and he has that funny walk, we're pretty sure he's straight, but we're not all *that* definite about Rinty. Lassie, of course, is a drag queen from *way* back."

Waverley said that he had been very depressed since he and his last lover had split up. At first he had just sat around feeling sorry for himself, typing by day and jerking off by night. "Then I decided, the hell with that. I did something I've never done before. I went out cruising in all the bars. Did all the things I've always wanted to do. I felt justified because I was tired of living like a vegetable."

"You wanted to live like a piece of meat," Oreo said.

Waverley nodded appreciatively. "Oh, you are evil, *e-vil!* Anyway, I had all kinds of guys. In the third week, I had my first Oriental."

"Is it true what they say about Oriental men?"

"What?"

"That their balls are like this"—she placed one fist on top of the other—"instead of side by side?"

Another nod, another "Evil, *e-vil!*" He said he would top that by starting a rumor that Castilian fags had a double lisp. Then he opened his wallet. "Let me show you some pictures." He smiled as he looked at the first one. "These are two of my best friends, Phyllis and Billie."

Oreo nodded. "Phyllis looks like Ava Gardner."

"That's Billie, with an *i-e.* Phyllis is the one who looks like a truck driver. But that just goes to show you looks are deceiving. Phyllis doesn't drive trucks. She fixes them. My mother got hold of this one—she's always popping in on me, snooping around, but that's another story. Anyway, when she saw this, I had to tell her Phyll was Billie's *boy*friend. But if you look close, you can see her bra strap through the tee shirt. I showed it to Phyll's ex-husband. I thought he would wet his drawers, he laughed so hard. He's gay, too. A real swish, honey. He's Filipino and they were going to send him back to the islands. He wanted to stay here and he and Phyll were good buddies, so she married him." He shook his head, remembering. "You should have seen her at the wedding. She let her hair grow long and looked pretty good, for her. Joe, that's the guy she married, had to buy her a girdle and stockings and show her how to walk in heels. When she walked, it was a complete panic." He stood up and did a hoarse, deep-voiced cowhand on stilts. " 'By God, when I get out of these damn things, I'll never put them on again.' This was years ago, when girls used to wear dresses to work. But old Phyll would always wear her overalls. Of course, she *was* a mechanic. If her bosses knew she was a girl, they weren't saying. She was a damn *good* mechanic."

"She looks tough," said Oreo. "Does she give Billie a hard way to go?"

Waverley looked genuinely shocked. "Of *course* not. *Billie's* the butch. Phyll's the sweetest girl you'd ever want to meet. She taught me how to knit. Gives cooking lessons to anyone who asks her. She didn't *have* to marry Joe. And then there was the baby—"

"The baby?"

"Sure. Joe said he always wanted one, so Phyll said okay. She made the right decision too. Joe's the best mother a baby could want. But that Billie—she'd break your balls as soon as look at you."

"Or twist your tits," Oreo said.

"What?"

"Never mind—a failure of empathy."

Waverley went on with his adventures. All his talk of cocks he had known and loved reminded Oreo that she had forgotten to pack the gift she had for her father. It was a plaster of Paris mold of Jimmie C.'s uncircumcised penis. Helen had refused to let the hospital take a hem in her son's decoration, saying that she considered it mutilation and that when he was old enough, she would let him decide whether he wanted to have it done. He had not decided because Helen had not put the question to him. Helen had not brought it out in the open because she still did not consider Jimmie C. old enough to decide. Jimmie C. brought it out in the open only to go to the bathroom and to conform to Oreo's special request—no, threat—for a mold. He conformed to her special request because he loved his sister and because she threatened to tell him one of the "suppose" lines that she had been saving up to make him faint. He, in turn, had a special request, which he sang with a hauntingly sweet melodic line: "Nevertheless and winnie-the-pooh, whatever you do, don't paint it green." For one fiendish moment, Oreo had contemplated doing just that, but she contented herself with deciding which of two questions she would put to Samuel when she gave him the mold: "How do you like that *putz?*" or "How do you like *that, putz?*" She had been leaning toward the second, but now all that was moot, since she had forgotten the *putz* in question.

As the train approached the next stop, Waverley said, "Well, this is it. Today Newark, tomorrow Rahway. Could *you* stand such excitement?" They exchanged addresses, and he pulled his black case down from the overhead rack. "Ooo, do I have to pee—the first bar I come to gets the gold," he said piss elegantly.

"Any pot in the storm," said Oreo. She had no shame. She watched Honor bound for a tearoom.

Oreo's gift was
mad of Jimmie C
penis

FRANKLYN AJAYE

be black, brother, be black
1977

be black, brother, be black. My name is an African name, but it's real, see. I had it before it was worthwhile to have it, see. I struggled with it for years. You know what I mean? Because before it was hip to have an African name it was a disgrace to have it. Shit, I had to carry the burden on my ass, you know? But then it got hip, see, and brothers started changing their names, which I didn't mind except they wouldn't give me no warning. Overnight they'd just become another person, you know?

You say, "Hey Willie, what's happenin'?"

"My name ain't Willie."

"Goddamn, you sure do look like that dude."

Can't be two dudes that ugly in America.

"Willie, why you bullshittin'?"

"My name ain't Willie, it's Mbutu Yata. Got meaning. I got a name with meaning. I got it out the book last night I was just reading."

"Oh yeah, what does it mean?"

"It means Warrior with Good Jump Shot. Got meaning, man. It's about my people. I ain't going to answer to that slave shit 'Willie' no more, you dig?"

Then a chick would go by, "Hi Willie. How are you?"

"Oh, I'm all right. Looking good, looking good, baby."

I took black history, hardest class in the school, learned a lot of interesting facts though . . . found out that a black man, Matthew Henson, was actually the first man to actually set foot on the North Pole. A black man, you all didn't know that, nyeah, nyeah. Learn that, man. But you got to take that with a grain of salt, you know, because you got to know that the only reason Matt Henson was the first one allowed to set foot on the North Pole was because Admiral Peary went, "Hmm, that ice looks a little thin up there, doesn't it? Naw, keep the dogs back. Hey Matthew, come here! Put the skillet down, Matthew, and come on up here."

disneyland high
1977

Went to disneyland high. You know, that was hip. Went on psilocybin. Dropped psilocybin. One time. Never will do it again. Too weird, man. Too weird, brother. Mushrooms. Too weird, know what I mean? Me and Tre we went. When you're on psilocybin you really be trippin', you'd be thinking really strange things. We came to the conclusion that everybody at Disneyland was ugly but us, okay? We agreed. We said, "Right!" You know, 'cause we was looking at cats.

"Man, check that out over there, man. They better not ever have no kids."

"Who you tellin', jack? That'd be illegal, man."

"Ah man, to the left, to the left! Don't look long, man. Don't look long, all right? It's bad for the eyes! Bad for your eyes."

We was trippin', man. We was having a good time, man. We was freaking and everything was mellow until this giant mouse came up to us, okay? We just holding on to reality anyway just by a thin thread, okay? Just holding on to what's really going on, you know? And this giant mouse just went, "Snip! Snip!" and cut that thread. 'Cause he just came up, "*Haaa-ah Haaa-ah! Hoooeeeee!,*" skippin', "*Wooooo wooooo! Wooooo!*"

And Tre freaked. Tre just went, "Ah! No! No, I don't believe this, man! Hey! Man! Hey! No!"

And I went, "Hey maintain, Tre. Maintain. It's just a mouse, man; we can whip him, shit. Come on."

He went, "You right, man. You right. You right."

And Mickey he went, "*Hi guys! Tell me have you seen Minnie?*"

Tre went, "Uh, this ain't going to mess with my sex drive now, is it? Come on, man, let's get high. You all right, you know?"

We grabbed Mickey and took him behind the Matterhorn. He was fightin'. "*Come on guys, let me go! Let me go! Come on! Come on!*"

We got Mickey Mouse high, boy, that little sucker freaked, really freaked. Man he got cool, cool, cool. He started walkin' around Disneyland, *"Where is that bitch? Shit, where is that ho? All right, all right. Donald Duck, come here, man. Come here, man, Why don't you buy some pants, Donald? I'm tired of looking at your ass, you know what I mean? Fuck you, Goofy! I don't want to hear shit you got to say, you bucktoothed motherfucker! That's right, I'm talking to you! Don't call me Mickey no more, goddammit, my name is Michael. Shit, man, I'm fifty years old. Show me some respect, man, you dig? Tell your faggot friend Pluto that shit too. Yeah, I saw you the other day. Fuck, I got pictures. Hey Snow White! Snow White, come here, mama. Looking good, looking good, jack. Oh yeah, looking good. Wooo shit, I been checking you out for thirty-five years, you know that? You know what I'm talking about? Well, you know, I'm kinda slow. When we gonna get down? What you mean, you don't know? Shit, you fucking seven dwarves, I'm sure you can work me in."*

So I started throwing up. It was just too much for my nervous system at the time. Seeing this, a giant mouse cursing people out and shit. I said, "I can't go through this." I just started throwing up, "Yaaaggghhh!" Everybody was looking at me. People were stopping. Little kids thought I was a new attraction.

"Oh Daddy, I want to ride that black one! Come on! Come on!"

"Come here, boy. I don't have coupon for that one. I'll have to go to one these booths. You got a ticket for that nigger ride over there? He's not a ride, hunh?"

I went back to Disneyland this year, man, just to mess around. I checked out Mickey Mouse, you know, he's a junkie now. He just hangs around Jungleland, *"What's happenin', Franklyn? What's happenin'? Gimme four, man, gimme four. All right. All right. Yeah, man. You want some blow, brother? It's cut with cheese, man. Open your nose, but close your ass right up, jack. Won't be nothin' getting out."*

I said, "Why you getting loaded so much now, man? What's wrong with you?"

"Hey, I'm depressed. Have you ever dealt with the fact that you're a mouse, man, you know what I mean? Wearing gloves and shit, you know what I mean? I mean what am I going to do in this country? A mouse ain't going nowhere in this country. My future is limited. Best I can hope for is to lead parades and shit. That's about the only form of employment I can get. Minnie left me and shit. I can't cook for myself. Then the worst blow of all happened last week, man. Worst thing, man. I went over to Snow White's last week, man. I was ready, man. I was ready, jack. I

started lovin' on her, man. Got her turned on, jack, man, hey. I took off my clothes, man. I looked down I didn't have no dick. Motherfucker didn't draw one on, man. I don't know what he was thinkin' about. I really don't know what he was thinkin' about, he sure wasn't thinking about me."

cartoons
try to
bang to dick.

from platitudes
1988

g ray desks and chairs on gray rubber mats stripe the glossy, hardwood basketball-court floor. The glass bricks in the walls burn white and the ten lamps hanging from the high, high ceiling—all as big as tin trash cans—hum under the talk of the nervous sophomores.

Please take your seats, people, says Mr. Morgan as he taps the chalkboard rolled in especially for the occasion. This is the Preliminary Scholastic Aptitude Test or PeeEssAyTee, as you prefer. If you are here for any other reason, I bid you good day. [The students all laugh simultaneously, producing not one big laugh but a low, warbled hum that rattles the windows.] Today I am not Mister Morgan your Thespian Arts instructor or Mister Morgan your homeroom babysitter, I am Mister Morgan the Law. I am the head proctor of you twenty-score miscreants, and I intend to fulfill my duties utterly . . . By the way, if you do not know what *miscreant* means, I shan't assist you. For your sake, I hope the word does not appear in the vocabulary section of this examination. [More window rattling.] You shall have three hours to complete the examination. After one and a half hours there will be one break of ten minutes. Other than during that break there will be absolutely no talking, palavering, or chitchatting whatsoever. Your answer sheets are being distributed forthwith. You shall not, I repeat, not, touch them with your finely sharpened number-two pencils or any other marking instrument until you are explicitly told to do so. Once these sheets are filled out, you will each receive a sealed test booklet. If your test book's seal is broken, you will have exactly thirty seconds in which to inform the nearest proctor: Failure to inform him or her of the tampered booklet in time will result in your being asked to leave the test premises. [The combined whispers of fear do not rattle the windows.]

As I mentioned earlier, and as you all undoubtedly know, a number-two pencil and only a number-two pencil may be used to complete this examination. Any marks made by other writing instruments will not be read by the Educational Testing Service computer and you will receive no score. Do not mark the answer sheet other than in the loci provided, otherwise the computer may misjudge your answers and thus lower your score. Of course it may also raise your score, so the less bright of you may just be providential. You may mark the test book if you wish and use it for scrap paper; however, since it is not graded, any answers not transferred to the answer sheet are answers unseen—hence, useless. You may look at your neighbors' answer sheet to your plagiaristic heart's content, but it will not assist you in the slightest, since there are many different versions of the tests, hence no one in your environs will have an answer sheet that even remotely resembles your own. Some of the questions are experimental and have been inserted by the Minority Testing Fairness Coordinating Committee Council. They will not count against your score, but I caution you to try your best on *all* questions, since you cannot be certain which they are. I presume you people know where to locate the lavatories, and for those of you fortunate enough not to be strapped by harried schedules so as to not necessitate wearing a timepiece, I shall display the hour on this green blackboard every fifteen minutes per each of the six sections. At the end of each section I shall say *Stop* and you shall all stop. If you are found to be still writing, you shall be asked to leave the test premises and your test will be invalidated. Finally, though we have laid down rubber matting, the gymnasium floor is slick, so be careful your chairs do not slip, or, in your own parlance—*Keep the four on the floor.* Is everything clear?

Preliminary Scholastic Aptitude Test

Test Booklet #dE101bR-H

NOTE: You MAY mark the test booklet, but these marks are NOT graded by the Educational Testing Service.

SECTION ONE (1): Verbal Relationships. Choose the words whose relationship most CLOSELY resembles the first cluster group conglomerate.

EXAMPLE:

MISCEGENATION: CRIME

a. black: beige

b. zebra: ape

c. Jane Russell: a sexy woman

d. jellyroll: gatemouth

The correct ANSWER is (c) because just as miscegenation used to be a crime, Jane Russell used to be a sexy woman.

Minutes: 20

Questions: 14

1. STRIKINGLY: GOOD-LOOKING
    a. cordially: invited
    b. thoroughly: enjoyed
    c. firmly: believed
    d. terribly: British

2. DEVOTED: FAN
    a. grueling: regime
    b. alarming: rate
    c. voracious: reader
    d. extolling: virtues

3. INSECURE: LOOSE
    a. piebald: apple tart
    b. sinecure: facial
    c. phonetics: turntable
    d. him: her

4. ANC: SAA
    a. TWA: CIA
    b. FCC: NRA
    c. FBI: AAA
    d. PBS: RPG

5. SPEISS: SPORAN
    a. tocher: toric
    b. exuviate: exoteric
    c. liberate: lixiviate
    d. blench: blowsy

6. RECEPTACLE: LOVEMAKING
    a. ephemeral: gauze
    b. quixotic: Spain
    c. firehose: Selma
    d. bulk mail: philately

7. NARRATIVE: PLATITUDES
    a. hot dog: shish kebab
    b. indict: corruption
    c. still life: montage
    d. monochromatic: piebald

8. CUTESY: WOOTSY
    a. boogie: woogie
    b. itsy: bitsy
    c. teeny: weeny
    d. artsy: fartsy

9. SLENDER: WAIST
    a. shapely: breasts
    b. knobby: knees
    c. broad: shoulders
    d. delicate: wrists

10. SCORCHING: SUN
    a. licking: flames
    b. howling: winds
    c. raging: clouds
    d. crashing: waves

11. MARTIAL: MARITAL
    a. siren: Siren
    b. fiend: friend

12. CHOPHOUSE: GRILLROOM
    a. eatery: bistro
    b. misogyny: feminism

    c. enamored: enameled   c. brasserie: diner
    d. black: mail   d. beanery: cookshack

13. BEBOP: MUZAK   14. MOUTH: GAPING
    a. maverick: mule   a. grin: mischievous
    b. heretic: Jesuit   b. smile: radiant
    c. amorphous: tenuous   c. smirk: evil
    d. Coney Island: Great Adventure   d. laugh: scornful

STOP!

End of Section One (1)

You may review THIS and ONLY THIS section.

DO NOT go on to the next section until told to do so.

section two (2): Sentence-building. Choose the word that most CLOSELY fits the blank in the following sentence group clusters.

EXAMPLE:

The robust man _____ another guest wearing black Romanic leather sandals and fluorescent yellow socks who said, "But darling, Foucault was last year."

a. wheeled upon

b. whistled shrilly at

c. huffed, rolled his eyes toward

d. assaulted

The correct ANSWER is (c).

Minutes: 30

Questions: 17

1. The civil-rights leader was _____ to believe the police officer when he said he "liked the colored."
   (1) a. naïve
        b. insinuated
        c. onomatopoeia
        d. paid

2. The black boy knows that _____ .
   (2) a. "Our top story tonight: The Van Camp's bean factory exploded this afternoon soon after their annual All-You-Can-Eat-What-A-Taste-

Treat charity bean-a-thon. Fire inspectors call the blaze ''suspi-cious.''

   b. deep, deep, way down, we are all one and the same.

   c. it ain't the meat, it's the motion that makes your mama want to rock.

   d. yes, oh golly, yes! He would soon meet that special someone who would lead him not into temptation but deliver him into the wonderful world of hand-trembling, glass-shattering, adolescent lovemaking.

3. Though a boy of (3) _____ outward appearance, he knows that if the others understood how (4) _____ and (5) _____ he was, he would soon be loved by all.

   (3) a. ebullient   (4) a. boring   (5) a. slipping

       b. intravenous   b. vapid   b. just a smidgin

       c. unremarkable   c. complicated   c. interesting, almost brilliant

       d. piglike   d. interwoven   d. ribbed, colored, and scented for hours of added enjoyment

6. He often feels (6) _____ because of his perverse sexual urges, but at other times he thinks he is (7) _____ and just passing through the all-too-common rite of passage to manhood.

   (6) a. soluble   (7) a. St. Zenobi, King of the Wild Frontier

       b. different, sick   b. pretty as a picture

       c. an intense desire to win   c. hopelessly normal, and win big   replaceable

       d. himself   d. plátanos fritos

8. Though usually a man of his word, the homeroom teacher was less than honest when he said, ''_____.''

   (8) a. *Ptou*

       b. Mama's baby, papa's . . .

       c. At Morgan's Chevrolet and Used Cars ''fidelity'' is our middle name

       d. Janey's pregnant?

9. Opening his bedroom door _____ , he was surprised to see a white nude Heimlich instructor giving his wife a lesson.

   (9) a. quick as all get-out

       b. with the wind at his back and a good, stout ship under his feet

   c. flowers and chocolates in hand, after having made reservations for two
      at Windows on the World, chirping, ''Happy anniversary, honey!''
   d. like a bat out of hell

10. The _____ , the disillusionment with a movement that once filled him with
such joyous and foolish optimism, is to what he attributes his current and
unshakable cynicism.
(10) a. look of love
     b. aroma of fresh-baked taste treats
     c. pieces of the puzzle were finally coming together
     d. dream deferred once more

11. He _____ bumps into her in a public place just before the music swells
and the camera CUTS to the tight close-ups of their faces revealing that
dreamy surprise of finding that certain someone of your waking and sleeping
dreams.
(11) a. unexpectedly
     b. perfunctorily
     c. knowingly
     d. always

12. The American commando (12) _____ leafs through *Mein Kampf* on a train
lurching through war-torn and enemy-occupied France when (13) _____ ,
a sinister-looking man in a black trench coat, a fedora pulled low over his
bony face, small, round glasses, and an unshaven mug barks, ''Your paperz!
Your paperz! Rrrraus!''

(12) a. nonchalantly   (13) a. contusely
     b. tepidly   b. ponderously
     c. placidly   c. suddenly
     d. tranquilly (yet inside he's a   d. not available in stores
        bundle of nerves)

14. ''C'mon,'' said the rugged hero, clutching his Beretta in one hand, his
woman in the other. ''Let's get out of here!''
    They (14) _____ themselves through the passageway as Dr. Bülow's
evil fortress shook mightily; rocks fell everywhere. Once outside, they dashed
for their lives, he nearly flying her by her arm behind him like a kite when KA-
BOOM! the fierce explosion dashed them to their feet. Moments later they
(15) _____ rise to find just a charred, smoking hole where the mad,
misguided doctor's laboratory once stood.

(14) a. rushed   (15) a. dazedly
     b. hurtled   b. groggily
     c. flung   c. wearily
     d. raced   d. stunnedly

16. Even though the towering monster walked _____ , and the girl was an
    Olympic silver-medalist miler, he caught her and began to strangle her at
    arm's length.
    (16) a. slowly, arms akimbo
         b. ponderously, arms outstretched like a sleepwalker's
         c. like a regular live wire, a real wisenheimer
         d. lethargically, yet each mighty footfall quaked the earth

STOP!

End of Section Two (2)

You may review THIS and ONLY THIS section.

DO NOT go on to the next section until told to do so.

SECTION THREE (3): Reading Comprehension. Read the following passage snippet
    excerpts to come, then answer the questions based on a foundation grounded in
    what you have read.

EXAMPLE:

Most people do not know the interesting origins of Nabisco's Oreo cookie, one of
the world's most-eaten dessert snack biscuits. If people realized that it was
invented by a wealthy Afro-American baker and leader of the pro-assimilation
movement of the 1940s, they might think twice before unscrewing the chocolate
wafers and eating the cream filling separately.

The author probably believes that . . .
    a. "Whitey is de devil."
    b. Today is the first day of the rest of your life.
    c. The already-troubled black bourgeoisie is now in danger of assimilating
       itself to smithereens.
    d. The best things in life are free, me bucko, the best things in life are free.

The correct ANSWER is a matter of heated debate.
Minutes: 40
Questions: 12

One of the most charming and endearing of the many humorous anecdotes to come out of the civil-rights era concerns a certain Georgia church deacon, one of those fiery, uncompromising few who symbolized that struggle to make old Jim Crow take
(5)   wing and fly from this Land of the Free.

It seems that his town's major department-store diners and restaurants continued to refuse to serve Afro-American customers, even though similar changes had already been made all over the South in the wake of the now-legendary boycotts and sit-ins. Well, that firebrand of a man, Deacon _____, took it upon himself to rally the hardworking Afro-American community to boycott every downtown store until they ''changed their tune.''

The town's level of tension was at an all-time high. The
(15)   Deacon, who did not own an automobile himself, valiantly and effectively organized those in the Afro-American community with vehicles to drive the fifty miles to newly integrated Macon to buy all their dry goods and sundries.

After two weeks of the boycott, the Deacon was called to meet the town's Caucasian elders. Three hours later, the Deacon emerged and told his loyal and good-natured, trusting flock, ''Brethren, who wants to eat at their old smelly lunch counters anyway? Shoot, I would not eat their old smelly food even if you promised me a key to the gates o' heaven itself. Let
(25)   us all go home and forget all this talk about boycotts. We will fight them old white folks when it is really important.''

And the funny end of the story came one month later, when the stores *did* change their Jim Crow policy without seeming to bow to Afro-American pressure, and that fiery stalwart, the Deacon, won a brand-new, soft-blue Cadillac convertible in the Chamber of Commerce's First Annual Negro Car Lottery!

1. The tone of the narrative is . . .
   a. jocular
   b. bitingly sarcastic
   c. caustic
   d. conversational

2. The Deacon is described as
    a. fiery
    b. corrupt
    c. valiant
    d. all of the above

3. The most precise title for this passage is
    a. Glory! One Chapter in the Struggle
    b. The Deacon's New Car
    c. Shameless: The Buying of Deacon _____
    d. Free at Last: ''I Won't Be Takin' No Bus No Mo'!''

4. In line 17 ''integrated'' means
    a. your daughter can now marry anyone
    b. improved
    c. Afro-Americans have no more excuses
    d. all of the above

5. In line 22 the Deacon's speech is
    a. fake, contrived, as if written by a Northerner
    b. not even remotely believable, but brilliantly inciteful nevertheless
    c. wholly believable and effective, except that ''key to the gates o' heaven'' business
    d. good. I liked it very much

6. The anecdote itself is
    a. absolutely believable
    b. believable, but a bit overdone, especially the end
    c. true, trust me, I'll even tell you his real name if you want
    d. true, but not such a big deal as the author would have us believe. After all, they did get what they wanted

> ''We are both of us so rich and possessing such impossibly good looks, let us make love like a proud stallion and a mare, or perhaps like two Greek statues newly come to life,'' husked Wayne as he sipped his Moët in his 150-foot yacht bound for
> (5)   Portofino.
>   ''Zere's nothing Greek about what we're going to do, *mon cher*,'' chortled Monique as she let slip her diamond-sequined ball gown, revealing two perfect globes of lust, then stepped

into the life raft filled with caviar and thusly concealed her neatly trimmed, keystone copse.

He untied his Giorgio Armani black-silk bow tie and tossed it into the churning wake of the expensive ship, then disrobed from his Pierre Cardin double-breasted tuxedo and threw the entire suit into the sea, leaving himself naked save for the silk, (15) custom-made shoulder holster cuddling his Beretta 48C he had nicknamed ''Sinbad.''

''Zon't zou zare throw my gown overboard, bee-cauze iz ze ony clothz I bring,'' throated the naked Frenchwoman.

Wayne picked up her Yves Saint-Laurent original, the sequins twinkling in the moonlight, and unceremoniously balled it up. ''Neither of us will be needing any clothing on this trip,'' he cooed deeply as he pitched the shimmering frock into the turbulent waves, which made him recall his rough-and-tumble childhood bouncing from foster home to reform schools, mak- (25) ing friends only by being the best sandlot pitcher and hardest hitter in all of West Philly.

''*C'est la vie, mais* come on zin, ze *l'eau* iz fine,'' nasaled Monique sexily as she splashed herself with the Russian beluga, then fingered some caviar off her proud and jutting pencil erasers and licked her fingers clean.

''In a minute, froggy,'' gruffed Wayne as he donned his wet suit and scuba gear. ''I've got an illegal underwater plutonium-mining operation to blow up.''

7. Monique is
   a. a tease
   b. Mata Hari
   c. a whale of a gal
   d. typical

8. If Monique had succeeded in luring Wayne into the caviar bath,
   a. *he* would have stealthily disconnected *his* twin prosthetic breasts and deeply growled, ''Secret agent man, the jig is up. Did you forget I, your evil nemesis, Dr. Zamboni's thick calves so soon?''
   b. she would have made love with him wildly, then tried to sever his brain stem with a hairpin just as he gruffly grabbed her wrist, made her cry, and spilled the beans.

    c. she would have looped her arms around his neck and kissed him softly, then pulled him gently on top of her, arched her muscular, smooth, tanned back, and guided him gently into her valley of the shadow of Love.

    d. she would have run her arms over his rippling biceps sprinkled with scratches and scars and asked where each wound came from, then kissed each scarred arm, then his chest, his stomach, and down and down, until he would no longer remember his name, nor would he care.

9. How many times has ''globes of lust'' (line 8) appeared in print?
    a. just this once
    b. twice
    c. in *Squirt* magazine alone, 3.5×10^4 (as of 3/1/84)
    d. more times than I care to remember, thank you

10. How did Wayne get so wealthy if he grew up in foster homes and reform schools? (line 24)
    a. One day, a large yacht moored on the lake near his last juvenile hall. He stowed away on the vessel, and when he was discovered, the yacht's owner so admired his chutzpah, he adopted him.
    b. He was a hustling and scamming ragamuffin, stole when he had to, extorted when the need arose, amassed a large fortune eventually, but when the Internal Revenue Service caught wind of his little scam and was hot on his trail, they offered him one last out: ''Work for us,'' they said, ''and you won't go to the hoosegow.''
    c. Attending Stanford University on a basketball scholarship, his gregarious nature and winning good looks soon earned him a berth in the easy elitism of the school's fraternity system. Through these contacts, he met and married a meat-packing mogul's homely daughter, Megan Winston, who wound up the victim of a tragic gangland slaying.
    d. A good-looking boy of fourteen, he would mow lawns of the mansions on the other side of the tracks. One day, a wealthy divorcée paid him $100, saying, ''I've got a lawn to mow inside too.'' (Repeat)

       The good, homely folk of Lowndes County never expected they would ever get a gander of the likes of this here. Little Eehssi Robinson, Pernice's baby daughter, burning down Route 69 in a brand-new, shiny red foreign number, coming in even faster

(5)   than she had fled their quaintproudnoblesimplejoyousglorious- triumphalnice hamlet ten years before to attend university. They

all knew she was living in California; probably in one of those
big, fancy old houses up on those hills they'd seen in the moving pictures every Sunday, and she'd become right famous and
won prizes, and her books were in the library and all, but no
one, not even the boozy preacherman, expected such a shiny
red sports car.

    So there they were, the whole town out on their clean-
smelling front stoops watching that shiny red streak and the
(15) plume of dust that followed close behind like Ham's ghost.
The streak and that ghost—that brown cloud of memory—
finally slowed down to brave the cratered drive up to the house
from where the writer was birthed.

    "He-llo, Ma-ma," enunciated the jubilant writer. "I am ab-
solutely fatigued after such a long journey . . . Oh, and, Mama,
'fatigued' means tired."

    Mama, her nostrils proudly flaring like a holy god's chariot-
pulling mare, her heavy, joyous bosom rising and falling with
every profound breath of that sweet Georgia wind, her legs as
(25) strong and as stout as the mighty Georgia pines, exuberantly
hoisted that heavy iron skillet high over her kerchief-covered
head, the skillet from which she had fried the eggs and bacon
and ham and apples and cornbread, and had cooked the grits
and greens and black-eyes and chit'lin's and okra for her thirty
healthy children, and she swung that skillet down with a quickness far beyond her seventy years onto the hot-combed hair
of her youngest daughter, Eehssi, killing the child with
a *clonk*.

    " 'Fatigued,' my ass."

11. How would you describe the style of this passage?
   a. neoclassical
   b. postmodern
   c. Afro-Baroque
   d. mock Afro-Baroque

12. If Eehssi had not said, " 'Fatigued' means tired" (line 21), how would the
    story have ended?
   a. Little had changed in her sleepy little hamlet. Where she had expected
      envy and ignorance, she found instead a spirituality that had been missing

from her life ever since she had left. It was precisely at this moment that she decided to return—not once a decade as she had previously done—but every summer; not for the people, not even for Mama, but for her own now-blossoming soul.

b. The sun was warmer here, the air sweeter, and the smiles so much broader, and it was then and only then that Eehssi could not remember why it was she had ever left.

c. ''Welcome home, child,'' said Mama quietly. Eehssi glowed. Somewhere in the distance, watchful hounds barked. They too welcomed her home.

d. An old turkey buzzard circled aimlessly in the endlessly blue sky as the smell of cooking molasses—the best smell in the whole wide world, she thought to herself—tickled her nostrils with sweet, deliciously sweet memories of a little pigtailed girl with honey knees and ashy elbows who one day said to no one in particular, ''I-am going to be-a writer.''

STOP!
End of Section Three (3)
You may review THIS and ONLY THIS section.
DO NOT go on to the next section until told to do so.

any lit
1991

You are a ukulele beyond my microphone
You are a Yukon beyond my Micronesia
You are a union beyond my meiosis
You are a unicycle beyond my migration
You are a universe beyond my mitochondria
You are a Eucharist beyond my Miles Davis
You are a euphony beyond my myocardiogram
You are a unicorn beyond my Minotaur
You are a eureka beyond my maitai
You are a Yuletide beyond my minesweeper
You are a euphemism beyond my myna bird
You are a unit beyond my mileage
You are a Yugoslavia beyond my mind's eye
You are a yoo-hoo beyond my minor key
You are a Euripides beyond my mime troupe
You are a Utah beyond my microcosm
You are a Uranus beyond my Miami
You are a youth beyond my mylar
You are a euphoria beyond my myalgia
You are a Ukrainian beyond my Maimonides
You are a Euclid beyond my miter box
You are a Univac beyond my minus sign
You are a Eurydice beyond my maestro
You are a eugenics beyond my Mayan
You are a U-boat beyond my mind control
You are a euthanasia beyond my miasma
You are a urethra beyond my Mysore
You are a Euterpe beyond my Mighty Sparrow

You are a ubiquity beyond my minority
You are a eunuch beyond my migraine
You are a Eurodollar beyond my miserliness
You are a urinal beyond my Midol
You are a uselessness beyond my myopia

jinglejangle
1991

ab flab abracadabra Achy Breaky Action Jackson airy-fairy
  airfare
Asian contagion analysis paralysis Anna banana
  ants in your pants
Annie's Cranny Annie Fanny A-Okay ape drape argle-bargle
artsy-fartsy awesome blossom

backpack backtrack Bahama Mama balls to the wall bam-a-lam
  bandstand
Battle in Seattle beat the meat bedspread bee's knees
  behani ghani best dressed
best in the West BestRest Best Western Betsy Wetsy
  Better Cheddar Big Dig bigwig
bird turd black don't crack blackjack blame game boho
  boiling oil
Bone Phone Bonton Bony Maroni boob tube boogie-woogie
  boohoo book nook
boon coon Bot's dots Boozy Suzy bowl of soul bow-wow
  boy toy brace face
brain drain bric-a-brac bug jug bump on the rump
  Busty Rusty

cachi-bachi caffe latte cake bake candy's dandy Care Bear
  cash for trash Cat in the Hat
chalk talk Chatty Cathy cheers & jeers cheaper to keep her
  cheat sheet Chester the molester
chewy gooey chick flick Chilly Willy chips & dips chitchat
  chock-a-block

Choco Taco chop shop chrome dome Chubby Hubby
　　Chuck & Buck chugalug Chunky Monkey
cigar bar Cinni Mini claptrap Click & Clack clink-clank
　　clipclop Coca-Cola cock block
cock doc cock sock cookbook Cool Yule Cracker Jack
　　crack shack crack's wack creature feature
crick-crack crinkly wrinkly crisscross crop top crumb bum
　　Crunch 'n Munch
culture vulture curly-whirly

date rape deadhead deep sleep dikes on bikes dilly-dally
　　ding-a-ling ding-dang dingle-dangle
ding-dong dirty birdy Dizzy Lizzy dog log Don Juan
　　Donut Hut double trouble downtown dramarama
　　drape shape dream team Dress for Success drill & kill
drip-drop drunk skunk dry eye

eager beaver Earl the Pearl easy greasy Eat a Pita
　　eenie-meenie Etch-a-Sketch
Evel Knievel Even Stephen Eye in the Sky

fag hag fair share Fakin' Bacon fancy pants Fast Gas fat cat
　　Fax Pax Fay Wray
fender bender fews & twos fiddle-faddle fight or flight Fiji
　　file or pile fill the bill fine line
finer diner fine wine Flavor Saver Fleet Street flim-flam
　　flip-flop Flirty Gerty Flo Jo
flower power flub-dub fly-by fly-by-night fly guy fogdog
　　four-door four-on-the-floor
Foxy Roxy frat rat Freaks & Geeks freaky-deaky free bee
　　frick & frack
fried, dyed, laid to the side fright night Froot Loops FuBu
　　fuck a duck fuddyduddy
fungus among us fun in the sun funny money fur burger
　　fuzzy wuzzy

gal pal gang bang gas grass or ass gator bait gay for pay
　　Geechee gender bender

Georgie Porgie gewgaw gherkin jerkin gibber-jabber glad pad
    gloom & doom goof proof
googly-moogly Gorgeous George gory story Greeks & geeks
    Greek Week green bean
Green Jeans grinning & skinning

Hackensack hackmatack hackysack hair care hairy fairy
    Handy Andy
handy dandy hanky-panky hari-kari Happy to Be Nappy
    harum-scarum
haunch & paunch haste makes waste heart smart
    Heckle & Jeckle heebie-jeebies
Hegel's Bagels hell's bells helter-skelter Henny Penny
    herky-jerky heyday hickory-dickory
hi-fi higgledy-piggledy high & dry hinky dinky hip hop
    hippy dippy hobnob hobo
Hobson-Jobson hockey jockey hocus-pocus hodgepodge
    hoi polloi hoity-toity
HoJo Hokey Pokey holy mole holy moley Home Alone
    honey bunny Hong Kong honky-tonk
hoodoo hooked on books hook or crook hootchie-kootchie
    hotch-potch Hotel No Tell hot pot
hot shot Hottentot How now brown cow hubbub
    Hubba Bubba hubble-bubble Huckabuck
huff & puff hugger mugger Huey, Dewey, Louie Hully Gully
    humdrum hump & dump
Humpty-Dumpty hurdy-gurdy hurly-burly Hurry Curry
    hurry-scurry hustle & bustle

Icky Ricky I Like Ike ill pill ill will Increase the Peace
    inky-dinky
ism jism I Spy itsy-bitsy itty-bitty

jai alai Janet's Planet jeepers creepers Jeez Louise jelly belly
    jet set Jew canoe jig rig jimjams
jinglejangle Joe Blow Joe Schmoe Juicy Lucy June gloom
    June moon junkie's monkey
junk in the trunk junky punky

killer-diller King Kong Kit Kat kiwi knickknack knob job
    Koo Koo Roo
kowtow Krik? Krak! kudu Kundun

Laffy Taffy lame brain large & in charge late great later gator
    Lazy Daisy
Lean Cuisine lean & mean lean mean machine legal eagle
    Leggo my Eggo
Lexis Nexus lick dick Lickin' Chicken licking stick
    Liddle Kiddle liquor's quicker
lit crit liver quiver lizard's gizzard local yokel long dong
    Loony Toons Loopy Doopy
loose screws loosey-goosey lovie-dovie low blow lucky duck
    lump sum lunch bunch
lust in the dust Lynyrd Skynyrd

Mac Attack mad dad made in the shade Magilla Gorilla
    mainframe maitai Mango Tango
Manila Thriller Mantan Mars bars master blaster Maui Wowie
    May Day Meal Deal
Meals on Wheels mean green meet & greet mellow yellow
    Messy Bessy
Micmac might makes right Mighty Aphrodite miles of smiles
    Milli Vanilli
Mingus Among Us mishmash Missy-Pissy mock croc
    Mod Squad mojo moldy oldie
Money Honey moose on the loose mop top Mork from Ork
    motor voter muckamuck
muck chuck mukluk multi-culti mumbo jumbo mu shu
    mushy-gushy my guy

namby-pamby name game nature nurture near beer nice price
    night light
nig-nog niminy piminy nitty-gritty nitwit
    no finance, no romance
no glove, no love no go no muss, no fuss no pain, no gain
    no show no way, Jose
nudie cutie Nut Hut Nutter Butter Nutty Buddy

Ocean Potion odd jobs Oingo Boingo okey-dokey old gold
  ooga-booga
Only the Lonely oodles of noodles Oshkosh B'gosh

Paco's Tacos page gauge pale ale paranoid android
  Parappa the Rapper party hearty Patel hotel
paunch & haunch payday pay & play pee & see peewee
  peg leg pell-mell peter beater
Phantom Anthems phone home phony baloney Pick Up Sticks
  picnic pie in the sky, by & by
Piggly Wiggly ping-pong pit-a-pat pitter-patter Plain Jane
  plaster caster plastic fantastic
play as it lays pocket rocket poet don't know it pogo
  pooper scooper pot shot pope-soap-on-a-rope
Pop Shop poptop Post Toasties powwow poxy doxy prime
  time pump & dump psychedelic relic Puff 'n Stuff

Queen of Mean quest for the best Quick Pick quick trick
  quiet riot quirky quarky

racket-jacket ragbag Ragin' Cajun ragtag ramble-scramble
  Randy Andy rape & scrape
rat-a-tat razzle-dazzle razzmatazz real deal redhead
  Reese's Pieces reet pleat
retail detail Rhymin' Simon rich bitch rickety-tickety rickrack
  riffraff
ring-a-ding ringer dinger rinky-dink Rin Tin Tin riprap
  roach coach
Rock Around the Clock rocket pocket Rolled Gold roly-poly
  Ronald McDonald
rooty-tooty rope-a-dope rough & tough rough stuff
  rub-a-dub Rufty Tufty rusty dusty

saggy baggy Sally's Alley sandman sassafras scarlet harlot
  sci-fi scot & lot
Scrapple from the Apple screen scene screwy Louie screw you
  Sea & Ski
seedy tweedy seesaw self help sexy Rexy shady lady
  shake it, don't break it

Shake 'n Bake Shedd's Spread shilly-shally shipshape
　　shirk work shit fit
shit, grit, motherwit shock jock Shy Di sin-bin Sin Den
　　singles mingle singsong
skag hag skimble-scamble skinflint skinny mini skunk funk
　　sky high slammer jammer
Slice o' Rice slice & dice Slick Rick Slim Jim slo-mo
　　SmarteCarte snack pack
snail mail snail trail Smothers Brothers smut-butt smut slut
　　sneak peek snowblower
snug as a bug in a rug soap-on-a-rope SoHo space is the place
　　space race Spamarama
Spam in a can SpecTech speed reader spit-spot splish-splash
　　spring fling Spruce Goose
squeegee Stan the Man stars & bars steam clean Stinky Pinky
　　Stix Nix Hix Pix stranger danger
Stormin' Norman street beat stun gun stupid Cupid Style File
　　suck and tuck Suds Your Duds
sugar booger sump pump super duper Superloopers sure cure
　　surf & turf Swatch watch sweater weather sweetmeat
　　Swiss Kriss Swiss Miss

ta-da Tears for Fears tea tree teeny peeny teeny-weeny teepee
　　teeter-totter telltale Temporary Contemporary tent event
　　Texas Exes Tex-Mex thigh high think pink thinktank
　　thin's in, but fat's where it's at
thin skin thrill kill thrills & chills Throat Coat tib-fib Tictac
　　ticky-tacky
ticktock tie dye tin tan tan tiptop titbit tit for tat tittle-tattle
　　ton of fun tough enough tough stuff town & gown
　　Tragic Magic
treat and street Tricky Dicky true blue trust buster
　　turkey jerky tussy-mussy tutti-frutti
Twine Time

ubble-gubble Ubby Dubby Ugh Bug ugly-mugly
　　undone unfun urge to purge use it or lose it

Vanessa the Undresser vice price vomit comet voodoo

Wacko Jacko wacky shack wacky tobacky walkie-talkie
  Wavy Gravy waylay
wear & tear Weegee Whack Pack whale tale wham bam
  whammer-jammer
wheeler dealer whimwham white flight white knight
  Wicked Pickett
weird beard wild child willy-nilly Wilt the Stilt
  wining & dining
wingding Winken & Blinken wishy-washy womb to tomb
  wonton
Wooly Bully Writing Is Fighting

X-sex

Yak Pak yank the crank Yertle the Turtle ying-yang yoohoo

zero to hero zigzag zip your lip Zoo Doo zoot suit Zulu

kamasutra sutra
1991

This is a story I have heard:

Entwined in a passionate embrace
with his beloved wife,
the holy one exclaimed,
"I have reached enlightenment!"

His devoted partner responded,
"I'm truly happy for you, my love,
and if you can give me another minute,
I believe I'll get there too."

souvenir from anywhere
1991

People of color untie-dyed. Got nothing to lose but your CPT-shirts. You're all just a box of crayons. The whole ball of wax would make a lovely decorator candle on a Day of the Dead Santeria Petro Vodou altar. Or how about these yin-yang earrings to balance your energy? This rainbow crystal necklace, so good for unblocking your chi and opening the chakras? Hey, you broke it, you bought it! No checks accepted. Unattended children will be sold as slaves.

devotees in the garden of love
1991

The Lovers

LILY

GEORGE, later PATTY

MADAME ODELIA PANDAHR, A PANDERER

A.

A garden on a hilltop. In the middle of nowhere. Lily, a teeny tiny older woman in a wedding dress, sits in an old-time wheelchair. George, a much larger, much younger woman in a wedding dress, sits on a camp stool practicing conversation.

LILY: Ooooohlukater. Huh. Thuh huzzy.

GEORGE: Oooooh. *Mon nom? Ah, Monsieur, je m'appelle*—George. Jooooorrrrge.

LILY: Who does she think she is. Bein down there.

GEORGE: *Et vous? Comment vous appelez-vous?*

LILY: Down there amongst thuh action.

GEORGE: *Monsieur Amour? Oooh là là, Monsieur Amour! "Monsieur Amour"—très romantique, n'est-ce pas?*

LILY: Down there amongst thuh action where she do not belong.

GEORGE: *L'amour est très romantique. La romance est la nature de l'amour. Et vous, Monsieur Amour, vous êtes le roi d'amour.*

LILY: In my day uh woman spoke of her table. And that was all.

GEORGE: *Est-ce que vous êtes le roi d'amour?*

LILY: We did things thuh old-fashioned way. In my day. Thuh old-fashioned way was even "old-fashioned" back then. I go way back. Huh. Who thuh hell is she pretendin tuh be way down there in thuh thick of it.

GEORGE: *Vous êtes le roi d'amour, et je serai votre reine.*

LILY: Upstart, George girl. At high noon.

GEORGE: *Oooh là là Monsieur Amour! Oui oui! Oui oui!*

LILY: Look at that upstart! George! Uh upstart. In white even. At high noon. Huh. Thuh huzzy. Huh. Thuh upstart.

GEORGE: Starting up?! Not without my say so they dont!

LILY: Huh?

GEORGE: Start up?! Not without my say so!

LILY: Upstart. Uh huzzy.

GEORGE: Oh.

LILY: See?

GEORGE: *Oui oui! Oui oui!*

LILY: See?!

GEORGE: *Oui.* I see. In my heart. Madame Odelia Pandahr says that because all the eyes of the world are on the heart of the bride-who'll-be's heart thuh bride-who'll-be's heart thus turns inward, is given to reflection and in that way becomes an eye itself. Seeing inward to examine her most deepest thoughts and feelings and seeing outward too tuh give her form and grace thatll guide her in her most natural selection, that is, her choice of suitors.

LILY: Drop that lorgnette girl and use thuh bo-nocks. See?

GEORGE: *Oui!*

LILY: BO—NOCKS!

GEORGE: Oh.

LILY: HIGH NOON!

GEORGE: High noon?

LILY: HIGH NOON!

GEORGE: High noon.

LILY: Not your time! My time! High noon my time my time! George girl get over here and—ooooooooooh! Thuh huzzy. Right *in* thuh thick of it.

GEORGE: Thuh woman?

LILY: Thuh huzzy.

GEORGE: In white?

LILY: In white.

GEORGE: Mama Lily?

LILY: Right in thuh thick of it.

GEORGE: Mama Lily thats Madame Odelia Pandahr Mama. Oooh
   hooo, Madame! *C'est moi*! Joooooooorge! Oooh hoo! Oooh hooo!

LILY: Gimmieuhminute. Wheremy specs.—.Huh. Huh.—.Well.

GEORGE: Madame Odelia Pandahr ssgonna be monitoring thuh
   situation play by play.

LILY: Play by play.

GEORGE: Madame Odelia Pandahr says that thuh ultimate battle of love
   requires uh good go between. In thuh old days Madame Odelia
   Pandahr says they had matchmakers and messengers—

LILY: Them old days was my days.

GEORGE: Madame Odelia Pandahr says that our new days require thuh
   kind of reportage that shes doing. "Reportage." Ha! Madame
   Odelia Pandahr, you know, shes French.

LILY: I guess they just do things different.

GEORGE: They do. *Enchanté de faire votre connaissance, Monsieur.*

LILY: Look. They all lookin at us. Look.

GEORGE: You think they can see us way up here?

LILY: They all lookin our way.

GEORGE: Ooooh! *Bonjour! Bonjour! Bonjour! Bonjour!*

LILY: Honey?

GEORGE: Huh?

LILY: Theyre waitin for your signal.

GEORGE: Thuh hankie?

LILY: Thuh hankie

GEORGE: *Oui oui! Oui oui!*

LILY: Let it drop like we talked uhbout.

GEORGE: Madame Odelia Pandahr says that uh hankie should be
   dropped—

LILY: Go on then.

GEORGE: *Comme ça!*

   (*The battle begins*)

LILY: Thatll do. (*Pause*) And it's begun. (*Pause*) See? See?

GEORGE: You may, now, Sir, return my handkerchief to my hand now
   Sir.

LILY: See?

GEORGE: In my heart. Madame Odelia Pandahr says that—

LILY: Out there. Look.

GEORGE: In my heart—

LILY: Take uh look see through this. Go on. Lookie. Use your right eye. Put your hand over your left. Thats it. Figet thuh focus. Thats it. Now look-see. See!? See?!

GEORGE: Uh—

LILY: Try these. Go on. Both eyes on um. I used this pair tuh watch your daddy triumph over his rival. Ah—ooooooooooooooh!

GEORGE: *Oooh là là!*

LILY: KERBLAM! Sweet Bejesus! Scuze my French! Sweet Bejesus answer my prayers looks like ThatOne done sunked ThisOnes battleship rockum sockum rockum sockum—ONE OCLOCK love of uh girl! ONE OCLOCK!

GEORGE: One oclock.

LILY: My time!

GEORGE: Your time.

LILY: Off lookin at nothin at 19:45. They say love makes yuh blind. Only ever made me sweat. In my day my motherud say 16:15 and there wernt no question that it was 16:15 her time. Thuh time helpin tuh tell you where you oughta be where you oughta be lookin and whatcha oughta be lookin at. Frenchiz in uh different time zone. Seems tuh me. Must be. Huh. All that *français*. Dont belong on uh field uh battle. Tuck it outa sight. For now. We got our own lingo and what we cant say with our own—hometown lingo just wont get said. For thuh time being. Go on. Tuck thuh *français* away—WOOOOOOOOOOOH! And there it all is. Raging. 2 O CLOCK LOVE OF UH GIRL! KERBLAM! See?! SEE?!

GEORGE: Ooooooh—

LILY: Impressive. Impressed?

GEORGE: Rockets red blare at 2 oclock, Mama Lily. Makes my heart sing.

LILY: Thats my girl!

GEORGE: Our word is "Devotion." My match was made in heaven.

LILY: Thats my George!

GEORGE: We will hold fast unto thuh death. We will not come all asunder. We wont flinch.

LILY: Thats my George! Lookie lookie lookie: bombs bursting in air at 10:25. Just like thuh ditty.

GEORGE: Oooooooooooh!

LILY: KERBLAM! Direct hit! Makes it all worthwhile.

GEORGE: Mama?

LILY: AH-AH-AH-AH-AH-AH-AH-AH. RAT-TA-TAT-TAT.

GEORGE: Mama Lily? At 9 oclock?—My time. I think I see an instance of uh bodily harm.

LILY: You crossed your legs before you held your head up. First steps you took you took with uh board on your head balanced there as an insurance of premiere posture. Preschool charm school with all the trimmings we couldn't afford it so, thats my girl, thats my George, bless your sweet heart, sweetheart I taught you your basics. How tuh lay uh table. How tuh greet uh guest. Thuh importance of uh centerpiece. How tuh fix uh "mess." Thuh difference between "mess" and "messy."

GEORGE: "Mess" means food and should be plentiful. "Messy" means sloppy and should be scarce.

LILY: How, if you went tuh uh party and arrived early, how not tuh go in and catch thuh hostess unawares but tuh walk up and down thuh sidewalk until 20 minutes after thuh affair had begun.

GEORGE: The importance of being fashionably late.

LILY: Every affair is uh battle—

GEORGE AND LILY: And every battle ssgot tuh have uh battle-*plan*.

LILY: Even learned you uh little bit uh fan work. Then it was off tuh Madame Odelia Pandahrs. On full scholarship!

GEORGE: *C'était magnifique!*—It was wonderful!

LILY: My George finishes Madame Odelia Pandahrs Finishing Academy at thuh top of her class! Planning dinner parties for uh hundred and forty! Knowed thuh places for settings I'll never lay eyes on. Didnt have them places back then. *Au courant* we calls her. Thats my George. Thats my girl.

GEORGE: 9 oclock. Mama Lily. Looks like weve got ourselves uh premiere example of uh decapitation.

LILY: So it is. So it is.

GEORGE: Major dismemberment at 9:05.

LILY: So it is. So it is.

GEORGE: Blood. Blood. Blood. Dust. Ashes. Thick smoke.—Carnage.

LILY: Conclusion, Miss George?

GEORGE: In conclusion, Mama Lily, I'd say that the fighting is well underway.

LILY: Further?

GEORGE: Further, Mama Lily? If I'd go further I'd say "fierce."

LILY: Prognosis, Miss George?

GEORGE: Prognosis, Mama Lily? Well—looks like I just may be married in thuh mornin, Mama.

LILY: Makes my heart sing.

GEORGE: *Mon coeur est plein d'amour!*

LILY: Hold off until thuh peace talks please love of uh girl.

GEORGE: They may not be peacing by morning though. My match by morning may not be made. Madame Odelia Pandahr says there arent 2 suitors alive more well matched than ThisOne and ThatOne. While any other suitor in thuh area of conflict would be smote right down for dead ThisOne has uh move which ThatOne counters and ThatOne has uh counter to which ThisOne always gives reply. From what Madame Odelia Pandahr says ThisOne and ThatOne are even steven one for one move for move uh perfect match.

LILY: Keep your eyes stuckd inside them bo-nocks my sweet thing. Down theres where thuh action is.

GEORGE: It could be uh protracted engagement down there. I may be sittin uhround protractedly engaged up here. — .But I think thingsll wrap theirselves up nicely.

LILY: And how come?

GEORGE: How come cuz thuh cause of Love thats how come. L-O-V-E. ThatOne could start uh charge on ThisOne and ThisOne would rally back. Cuz thuh cause of Love. ThisOne may sever thuh arms and legs off uh all uh ThatOnes troops and those maimed and mismangled arms and legs would riiiise up uhgain and return to their trunks like uh child coming home for supper when thuh triangle bell was rung. Cuz thuh cause of Love. Guns with them knives on thuh ends may run through lines and lines of thuh faithful piercing through and through and through and fingers and toes may travel to foreign countries where we aint never been, Mama Lily, puss green-slimed bile and contagion may grow from thuh wounds of thuh wounded seep intuh thuh ground and kill and kill and kill and kill and kill and kill and kill and thuh

cannons may roar thuh wind may moan thuh sky may shake and
spit fire and crack open and swallow um all up but itll all end
nicely. Our word is "devotion." My match was made in heaven.
We will hold fast. Unto thuh death. We will not come out all
asunder. We wont flinch. How come? Cuz thuh cause of Love.

LILY: Seems all quiet now. Must be taking uh lunchtime. Nobody
down theres movin. Huh. In my day things were just as interesting.
Dont think twice uhbout that. Thuh lucky ones were pursued.
Thuh unlucky ones had tuh make do. Ssallways been like that. My
suitor fought for me and its only right that you oughta be so sought
after. If I havent given you you nothin else at least I've made sure
uh that. George? GEORGE!? Where you gone off to? Thuh gettin
was just gettin good. Theys takin uh break we kin sit here in watch
em lick their wounds. Shoot. Uh dogs lickin on that one. Werent
no dogs uhllowed on thuh field uh battle in my day. Everythings
gone tuh pot. De-volution. Huh. Where you been?

GEORGE: Had tuh get my hope chest.

LILY: Had tuh get your hope chest. Thats my George.

GEORGE: As uh bride-who'll-be I'm waiting at thuh ready. Ready for
uh inspection. As bride I expect my groomll inspect me. Maybe
you could inspection my wares while theyre getting reinforcements.

LILY: Could do. Go on—lounge uhround like you didnt know it was
coming. Lounge girl, go on. Madame Odelia Pandahr didnt cover
lounging?

GEORGE: Given thuh ensuing conflict she questioned its ethical nature.

LILY: Huh.—.Sit on thuh grass pick daisies look right on off intuh
thuh 3 oclock. Smoke uh cigarette. Sing.

GEORGE: Sing?

LILY: La de de la de dah and et cetera.

GEORGE: La de de la de dah la de de la de dah.

LILY: La de de la de dah la de de la de dah ssjust uh normal day who
knows what may be up next.

GEORGE: La de de la de dah la de dah dah le deee—

LILY: SPEC-SHUN!

GEORGE: YES, MAAM.

LILY: Gimmie gimmie gimmie. Bring it over here lets see whatcha got.
2 tablecloths: Irish linen. 1 tablecloth: fancy lace. Napkins tuh
match. Place settings for—40–42—.

GEORGE: Some may break.

LILY: Thats my George! Thats thuh battleplan! Ah ha: uh brown sac uh peppermint candies. For fresh breath?

GEORGE: For fresh breath.

LILY: Reason bein?

GEORGE: Reason bein cuz after battle my suitor may be uh little in need of refreshin. Madame Odelia Pandahr says that theres only one thing staler than thuh mouth of uh suitor—ha—and thats thuh mouth of thuh one that lost thuh fight. Ha ha ha ha. Aaah.

LILY: Yummy. Dont mind if I inspect thuh taste of thuh brown sacked mints for fresh breath do you Miss George. Uh set of informal nappi-kans. Everyday *serviettes*. Matchin everyday tablecloth. Plenty of sheets: handsewn. Doilies hand done. Extra bedsprings for thuh— wedding night. Bloomers xtra large hand sewn. Only one pair. Practicin economy. Brassieres galore tuh match. Why you got so many uh these things I will never know. You only got 2 tits girl.

GEORGE: Uh war brides gotta point thuh way.

LILY: Didnt we pack you uh pair of white elbow-length gloves?

GEORGE: Uh huhnn. Madame Odelia Pandahr borrowed um. She said ThisOne and ThatOne needed em. You know, tuh slap each others faces with and throw down and challenge.

LILY: Throwin down thuh gauntlet! Thats thuh old style! Ah! And thuh silver! 84 piece set. Stole it one by one from—well they aint never gonna know now is they. They aint noticed yet and they aint never gonna know cause we aint never gonna tell. Nicely polished. Shinin like thuh lake. In my day thuh first vision uh future battle bride envisioned was her table. Her place settings was thuh place holders for her company. Who would come tuh dine throughout her generations. Seein thuh vision of her table was thuh most important thing. Guess it aint like that now. Now you got— technology. Huh. Lets see now: uh few jewels for adornment. And your bridehead: intact. Intact, Miss?

GEORGE: I aint touched it. Seal on thuh jar iduhnt broke izit?

LILY: Hmmmmm. Hmmmmmmmmmm. HMMMMMMMMMMMM. HMMMMMMMMMMMMMMMMM. Huh. Nope. Ha! Makes my heart sing, Miss George. Love of uh girl. Ha ha ha ha ha—whasszis?

(A TV!)

GEORGE: Madame Odelia Pandahr says todays battle bride oughta be adequately accoutrementalized by thuh modern age.

LILY: Thuh modern age.

GEORGE: Madame Odelia Pandahr says there iduhnt nothin like watchin thuh conflict play by play like.

LILY: We got thuh spy glass. We got thuh bo-nocks. I used these bo-nocks when I watched your Daddy triumph over his rival.

GEORGE: Madame Odelia Pandahrs even featured this year. We may be sittin up here on thuh sidelines so tuh speak but Madame Odelia Pandahrs down there representing thuh modern age. Shes gonna be in charge of thuh regular broadcasts.

LILY: My day we had messengers. Skinny mens and womens who earned uh cent or two by running up and down thuh hillside. In my year I had me uh particular favorite. Nothin but bones by thuh time it was all through. That messenger came rippin up here at all hours. In thuh dead uh night! In thuh crack uh dawn! Would report—you know—thuh important stuff. Who said what, reenact ThissuhBodys troops last gasp or show me how one uh Thatuh-Bodys troopers kept walkin for hours with uh flag run through their guts and how thuh run through flag had pinned uhnother tuh his back so he was walking for two—with one piggy back, you know. Like uh shishkebob. That messengers speciality was thuh death throes. Kept us in stitches up here showing us who dropped dead and how. And they was droppin dead down there like flies drop so that messenger kept busy. Runned up here tuh tell me thuh news. Whuduhnt nothin but bones by battles end. Last time that messenger runned up here just his bones was doin thuh runnin and thuh stuff that holded thuh bones tugether was all used up as fuel tuh get them bones up thuh hill. We didnt bury thuh messenger. Gave him uh higher honor. My corset is from that messengers bones, you know. In my day we didnt waste.

GEORGE: Madame Odelia Pandahr says that uh unit like this can do double duty: keep us up here abreast of thuh action and after thuh wedding serve as uh device for entertainment.

LILY: Enter-whut?

GEORGE: Entertainment. Fun.

LILY: Oh. Serves uh double duty do it?

GEORGE: So she claims. Just pull thuh knob. And: presto.

LILY: Just pull thuh knob. Huh. Pres-to.

GEORGE: And enjoy.

LILY: Huh. Pres-to.

B.

At the Front. Madame Odelia Pandahr, the panderer, in a wedding dress with microphone in hand, broadcasts live.

ODELIA PANDAHR: Rat uh tat tat and kerblam kerblooey. As someone said long ago: "Thems fighting words." That adage today has well proven true. There is only one way to describe the scene here the scene that began shortly over 5 days ago and seems well intended to last at least through the night. What began as what could be characterized as a border skirmish, a simple tribal dispute, has erupted into a battle of major consequence. High high up above me is the encampment of the bride-who'll-be who has been keeping watch on this situation. The actual area of our attention is not high high up but right down here right down here in, so to speak, "the thick of it." In the area just behind me through this thick veil of deadly deadly smoke you can just make out the shapes of the 2 opposing camps and of course we are speaking of the camps of ThisOne and the camps of ThatOne. The two suitors vying for the hand of Miss George the beautiful most sought after bride-who'll-be who watches now from high above us with her mother, Ms. Mother Lily, from that far high hilltop. There is one word that, I guess you could say, sums up this brilliant display this passionate parade of severed arms and legs, genitals and fingertips, buttocks and heads, the splatterment the dismemberment, the quest for an embrace for the bride-who'll-be which has, for many, ended in an embrace of eternity, and that one word I think we could say that one word is "Devotion." This is Ms. Odelia Pandahr. At the Front.

C.

In the garden.

GEORGE: Dont run from me Mama.

LILY: Aint runnin.

GEORGE: Dont roll from me.

LILY: Mmon uh roll.

GEORGE: Gimmie.

LILY: Not thuh place settings George honey.

GEORGE: Gimmie.

LILY: I got my wheels dug in George.

GEORGE: Sseither them knives and forks and spoons and butter-knives and salad tongs and pickle prongs and lobster tools sseither thems or my brassiere and they aint getting my brassiere.

LILY: In my day we went without.

GEORGE: She aint gettin it.

LILY: In my day thuh table was of most importance.

GEORGE: Uh bride like me ssgotta point thuh way and I intend tuh point thuh way so gimmie. Gimmmmmmmmmmmie!

LILY: You kin give her thuh model of your dream home.

GEORGE: Ssalready been gived.

LILY: Thuh nap-pi-kans. *Serviettes*, love of uh girl?

GEORGE: Mopped up thuh sap of thuh wounded.

LILY: —bloomers?

GEORGE: Turned intuh flags.

LILY: They had tuh know who was who huh?

GEORGE: Gimmie.

LILY: In my day thuh first thing thuh very first thing uh bride-tuh-be envisioned was her table. Thuh shape or size, thuh dimensions of her table were not thuh question. Uh table could be round and of uh cherry wood or square and of oak. Thuh one I always seed was oblong, I was uh little fancy for uh war bride. Oblong and of pine. But thuh materials and dimensions were not really thuh center of thuh envisioning. No. You could have uh table and uh chair— traditional style—or just on uh blanket on thuh ground. Outdoors. Thats uh picnic. Thuh first thing was always her table. And when she had seen it she told her mother and her dear mother tooked it as uh sign that she would be—you know—uh bride. Uh bride with uh groom in all. Like on thuh cake top. On her table with thuh cloth stretched out she would see places for those who would come to mess with her, you know—

GEORGE: Eat.

LILY: In her envisioning she'd see how many there would be and where and what theyd all eat. (You could always tell thuh eats by thuh forks and knives and so on she saw laid out.) What tuh drink. If there was tuh be coffee or tea. And desserts. Thuh first vision was always thuh table. You girls dont see tables these days but I still see mines sometimes—not that I actually ever had no guests like that—but sometimes I still kin see it. Rows and rows of flatwear spiralin out like they was all holdin uh place for me. Holdin my place.

GEORGE: She can take thuh cake top. She can take thuh hope chest itself.

LILY: How unbout that book. Your *French Love Words and French Love Phrases?*

GEORGE: Uh uhnn.

LILY: Oh.

GEORGE: Ssunder my gown.

LILY: Oh.

GEORGE: Keepin my gut in.

LILY: Oh. Lets lay low. Maybe she wont want nothin.

(Enter Odelia Pandahr)

ODELIA PANDAHR: Madame Mother Lily. And thuh most fought over Mademoiselle Miss George.

LILY: Delighted, Maam.

GEORGE: *Enchanté de faire votre connaissance, Madame Pandahr.*

ODELIA PANDAHR: —. *Votre fille est si charmante, Madame Mama Lily.*

LILY: *Oui oui! Oui oui!* Well,—I dont—speak thuh language—.

GEORGE: You think they can see me way up here?

ODELIA PANDAHR: Of course they can, dear girl. The eyes of the heart can see across continents and through stone, Mademoiselle George! Your every breath your every whisper your every tear wink and sigh.

GEORGE AND LILY: Aaaaah!

ODELIA PANDAHR: ThisOne thanks you for the great gift of the tatted dishtowels. They have been reshaped and put into service as shifts

for the war captured. ThatOne is beholden to you for your gracious
coughing up of the salad plates which have been split pie shape
stood on end and now instead of serving salad serve as an
impediment to the advancing shoeless enemy. You both no doubt
have seen the most effective translation of the bridal bloomers?
Ripped in 2 and dipped in dye theyve created *voilà*: the bright
green flag of ThatOne and at 11 oclock the dark deep green of
ThisOne. It is only an extravagance of your devotion which offered
up the bloomers and now allows the troops to distinguish
themselves. Of your jewlery, most gracious Miss George, both
ThisOne and ThatOne have made great use. Both have pinned the
baubles to their respective bodies an act which literally transfixes
them. Pinned by desire, they are spurred on to new deeds of
devotion. Your jewels, George, also make the boys real shiny—
easier for my crew to track their night-time skirmish activities.

GEORGE: Skirmish.

ODELIA PANDAHR: Itll be upgraded to "conflict" any day now.

GEORGE: Skirmish.

ODELIA PANDAHR: We wont fail you Miss George. I know youve got
yourself set for the big win and we will not fail you. With but a
few more of your very dear contributions, my dear Mademoiselle,
I'll not only personally insure an upgrade but will promise promise
promise that youll be wed. To thuh Victor. By sunset tomorrow.
So gimmie.

GEORGE: Uh uhnn.

ODELIA PANDAHR: Ive schooled you in all aspects of Devotion
Mademoiselle George. Pouting was not one of those aspects.

GEORGE: We dont got nothin else.

ODELIA PANDAHR: And neither was hoarding. What will you be
donating today, Mademoiselle?

GEORGE: —.

ODELIA PANDAHR: Cough up.

LILY: What do they require, Maam?

ODELIA PANDAHR: With more ammo ThatOne claims he'll have the
whole skirmish—conflict—wrapped up by sunrise.

LILY: Ammo?

ODELIA PANDAHR: A melted down butterknife makes one hell of uh
bullet, Mother Lily.

LILY: In my day—

ODELIA PANDAHR: All ThisOne wants is a decent silver serving spoon. The medic says itll make a nice new kneecap. If you object tuh thuh weapons question ThatOnes troops need their teeth filled.

LILY: Thuh table.

GEORGE: We got thuh cake top.

ODELIA PANDAHR: Useless.

GEORGE: Dont suppose youd take thuh Tee Vee.

ODELIA PANDAHR: Weve got plenty.

GEORGE: You kin take thuh hope chest itself.

ODELIA PANDAHR: The morgue officerll come and pick that up this evening. Seems weve had a problem with animals exhuming and consuming the—well thats not a subject for a young ladys ears. *(Pause)* SILVER. Cough up.

LILY: Thuh table.

GEORGE: How unbout my brassiere. My last one howboutit.

ODELIA PANDAHR: A bride must point the way, Miss George!

GEORGE: Ssall we got.

ODELIA PANDAHR: Unfortunately brassieres are not what theyre requesting right now but well but well butwell it will most likely come in handy so go ahead and take it off. Keep it in the ready and I'll keep you posted. Anything could happen at this point! You know how skirmis-flicts are. You know.

GEORGE: We know.

ODELIA PANDAHR: Your generosity will not go unnoticed, Miss George. Perhaps I can even finagle a citation of some sort for you. For both of you. Would you like that? Hmmmm? What the troops need right now is something that will unquestionably smack of "Devotion." Smack of Devotion clear as day. Dont you think?

LILY: How uhbout my chair.

ODELIA PANDAHR: Weve got plenty.

GEORGE: Im gonna look all wrong. Be pointin at down 6 oclock instead of out at 9. You say they can see me from here. How they gonna know whats what?

ODELIA PANDAHR: Mama Lily. Surely you can help.

LILY: Uh table is—

ODELIA PANDAHR: Uhround your neck.

LILY: Oh.

ODELIA PANDAHR: May I? Thanks. Their eyes have been under such a—such a strain. These will do just the trick.

LILY: My bo-nocks. I watched your father triumph with them bo-nocks. They still got his winnin image in um somewheres.

ODELIA PANDAHR: I'll be on the 11 oclock update. I'm sure youll tune in.

LILY: Sure.

ODELIA PANDAHR: *Enchanté, Madame. Enchanté Mademoiselle George.*

GEORGE: *Enchanté! Enchanté! Oui oui! Oui oui!*

ODELIA PANDAHR: *Au revoir, Mademoiselle. (Exits)*

GEORGE: Oh. *Au revoir, Madame. (Pause)* Just turn thuh knob. And enjoy.

(George turns on the TV)

LILY: Huh. Presto.

D.

The Front. Odelia Pandahr broadcasts live.

ODELIA PANDAHR: At this hour there is silence. Silence from the guns and swords which only hours ago smote with such deathly volume. Silence from brave troops who only hours ago charged out with the whoops of battle in their throats. Many of those throats are cut now. At this hour. And the cries which spurred them on just hours ago have fled out through their wounds to find refuge in the silence. What began some years ago as a skirmish, what some years ago was upgraded to a conflict now has all the trappings of war. Last week the destruction of ThisOnes troops seemed imminent as the forces of ThatOne marched on and captured the enemy command post. Reports from the field claimed that ThisOne remained defiant vowing that the body could and would continue to fight—headless yes headless if necessary and that it did. What many of us believed and reported to you to be a "headless hen" certain to succumb with the sunset has become a very different bird altogether—striking again and again with an unbelievable fierceness and very much redefining this battle. For the Victor: comfort in the lap of the bride-who'll-be, and the bride-who'll-be is of course the most beautiful and most sought after Miss George who with her mother, Mother Lily, sits high above us on the hilltop just behind me, waiting and watching, watching and waiting. So for the Victor, comfort in the lap of the beloved and for the vanquished, for those who do not triumph, there is only comfort in the lap of the earth, here in this valley. They have renamed this valley "Miss George's Valley" after, of course, their beloved. Several minutes from now, when the troops rise and resume their positions, the wind will awake and unfurl the flags and the echo of Love will once again resound throughout Miss George's Valley. An echo like no other an echo that will not die and fall and forget and be forgotten. An echo that can only be called—"Devotion." This is Ms. Odelia Pan—

E.

The Garden. Lily and George watch TV.

GEORGE: Turn it off. *(Pause)* Zit off?
LILY: Ssoff. *(Pause)* Turn thuh knob. Hhhh. Presto.
GEORGE: Presto.

(Pause)

LILY: Ssdark.

(Pause)

GEORGE: Ssdark.

(Pause)

LILY: Ssquiet.

(Pause)

GEORGE: Ssquiet. *(Pause)* Zit off?
LILY: Ssoff. Love of uh girl.
GEORGE: Guess theys all dead. Or dying.
LILY: Or restin.

GEORGE: Ssquiet.

LILY: Uh huhnn. Ssquiet.

(Pause)

GEORGE: How come you called me George?

LILY: In my day we had rules. For thuh battle. Rule Number One:
No night fightin. Maybe theys observin Rule Number One.

GEORGE: How come you gived me George? As uh name?

LILY: Maybe theys lickin their wounded. I kin just hear thuh sound of
uh tongue on riddled flesh. Or maybe its uh dinner break. Maybe
what I hear is lips slurpin soup. Whisperin over thuh broth. So
quiet. So quiet.

GEORGE: I'm thuh only one I know named George. Seems like thuh
name went out uh fashion when you used it on me.

LILY: In my day—. Hhhh. Well. We iduhnt anywhere near them days
nowuhdays now is we. Hhh. Clear outa sight. Un-seed. I sure do
miss my bo-nocks, George.

GEORGE: Call me somethin pretty. Somethin with uh lift at thuh end,
K, Mama Lily? Somethin like—oh Idunno—. Patty? Patty got uh
French ring to it dont it?

LILY: George iz all we had.

GEORGE: Patty. Patty. Patty-Patty.

LILY: George iz all we got now, George. Huh. "Patty?" "Patty?" Huh.
Idunno. Gimmieuhminute.

GEORGE: Pattyssgot uh happy ending tuh it.

LILY: Huh. Love of uh girl. Love of uh girl. "Patty?" Huh.
Gimmieuhminute.

GEORGE: So quiet down there. HELLO? Huh. Just thuh echo. I waved
my handkerchief at um this noon. Then I dropped it. No one came
runnin. My etiquettes up here goin tuh waste. *French Love Words
and French Love Phrases.* Huh. *(Pause)* Quiz me.

LILY: Huh?

GEORGE: Quiz me. Quiz me before I forget.

LILY: Okay. Our lingo first. Tuh warm up. Suitor: "My sweetest
flower of the morning, when your eyes open it is the dawn and
when they close the sun cannot resist and sets with you. My
sweetest flower, you have dropped your handkerchief." Bride-
who'll-be?

GEORGE: "As the sun itself returns to its house after providing light unto the entire world, so may you, kind Sir, return my scented cloth unto my scented hand."

LILY: Uh—. More like this: "After providing light unto the entire world which wakes first for you then proceeds upon its course, so may you, kind Sir,—" and et cetera.

GEORGE: Oh.

LILY: Lets try uhnother, K? Suitor: "In my hand I hold a diamond in my heart I hold your image. You are infinitely more beautiful fair and precious than this most precious stone. Oh my heart would be the most basest and plainest of rocks if ever you did not move me." Bride-who'll-be?

GEORGE: "The earth moves—as do its consorts, the planets. Daily engaged in their revolving. By its very nature, Lover, Love itself revolves, revolves to bring you back, Lover, to me."

(Pause)

LILY: Uh uhnn.

GEORGE: Oh. Gimmieuhhint.

LILY: "My image—"

GEORGE: Oh oh oh. "My image—which you keep with such care in your heart, my image, fair as it may be is not so nearly as fair as—"

LILY: Uh uhnn. "My image, Sir, is merely a—"

GEORGE: "My image, Sir, is merely—a reflection in that safe keeping mirror of your heart."

LILY: Good.

GEORGE: "As gardens should be judged by their caretakers so should my image be judged by your care. Base rocks are bulwarks to the great ocean but they too sand in time. And time itself is a round thing, a round thing that—that—that—"

LILY: Thatll do. Now. —. Uh—*en français?*

GEORGE: *En français?*

LILY: Uh huhnn. Go on.

GEORGE: *Oui oui! Oui oui!* Uh—. *Monsieur.* —. Uh—*Monsieur*—. Uh—. Gimmieuhminute.

(Enter Odelia Pandahr)

ODELIA PANDAHR: Madame Mama Lily and the most fought over
Mademoiselle Miss George! I arrive today triumphant gather round
gather round! I bring you: Yes! The Victor! The Victor, Miss
George, the true suitor who has won through the truest test your
hand! The Victor, Miss George, smiter of the victim! Stand back
stand back! Now! Wait right here!

LILY: "Patty." "Patty." We'll call ya "Patty," Patty. Patty?

PATTY: How I look? Wedable?

LILY: Patty. Love of uh girl.

PATTY: I look all right?

LILY: Like uh happy ending.

PATTY: Huh. Thatll do. Whats our word? Our words "Devotion." We
will hold fast. Unto thuh death. We will not come all asunder. We
wont flinch. I'll see him and he'll see me. We will exchange words
of love and fall fall fall into eachothers arms—.

LILY: Thats my girl. Here they come, honey. —. Suck in your gut.

ODELIA PANDAHR: May I present to you Madame Mother Lily and
beautiful most fought over bride-who'll-be Mademoiselle Miss
George: The Victor!

PATTY: Thuh Victor!

LILY: Thuh Victor!

ODELIA PANDAHR: *Voilà!*

PATTY: *Voilà!*

LILY: *Voilà!*

(Odelia Pandahr uncovers a head on a platter)

PATTY: Oh.

LILY: Presto.

PATTY: Wheres thuh rest of im, Madame?

ODELIA PANDAHR: He's full of love for you, Mademoiselle George. His
lips are pursed in a kiss. His eyes only for your fair image,
Mademoiselle. I recounted to him the story of your waiting. The
history of the gifts you gave. The story of the tears you shed for
him. The tale of your devotion. The way you wrung your hands.
There is only one word for such a show of bravest bravery,—

PATTY: Wheres thuh rest of im?

ODELIA PANDAHR: There is only one word for such a show of bravest
bravery, Mademoiselle George—

PATTY: Patty.

ODELIA PANDAHR: Patty?

LILY: Presto.

ODELIA PANDAHR: —Patty—. There is just one word for such valorous valor just one word for such faithful faith just one word, Mademoiselle George for—

PATTY: Patty.

LILY: Patty.

ODELIA PANDAHR: Patty?

PATTY: Patty.

LILY: Turn it off.

ODELIA PANDAHR: Now your suitor, Mademoiselle—Patty, may be just a head—a head kept alive by a wealth of technology, the fruits of our modern age. Your suitor may be just a—head—uh head-stone of thuh former self but as we are schooled in Madame Odelia Pandahrs, the head is the place where sit thuh lofty—the lofty-most thoughts. Weve, you could say, done away with thuh base. We would do away with this base but then of course your handsome and devoted suitor would have difficulty standing you understand.

LILY: Turn if off. Turn it off Patty.

PATTY: Patty. Pattysgot uh happy ending to it. Arent him and me supposed tuh fall into eachothers arms?

ODELIA PANDAHR: It is true that in the rage of battle suitors ThisOne and ThatOne were thick as tigers around an old gum tree. Even steven blow for blow a perfect match! They always did look uh bit uhlike, Mademoiselle—Patty. There has been a bit of debate down in your valley as to just which one this is. Some say ThisOne some say ThatOne. There is talk of the two opposing camps taking up arms to settle the matter. But that is not our affair now is it. I myself think well I myself know this to be ThatOne. I am after all his mother.

LILY: Turn it off. Turn it off. Zit off?

ODELIA PANDAHR: PATTY! Patty!? ThatOne looks as if he's uhbout to speak!

LILY: Speak?!

ODELIA PANDAHR: Words of love!!

PATTY: Love?!!

ODELIA PANDAHR: Lean in close, love of uh girl. LEAN IN CLOSE.

Some need a little prodding I understand. Ive seen it all. LEAN.
IN. CLOSE.—. See? See? Thuh lips twitch. Oh—sssssssssh! Hear?
Hear? —. —. Now hows that? Uh happy ending!
PATTY: Oh. Oh. Mama? Oooh. Mama? He said: "Be Mine."
LILY: Oh! "Be mine!"

F.

At the Front. Patty with a microphone.

PATTY: Once upon uh time way up there in uh garden in thuh middle
of nowhere there were 2 who got married. After thuh marriage
thuh boy it seemed soon forgot his home-town lingo. To woo her
he had used thuh words "be mine." Now "be mine" is fine for uh
woo but it iduhnt enough tuh build anything longlasting and stable
on. Sheud ask him tuh say something. Sheud plead with him tuh
say anything. He'd just say "be mine" and although they were in
love that "be mine" got rather old rather quick. Soon even his "be
mine" dried up. And she realized that he had forgotten his home-
town lingo. And she realized that he couldnt pick it up again. So
she did what she had to do. She left her wordless husband and went
journeying. Abroad. To Gay Paree. And lived over there amongst
them. For 12 long years. Full of her new words and phrases she
then came home to him. Where he waited. She took off her
traveling cloak and did what any anybody would do, that is, she
taught him French. It was rough going at first, but he was eager.
And soon they could make decent conversation. They became
close. In their way. Made a go of it. Raised uh family. Thuh usual.
He told his war stories *en français*. She opened up uh finishing
academy and they prospered. And they lived that way. Lived
happily ever after and stuff like that. Talking back and forth. This is
Ms. Patty. At thuh Front.

WILLIE PERDOMO

nigger-reecan blues
1996

—Hey, Willie. What are you, man? Boricua? Moreno? Que? Are you
   Black? Puerto Rican?
—I am.
—No, silly. You know what I mean: What are you?
—I am you. You are me. We the same. Can't you feel our veins drinking
   the same blood?

   —But who said you was a Porta-Reecan?
   —Tu no ere Puerto Riqueño, brother.
   —Maybe Indian like Ghandi-Indian?
   —I thought you was a Black man.
   —Is one of your parents white?
   —You sure you ain't a mix of something like Cuban and Chinese?
   —Looks like an Arab brother to me.
   —Naahhh, nah, nah . . . You ain't no Porty-Reecan.
   —I keep tellin' y'all: That boy is a Black man with an accent.

If you look real close you will see that your spirits are standing right next to
our songs. Yo soy Boricua! Yo soy Africano! I ain't lyin'. Pero mi pelo is
kinky y curly y mi skin no es negro pero it can pass . . .

   —Hey, yo. I don't care what you say. You Black.

I ain't Black! Every time I go downtown la madam blankita de Madison
Avenue sees that I'm standing next to her and she holds her purse just a bit
tighter. Cabdrivers are quick to turn on their *Off-Duty* signs when they see
my hand in the air. And the newspapers say that if I'm not in front a gun
you can bet I'll be behind one. I wonder why . . .

—Cuz you Black, nigger!

Don't call me no nigger. I am not Black, man. I had a conversation with
    my professor and it went just like this:
"So, Willie, where are you from?"
"I'm from Harlem."
"Ohhh . . . Are you Black, Willie?"
"No, but we all the same and—"
"Did you know our basketball team is nationally ranked?"

—Te lo estoy diciendo, brother. Ese hombre es un moreno. Miralo!

Mira, pana mia, yo no soy moreno! I just come out of Jerry's Den and the
coconut spray on my new shape-up is smelling fresh all the way up 125th
Street. I'm lookin' slim and I'm lookin' trim and when my compai Davi
saw me he said: "Coño, Papo, te parece como un moreno, pana. Word up,
kid, you look just like a light-skin moreno."

—What I told you? You Black my brother.
Damn! I ain't even Black and here I am suffering from the young Black
man's plight / the old white man's burden / and I ain't even Black, man / a
Black man I am not / Boricua I am / ain't never really was / Black / like
me . . .

—Y'all leave that boy alone. He got what they call the "nigger-reecan
    blues."

I'm a spic! I'm a nigger!
Spic! Spic! Just like a nigger.
Neglected, rejected, oppressed and dispossessed
From banana boats to tenements
Street gangs to regiments
Spic, spic, spic. I ain't nooooo different than a nigger!

DANZY SENNA

the mulatto millennium
1998

Strange to wake up and realize you're in style. That's what happened to me just the other morning. It was the first day of the new millennium and I woke to find that mulattos had taken over. They were everywhere. Playing golf, running the airwaves, opening their own restaurants, modeling clothes, starring in musicals with names like *Show Me the Miscegenation!* The radio played a steady stream of Lenny Kravitz, Sade, and Mariah Carey. I thought I'd died and gone to Berkeley. But then I realized. According to the racial zodiac, 2000 is the official Year of the Mulatto. Pure breeds (at least the black ones) are out and hybridity is in. America loves us in all of our half-caste glory. The president announced on Friday that beige is to be the official color of the millennium. Major news magazines announce our arrival as if we were proof of extraterrestrial life. They claim we're going to bring about the end of race as we know it.

It has been building for a while, this mulatto fever. But it was this morning that it really reached its peak. I awoke early to a loud ruckus outside—horns and drums and flutes playing "Kum ba Yah" outside my window. I went to the porch to witness a mass of bedraggled activists making their way down Main Street. They were chanting, not quite in unison, "Mulattos Unite, Take Back the White!" I had a hard time making out the placards through the tangle of dreadlocks and loose Afros. At the front of the crowd, two brown-skinned women in Birkenstocks carried a banner that read FOR COLORED GIRLS WHO HAVE CONSIDERED JEW BOYS WHEN THE NEGROES AIN'T ENOUGH. A lean yellow girl with her hair in messy Afro-puffs wore a T-shirt with the words JUST HUMAN across the front. What appeared to be a Hasidic Jew walked hand in hand with his girlfriend, a Japanese woman in traditional attire, the two of them wearing huge yellow buttons on their lapels that read MAKE MULATTOS, NOT WAR. I trailed behind the parade for some miles, not quite sure I wanted to join or stay at the heels of this group.

I guess I should have seen it coming. Way back in the fall of 1993, *Time* magazine put on its cover "The New Face of America," a computer-morphed face of fourteen models of different racial backgrounds, creating a woman they named Eve. The managing editor wrote:

> The woman on the cover of this special issue of *Time* does not exist except metaphysically . . . The highlight of this exercise in cybergenesis was the creation of the woman on our cover, selected as a symbol of the future, multiethnic face of America . . . As onlookers watched the image of our new Eve begin to appear on the computer screen, several staff members promptly fell in love. Said one: "It really breaks my heart that she doesn't exist." We sympathize with our lovelorn colleagues, but even technology has its limits. This is a love that must forever remain unrequited.

Of course, anyone could see that women just like the computer face they had created did exist in Puerto Rico, Latin America, and Spanish Harlem. But the editors at *Time* remained unaware of this, seeming to prefer their colored folk imaginary, not real. As I read the article, it reminded me of an old saying they used to have down South during Jim Crow: "If a black man wants to sit at the front of the bus, he just puts on a turban." Maybe the same rule applied here: call yourself mixed and you just might find the world smiles a little brighter on you.

Mulattos may not be new. But the mulatto-pride folks are a new generation. They want their own special category or no categories at all. They're a full-fledged movement, complete with their own share of extremists. As I wandered at the edges of the march this morning, one woman gave me a flyer. It was a treatise on biracial superiority, which began, "Ever wonder why mutts are always smarter than full-breed dogs?" The rest of her treatise was dense and incomprehensible: something about the sun people and the ice people coming together to create the perfectly temperate being. Another man, a militant dressed like Huey P. Newton, came toward me waving a rifle in his hand. He told me that those who refuse to miscegenate should be shot. I steered clear of him, instead burying my head in a newspaper. I opened to the book review section, and at the top of the best-seller list were three memoirs: *Kimchee and Grits*, by

Kyong Washington, *Gefilte Fish and Ham Hocks*, by Schlomo Jackson, and at the top of the list, and for the third week in a row, *Burritos and Borsht*, by a cat named Julio Werner. That was it. In a fit of nausea, I took off running for home.

Before all of this radical ambiguity, I was a black girl. I fear even saying this. The political strong arm of the multiracial movement, affectionately known as the Mulatto Nation (just "the M.N." for those in the know), decreed just yesterday that those who refuse to comply with orders to embrace their many heritages will be sent on the first plane to Rio de Janeiro, Brazil, where, the M.N.'s minister of defense said, "they might learn the true meaning of mestizo power."

But, with all due respect to the multiracial movement, I cannot tell a lie. I was a black girl. Not your ordinary black girl, if such a thing exists. But rather, a black girl with a Wasp mother and a black-Mexican father, and a face that harkens to Andalusia, not Africa. I was born in 1970, when "black" described a people bonded not by shared complexion or hair texture but by shared history.

Not only was I black (and here I go out on a limb), but I was an enemy of the people. The mulatto people, that is. I sneered at those byproducts of miscegenation who chose to identify as mixed, not black. I thought it wishy-washy, an act of flagrant assimilation, treason, passing even.

It was my parents who made me this way. In Boston circa 1975, mixed wasn't really an option. The words "A fight, a fight, a nigga and a white!" could be heard echoing from schoolyards during recess. You were either white or black. No checking "Other." No halvsies. No in-between. Black people, being the bottom of the social totem pole in Boston, were inevitably the most accepting of difference; they were the only race to come in all colors, and so there I found myself. Sure, I received some strange reactions from all quarters when I called myself black. But black people usually got over their initial surprise and welcomed me into the ranks. It was white folks who grew the most uncomfortable with the dissonance between the face they saw and the race they didn't. Upon learning who I was, they grew paralyzed with fear that they might have "slipped up" in my presence, that is, said something racist, not knowing there was a Negro in their midst. Often, they had.

Let it be clear—my parents' decision to raise us as black wasn't based on any one-drop rule from the days of slavery, and it certainly wasn't based on our appearance, that crude reasoning many black-identified mixed people use: if the world sees me as black, I must be black. If it had been based on appearance, my sister would have been black, my brother Mexican, and me Jewish. Instead, my parents' decision arose out of the rising black power movement, which made identifying as black not a pseudoscientific rule but a conscious choice. *You told us all along that we had to call ourselves black because of this so-called one drop. Now that we don't have to anymore, we choose to. Because black is beautiful. Because black is not a burden, but a privilege.*

Some might say my parents went too far in their struggle to instill a black identity in us. I remember my father schooling me and my siblings on our racial identity. He would hold his own version of the Inquisition, grilling us over a greasy linoleum kitchen table while a single, bright lightbulb swung overhead. He would ask: "Do you have any black friends?" "How many?" "Who?" "What are their names?" And we, his obedient children, his soldiers in the battle for negritude, would rattle off the names of the black kids we called friends. (When we, trying to turn the tables, asked my father why all his girlfriends were white, he would launch into one of his famously circular diatribes, which left us spinning with confusion. I only remember that his reasoning involved demographics and the slim chances of him meeting a black woman in the Brookline Public Library on a Monday afternoon.)

But something must have sunk in, because my sister and I grew up with a disdain for those who identified as mulatto rather than black. Not all mulattos bothered me back then. It was a very particular breed that got under my skin: the kind who answered, meekly, "Everything," to that incessant question "What are you?" Populist author Jim Hightower wrote a book called *There's Nothing in the Middle of the Road but Yellow Stripes and Dead Armadillos.* That's what mulattos represented to me back then: yellow stripes and dead armadillos. Something to be avoided. I veered away from groups of them—children, like myself, who had been born of interracial minglings after dark. Instead, I surrounded myself with bodies darker than myself, hoping the color might rub off on me.

I used to spy on white people, blend into their crowd, let them think I was one of them, and then listen as they talked in smug disdain about black folks. It wasn't something I had to search out. And most white people, I found, no matter how much they preach MLK's dream, are just as obsessed with color and difference as the rest of us. They just talk about it in more coded terms. Around white folks, I never had to bring up race.

They brought it up for me, and I listened, my skin tingling slightly, my stomach twisting in anger, as they revealed their true feelings about colored folks. Then I would spring it on them, tell them who I really was, and watch, in a kind of pained glee, as their faces went from eggshell white, to rose pink, to hot mama crimson, to The Color Purple. Afterward, I would report back to headquarters, where my friends would laugh and holler about how I was an undercover Negro.

There had been moments in my life when I had not asserted my black identity. I hadn't "passed" in the traditional sense of the word, but in a more subtle way, by simply mumbling that I was mixed. Then the white people in my midst seemed to forget whom they were talking to, and countless times I was a silent witness to their candid racism. When I would remind them that my father was black, they would laugh and say, "But you're different." That was somewhere I never wanted to return. There was danger in this muddy middle stance. A danger of disappearing. Of being swallowed whole by the great white whale. I had seen the arctic belly of the beast and didn't plan on returning.

One year, while working as an investigative journalist in Hollywood, I even made up a list, evidence I've long since burned. These days such a thing would mean sure career death—luckily, it was never published. It was an exposé of who is passing in Hollywood. I called it "And You Thought It Was Just a Tan?" There were three categories:

Black Folks You May Not Have Known Are Black

Mariah Carey	Johnny Depp
Jennifer Beals	Michael Jackson
Tom Hanks	Kevin Bacon
Carly Simon	Robin Quivers
Slash	Elizabeth Berkley
Arnold Schwarzenegger	Paula Abdul

Black Folks Who May Not Know They Are Black

Mariah Carey	Johnny Depp
Jennifer Beals	Michael Jackson
Tom Hanks	Kevin Bacon
Carly Simon	Robin Quivers
Slash	Elizabeth Berkley
Arnold Schwarzenegger	Paula Abdul

Black Folks You Kinda Wish Weren't Black

O. J. Simpson   Gary Coleman

Michael Jackson   Robin Quivers

Needless to say, my list wouldn't have gone over too well with the M.N. posse. But I put decent research into the article and was proud of my results. It was nearly published in a local news weekly, but the editors balked at the last minute, for fear of lawsuits. I bet they're thanking their lucky stars now that they didn't print it. Essentialism is out. In this age of fluidity, it doesn't pay to be blacker than thou.

Just the other night, I was taken in for questioning by some M.N. officials. They wanted to question me about my "dark past." I tried to explain to them in as clear terms as possible why I had done it: denied my multiculti heritage for this negritudinal madness. I tried to explain to them that in Boston in the 1970s, racism was pervasive, blatant, dangerous, palpable. The choice of multiracial was simply not an adequate response to racism. In my mind, there were only two choices—black or white. Those choices were not simply abstractions. They had real consequences and meaning in my everyday world.

But the M.N. officials didn't buy it. They kept me at the station all night, in a small white room with a bright light. In the corner, there was a video monitor showing Grover and a gang of toddlers singing that old *Sesame Street* song over and over again: "One of these things is not like the other / one of these things isn't the same . . ." One of the agents, a big guy with a blond Afro and orange-tinted glasses, kept shouting at me, his spittle spraying across my face, "But why black? I mean, why didn't you identify as white if you were gonna identify as only one thing? Isn't that reverse racism?" I told him that multiculturalism should be about confronting racism and power, not about plates of ethnic food.

The Grover gang was beginning to have its desired effect. I was beginning to sing along, despite myself. " 'One of these things is not like the other . . .' " But I clenched my eyes shut and tried my best to explain to the man. I told him that all this celebration of mixture felt to me like a smoke screen, really, obscuring the fundamental issue of racism, and for that matter, class divisions. It seemed to me we spent so much time talking about kimchee and grits, we forgot to talk about power.

But the agent only whispered to me (his breath smelled of falafel), "Class analysis isn't quite as sexy as a grinning mulatto on a golf course."

He even admitted to me that multiracialism was a terrific marketing tool, the best way to sell to as many types of people as possible. "It's ingenious!" he shouted, grinning, carried away by his own ideas. "This will change the face of marketing forever!"

But my experience, I told him, feeling broken now with exhaustion, could never be reduced to cute food analogies (Wasp cooking, I've come to realize over the years, can go well with almost anything because it has no flavor). My mulatto experience, I argued, was difficult not because things were confusing, but rather because things were so painfully clear. Racism, as well as the absurdity of race, were obvious to me in ways that they perhaps weren't to those whose racial classification was a given. Racism, I told him, is a slippery devil. Like Madonna, it changes its image every couple of years. Today, sans burning crosses and blatant epithets, racism is harder to put one's finger on. But I know it when I feel it. In all this mulatto fever, people seem to have forgotten that racism exists with or without miscegenation. Instead of celebrating a "new race," I told the agent, can't we take a look at the "new racism"?

When I was finished with my monologue, he just laughed. He told me I was imagining things. He told me there was no such thing as "new racism." He told me that if I couldn't show him a burning cross, he didn't want to hear about it. Then he was gone, locking the door behind him. The room was completely empty except for a video display monitor in one corner and a camera pointed at me in the other. At some point during that long, agonizing night, the video monitor switched from Grover and the gang to something far more sinister. It was a montage of Gary Coleman, Michael Jackson, Julie Andrews, and Sinbad, their faces flashing across the screen quicker and quicker until they seemed to blur into the smiling face of Juan Epstein. Eventually I fell into a fitful sleep and had a nightmare that I was buried under forty feet of snow.

But their tactics must have worked. I'm no longer a black girl. At least according to my new driver's license and birth certificate. The "black" has been smudged out and the word "quadroon" scribbled in. I told the woman at the DMV—auburn cornrows, vaguely Asiatic features—that I wasn't comfortable with that term "quadroon." I told her, as politely as I could, that it reminded me of slave days, when they used to separate the slaves by caste. She just laughed and told me to be happy I got "quadroon." "You don't know how lucky you are, babe," she said, puffing on a Marlboro and flipping through her latest issue of *Vibe* magazine. "They're being picky who they let use that term. Everybody's trying to claim something special in their background—a Scottish grandfather, a Native American grandmother. But the M.N. is trying to keep it to first-generation mixtures, you know. Otherwise things would get far too confusing." Then she had me sign some form, which I barely read, still reeling from my night before the video monitor. It said something about allowing my image to be used to promote racial harmony. I left the DMV in a daze.

These days, there are M.N. folks in Congress and the White House. They've got their own category on the census. It says "Multiracial." But even that is inadequate for the more extremist wing of the Mulatto Nation. They want to take it a step further. I guess they have a point. I mean, why lump us all together as multiracial? Eskimos, they say, have forty different words for snow. In South Africa, during apartheid, they had fourteen different types of coloreds. But we've decided on this one word, "multiracial," to describe, in effect, a whole nation of diverse people who have absolutely no relation, cultural or otherwise, to one another. In light of this deficiency, I would like to propose the following coinages. Perhaps the Census Bureau should give them a try.

Variations on a Theme of a Mulatto

Standard Mulatto: white mother, black father. Half-nappy hair, skin that is described as "pasty yellow" in the winter, but turns a caramel tan in the summer. Germanic-Afro features. Often raised in isolation from others of its kind. Does not discover his or her "black identity" till college. At this point, there is usually some physical change in hair or clothing, and often speech, so much so that the parents don't recognize their child when he or she arrives home for Christmas vacation. (E.g., "Honey, there's some black kid at the door.")

African American: The most common form of mulatto in North America, this breed is not often described as mixed, but is nevertheless a combination of African, European, and Native American. May come in any skin tone, and of any cultural background. Often believe themselves to be "pure" due to historical distance from the original mixture, which was most often achieved through rape.

Jewlatto: The second most prevalent form of mulatto in the North American continent, this breed is made in the commingling of Jews and blacks who met while registering voters down South during Freedom Summer or at a CORE meeting. Jewlattos will often, though not necessarily, have a white father and a black mother (as opposed to the more common case, a black father and a white mother). Will also be more likely to be raised in a diverse setting, around others of his or her kind, such as New York City (Greenwich Village) or Northern California (Berkeley). Have strong pride in their mixed background. Will often feel that their dual cultures are not so dual at all, considering the shared history of oppression. Jewlattos are most easily spotted amid the flora and fauna of Brown University. Famous Jewlattos: Lenny Kravitz and Lisa Bonet (and we can't forget Zoe, their love child).

Mestizo: A more complicated mixture, where either the black or white parent claims a third race in their background (e.g., Native American or Latino) and therefore confuses the child more. The mestizo is likely to be mistaken for some other, totally distinct ethnicity (Italian, Arab, Mexican, Jewish, East Indian, Native American, Puerto Rican) and in fact will be touted by strangers as a perfect representative of that totally new race. (E.g., "Your face brings me right back to Calcutta.") The mestizo mulatto is more prevalent than commonly believed, since they often "disappear" into the fabric of American society, wittingly or unwittingly passing as that third, "pure," totally distinct race. It takes an expert to spot one in a crowd.

Gelatto: A mixture of Italian American and African American, this breed often lives in either a strictly Italian neighborhood if the father is white (e.g., Bensonhurst) or in a black neighborhood if the father is black (e.g., Flatbush). Usually identifies strongly with one side of the family over the other, but sometimes with marked discomfort becomes aware of the similarities between the two sides of his cultures, and at this point, often "flies the coop" and begins to practice Asian religions.

Cultural Mulatto: Any American born post-1967. See *Wiggers.*

Blulatto: A highly rare breed of "blue-blood" mulatto who can trace their lineage back to the *Mayflower.* If female, is legally entitled to membership

in the Daughters of the American Revolution. Blulattos have been
spotted in Cambridge, Massachusetts, and Berkeley, California, but
should not be confused with the Jewlatto. The Blulatto's mother is
almost always the white one and is either a poet or a painter who disdains
her Wasp heritage. The father of the Blulatto is almost always the black
one, is highly educated, and disdains his black heritage. Unlike the
Jewlatto, the parents of the Blulatto are most likely divorced or separated,
although the black father almost always remarries another blue-blood
woman much like the first. Beware: The Blulatto may seem calm and
even civilized, but can be dangerous when angry. Show caution when
approaching.

Negratto: May be any of the above mixtures, but is raised to identify as
black. Negrattos often have a white mother who assimilated into black
culture before they were born, and raised them to understand "the trouble
with whitey." They will tend to be removed from the white side of their
family and to suppress the cultural aspects of themselves that are considered
white. Will tend to be more militant than their darker brothers and sisters
and to talk in a slang most resembling ebonics circa 1974. Has great disgust
for the "so-called mulatto movement" and grows acutely uncomfortable
in the presence of other mulattos. Despite all of this posturing, there is a
good chance that they have a white lover hidden somewhere in their past,
present, or future.

Cablinasian: A rare exotic breed found mostly in California. This is the
mother of all mixtures, and when caught may be displayed for large sums
of money. The Cablinasian is a mixture of Asian, American Indian, Black,
and Caucasian (thus the strange name). A show mulatto, with great
performance skills, the Cablinasian will be whoever the crowd wants
him to be, and can switch at the drop of a dime. Does not, however,
answer to the name Black. A cousin to other rare exotic mixes found only
California (Filipino and Black; Samoan and Irish; Mexican and Korean).
Note: If you spot a Cablinasian, please contact the Benetton Promotions
Bureau.

Tomatto: A mixed or black person who behaves in an "Uncle Tom-ish"
fashion. The Tomatto may be found in positions of power, being touted as
a symbol of diversity in otherwise all-white settings. Even if the Tomatto

has two black parents, his skin is light and his features are mixed. If we are ever to see a first black president, he will most likely be a Tomatto.

Fauxlatto: A person impersonating a mulatto. Can be of white, black, or other heritage, but for inexplicable reasons claims to be of mixed heritage. See *Jamiroquai.*

Ho-latto: A female of mixed racial heritage who exploits and is exploited sexually. See any of Prince's Girlfriends.

The categories could go on and on, and perhaps, indeed, they will. And where do I fit into them? That's the strange thing. I fit into none and all of the above. I have been each of the above, or at least mistaken for each of them, at different moments in my life. But somehow, none of them feel right. Maybe that makes me a Postlatto.

There are plans next week to paint the White House rainbow colored. And just last month, two established magazines, both bastions of liberal thought, had cover stories predicting "the end of blackness." Not too long ago, *Newsweek* officially declared it "hip" to be multiracial. Race relations have been boiled down to a game of semantics—as if all that matters is which box one checks on the census.

And me? I've learned to flaunt my mixedness at dinner parties, where the guests (most of them white) ooh and aaah about my flavorful background. I've found it's not so bad being a festishized object, an exotic bird soaring above the racial landscape. And when they start talking about black people, pure breeds, in that way that used to make me squirm before the millennium, I let them know that I'm neutral, nothing to be afraid of. Sometimes I feel it, that remnant of my old self (the angry black girl with the big mouth) creeping out, but most of the time I don't feel anything at all. Most of the time, I just serve up the asparagus, chimichangas, and fried chicken with a bright, white smile.

JOHN RODRIGUEZ

how to be a street poet
1999

If you're going to be a street poet
make sure you have lots of friends
who drink fight steal or sell drugs.
They will always have problems
with the law, and you can write
poems about them.

Make sure one of them is a crackhead
cokehead dope fiend, they are sure to
take a really bad hit or a really good
hit and die, and then you can write
a poem about it.

Get a quiet, light-skinned girl from Yonkers
or Long Island to fall in love with you. Ask
her, occasionally, for her opinion on your
friends and your poetry. She will probably
say something naive. That's how you'll know
you're on the right track.

Meanwhile get a loud, brown girl
from 'round the way to have your
baby, and then break up with her.
She will quite possibly stress you
whenever she can. Should the street
muse ever fail to keep its appointment
with you, you can call your baby

mama and ask her why she hasn't
let you see your child. She will
immediately go into single strong
independent brown mother woman
mode and GO OFF on that ass. This
will make you regret calling her, but
then you can write a poem about it.

Your child will grow up hating
you for being a part time dad—
good for happy meals and maybe next times twenty-six weekends a year—instead of being a
live-in dad like the ones on tv.
You will forget her/his birthday
and sometimes her/his age, and
otherwise break her/his heart.
You'll be able to write poems
about that, too.

Keep odd hours, making sure to walk
into your parents' home menacingly
Sunday mornings, until you find sudden
travel bags filled with your underwear.
This will allow you to spend more time
at friends' houses on rooftops park benches
subways and in shelters where you can
further develop your street poet resume
and, of course, write more street poems.

But that's okay because you can tell
your friends about all your street issues
as you sit in front of the corner store
with an almost-like-mom's dinner from
the caridad playing dominoes with your
friends who are still drinking fighting
stealing selling drugs unless they're in
jail, in which case they're still drinking

fighting stealing selling drugs, or dead.
When the store closes, ending the game,
you will make a final trip to the liquor
store next door to the corner store to buy
rum from an island you've never known
in order to feel like you belong there and
drag yourself to your solitary apartment
to pass out to wake up the next day with
a hangover and still another street poem.

DARIUS JAMES

from froggie chocolates'
christmas eve
2003

S tooped, wrinkled and arthritically slow, the old man clasped the little boy's hand in the weathered claw of his own; and, with the assistance of a cane, creaked at snail's pace through the shopping mall's spacious halls. Oblivious to the crush of holiday crowds, the old man's eyes twinkled in wonder. His grandson only wondered why.

The little boy's grandfather was nearly as old as the dirt under the mall's concrete foundation. How could a man of his years get misty-eyed over a film as wantonly repugnant as the one that had just unspooled on screen? Had it been "It's a Wonderful Life," "Miracle on Thirty-Fourth Street," "A Christmas Carol" or, even, "Santa Claus Conquers the Martians," the little boy might have understood his grandfather's addled wonderment.

But "Santa's Showdown in the Sand"? It had given him a headache. And he was only nine!

The preceding summer's teaser—a black screen, an exploding fireball and a jolly Ho! Ho! Ho!—promised fun 'n guns galore for the whole family. Once it was announced California's Austrian governor would flex his considerable muscle behind the camera instead of in front of it, "Santa's Showdown . . ." was the most highly anticipated release of the Christmas season. And, on opening day, popcorn sales soared.

The little boy, however, was not fooled.

As he suspected, "Santa's Showdown . . ." was humbug sold as "light-hearted comic-fantasy." Or so grinned the gap-toothed "gouvernator." Along with martial arts sequences highlighted by troupes of flying acrobats; an overuse of computer-generated animation; and a two-gun Santa blasting away in slo-mo as if he were trying to keep it real for MTV's hiphop generation, there were elaborate song and dance routines with crotch-grabbing elves and rappin' reindeer.

Oh, how the pain in his head throbbed!

Even before the film's introductory title and credits, the little boy realized this Santa was going to be difficult on his stomach when, the gouvernator, anxious to show off his erudition as a cineaste, referenced the early efforts of Brian DePalma by opening with a split-screen of the President of the United States in the Oval Office speaking with Santa at the North Pole.

"Those swarthy camel jockeys are at it again, Santa!" the president said. "They're hatching another nefarious plot against the peoples of the free world! And you've gotta stop 'em!"

"Ho! Ho! Ho! Precisely how 'nefarious,' Mr. President?"

"Frankly, I have no idea what 'nefarious' means," the president replied without embarrassment, despite his expensive Ivy-League education, "but my advisors say it ain't good. Our intelligence sources, in any case, have informed us those nasty little sand-boogers are out to steal Christmas from the Infidels! And I have a suspicion those snaileatin' French are behind it—even if they are Catholics!"

"Ho—uh—oh no!"

"That's right, Santa, you'll be out of a job! No more cookies and milk set by the fireplace for you! No more quick nips out of that flask of hot spiced-rum you keep hidden in your winter overcoat while your reindeer fly through those snowy nighttime skies! And, most important of all, no more fat residual checks from those nice people at the Coca-Cola Corporation! You'll just be a forgotten, lonely old man stripped naked and left to die on an ice floe in the Arctic—a bloated blue has-been fossilized in a colossal block of ice!

So load your sleigh with the most advanced military weaponry the U.S. government can buy; round up the roughest and toughest gang of the most ornery elves you can find; water up your reindeer and high tail it over to the Middle East! Spare the U.S. taxpayer no expense! Nothing's too good for our Santa! Now, hop to it!"

"Right away, Mr. President!"

"Did I mention those swarthy, fig-eatin' towel heads were 'nefarious' . . .?"

As the title and credit sequence scrolled in a tricolor-shimmer of red, white and blue stars; stripes; snowflakes and Holly branches, accompanied by a heavy-handed score evoking strains of "The Star-Spangled Banner," "Jingle Bells" and Ennio Morricone's "Man with a Harmonica," the white-whiskered fat man, unseasonably attired in his ermine-fringed red suit and seal-skin snow boots, was dispatched to the Middle East.

During a cheerful ditty about assailing the Taliban with a down pour of wet reindeer-dung, Santa ran into the first of his complications when his team of reindeer, in mid-air flight, suddenly died of heat exhaustion. And Santa, sleigh and gang of cut-throat elves—as well as inert reindeer stiffening in rigor mortis—fell from the sky; plummeting into a massive sand dune.

With their food and medical supplies scattered across the desert, and sinking beneath the sands, Santa and his elves were forced to disrobe in the sweltering heat. Further, to stave off infection, as the fall had left them scratched, battered and bruised, they stood in a circle, fusing in a cluster of chubby pink bodies, and showered each other in a brine of steaming urine. For the next three days, compressed into time-lapsed montage, they subsisted on the maggot-ridden remains of the reindeer's mangled carcasses. It was during this sequence of over-saturated Sergio-Leone sunglare the little boy's stomach turned for the worse.

Soggy with dripping Santa piss, the naked elves, skin puckered and wrinkled, gorged themselves on a mound of maggots left to dry a crispy brown under the sun. Upon witnessing this scene, the color in the little boy's face turned a pallid green. And a volley of rancid bile spewed from his mouth in an ever-increasing arc of half-digested popcorn; artificially-flavored grape soda; animal-shaped jelly candies; and a McDonald's Happy Meal with an extra-large chocolate shake. This fetid frappé rained down on a pigtailed seven-year-old seated three rows ahead.

Squalling in abject horror, the little girl fled the auditorium in a carapace of semi-congealed putrescence with her pigtails trailing stiffly in the wind.

The little boy, mercifully, fainted.

Unaware of what transpired, despite his grandson's unconscious status, and the residual stench wafting under his hairy nostrils, the old man remained seated with his eyes riveted to the screen.

As the old man and his grandson walked through the shopping mall's crowded halls, inundated by displays of flashing lights, artificial evergreens and cycloramas of robotic Christmas critters, the old man nudged his grandson with a wink and enthused: "That was one hot pistol of a movin picture, huh, Froggie?"

The little boy's grandfather called him "Froggie." Or "Froggie Chocolates." He didn't know why.

"There's nothin' like a good Christmas picture to put you in the holiday spirit!"

Froggie said nothing. His stomach tossed like a ship on angry seas. And his vision spun in the wayward circles of an erratic gyroscope. His legs wobbled as if made of pliant rubber. And the inside of his mouth tasted like, well, a McDonald's Happy Meal.

"That was a real whiz-bang of an ending, too!" his grandfather continued. "It had plenty of piss and vinegar! Santa showed them sand monkeys they can't mess with Christmas and get away with it!"

Froggie didn't need reminding. Just as Santa was about to defend himself and the sanctity of Christmas against Osama bin Laden in a no-holds-barred cage match to the death, Froggie, recovering from his nauseous faint, opened his eyes on a Santa stripped to the waist. Thick curly tufts of white hair grew on Santa's back. His belly's excessive corpulence sagged over a loin-cloth. The loincloth enfolded his flabby fish-white haunches like a baby's diaper. Osama stood in a corner laughing at the bearded fat man with his boys, smoking a hookah. The hookah was packed with chalk-colored gravel. He asked Santa if he wanted to "beam up" before the brawl.

Behind the iron bars of the cage, a turbaned supplicant caterwauled on a prayer mat. This was the signal for the match to begin. Osama sprang out of his corner like a bat-winged Ferret; gouging out Santa's left eye. Santa bellowed like a shot Moose. The empty socket gushed spurts of crimson, turning his fabled white beard into a cone of bright red cotton candy. Tendrils of optical nerve fastened to his cheek in a spatter of coagulating blood. Osama butted him in the mouth. And Santa spat out thirty-two kernels of loosened teeth in a gelatinous wad of mucus and blood, stumbling about the cage like a drunken bear.

Santa's face, awashed in blood, was pained, toothless and contorted in despair.

Unexpectedly, Santa began to cry. Tears streamed down his cheeks. Mucal-bubbles popped in his nostrils.

Osama had proved too much for the once-jolly fat man. Santa accepted defeat without grace; surrendering all he once held dear—Christmas, children, the American way of life—to the hookah-huffing Face of Evil.

Osama sneered in triumph.

The Cineplex audience joined in one thundering voice and booed the spineless Santa. Even the little boy felt a twinge of outrage. Santa had let down America. He let down Christmas. Most of all, he let down all the children of the world.

Then Osama delivered the final blow of humiliation. He mimicked Santa's falsetto boo hoo-hoos, stripped him of his loincloth and exposed the shriveled worm of his nakedness!

However, in one of those predictably "ironic" turn-arounds common to Hollywood fare, a letter fluttered from under the folds of Santa's linen loincloth. It was addressed to a "Mr. Jolly Man" in care of the North Pole. And sent by a child who had lost all four limbs during an attack on his jungle village in the Congo. The letter was a painstakingly-written scrawl; smudged with imprints of the child's lips. Clearly, he had written it with a leaky Bic pen gripped between his teeth. It read:

Dear Mr. Jolly Man:

How is Mrs. Jolly Woman? How is the borned animal with the red nose that lights up and goes on and off? My life is not good. Soldiers chopped off my arms and legs. And ate them. For Christmas, I want to live with you and Mrs. Jolly Woman and all your little jolly men and make free stuff to give away to all the children of the world. I have no hands or feet but you would be surprised by what I can do with my mouth.

Your friend,
Pete

Upon reading this letter, Santa had decided then and there to raise the child in the snowy climes of his North Pole reindeer ranch. He and Mrs. Claus would feed him heartily on a diet of Caribou chops, Walrus steaks and quivering globs of Beluga-whale blubber. He would teach him to fish by dunking his head in icy waters, coming up with a fresh catch clenched, like a seal, between his teeth. He would not only employ the child in his enchanted workshop making wondrous and magical toys but he would bring him along on his sleigh for his yearly mission of spreading joy and good cheer. All his plans came flooding back into memory as the letter floated into blood-shot view. Now his tears of self-pity seemed ridiculous compared to the suffering of that limbless Congolese child. Santa's resolve returned with the fury of an Olympian god.

"No!" he dry whispered to the sneering Osama in his best Clint Eastwood voice. "I ain't goin' out like a sucka!" He raised his fists in the air and roared a mighty "Ho! Ho! Ho!" Then rushed the surprised Osama with the swiftness and power of a rhino. He kneed Osama in the groin, knocked him to the floor and grabbed him by the shaft of his manhood.

He gloatingly, savagely, tore it out by its root.

As Osama shrieked in agony, bleeding like a menstruating woman, the one-eyed and toothless Santa waved the bloody trophy high above his head, dancing the primate's dance of victory.

Froggie—once again—fainted.

Assisting his grandfather, Froggie inched towards the shopping mall's exit. The old man leaned the bulk of his weight on Froggie's small shoulders, encumbering the little boy. The exit was somewhere far off in the distance. Froggie found it curious his grandfather's feet moved in the same stumbling way as a two year old first learning to walk.

Froggie was appalled by "Santa's Showdown . . ." It was not only because his geriatric grandfather enjoyed this crap but he also couldn't believe a "responsible adult" would expose a precocious yet impressionable child to such puerile madness. What was the purpose of the Motion Picture Association's "rating code"? He thought it was there to protect him. Had the "gouvenator" or the studios paid them off? And what did any of it have to do with the spirit of Christmas? Maybe he missed something.

"What's Christmas, grandpa?" he asked. "And what does it have to do with that movie?"

"What kind of fool question is that?" his grandfather snapped, lapsing into the Never-never Land of senility. "Why Christmas is when the whole family gets together with rubber masks of Michael Jackson and Ronald Reagan pulled over their heads an' go out searchin' for roast turkeys hidden in the bushes! It's when you throw rabbits at your neighbors' windows an' set off fireworks on their front porch if they don't give you any painted eggs while singin' We Shall Overcome for the Negroes! It's that time of year we thank God we got all the good stuff because the commies don't deserve it! But, most of all, Christmas is holiday specials on TV!"

Froggie surprised himself with the words he heard himself say next.

"Christmas is about Jesus!"

His voice was shrill and impatient. He had no idea what provoked his outburst. He was not particularly religious. However, he was irate.

"What was all that nonsense about Arabs stealing Christmas?!! And where do you learn Kung Fu at the North Pole? From Chinese elves?

What did all that have to do with Jesus? Wasn't he born in the Middle East? Doesn't that make Jesus an Arab, too?"

In loud reverberations, Froggie's voice echoed throughout the shopping mall's cavernous halls. His voice bounced from wall to floor to ceiling and back again in rapid ricochet; shocking its denizens into stony silence.

"Doesn't that make Jesus an Arab, too? . . . too? . . . too? . . . too?"

No one moved. No one said a word.

Out of nowhere, a human stinkball in rags shoved a picture of Jesus in Froggie's face. Jesus' skin was painted the color of pink bubble gum. His hair was long, wavy and straight. His hands gestured in mudras of blessing and grace. Jesus' eyes tilted piously towards the heavens. A wreath of thorns choked the bleeding muscle of his heart.

"Does this look like an Ay-rab to you?" asked the ragged Stinkball. Its smell was one Froggie hadn't thought possible for a human being.

"No," Froggie replied. "He looks like he plays guitar for one of those stupid bands on MTV!"

"You're an evil child!" spat the Stinkball. "Don't you know what happens to bad children on Christmas Eve?"

"No" replied Froggie. "I don't."

"Well, tonight's the night!" cackled the Stinkball, wagging a crooked finger. "And you'll find out!"

"Does it involve . . ."—Froggie's grandfather asked—"bathing with people like you?"—before his cane crashed down on the Stinkball's skull.

Froggie and his grandfather stepped from the bubble-topped black and white without the aid of the two officers. On the front lawn, a Santa suit stuffed with straw crowned by a grimacing and candle-lit pumpkin sat on a throne built of snow. The policemen sat and watched, muttering sarcastic jokes. Froggie, as best he could, helped his grandfather steer the icy path to the door of their gray-shingled house.

After cracking the skull of the malodorous "Christian," the old man and his grandson were surrounded by a mob of hostile holiday shoppers. They threatened with umbrellas; stuffed animals; ribboned packages; Swiss koo-koo clocks; candied apples; remaindered cookbooks; and oversized peppermint sticks. Even the rum-hound hired as the resident Santa of "Christmas Village" took part in the festivities. Imitating Santa's testosterone imbalance, a three year old pelted Froggie and his grandfather with oblong slabs of candy fired from a Pez dispenser.

"DIE! DIE! DIE!" screamed the three year old, "YOU IZZWOMIC SCUM!!!"

And continued his assault with artificially-flavored projectiles launched from Bugs Bunny's neck.

Local police were called to quell the disturbance.

When the police arrived, the mob complained the two were terrorist sympathizers and that the "heretical" little boy had called Jesus an Ay-rab. The policemen peacefully dispersed the crowd by reminding everyone it was Christmas Eve.

"Go home,' the policemen said. "And watch 'It's A Wonderful Life.' If you hurry, you can still catch 'A Charlie Brown X-Mass'; 'The Grinch Who Stole X-Mass' and that 'Honeymooners' episode where all the characters from 'I Love Lucy,' 'Amos 'n' Andy' and "The Untouchables' get together with Ralph Kramden and Ed Norton for a special X-Mass celebration in Ed's sewer. It's the one with that famous scene of Lucy kissing the Kingfish. And he says, 'Holy Mackerel! I been kissed by a white woman! They gon' cancel our show for sho' now!' before Elliot Ness caps 'im in the butt with a submachine gun."

The mob laughed at the policeman's impersonation of the melanin-skinned malaprop and went home.

The security staff of the White Woods Suburban Mall didn't press charges; however much they liked the idea. They realized it would be bad publicity for the mall. "Old Man Jailed For Defending Nine Year Old Against Deadly Ball of Human Rags!" Christmas morning's headline would not look good.

Instead, the Stinkball was charged with air pollution; driven to a nearby dump and left to fend for itself against a pack of prowling dogs. The dogs ate well that Christmas Eve.

When Froggie and his grandfather reached the door of their home, Froggie looked up and asked: "So what's supposed to happen to bad children on Christmas Eve, huh, grandpa?"

"The Giant Easter Rat gets them!" His grandfather popped out his dentures. He tried to make a scary face by baring his false teeth like the fangs of a snarling animal but only succeeded in looking stupid. "He's six feet tall with sharp yellow claws!"

Froggie rolled his eyes and decided not to ask his grandfather any more questions.

Inside, the Christmas tree, as one of his father's "innovative" space-saving ideas, was suspended upside down from the living-room ceiling. It had the frosty glow of the musical mothership in "Close Encounters of the Third Kind." A pile of presents in metallic wrapping was heaped on the floor underneath.

Froggie's father was watching television clutching a can of beer when he and his grandfather walked in. By way of greeting, his father grunted and belched. His eyes hadn't strayed from the screen.

The television set was a point of contention between Froggie's father and grandfather. Though the set broadcast in color, it's monitor was housed inside of a scratched wooden cabinet. And it was so old, it couldn't connect to cable or hook up to a vcr. They had picked it up at a yard sale for three bucks.

Froggie's father said the TV-set was a real find; a faux art-deco design of the early sixties. A true collector's item. Froggie knew instinctively his father had no idea what he was talking about. His father made up that stupid "art deco" story because he was cheap. His father's cheapness was what finally drove his mother away. That was when he and his father moved into his grandfather's house. His mother hadn't even sent a postcard.

For the past nine months, tired of bending the TV's rabbit-ear antennae, Froggie's grandfather nagged Froggie's father to get off his lumpy beer-swilling butt and, instead of living off his grandfather's old age pension, find a job and buy one of those digital flat-screen models.

"Why?" the younger asked the elder. "They cost five-thousand bucks."

"The Playboy Channel!" Again, the grandfather popped out his dentures—this time with a grotesque leer and lecherous wink.

"Why do I need the Playboy Channel? I got a stack in the closet. Plus I got some Hustlers, Gents and Nuggets, too. You can look at them any time you want. Miss June '67 is a bra-buster."

"Better picture resolution. Tsitskehs so clear you can reach out and touch 'em!"

"Just go in the closet. I'll loan you the Vaseline."

"HBO and Showtime!" the grandfather countered.

"Watch those movies six months down the line on the free channels."

"Pay-per-view!"

"On whose dime?"

"I know a guy can hook us up if we toss him a few bucks. Free movies twenty-four hours a day. Uncut. Uncensored. And not one commercial explaining how you can relieve the pain of hemorrhoid irritation!"

"I'm on parole, Pop! I could go back to prison just for being in the same room with you; listenin' to that criminal idea!"

So it went. Back and forth. Nine months. Every day. And no flat-screen with cable connection and VCR hook-up.

On the clunky television set, Sammy Davis, Jr., in a red leather suit, tap-danced up a storm. It was an old movie from the sixties. He was an emissary of Hell: "Hey, baby! On behalf of his infernal hotness, gimme som' skin on the charcoal side!"

"So he really did have horns and a tail!" Froggie's grandfather exclaimed.

"What are you talking about?" Froggie's father asked, irritated. "I don't see any horns!"

"You would if we had a flat-screen TV!"

Thinking of devils and red suits, Froggie decided to gamble and go for broke. He shook his dice, threw and asked his father those pesky Christmas questions. As his father wasn't really paying attention, Froggie came up snake eyes.

"The crucifixion was a set up," his father belched. "Poor schmuck walked right into it. What did Jesus say when the Romans flogged him on the way to Golgatha? I'm just a patsy? Where have we heard that one before? The rest of that hocus-pocus was a black psyche-op cooked up by a secret-service agent. The agent flipped out on the way to Damascus. It was an early Mk-Ultra job. They slipped him Matzoh baked with wheat rust. Saw a blazing wheel of fire. And this thing with wings and four heads. Thought it was Jesus. Made the crooked bastard a saint."

"Where did you get that crazy story?" Froggie's grandfather asked.

Froggie's father lifted his leg and farted. "Off the web. Where else?"

In disbelief, Froggie slapped his hand against his forehead. His father not only mixed up the story of Saul's conversion on the road to Damascus with Ezekiel's fire, he confused biblical lore with an episode of the X-Files!

That night, before he went to sleep, Froggie wrote a letter and left it under the upside-down Christmas tree with a glass of milk and a plate of Little Debbie cookies he had purchased in a Bodega. It read:

Dear Santa:

I'm trapped on a planet obviously meant for assholes. Help!!!

Your friend,

Froggie Chocolates

i am what i am

date unknown

e *mcee intro: It is time for the gospel program from the Peaceway Temple, Prophet Omega, founder and overseer.*

Friends seen and unseen, people that are ridin' along in yo' auto-mo-beels, people that are sittin' at the table, I greet with the holy word peace.

For with my intimate mind I thinks constructively. For yo' minds are my mind and my mind is yo' mind and I'm sendin' out my Christ mind to you, you and you. And I'm able to draw whatsoever I want into my immediately surroundin'. But I'm sayin' to you right now let the spirit in me be in you. Yes, on last night the spirit told me to tell you . . . the spirit told me to tell you to say these words, "I am what I am." Now repeat this behind me. I am what I am and that is all I am and I am IT.

It makes no difference who you are or what you're doin', what you're tryin' to do or want to do, repeat these words, "I am what I am, and that's all I am . . . is what I am. That's all I am, look that's all, that's all I am . . . is what I am. And I am it." Now repeat those words and if you repeat the words and continue to repeat those words blessings goin' come to you.

You got to remain to bein' yo'self. You cannot be nobody else. It ain't no use in tryin' to be no whirlwind and jumpin' here and playin' checkers with your own life. That ain't goin' to work, baby.

Now repeat these words behind me. "I am what I am." Now that's all you are. You are what you believes you are. Belief is intellectual process and faith involves action.

Now do you believe that on this afternoon when you come to 488 Lamont Drive that you goin' to receive a blessin' to pay them bills? Pay your car note, house note? Now if you repeat these words, "I am what I am," and come in a good spirit, GOD goin' bless you, GOD goin' make it work for you. GOD goin' heal your pockets. Goin' heal your mind, your ideals. For GOD is in the blessin' bidness. GOD is in the healin' bidness, and the whole facts about it GOD is in all the bidness . . . and to you all that been attendin' my service know what GOD has done. Let me straighten out a little few things. I said on yesterday to those that call me, that I call rather, Lord I didn't call nobody, those that call ME. Amen, receive the word "blood." For the blood of Jesus was a stain. The blood of Jesus will do many things for you.

Now listen to me, those that was at service on last Sunday night, amen, we gave you a blessin', and I told that the shoes that I already preached on was going to repeat themselves, I read from the ninth and sixth psalms and the fifth verse.

Now GOD is movin' in a mysterious way, and GOD is doing great things . . . all over Nashville. GOD is doing great things all over the universe and everywhere my voice is being heard and everywhere I go. Even though they call me long distance, Buffalo, New York, Miami, Floridy, New Orleans, Louisiana, and not only that there children in those place I have gone GOD is workin' all through Mississippi, Arkansas, Pennsylvania, Maryland, New York City, in Michigan, and Floridy, GOD is workin' miracles in folks' life.

Now down in New Orleans, amen, they got those ol' folks the people down there they call 'em the two-head folks, but I went down there with one head and amen, I tol' 'em, I said, "I'm gonna bury all these heads and gonna bring you JESUS CHRIST!" And I brought 'em Jesus Christ and GOD moved in a mysterious way.

If your happy with who you are god. will help and show you the way

swollen feets
date unknown

Well, i w a n t you to call up a friend now tell them that Omega is on the air, and that we are going to have a wonderful program this afternoon at 488 Lamont Drive, Apartment Q258. Now Christmas is approaching and it's later than you think. You want to start to preparin' yourself now for children's goods and yo' goods. Then meet this afternoon at 488 Lamont Drive in the Kentmount Apartments where the Peaceway Temple is conducting its service in apartment Q258. That's the Kentmount Apartments, 488 Lamont Drive, Apartment Q258.

And I'd like to pause here and make an announcement about the Shipp Movin' Company who is located on Old Lexington City Highway. They been in bidness since 19 and 54 and they specialize in movin' fine furniture, your furniture, which is fine furniture. Now for a courtesy move or quick move or a right now move, and some of y'all make the move tomorrah. Some of y'all most likely might need to move next week, week after next, a month from now. Then call Shipp Movin' Company. Got mens ovah there that are very courtesy and unnerstandin' and don't mind tryin' to satisfy you the customent. The company give you an estimation they don't charge you any extra money for that. And if the company move you, they don't charge you for a heavy piece, a heavier piece. And they got some beautiful girls ovah there doin' the packin' and unpackin', now this cost you extra. Now what is a little extra for safety ssss? Your glasses don't be broken, your silverware wrapped nice. And the very things that you treasure is wrapped neatly and nice. Wrapped and unwrapped. Took down and put up. Now that's the Shipp Movin' Company. You may call them at 242–5381, that's 243 . . . 242–5381, 242–5381, may God bless ya.

But for a spiritual blessin', for a spiritual healin' and advice on all problems, whether it's your marriage, whether it's crossed-up conditions, unnatural feelings . . . you think somebody did somethin' to you. And you tried doctors and they can't do it no good? Then call Prophet Omega, and I am Prophet Omega at 226–1832 and I pray for those that have swollen foots, swollen feet, swollen legs, swollen ankles, backache, headaches, cancer, heart trouble. Whatever your problem is I pray for it. And God has healed these problems. God has healed these conditions. Even if you have a financial worry, or financial problems, I pray for that too. All right, then meet me this afternoon at 488 Lamont Drive, Lamont Drive, Apartment Q258.

Now I'm supposed to be at Dr. Ross's church on Wednesday night and I'm goin' preach there and a lot of y'all like to have the address, you may call at 226–1832, 226–1832, and I will tell you exactly what the address of the place, but on Wednesday night we 'posed to be there. But tonight at six o'clock we goin' to have a divine service, a healin' service, a get what you want a get ahead service. Now is the time to start to preparin' for Christmas. Get ahead of the rest. Meet me at 488 Lamont Drive, right here in Nashville, Tennessee. And we want to dedicate this record right here to the sick and shut in, to those that are confined to their beds, to those that are behind prison bars, to those that havin' trouble in your homes, to you that are havin' trouble within yo' own self. And especial to the sick and shut-in. We also like to dedicate this to Mrs. Shelton who somehow has a swollen foot . . . a swollen toe rather, *Trouble Do Not Last Always*, by James Cleveland.

contributor notes

Franklyn Ajaye (1949–) is a comedian, writer, and actor with numerous television and movie appearances to his credit, most recently a recurring role on HBO's *Deadwood*. He has released three comedy albums to date: *Franklyn Ajaye, Comedian*; *I'm a Comedian, Seriously*; and *Don't Smoke Dope, Fry Your Hair*.

Elizabeth Alexander (1962–) is an award-winning poet who's authored three volumes of poetry: *The Venus Hottentot, Body of Life*, and *Antebellum Dream Book*. Presently, Ms. Alexander teaches in the Department of African American Studies at Yale University.

A staff writer for the *New Yorker*, Hilton Als (1961–) has published two books: *The Women*, a memoir, and *The Group*, a portrait of James Baldwin.

Kyle Baker is an illustrator and writer. *Why I Hate Saturn, The Cowboy Wally Show, Plastic Man: On the Lam* are just a few of his many titles.

Toni Cade Bambara (1935–1995) was a writer and social activist most noted for her collection of short stories *Gorilla, My Love* and the novel *The Salt Eaters*.

Amiri Baraka (1937–) is a writer and musicologist. He co-founded the Black Arts Liberation Theater. The former poet laureate of the state of New Jersey, Baraka has published several books, among them *Black Music, Blues People*, and *Transbluency: The Selected Poems of Amiri Baraka/Leroi Jones (1961–1995)*.

An Emmy-nominated television writer whose credits include *Get Smart, The Doris Day Show*, and *Newhart*, Gary Belkin (1927–) spent a good part of the sixties as Muhammad Ali's (then known as Cassius Clay) ghost-writer.

Tish Benson (1969?–) is an award-winning poet, screenwriter, play-wright, and solo and collaborative performance artist. *Wild Like That* is her most recent collection of poems. She also wrote *Hairstyles*, a short film produced by Lifetime television. Originally from Texas, she currently lives in Brooklyn.

Gwendolyn Brooks (1917–2000) was the Poet Laureate of Illinois. In 1949 she became the first African-American to win the Pulitzer Prize. Among her many collections of poetry are *Annie Allen* and *The Bean Eaters*.

Novelist and scholar Cecil Brown (1943–) is the author of *The Life and Loves of Mr. Jiveass Nigger, Days Without Weather,* and *Stagolee Shot Billy*. He lives in northern California.

H. Rap Brown (1943–) was the former chairman of SNCC (the Student Nonviolent Coordinating Committee). In 1971 he changed his name to Jamil Abdullah al-Amin. He was once quoted as saying, "Violence is as American as cherry pie."

Sterling Brown (1901–1989) was a poet, Howard University professor, and literary critic. His first collection of poems, *Southern Road*, was published in 1932.

Born in New Orleans, Steve Cannon (1935–) has made his home New York's Lower East Side for the last thirty-five years. He's the author of the underground classic *Groove, Bang and Jive Around* and director of The Gathering of the Tribes, Inc.

Wanda Coleman (1946–) is a Los Angeles-based writer. Her most recent publications are the novel *Mambo Hips & Make Believe*; a volume of poetry, *Mercurochrome: New Poems*; and a collection of essays, *The Riot Inside Me: More Trial & Tremors*.

W.E.B. DuBois (1868–1963) was a noted civil rights activist and public intellectual. In 1895 he became the first African-American to receive a Ph.D. from Harvard. His seminal collection of essays *The Souls of Black Folk* was published in 1903. In 1909 he helped found the NAACP and served as the editor of its official magazine, *The Crisis*, for twenty-five years. In his later years he renounced his American citizenship and moved to Ghana, where he died at age ninety-five.

The life of short-story writer Henry Dumas (1934–1968) ended tragically when he was shot by a police officer on the New York City subway. His most recent volume is *Goodbye Sweetwater: New and Selected Stories*.

A key figure in African-American letters, Paul Laurence Dunbar (1872–1906) counted Orville and Wilbur Wright and Frederick Douglass amongst his supporters. He died of tuberculosis aged thirty-four.

Cornelius Eady (1954–) is a prize-winning poet, His volumes of poetry include *Brutal Imagination, Autobiography of a Jukebox*, and *You Don't Miss Your Water*. He lives in New York City.

Erika Ellis (1965–) is a novelist who resides in California. Her novel *Good Fences* was adapted into a made-for-television movie starring Danny Glover and Whoopi Goldberg.

Trey Ellis (1962–) has penned three novels—*Platitudes, Home Repairs*, and *Right Here, Right Now*—and several screenplays, including *The Inkwell* and *The Tuskegee Airmen*. He currently lives in Southern California.

A celebrated novelist and essayist, Ralph Ellison's (1914–1994) novel *Invisible Man* won the National Book Award in 1953.

Percival Everett (1956–) is the author of more than fifteen novels and short story collections. He is a professor at the University of Southern California. The novels *Glyph, Erasure*, and *American Desert* are some of his more recent publications.

John Farris (1940–) lives and writes in New York City; his latest book is a collection of poems entitled *It's Not About Time*.

Rudolph Fisher (1897–1934) was a writer and radiologist. As a Harlem Renaissance personality he is known mostly for the short story "The City of Refuge" and his novel *The Conjure Man Dies*.

Hattie Gossett (1942–) is a poet, teacher, and recording artist. She lives in New York City and has published *Presenting . . . Sister No Blues*, a collection of poetry.

Sam Greenlee (1930–) is a novelist, poet, and educator who makes his home in Chicago. His books include *Baghdad Blues, Be-bop Man / Be-bop Woman: Poetry and Other Raps*, and *The Spook Who Sat by the Door*.

Chester Himes (1909–1984) began writing while incarcerated in an Ohio penitentiary for armed robbery. He authored over sixty short stories and almost twenty novels, among them *If He Hollers Let Him Go, A Rage in Harlem*, and *Pinktoes*.

Lightnin' Hopkins (1912–1982) was a prolific country blues recording artist known for his fast guitar style and mellow Texan drawl.

An acclaimed poet, playwright, and novelist, Langston Hughes (1902–1967) is synonymous with the Harlem Renaissance. He was inducted into the National Institute of Arts and Letters in 1961.

Born in Alabama, Zora Neale Hurston (1891–1960) was raised in Florida. She moved to New York City to study sociology at Barnard College, eventually becoming a key contributor to the Harlem Renaissance. Her works include *Mules and Men, Their Eyes Were Watching God*, and her autobiography *Dust Tracks on the Road*.

Darius James (1954–) is a novelist and essayist; he lives in Berlin, Germany. He is the author of *Negrophobia, That's Blaxploitation!*, and *Froggie Chocolates' Christmas Eve*.

James Weldon Johnson (1871–1938) was a poet, songwriter, novelist, diplomat, university professor, and civil rights activist. He is best known for his novel *Autobiography of an Ex-Colored Man*, for the poetry volumes *God's Trombones* and *Saint Peter Relates an Incident*, and for composing the "Negro national anthem," *Lift Every Voice and Sing*

Bob Kaufman (1925–1986) was an esteemed and enigmatic Beat poet who after the Kennedy assassination took a vow of silence that lasted until the end of the Vietnam War. His four collections of poetry are *Solitudes Crowded with Loneliness, Golden Sardine, Ancient Rain*, and *Cranial Guitar: Selected Poems*.

Etheridge Knight's (1931–1991) poetry collection *The Essential Etheridge Knight* won the American Book Award in 1987.

Spike Lee's (1957–) third feature film, *Do the Right Thing*, was nominated for an Academy Award for Best Screenplay. *4 Little Girls*, his documentary about the bombing of a Birmingham, Alabama, church in 1963, received an Oscar nomination for Best Feature Documentary in 1997.

Lord Finesse, a Bronx born rapper/producer, has four solo albums to his credit: *The Funky Technician, Return of the Funky Man, The Awakening*, and *From the Crates to the Files*.

Malcolm X (1925–1965) was a prominent Muslim minister and founder of the Organization for Afro-American Unity. His book *The Autobiography of*

Malcolm X was cited by *Time* magazine as one of the ten most important works of nonfiction in the twentieth century.

Harryette Mullen was born in Florence, Alabama, and raised in Fort Worth, Texas. Her volumes of poetry include *S*PeRM**K*T, Muse & Drudge,* and *Sleeping with the Dictionary,* which was named as a finalist for the 2002 National Book Critics Circle Award. She is a professor in the UCLA English Department.

Suzan-Lori Parks (1964–) is a playwright, screenwriter, and novelist. Her play *Topdog/Underdog* won the 2002 Pulitzer Prize for drama. She recently published her first novel, *Getting Mother's Body.*

Willie Perdomo (1967–) is the author of *Where a Nickel Costs a Dime, Postcards of El Barrio,* and *Smoking Lovely,* which won the 2004 PEN America Beyond Margins Award. His work has appeared in several publications including *Bomb, Urban Latino,* and the *New York Times Magazine.*

Prophet Omega (date of birth unknown) is the founder and overseer of the Peaceway Temple in Nashville, Tennessee. He is what he is.

Ishmael Reed (1938–) is a novelist, essayist, and poet. He teaches at the University of California at Berkeley and has written well over a dozen books, including *Mumbo Jumbo, Reckless Eyeballing,* and *Another Day at the Front.*

John Rodriguez (1973–) is a teacher and writer who lives in the Bronx, New York. He is the author of the chapbook *Purple 5,* and his work has appeared in many anthologies.

Fran Ross (1935–1985) was raised in Philadelphia and lived in New York City. *Oreo* is her only novel.

Journalist and novelist George Schuyler (1895–1977) was the editor of the *Pittsburgh Courier* from 1924 to 1966; he is most noted for the novel *Black No More.*

Born in Boston, Danzy Senna (1970–) presently resides in New York. She's written two novels, *Caucasia* and *Symptomatic.*

The Brooklyn-born civil rights activist Reverend Al Sharpton (1954–) was ordained as a minister at age nine and sermonized under the moniker

"The Wonder Boy Preacher." He was a candidate for the 2004 Democratic presidential nomination.

Patricia Smith (1955–) is a four-time winner of the national poetry slam; her volumes of poetry include *Life According to Motown, Big Towns, Big Talk*, and *Closer to Death*.

Sojourner Truth (c. 1797–1883) was born into slavery. She escaped to Canada in 1827, then later returned to the U.S. to become a celebrated activist in the women's rights and abolitionist movements.

In 1985 Mike Tyson (1966–) defeated Trevor Berbick to become the youngest heavyweight champion of all time. He held the title until 1990, when he was knocked out in the tenth round by the then unheralded James "Buster" Douglas.

Colson Whitehead (1969–) is a prize-winning novelist and essayist. He's written two novels, *The Intuitionist* and *John Henry Days*, and a travelogue, *The Colossus of New York*. He lives in Brooklyn, New York.

A vaudevillian who often performed in blackface, Bert Williams (1875–1922) was a groundbreaking entertainer. As a performer in the *Ziegfeld Follies*, he became the first African-American to headline on the Broadway stage. W. C. Fields once described him as being "the funniest man I ever saw, and the saddest."

Charles Wright (1932–) has written three novels: *The Messenger, The Wig*, and *Absolutely Nothing to Get Alarmed About*. He lives in New York City.

acknowledgments

I would like to thank the following folks for their guidance, encouragement, and assistance: Lydia Offord, Steve Cannon, Oscar Villaron, Lou Asekoff, Kofi Notambu, Eugene Redmond, Nichole Shields, Sonya Abrams, Tracy Sherrod, Bert Ashe, Danzy Senna, Josslyn Luckett, Darius James, Natalie Moskovich, Reginald Dennis, James Bernard, and especially, the incredibly patient Jin Auh.

Franklyn Ajaye: "Be Black, Brother, Be Black" and "Disneyland High" from *Don't Smoke Dope, Fry Your Hair*, copyright © Little David Records, 1977. Used by permission of the author.

Elizabeth Alexander: "Talk Radio, D.C.," from *The Body of Life* by Elizabeth Alexander. Copyright © 1996. Reprinted with permission of Tia Chucha Press.

Hilton Als: "The Only One," previously published in the *New Yorker*. Copyright © 1994 by Hilton Als, used with permission of the author.

Kyle Baker: "Sands of Blood (The Cowboy Wally Show)," from *The Cowboy Wally Show* © 1988, 1996 Kyle Baker. All rights reserved. Used with Permission of DC Comics.

Toni Cade Bambara: "The Lesson," copyright © 1972 by Toni Cade Bambara, from *Gorilla, My Love* by Toni Cade Bambara. Used by permission of Random House, Inc.

Amiri Baraka: "Wise 1," from *Wise, Why's, Y's*, copyright © 1995 by Amiri Baraka, reprinted by permission of Third World Press, Chicago, Illinois.

Gary Belkin: "Clay Comes Out to Meet Liston," written by Gary Belkin for recitation by Cassius Clay aka Muhammad Ali on "*I Am the Greatest!*" Columbia Records LP, 1963. Reprinted by permission of Gary Belkin.

Tish Benson: "Fifth-Ward E-Mail," from *Wild Like That*, copyright © 2003 by Tish Benson. Reprinted by permission of Fly By Night Press, New York, New York.

Gwendolyn Brooks: "at the hairdresser's" copyright © 1945 by Gwendolyn Brooks. "One Reason Cats" from *In the Mecca*, copyright © 1968 by Gwendolyn Brooks. "a song in the front yard" copyright © 1945 by Gwendolyn Brooks, reprinted by consent of Brooks Permissions.

Cecil Brown: From *The Life and Loves of Mr. Jiveass Nigger*, copyright © 1969 by Cecil Brown, used with permission of the author.

H. Rap Brown: *Die, Nigger, Die!*, chapter 2, by H. Rap Brown, Copyright © 1969, 2002. Used with permission of Lawrence Hill Books.

Sterling Brown: "Slim in Atlanta" and "Slim Lands a Job?," from *Southern Road*, copyright © 1932 by Harcourt, Brace & Co., copyright © renewed 1960 by Sterling Brown. Included in *The Collected Poems of Sterling A Brown*, selected by Michael S. Harper. Copyright © 1980 by Sterling A. Brown. Reprinted by permission of HarperCollins Publishers Inc. "Crispus Attucks McKoy" from *The Collected Poems of Sterling A. Brown*, edited by Michael S. Harper. Copyright © 1980 by Sterling A. Brown. Reprinted by permission of HarperCollins Publishers Inc.

Steve Cannon: From *Groove, Bang and Jive Around*, copyright © 1969 by Steve Cannon. Used with permission of the author.

Wanda Coleman: "April 15th 1985," "Identifying Marks," and "On That Stuff That Ain't Nevah Been Long Enuff for No Damn Body," from *Heavy Daughter Blues*. Copyright © 1990 by Wanda Coleman, Ballantine Books. Used with permission of the author.

W. E. B. DuBois: "On Being Crazy," from *The Crisis*, June 1923. Public domain.

Henry Dumas: "Double Nigger," copyright © 1965 by Henry Dumas, reprinted by permission of Eugene B. Redmond for the Henry Dumas Estate.

Paul Laurence Dunbar: "When De Co'n Pone's Hot," copyright © 1895 by Paul Laurence Dunbar, used with permission of Hakim's Bookstore, attn: Yvonne Blake.

Cornelius Eady: "The Cab Driver Who Ripped Me Off," from *Autobiography of a Jukebox* by Cornelius Eady. Copyright © 1997. Used by permission of Carnegie Mellon University Press.

Erika Ellis: "Blackflight" from *Good Fences*, copyright © 1988 by Erika Ellis, reprinted by permission of International Creative Management, Inc.

Trey Ellis: *Platitudes*, copyright © 1988 by Trey Ellis. Used by permission of the author.

Ralph Ellison: *Invisible Man* by Ralph Ellison, copyright © 1947, 1948, 1952 by Ralph Ellison. Copyright renewed 1975, 1976, 1980 by Ralph Ellison. Used by permission of Random House, Inc.

Percival Everett: *Erasure* by Percival Everett, copyright © 2002 Percival Everett. Reprinted by permission of Hyperion.

John Farris: "In the Park After School with the Girl and the Boy" by John Farris. Copyright © 1994 by John Farris. Used with permission of the author.

Rudolph Fisher: "The City of Refuge" from *Atlantic Monthly* 135, Public Domain.

Hattie Gossett: "yo daddy" from *Presenting . . . Sister No Blues*, copyright © 1990 by Hattie Gossett, used with permission of Firebrand Books, Ann Arbor, Michigan.

Sam Greenlee: *The Spook Who Sat by the Door* by Sam Greenlee, copyright © Allison & Busby, 1969. Reprinted by permission of the author.

Chester Himes: "Let Me at the Enemy—an' George Brown" and "Dirty Deceivers." UK rights: Reprinted by permission of Allison & Busby. US rights: From the book *The Collected Stories of Chester Himes*, copyright © 1990 Lesley Himes; appears by permission of the publishers, Thunder's Mouth Press.

Lightnin' Hopkins: "Big Black Cadillac Blues" aka "Black Cadillac." Written by Sam "Lightnin'" Hopkins, copyright © 1970 (renewed). Published by Tradition Music (BMI)/Administered by BUG. All rights reserved. Used by permission.

Langston Hughes: "Adventure" and "Pose-Outs" from *Simple's Uncle Sam* by Langston Hughes. Copyright © 1965 by Langston Hughes. Copyright renewed 1993 by Arnold Rampersad and Ramona Bass. Reprinted by permission of Hill and Wang, a division of Farrar, Straus and Giroux, LLC. Reprinted in the U.K. by permission of Harold Ober Associates Inc.

Zora Neale Hurston: " 'Possum or Pig?" "The Bone of Contention," and "Book of Harlem" as taken from *The Complete Stories* by Zora Neale Hurston. Introduction copyright © 1995 by Henry Louis Gates, Jr., and Sieglinde Lemke. Compilation copyright © 1995 by Vivian Bowden, Lois J. Hurston Gaston, Clifford Hurston, Lucy Ann Hurston, Winifred Hurston Clark, Zora Mack Goins, Edgar Hurston, Sr., and Barbara Hurston Lewis. Afterword and Bibliography copyright © 1995 by Henry Louis Gates. Reprinted by permission of HarperCollins Publishers Inc.

Darius James: "Lil' Black Zambo" from *Negrophobia*, copyright © 1992 by Darius James, Citadel Press. Used with permission of the author. *Froggie Chocolates' Christmas Eve* by Darius James, copyright © 2003. Used with permission of the author.

James Weldon Johnson: "Brer Rabbit, You's de Cutes' of 'Em All" from *Saint Peter Relates an Incident* by James Weldon Johnson, copyright © 1917, 1921, 1935 by James Weldon Johnson, copyright renewed © 1963 by Grace Nail Johnson. Used by permission of Viking Penguin, a division of Penguin Group (USA) Inc.

Bob Kaufman: "Heavy Water Blues" from *Cranial Guitar: Selected Poems*. Copyright © 1967 by Bob Kaufman. Copyright © 1996 by Eileen Kaufman. Reprinted with the permission of Coffee House Press, Minneapolis, Minnesota, *www.coffeehousepress.com*. "Abomunist Manifesto" by Robert Kaufman, from *Solitudes Crowded with Loneliness*, copyright © 1965 by Bob Kaufman. Reprinted by permission of New Directions Publishing Corp.

Etheridge Knight: "Dark Prophecy: I Sing of Shine," "Memo #9," "Rehabilitation and Treatment in the Prisons of America" are from *The Essential Etheridge Knight*, by Etheridge Knight, © 1986. Reprinted by permission of the University of Pittsburgh Press.

Spike Lee: *Do the Right Thing*, copyright © 1989 by Spike Lee, Fireside. Used with permission of the author.

Lord Finesse: "Return of the Funky Man," published by Technician Tunes, copyright © 1992 by Robert Hall, used with permission of the author.

Malcolm X: From "Message to the Grass Roots" by Malcolm X, excerpt pp. 21–24 (Pathfinder Edition), copyright 1965, 1989 by Betty Shabazz and Pathfinder Press. Reprinted by permission.

Harryette Mullen: "Any Lit," "Jinglejangle," "Kamasutra Sutra," and "Souvenir From Anywhere" from *Sleeping with the Dictionary*, copyright © 2001 by Harryette Mullen, used with permission of the Regents of the University of California and the University of California Press.

Suzan-Lori Parks: "Devotees in the Garden of Love" from *The America Play and Other Works* by Suzan-Lori Parks, copyright © 1991, used by permission of the Theater Communications Group.

Willie Perdomo: "Nigger-Reecan Blues," from *Where a Nickel Costs a Dime* by Willie Perdomo. Copyright © Used by permission of W.W. Norton & Company. "Should Old Shit Be Forgot," from *Smoking Lovely* by Willie Perdomo. Copyright © 2003 Rattapallax Press. Used by permission of author.

Prophet Omega: Public domain.

Ishmael Reed: *Yellow Back Radio Broke-Down*, Dalkey Archive Press. Copyright © 2001 by Ishmael Reed, used with permission of the author.

John Rodriguez: "How to be a Street Poet," copyright © 1999 by John Rodriguez. Used by permission of the author.

Fran Ross: From *Oreo*, copyright © by Fran Ross, 1974. Reprinted with permission of Gerald Ross Jr. and Richard Ross Sr.

George Schuyler: *Black No More* by George Schuyler, copyright © The Macaulay Company, 1935. Public domain.

Danzy Senna: "The Mulatto Millennium," copyright © 1988 by Danzy Senna. Used with permission of the author.

Al Sharpton: Reprinted with permission of the Commonwealth Club of California.

Patricia Smith: "Boy Sneezes, Head Explodes," from *Life According to Motown* by Patricia Smith, copyright © 1991. Reprinted with permission of Tia Chucha Press.

Sojourner Truth: Public domain.

Mike Tyson: Various sources including BBC Sport, ESPN.com, CNN, Sports Illustrated, Fox News, and the Nevada State Athletic Commision.

Colson Whitehead: *John Henry Days* by Colson Whitehead, copyright © 2001 by Colson Whitehead. Used by permission of Doubleday, a division of Random House, Inc.

Bert Williams: Bert Williams Jokebooks, n.d. Manuscripts, Archives and Rare Books Division, Schomburg Center for Research in Black Culture, The New York Public Library. Astor, Lenox and Tilden Foundations.

Charles Wright: From *The Wig*, copyright © 1966. Used with permission of the author.

a note on the editor

Paul Beatty is the author of two novels, *Tuff* and
The White Boy Shuffle, and two books of poetry,
Big Bank Take Little Bank and *Joker, Joker, Deuce*.
He lives in New York City.

a note on the type

The text of this book is set in Bembo. This type was first
used in 1495 by the Venetian printer Aldus Manutius
for Cardinal Bembo's *De Aetna*, and was cut for Manutius
by Francesco Griffo. It was one of the types used by
Claude Garamond (1480–1561) as a model for his Romain
de L'Université, and so it was the forerunner of what became
standard European type for the following two centuries. Its
modern form follows the original types and was designed for
Monotype in 1929.